Also by Arielle Guttman

Astro*Compatibility

The Astro*Carto*Graphy Book of Maps (with Jim Lewis)

Mythic Astrology (with Kenneth Johnson)

Mythic Astrology Applied (with Kenneth Johnson)

To VENUS
Who inspires love in us all

And to my mother, Fran
For her lifelong support of my endeavors
and for the encouragement of this project

♀★ ACKNOWLEDGEMENTS ♀★

To Joseph (Jose) whose pentagrams, dodecahedrons and icosahedrons opened up a whole universe and ignited the spark of Venus Star Rising; to Leslie Nathanson, whose fine Virgo editorial work gave order and direction to this volume; to Aline Fourier, Jaye Oliver and Janice St. Marie, whose artistic sensibilities and flair gave beauty to this work; to Diane Kennedy, Dawn Abriel and Jean Kotchision, the women of Natural Grace, who gave me guidance, support and direction during the years that this volume was taking shape; to Junko Fujisue Wells for her expertise and research; to Flannery Davis for her dedication to long hours of editorial review and suggestions; to Kenneth Johnson for mythological content review and recommendations, and to all the friends, family, students and supporters who have been patiently awaiting the birth of Venus Star Rising.

VENUS STAR RISING

A New Cosmology For The Twenty-First Century

Arielle Guttman

Sophia Venus Productions
Santa Fe, New Mexico

Venus Star Rising. A New Cosmology For The Twenty-First Century. Copyright ©2010 by Arielle Guttman. All rights reserved. No part of this book may be used or reproduced in any manner whatsoever, including Internet usage, without written permission from Sophia Venus Productions except in the case of brief quotations embodied in critical articles and reviews.

FIRST EDITION, SECOND PRINTING (2019)

Cover design by Jaye Oliver and Janice St. Marie
Cover images © Photograph of Venus de Milo by Arielle Guttman
Illustrations by Jaye Oliver
Book design and layout by Aline Fourier

Library of Congress Control Number: 2010917301
ISBN: 978-0-9830598-5-1
Library of Congress Cataloging-in-publication Data:
Guttman, Arielle
   Venus star rising: a new cosmology for the twenty-first century/Arielle
   Guttman p.   cm.
   Includes bibliographical references and index.

   1. Astrology, mythology. 2. Body, Mind, Spirit

Sophia Venus Productions
Santa Fe, New Mexico
www.VenusStarRising.com

Printed in the United States of America

…When his love he doth espy,

Let her shine as gloriously

As Venus of the sky.

--Shakespeare: A Midsummer Night's Dream III, II

Table of Contents

Preface..*x*

Introduction: A New Cosmology for the Twenty-First Century...............*13*

PART I – BACKGROUND OF THE VENUS STAR POINT THEORY......*19*

Chapter 1: **The Astronomy and Geometry of the Venus Star**..........*21*
    Venus: A Planet and a Star
    The Form of the Venus Star
    The Mechanics of the Venus Star
    The Numerical Values of Venus
    The Sacred Geometry of the Venus Star

Chapter 2: **The Mythology and Astrology of Venus**........................*36*
    The Mythology of Venus
    History and Myth
    The Dual Nature of Venus: Morning Star/Evening Star
    A Psychological Comparison between Morning Star and Evening Star
    Symbols of Venus and the Medieval Church
    Venus and the Astrology of the Mayan Calendar
    Venus Transits Across the Face of the Sun
    The Mayan Mythos of Venus
    The Astrology of Venus
    Measuring the Venus Star
    The Venus Return
    A Double Quincunx—Finger of the Goddess?
    The Venus Star As Eros

PART II – WORKING WITH THE VENUS STAR POINTS......................*63*

Chapter 3: **Discovering the Venus Star Points**................................*65*
    The Twelve Houses of the Zodiac Wheel
    The Current Venus Star—Sign of the Times
    World/Historical Trends and the Twelve Venus Star Points
    Finding Your Venus Star Point

Chapter 4: **The TAURUS Venus Star Point (1825 to 1934)**..........................*83*
    The VSP in Taurus: The Personal Realm
    The VSP in Taurus: The Historical Realm

Chapter 5: **The SAGITTARIUS Venus Star Point (1830 to 1923)**..................*93*
    The VSP in Sagittarius: The Personal Realm
    The VSP in Sagittarius: The Historical Realm

Chapter 6: **The CANCER Venus Star Point (1852 to 1961)**..........................*103*
    The VSP in Cancer: The Personal Realm
    The VSP in Cancer: The Historical Realm

Chapter 7: **The VIRGO Venus Star Point (1875 to 1984)**.............................*115*
    The VSP in Virgo: The Personal Realm
    The VSP in Virgo: The Historical Realm

Chapter 8: **The AQUARIUS Venus Star Point (1890 to 1982)**.......................*127*
    The VSP in Aquarius: The Personal Realm
    The VSP in Aquarius: The Historical Realm

Chapter 9: **The SCORPIO Venus Star Point (1926 to 2027)**........................*141*
    The VSP in Scorpio: The Personal Realm
    The VSP in Scorpio: The Historical Realm

Chapter 10: **The ARIES Venus Star Point (1929 to 2038)**............................*153*
    The VSP in Aries: The Personal Realm
    The VSP in Aries: The Historical Realm

Chapter 11: **The GEMINI Venus Star Point (1964 to 2073)**.........................*165*
    The VSP in Gemini: The Personal Realm
    The VSP in Gemini: The Historical Realm

Chapter 12: **The CAPRICORN Venus Star Point (1986 to 2078)**..................*177*
    The VSP in Capricorn: The Personal Realm
    The VSP in Capricorn: The Historical Realm

Chapter 13: **The LEO Venus Star Point (1987 to 2100)**..............................*191*
    The VSP in Leo: The Personal Realm
    The VSP in Leo: The Historical Realm

Chapter 14: **The LIBRA Venus Star Point (2022 to 2131)**...........................*203*
    The VSP in Libra: The Personal Realm
    The VSP in Libra: The Historical Realm

Chapter 15: **The PISCES Venus Star Point (2041 to 2133)**..........................*215*
        The VSP in Pisces: The Personal Realm
        The VSP in Pisces: The Historical Realm

PART III – RELATIONSHIPS ON THE VENUS STAR..........................*227*

Chapter 16: **How the Venus Star Defines Relationships**..........................*229*
        Yin or Yang
        Chinese Medicine, Feng Shui, and the Venus Star
        Using the Venus Star Relationship Data
        The Venus Star Relationship Principles
            The Karmic Star Relationship
            The Twin Star Relationship
            The Creative Star Relationship
        Venus Star Point and Relationships

Chapter 17: **Marriage and Partnership on the Venus Star**..........................*243*
        Connections to Our Star Partners
        How the Venus Star Gives and Receives

Chapter 18: **TAURUS Venus Star Relationships**..........................*248*

Chapter 19: **SAGITTARIUS Venus Star Relationships**..........................*256*

Chapter 20: **CANCER Venus Star Relationships**..........................*262*

Chapter 21: **VIRGO Venus Star Relationships**..........................*270*

Chapter 22: **AQUARIUS Venus Star Relationships**..........................*280*

Chapter 23: **SCORPIO Venus Star Relationships**..........................*288*

Chapter 24: **ARIES Venus Star Relationships**..........................*296*

Chapter 25: **GEMINI Venus Star Relationships**..........................*306*

Chapter 26: **CAPRICORN Venus Star Relationships**..........................*314*

Chapter 27: **LEO Venus Star Relationships**..........................*320*

Chapter 28: **LIBRA Venus Star Relationships**..........................*328*

Chapter 29: **PISCES Venus Star Relationships**..........................*334*

Chapter 30: **Groupings on the Venus Star**..........................*340*

APPENDIXES

Appendix I: **The Venus Star Program**..*346*
    The Venus Mantra
    The Venus Mudra
    The Venus Period
    The Venus Environment
    A Venus Song

Appendix II: **Venus Star Dates and Signs—1750 to 2050**................*353*

Appendix III: **Celebrity Birth Dates/Venus Star Signs**.....................*358*

Appendix IV: **Houses of the Venus Star Point**...................................*374*

ENDNOTES..*377*

GLOSSARY OF TERMS...*381*

SELECTED BIBLIOGRAPHY..*383*

LIST OF REFERENCES FOR CELEBRITY BIRTH DATA........*387*

ACKNOWLEDGEMENTS..*388*

INDEX..*389*

PREFACE

The Venus Star, a pentagonal pattern that Venus weaves as it moves about its orbit in the sky every eight years is of special significance. Venus has been repeating this Star, affecting human consciousness and historical events for many centuries. But of significance for our times is that it is presently positioned to rise in a special region of the heavens in the next ten to thirty years, sweeping like a vast wave over all humanity. Venus, the planet in our sky that represents love, will bring this much needed energy to earth and its inhabitants in these coming years. Preceding that event, we are presently witnessing the difficult and sometimes painful birthing – a transformation of humankind from a competitive, warring, survival-oriented species, governed in the body by the sacral centers, to a loving, compassionate species, governed in the body by the heart center. The painful transformation the earth is now experiencing is characterized by the position of the Venus Star in the zodiac, as this book will systematically reveal. The awareness of the Venus Star, the attunement to its five-fold rhythm, and the knowledge of how best to utilize its special frequency are all issues addressed in this book, and if practiced and undertaken by a large group of people, will also catalyze and assist the process of evolution that Earth itself is undergoing. An increased consciousness of Venus's core principle of love will assist each individual in their daily life to emanate from that love principle, which can in turn spread like a vast wave of energy, something that the world is hungering to experience. And, as more people awaken to the concepts of a peaceful, loving world based on a partnership model, rather than an angry, warring world based on a dominator model[1], a miraculous shift can occur, affecting millions of people and potentially changing the world. But certainly, the awareness of the Venus Star in one's own life can dramatically alter one's personal energies, one's relationships and can reinforce the feeling that each one of us is playing our part, giving our life the special meaning so many of us are searching for. Much is made in these times of "celebrity", but what of actual talent? The Venus Star Point™ reveals one's special talent in the world.

The Venus Star, simply stated, functions as a celestial heartbeat for Earth and the human race, even though most people are unaware of its effect on people and historical events. During my research, I grasped how well we as humans reflect the Venus Star under which we are born as Venus moves around the zodiacal wheel. This is particularly exciting because it takes the study of astrology to a new level. The Venus Star Point in one's chart is not the Venus of our natal charts; this Venus operates on a different dimension entirely. Never before has this particular point been examined so thoroughly and documented in such detail.

The basic premise of *Venus Star Rising* is that readers can be in better attunement with their life's purpose by learning what Venus Star they were born under and how they can use such knowledge to better understand and create harmony with others in various relationships, as well as contribute to love and harmony on Earth. Imagine how much better our lives would be if we surrounded ourselves with people whose Venus Star Points were in harmony with our own—in workplaces, family units, committees of organizations, or sports teams. Or think how helpful it would be to have information about the Venus Star Points of others to help us understand people whose views differ from ours. With such understanding, we could better communicate and resolve potential conflicts without judgment. If we could apply the contents of this book to our daily activities, it might go a long way towards creating more positive possibilities in our lives.

As I studied, I was equally astounded at how historical events on Earth mirror the pattern of the Venus Star in the sky. It seemed a perfect example of the well-known saying of ancient sages, "As above, so below." This book explores not only how the Venus Star works in our personal charts, but even more importantly, how the Venus Star affects collective human consciousness and historical timelines through its zodiacal star points.

In the following pages we will look deeply into the mythology of the planet Venus to rediscover what ancient mystery schools have told us about Venus—that her energy is not simply a metaphor for the energy of love, but that she transmits the energy of love. From such visual images, we can appreciate the mathematical perfection, beauty, and symbolism that Venus beams to love-hungry planet Earth.

My research on the Venus Star began just before the Venus/Sun conjunction during the retrograde period of June 2004, which was unique among Venus cycles. It marked the first of two periods of Venus to transit the Sun in our lifetimes, the next being in 2012. The last pair of Venus transits occurred in 1874 and 1882, and the next one won't occur until the early twenty-second century. Thus, this unique Venus period marked an auspicious moment for initiating my investigation. The Venus Star and the Venus Star Point (VSP) theory literally "asked" me to transmit this information, which was synchronistic with how Venus's energy was then operating in my own chart. In the Vedic system of planetary periods called *dashas*, as well as in the Western system of planetary periods, I had arrived at my Venus period, an example of a rare occurrence of the same planet period in the Vedic and Western systems simultaneously. And, at the same time came the arrival of my life-mate, Joseph, who possessed a passion for sacred geometry. In his lectures concerning the pentagram, I immediately thought of Venus. The language used by Joseph to describe the energy flow of the pentagram could have also been voiced by an astrologer describing the meaning of the planet Venus, or an astronomer or mathematician giving a discourse on how the Venus orbit equates with the phi ratio. The task I subsequently undertook was an exploration of the geometry, astronomy, mythology, and astrology of Venus.

In *Venus Star Rising*, the ancient myths about Venus and her subsequent astrological meaning are correlated through a thorough examination of her astronomical orbit and the geometrical pattern formed by that orbit. It is this very message that I hope to convey as powerfully and accurately as possible. I hope to underscore how Venus exists in a very special relationship to Earth, and how important it is to recognize its significance for humanity at this particular period of history, given the numerous challenges the world is now facing.

I have sought to present material about the Venus Star in an interesting, informative, and accessible manner for general readers, as well as for astrology practitioners. Once they study aspects of the Venus Star, I am hopeful that practitioners will include this material in their astrological analysis. Once people are aware of the multidimensional aspects of the Venus Star pattern and how it can be used to enhance the horoscope, perhaps similar studies will be undertaken with the other planets to reveal the special significance of their orbital patterns in our lives and on Earth.

Meanwhile, we now have the Venus Star and all its intricate workings to study, to absorb and to enhance our life, our special relationships and to give meaning and understanding to the particular timeline in history we are currently experiencing.

ARIELLE GUTTMAN
JULY 2010

Introduction

VENUS STAR RISING

A New Cosmology For
The Twenty-First Century

Star light, star bright, first star I've seen tonight,
I wish I may, I wish I might,
Have this wish I wish tonight.

Most of us, as children, went outside just after sunset on warm summer evenings to wish upon a star, reciting the verse above. There's a very good chance that the star we focused on was Venus, because Venus is the brightest object in the night sky besides the Moon, and at certain times appears as the "evening star" right after sunset.

Although Venus is not technically a star, but a planet whose light is reflected from the Sun, in her orbit around the Sun she traces a beautiful, almost perfect five-pointed star pattern every eight years, a process that is repeated throughout time. So even though Venus is not a star, we were really not incorrect by wishing upon a star while focusing on Venus.

Venus is known as a planet appearing in the morning or evening sky, which is not only beautiful to gaze at but that inspires expressions of love, beauty, and feminine principles. She has been celebrated in some of the world's greatest musical compositions, poems, and paintings by great masters of the world. Further, Venus is the goddess of the ancient world who perhaps is most recognized and revered still today because of her associations with love, without which life would be lonely, bitter, and hopeless.

In both our night skies and in astrology, the domain of love belongs to Venus. The position of the planet Venus in a person's birth chart tells us a great deal about how successful that person will be in matters of love and relationships throughout life. We can expand our understanding of Venus's influence by combining some basic astronomy, astrology, geometry, mathematics, and mythology to realize the significance of Venus' unique star pattern, the Venus Star. In doing so, we can obtain a more comprehensive view of the effect of Venus on the lives of individuals and on historical developments. It is only since the beginning of the industrial revolution that astronomy and astrology have been separate disciplines. Prior to this it was assumed that properties of a planet and its motion relative to Earth (astronomy) affected people and conditions on Earth (astrology). In this book, we are once again integrating astronomy and astrology to expand our understanding of Venus.

Part I of this book focuses on aspects of astronomy, geometry, mythology, and astrology in relationship to Venus, emphasizing lesser-known mysteries about the planet. In Chapter 1, the geometrical characteristics of the five-pointed star pattern and its meaning are discussed. Venus's orbit in connection to Earth possesses a particular geometry and mathematical quality that is equated with harmony, beauty, love, and peace. This is also how the archetype of Venus has come down to us through the ages and how astrology continues to use it. Further, the diagram of Venus's circular orbit around the Sun is shown, illustrating how it pauses, turns retrograde for about forty days, and "kisses" the Sun, creating what in this book is termed the Star Gate, or Venus Star Point (VSP). Perhaps the most significant aspect of the theories in this book are the implications of the orbit of Venus and its astrological correlations for individuals and the world. Each time Venus moves a degree or two clockwise around the circle from where she completed her previous star pattern, she creates another beautiful five-pointed star, which dramatically affects Earth and its inhabitants. Although most people do not even know the star pattern is occurring, some are perceptive enough to feel it, even if they can't see it. This is a beautiful matrix in which to live life, surrounded by Venus's loving embrace. Just like the ancient mythological female weavers called The Fates by Greeks, who were said to spin the webs of destiny, Venus, our feminine archetype of love and everything beautiful in our world, is doing this in the sky.

Finally, Chapter 1 also explores the background of the Venus Star Point theory by delving into how the planets embody a multidimensional energy field, which is currently being researched in the fields of quantum physics and astronomy.

Chapter 2 looks at myths and stories about Venus that have been passed down from ancient times and how astrology and cosmic elements played an important part in inspiring them, including clues about the significance of the Venus Star.

Part II of *Venus Star Rising* will reveal in great detail how the star points influence your life. For instance, if you were born when the Venus Star Point was in Aries, you may forever go through life with the eyes of a child, constantly discovering new worlds and reinventing yourself as you push down on the accelerator of life. You astound others with your numerous accomplishments in a relatively short time, but are always reinvigorated by pioneering new paths. If you were born on the Virgo Star Point it is likely people fall in love with your devotion, your skills, your analytical sharpness and endless service to others, but perhaps you need to take more time for yourself. If you were born on the Cancer Star Point, you will know that home is where the heart is, that finding the right nest and having a large family system are primary to your life's aim, even though this can be challenging to the expression and expansion of your own individuality. If you were born on the Scorpio Star Point, you endure intensely fiery emotions in relation to partnerships; you are motivated by transformation and change and are excited by the mysterious and dangerous, unafraid to penetrate life's dark mysteries. If you were born on the Aquarius Star Point, you possess a highly charismatic nature that people find hard to resist. You easily gain a following, becoming the voice for your group. You can lead others in new directions in a detached, non-emotional, but sometimes self-righteous way. If you were born on the Gemini Star Point you are multitalented and need to find numerous outlets in which to integrate and express all you have learned. Although your life story, something you would love to tell, involves fiery sibling relationships, you tend to partner with sibling types, that is, people who remind you of a brother or sister and with whom your relationship dynamics reflect how you interact with your brother/sister. These brief summaries are taken from the six most populous groups of stars living today.

Chapter 3 concentrates on the construction of the Venus Star and tracks its time line. With the precision of a Swiss clock, the Venus Star's movements through the ages affect changes on Earth and influence the traits and life aspirations of its inhabitants. Although it is not necessary to understand all the scientific technicalities of the Venus Star and its points, it is important to discover the qualities of the Venus Star under which you were born in order to see how it is operating in your life. Tables for determining your Venus Star Point are included at the end of Chapter 3.

Chapters 4 through 15 discuss the Venus Star Point as it relates to each of the twelve signs of the zodiac. To determine how the Venus Star Points affect one's personal life, the reader can focus on the Venus Star Point under which they were born. In this way, one can become better attuned to their true life's purpose, as well as live in greater harmony with others.

To know exactly how someone else fits into the matrix of the Venus Star design, all that is needed is one's date of birth. Once you know your Venus Star Point, you will need only the birth date of anyone else of importance in your life to better understand your talents and theirs as expressed by the Venus Star placement at birth (Part II). These can include your mate, your children, your siblings, parents, best friends, co-workers, or even your favorite celebrities or inspirational teachers. You will also gain a much richer appreciation of how your relationship with each of these individuals works, who feeds whom, who is fed by whom, or even why the attraction or connection exists at all.

Thus your Star Point influences your point of view, identifies your talents, and leads you to fulfill your life's purpose. It also connects you to people of other Star Points, allowing you to better understand your personal relationships and experience the power and harmony of the Venus Star in its totality.

In deciphering the complexities and meaning of the Venus Star, I have collected data on approximately 1,500 celebrity birthdays so readers can see the Venus Star reflected in people they admire or are inspired by. How the Venus Star Points affect individuals I have labeled their motivating life principle, which is demonstrated through numerous examples in the chapters of Part II.

To better understand how the Venus Star Point affects historical events and trends, Part II contains a large section focusing on history. Although the emphasis is on U.S. history, because as an American it is much more familiar to me, readers will be able to correlate these historical events to major events all around the world, learning how important historical events in many countries synchronize precisely with the Venus Star cycles. Certain historical patterns became obvious during the Venus Star Point transit of a particular sign, allowing an understanding of why the views of one generation differed radically from those of another.

Part III deals with how the Venus Star influences our relationships. I have analyzed over 500 couples to determine how the Venus Star affects partnership dynamics. Chapter 16 focuses on the five-pointed star as it operates in other disciplines, such as Oriental medicine. It also delves into the three types of relationships that exist on the Venus Star.

Appendix I includes various additional, alternative avenues for relating to the Venus Star, such as through mudras and mantras, and on ways to create an appropriate Venus environment.

Appendix II lists the Venus Star Point dates from 1750 to 2050, allowing the reader to look at any figure, past, present or future to determine their VSP.

Appendix III lists nearly 1,500 celebrity birth dates, their Venus Star Points and their Morning Star (MS) or Evening Star (ES) designation.

Appendix IV is designed for readers who know their astrological houses, as the meaning of the Venus Star Point in each house further establishes an individual's heart-centered offering and unique talent.

Ultimately, Venus's design is what the soul longs to look at and experience and what the soul perceives as beautiful. What is beautiful heals. What is harmonious soothes and calms. What is perceived by humans as beautiful is pleasant, and I would say that what is perceived as beauty and harmony brings peace. This routinely occurs in nature. It occurs in music. It occurs in light and color. And it occurs in the human, whose design is based on a replica of the Venus Star design, with our five senses and the five appendages emanating from our heart center. When all five senses are simultaneously activated, we are able to transcend the physical senses and achieve perception of higher dimensions.

Part I

Background of the venus star point Theory

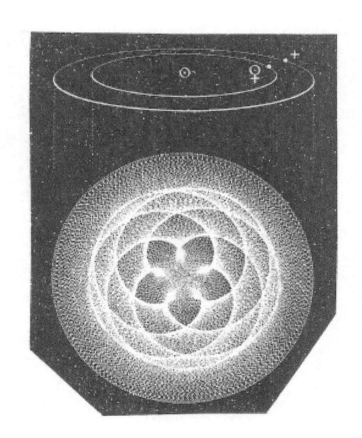

1 THE ASTRONOMY & GEOMETRY OF THE VENUS STAR

Figure 1.1: Venus/Earth Orbit

Venus—A Planet and a Star

Venus is, by far, the brightest object in the sky after the Sun and Moon. This dazzling brilliance contributes to the power and intensity this planet possesses. By scientific definition, Venus is not a star but a planet, a celestial orbiting body that shines by the reflected light of the Sun. However, in relationship to Earth, Venus produces a pentagram, the five-pointed geometrical shape that we refer to as a star. The ancient sky watchers referred to Venus as a star, more specifically, the Morning Star or Evening Star, depending upon at what point of the night she was visible. These two faces of Venus were seen as embodying different characters: the Morning Star was likened to the warrior, and the Evening Star was viewed as the lover, both of which will be examined in this work.

The Form of the Venus Star

One of the most extraordinary aspects of Venus is the Venus Star, a series of repetitive pentagrams that are formed by the Venus orbit in relationship to Earth. Similarly, the orbital patterns of other planets, in combination with that of the Earth, produce beautiful geometric shapes of six, seven, and eight points, but Venus is unique in that she creates a five-pointed star. This is a number with special significance that will be explored more thoroughly in Chapter 2. This Venus star pattern can also be compared to a rose or other flower, such as the daisy, morning glory, or hibiscus (see Figures 1.1 and 1.17).

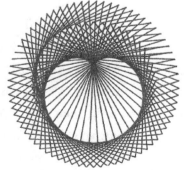

Figure 1.2: The Venus Earth mandala full cycle

The five-pointed patterns diagrammed in figures 1.1 and 1.3 suggest a universal design. In a religious context, universal design is God's way of manifesting one aspect of what people call the heart of God. As scientists discover more about the secrets of nature and the cosmos, many tend to agree that the designs of God's hand produce precise mathematical proportions and beautiful geometrical shapes. Mario Livio poses the question, "Is God a mathematician?" in his book *The Golden Ratio*.[2]

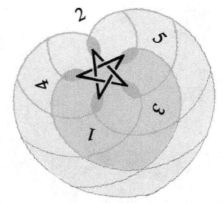

Figure 1.3: The Heart and Star of the Venus Orbit

The center of the computer-generated design shown in figures 1.2 and 1.3 are reminiscent of the shape of a human heart or a human embryo, which is apt, since Venus is associated with love, the language of the heart, and with creation, birth, and regeneration.

Figure 1.4: The human heart

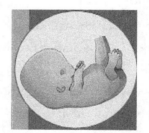

Figure 1.5: The human embryo

The Mechanics of the Venus Star

The Venus Star is a fascinating mechanism engineered with the precision of a giant celestial clock, illustrating the continual dance between Earth and Venus as they orbit around the Sun. Pictured against the backdrop of the twelve constellations of the zodiac, the Venus Star advances through time in a clockwise direction, retrograde from Earth's point of view. In this rendezvous, as Venus moves clockwise around the zodiac, the Sun moves counterclockwise. At the appointed moment of their encounter they kiss or embrace, punctuating one point of what will ultimately culminate in five such encounters, becoming the five-pointed star. Venus and the Sun repeat this same encounter over an eight-year period just one to two degrees clockwise from its previous degree, continuing around the zodiac until the entire star replicates itself 1,250 years later. Every 1,250 years, which constitutes one

The Astronomy & Geometry of the Venus Star

Figure 1.6: Venus-Earth Mandala

complete revolution, the Venus Star returns to the exact same alignment. We could call this a major Venus age, just like we have the Precessional Age of 26,000 years.

During the retrograde cycle of Venus, Venus conjoins the Sun in what is known as the inferior conjunction, an event that occurs when Venus is closest to the Earth and is about to emerge as a Morning Star. Five of these inferior conjunctions with the Sun produce the Venus Star over an eight-year period. The computer-generated Earth/Venus mandala, repeated in figure 1.6, shows an image of the entire 1,250-year cycle of Venus's consecutively formed pentagrams that come into alignment from our view on Earth.

Figure 1.7 illustrates the precision and beauty of the Venus Star pattern over a forty-year period (five full stars). Broken down into five parts, the arms of the star rotate clockwise and repeat the zodiac sequence every 250 years. In that 250-year time frame (one-fifth of the Star), the Star rotates so that the Aries arm of Figure 1.7 becomes the Capricorn arm, Capricorn becomes Scorpio, and so on.

Figure 1.7: A forty-year period of the Venus Star

23

In *The Book of Hiram*, authors Christopher Knight and Robert Lomas say the following about the importance of the Venus cycle:

> *Venus is the metronome of our world. Understand its movements and you can understand such vital functions as the seasons and the tides. It makes you master of your environment both in terms of farming and seamanship, and thereby ensures that you eat well and trade efficiently. In many ways it is the centerpiece of civilization.*[3]

Looking at this same five-star, eight-year pattern in another way, the way that Venus orbits around the Sun viewed from Earth, we might draw a comparison between the eight-year orbital cycle of Venus and the nautilus shell (figure 1.8). Significantly, Venus pauses for forty days in the retrograde period of the 584-day cycle, punctuating a point of the circle called a star gate or a Venus Star Point at precisely 1.6 turns around the wheel. This ratio of 1.6, the Venus Star cycle, is an important numerical value in math, art, design, and nature. Nature reflects this 1.6 design in numerous ways, but perhaps none more pleasing than the nautilus shell, a perfect 1.6 spiral.

Figure 1.8: A nautilus shell

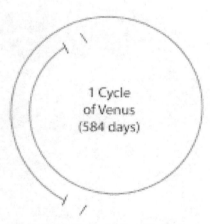

Figure 1.9a: One orbital cycle of Venus

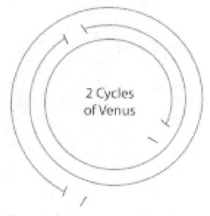

Figure 1.9b: Two orbital cycles of Venus

The Astronomy & Geometry of the Venus Star

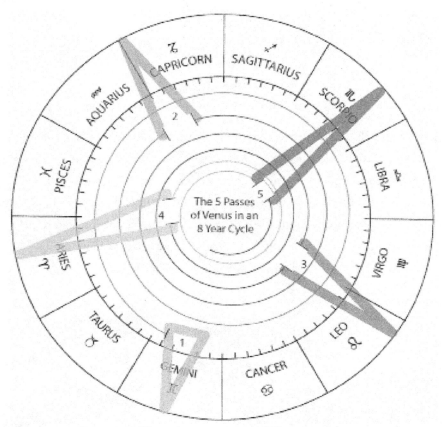

Figure 1.10: The stations or star gates of Venus over eight years

From observing these cycles, it is clear that when a planet—in this case Venus—is moving forward there is no special relationship to Earth other than the harmonic relationship with the Sun/Earth axis around its yearly cycle. But when the direct to retrograde motion is considered from Earth's point of view, this stationary pause amplifies Venus's power while etching another point of the star onto the zodiac.

Figure 1.9a illustrates one of Venus's 584-day cycles around the Sun, from retrograde to retrograde, while Figure 1.9b portrays two complete 584-day cycles. Figure 1.10 portrays five complete Venus cycles as measured against the zodiac, and which clearly illustrates the Venus Star Points that we will be referencing in this book. In the language of mathematics or geometry, the result is a five pointed star. The same form, represented by an artist, would be a spiral. Clearly, the spiral is related to Venus and is further exemplified by the shape we draw to represent a heart. When we draw a heart, we are actually drawing two spirals facing one another and joined together.

Another way to look at the math involved is to divide 584 days (one complete Venus cycle) by 365 (the number of days in a year) or vice versa to get the following:

$$584 \text{ divided by } 365 = 1.6$$
$$365 \text{ divided by } 584 = .62$$

Interestingly, this is the same ratio as the metric conversion system, whereby 1 kilometer = .62 miles or 1.6 kilometers = 1 mile. The .6 or 1.6 ratio that occurs repeatedly in nature has been used extensively in historic construction and architectural creations. Egypt's Great Pyramid, Greece's Parthenon, and the Solomon Guggenheim Museum in New York are examples of the divine proportion of 1.6 in architecture, a proportion said to produce harmony. The 1.6 ratio occurs repeatedly in the Gothic cathedrals of France and most likely was patterned after the architectural design of Solomon's Temple.

Figure 1.11: The Great Pyramid, the Parthenon, the Solomon Guggenheim Museum in New York

The Venus cycle with its retrograde pattern is also reminiscent of a labyrinth (Figure 1.12[4]) There are both twelve-circuit labyrinths and seven-circuit labyrinths. Twelve is the number of the signs of the zodiac, while seven is the number of the original planets, which includes Sun and Moon. Interestingly, many monuments considered to be sacred places or places of power on Earth possess design qualities that mirror cosmic patterns in the sky[5], exemplifying the dictum, "As above, so below." For example, navigating a labyrinth often involves a clockwise movement followed by a counter-clockwise movement and then again a clockwise movement, replicating planetary motion as seen from Earth (Figures 1.9 and 1.10).

The Astronomy & Geometry of the Venus Star

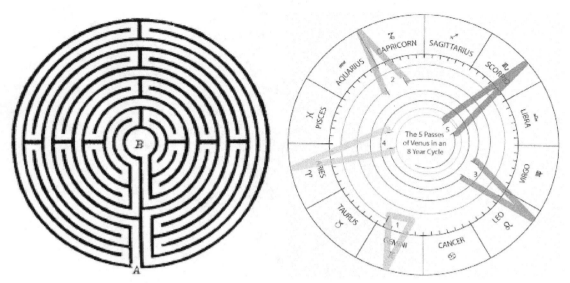

Figure 1.12: A labyrinth compared to the Venus star gates in Figure 1.10 (from above)

During Venus' 584-day cycle there are two conjunctions of Venus to the Sun, one inferior (closest to Earth) and one superior (farthest from Earth). The inferior conjunction produces the subsequently occurring Morning Star, while the superior conjunction gives birth to the Evening Star. (This is the rhythmic alternating heartbeat of Venus as applied to Earth, mentioned in the Introduction.) During both conjunctions there is a period when Venus is invisible to us, concealed in the radiance of the Sun. The reappearance of Venus in the morning sky after its kiss with the Sun occurs fairly rapidly, in about five to ten days, while the visibility of Venus in the evening sky after its same embrace with the Sun takes approximately sixty days.[6] The effects of this on the individual will be discussed in greater detail in Chapter 2. These two conjunctions form two stars interwoven like a shadow or mirror image, as illustrated in figure 1.13, which shows one complete eight-year Venus Star period from 2000 to 2008.

Figure 1.10 illustrates how Venus pauses at a Venus Star Point for forty days in her retrograde cycle five times in an eight-year period. Figure 1.13 illustrates the same sequence against the backdrop of the zodiac. In this scheme, point one, where Venus stops then moves in retrograde (from Earth's point of view) for forty days is the Scorpio Venus Star Point or Scorpio VSP. At this point Venus is at its closest position to Earth, and is seen from Earth as

Figure 1.13: The alternating Venus Star: Morning Star/Evening Star pattern against the zodiac

if it were "kissing the Sun." Then Venus starts a new 584-day cycle, moving 1.6 revolutions around the circle before stopping at point two, the Gemini VSP, for forty days; repeating the process at point three, the Capricorn VSP; point four, the Leo VSP; and point five, the Aries VSP. In this way Venus has replicated its star in our heavens for eons.

Figure 1.14: The Venus Star against the zodiac

If we were to draw any star, we would most likely draw it in the same way Venus's orbit is drawn in the sky pattern as shown in figure 1.13, beginning at point one, then moving to point two, three, four, and five. In this book, we will consider Venus as point one progressing toward or *feeding* point two, and point two feeding point three, and so on. From this point of view, in figure 1.14 Scorpio feeds Gemini, Gemini feeds Capricorn, Capricorn feeds Leo, Leo feeds Aries, and Aries feeds Scorpio. We will call these star relationships, in which signs either feed or are fed by another, "star mates." Part III, "Relationships on the Venus Star," covers the concept of star mates in greater detail.

The Numerical Values of Venus

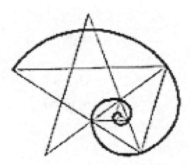

Figure 1.15: The spiral and the star

Logicians, mathematicians, and scientists from Pythagoras, Euclid, and Plato to Albert Einstein and Stephen Hawking have stated that the secrets to unlocking the mysteries of the universe are embedded in its mathematical patterns. Significantly, Venus is associated with two fundamental mathematical relationships: the pentagonal star and the equiangular spiral, as shown in figure 1.15.

This relationship, called the "divine proportion," "the golden mean," or "the golden section," is a mathematical sequence determined by tenth-century Italian mathematician Leonardo Fibonacci:

The Fibonacci Series:
0, 1, 1, 2, 3, 5, 8, 13, 21, 34, 55, 89, 144, 233, 377, 610, 987, 1597, and so forth.[7]

In this sequence, there is a 1.6 relationship from one number to the next. That is, dividing any number in the sequence by the preceding number will yield a 1.6 ratio. It is a ubiquitous ratio found not only in metric conversion tables and the piano keyboard, with each octave containing thirteen keys of eight white and five black, but it is frequently found in the natural world and especially in the construction of the human body. It's the magic number that keeps all the forces of nature working in harmony.

Not surprisingly, the five-pointed star formed by Venus also contains the golden mean. Measuring any line in relationship with another larger or smaller line in the star will result in the 1.6 ratio. Further, if we start with any cross-section of the inner part of the star and draw an arc line outward to the next line crossing, we will end up with this particular phi ratio (1.6) spiral.

Moreover, other numbers connected to Venus have special significance. The numbers five, eight, and thirteen found in the Fibonacci sequence also occur in relationship to Venus. The five points of the Venus Star are created in eight Earth years, which equals thirteen Venus years. Venus spins very slowly on its axis, from Earth's point of view, with five Venus days taking 584 Earth days, which translates into 19.4 months on our current calendar (twenty months on a lunar calendar), a number familiar to astrologers from the cycle of eclipses and transiting lunar nodes.

Interestingly, close to one-half of that cycle, from inferior conjunction to superior conjunction, constitutes the embryonic growth cycle in humans from conception to birth. This is one of the many connections Venus has to love, mating, reproduction, and growth, including being seen as a fertility goddess of antiquity. Using a lunar calendar month, the 29½-day lunar month multiplied by 20 gives us 584 days, one complete Venus cycle. Thus we have: Moon x 20 = Venus and Venus (584) x 20 = 11,680 days, or precisely thirty-two years, four complete Venus Stars. As we will observe in Chapter 2, the Maya, who were great observers of the Venus cycle, placed a great deal of importance on the number 20 in their calendrics, a possible indication that they were very precisely tracking both the Moon and Venus.

The Sacred Geometry of the Venus Star

The sacred geometry of the Venus Star is reflected in the human body as demonstrated by Renaissance genius Leonardo da Vinci's fascination with the "Vitruvian Man"[8] shown in figure 1.16.

In this illustration da Vinci demonstrated the occurrence of the number five and the golden mean in the human body. We note five extended appendages—head, two arms, and two legs. Replicating each of those, we note at the end of each another set of five—five fingers at the end of each arm, five toes at the end of each leg, and five sense organs on the head.

The Astronomy & Geometry of the Venus Star

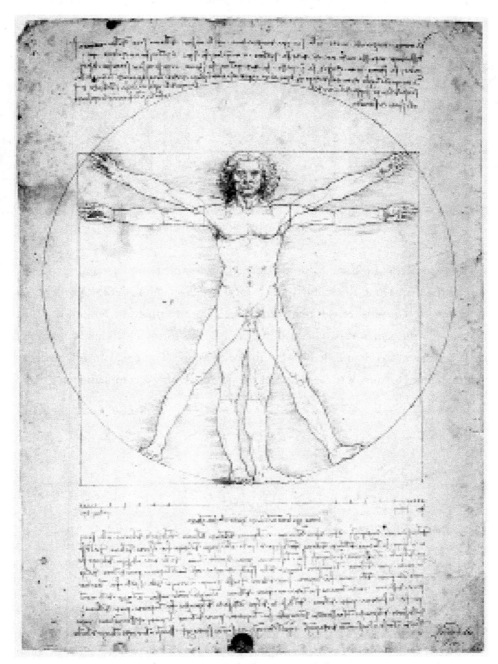

Figure 1.16 The "Vitruvian Man"

Countless species in nature embody these same proportions and principles, as can be readily seen by studying the forms of plants or fruits, as shown in figure 1.17.

Figure 1.17: Hibiscus, an apple, a starfish

The geometry of the star form is particularly relevant for understanding the harmony of the Venus Star. Regarding the star form, Michael Schneider's *A Beginner's Guide to Constructing the Universe*[9] reveals that the pentad is born through the *vesica piscis*, the almond shape in the center of two overlapping circles. This form, which has been revered throughout the ages, has been called the "womb of creation." Two equal circles are drawn, one circumference crossing over the center of the other, forming a complementary shape as shown in figure 1.18.

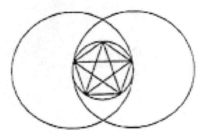

Figure 1.18: The vesica piscis containing the pentad and the star

The *vesica piscis*, or mandorla (almond) is the mother of the five platonic solids from which all material creation is born. One of these solids, the dodecahedron shown in figure 1.19, consists of twelve five-sided faces, or pentagons. If you were to draw a line from one point of the pentagon, skip the next point, and connect the line to every other point, we would have a five-pointed star.

Figure 1.19: Three-dimensional view of a dodecahedron

Schneider also reveals that from ancient times this five-pointed star has been a magical symbol for warding off evil in many parts of the world, including Babylon, Egypt, Greece, India, China, Africa, and the Americas. He concludes that not only does the flag of the United States contain fifty such stars, sixty countries have put this star on their flag.[10]

Medieval magicians and alchemists were also aware of the five-pointed star's power to ward off evil and to attract wealth and power. The upward-pointing star or pentagram was said to bring good fortune and protection, while the downward-pointing pentagram was thought to attract ill fortune (see figures 1.20a and b).

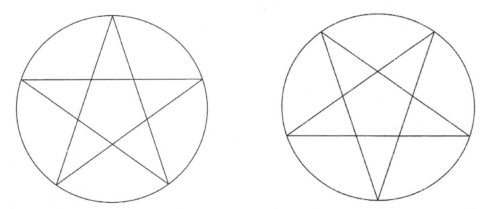

Figure 1.20a: Upward pointing pentagram compared to downward pointing pentagram, Figure 1.20b

Furthermore, when all the points of the star are connected with straight lines, as in figure 1.22, the five-pointed star becomes a pentagon.

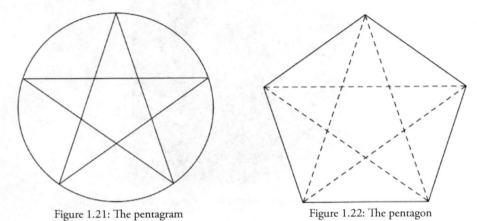

Figure 1.21: The pentagram   Figure 1.22: The pentagon

Notice how the image has a different effect when enclosed by a circle versus a series of straight lines, as shown in figures 1.21 and 1.22. When the star is enclosed by a circle, there is a flow consistent with nature, a feeling that is absent when it is enclosed in straight lines. When the outreaching arms of the pentagram are enclosed in a pentagon, the result is a powerful defense system and an invocation of the power of the pentagram to attract what is desired. It's interesting that the U.S. Department of Defense is housed in a building of this shape called the Pentagon and that more funding has been allotted to support the agency's military campaigns than any other department of the U.S. government.

Further, the Earth-Venus five-pointed star mimics the human desire to reproduce in that its form can be replicated endlessly by connecting the lines and points as shown in figures 1.23a and b.

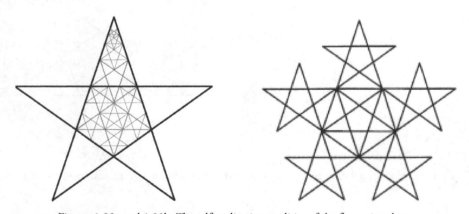

Figures 1.23a and 1.23b: The self-replicating qualities of the five-pointed star

The pattern, endlessly repeating itself inwardly in Figure 1.23a, mimics human and biological cell regeneration in the internal repetition of the star. Figure 1.23b illustrates the external representation of the star, reaching out to attach itself to another star, replicating a deep human desire to reproduce itself in one form or another, be it through one's offspring, one's artistic creations, or one's inventions. In this manner, the human fear of death is assuaged in that life continues through one's offspring. Thus, the Venus Star represents magnetism, fertilization, conception, life, and immortality.

Figure 1.24: The morning glory: the heart & star of Venus

The Birth of Aphrodite, Sandro Botticelli, 1485

2 THE MYTHOLOGY AND ASTROLOGY OF VENUS

The Mythology of Venus

My twenty-five years of researching mythic astrology, connecting the mythology of the zodiac and planets to stories created about them by ancient cultures, has made me see that our ancestors' knowledge of celestial events, without benefit of modern technology, is astonishing.

Figure 2.1: Venus of Laussel, c. 22,000 BCE

Instead of TV, the ancients were watching the theater of the night sky with its stars and planets reflecting myths and projecting energetic forces that helped shape stories of who we are and where we came from. We know that these ancient sky-watchers were especially captivated by Venus, as there is no shortage of material concerning that planet that has come down through the ages.

The planet that this book is dedicated to was named Venus by the Romans. It was this same planet that the Greeks called Aphrodite, that the Babylonians worshipped as Ishtar, and that the Sumerians honored as Inanna. Astarte and Ashtaroth were other names bestowed upon her in the Near East, but she existed all around the world in every culture, named differently, but meaning the same thing. Reaching even farther back into prehistory, she was known simply as the Great Goddess. The attributes, mythologies, and characteristics of all of these differently named goddesses have combined to create a lineage of what present-day Venus carries with her.

Images of Venus have come down to us much more frequently than any other mythological archetype over the millennia. Figures 2.1 through 2.14 show some of the images of Venus and associated goddesses over the past twenty-five thousand years.

Venus has been represented in many forms in Western mythology from ancient times to the classical era of Greece and Rome and the present. The earliest representations of Venus, such as those embodied by the goddesses Ishtar, Inanna, Isis, Astarte, and Aphrodite, are all associated with sensuality, fertility, and the female principle and are often portrayed bare-breasted with nothing more than the hint of a garment concealing their private parts. But once the religious patriarchy of Judaism, Christianity, and Islam was established as the arbiter of moral codes, images of Venus showed the goddess clothed and increasingly associated with love rather than sensuality and fertility. During this era, Venus became more virginal, always clothed and shrouded, so that no part of her body was visible except her hands and face. Despite this tendency, there were a few periods in which her image was less constrained, such as the era of the knights and troubadours, and the Renaissance, when artists and poets focused on her romantic beauty and her associations with love. However, by the modern era Venus has become pornographic, as the images of female nudity are often represented as purely sexual. Such portrayals lack artistic beauty and love. Porn websites, which proliferate on the Internet, are the most sought after sites on the Web.

Figure 2.2: Venus von Willendorf, c. 20,000 BCE

Figure 2.3: Medici Venus Aphrodite

History and Myth

For the purposes of this book, the mythology of Venus is predominantly drawn from the Greek Aphrodite, as the Greek system of mythology meticulously tracked and recorded a very rich and textured portrayal of their gods. Furthermore, the ideas of the Greeks have largely informed Western thought, and to a great extent, contemporary astrology. However, the planet that has brightly lit the morning or evening skies for millennia is named Venus from her

Figure 2.4: Capitoline

The Mythology and Astrology of Venus

Roman roots, even though her mythology is practically identical to Greek Aphrodite. And so there exists a marriage of sorts, Venus and Aphrodite melded into one shining planet goddess archetype.

Aphrodite came to the Greeks from the east, which may be why they connected her to Cyprus, an island in the far eastern Mediterranean, in proximity to the goddesses Ishtar, Inanna, and Astarte from Babylonian, Sumerian, Mesopotamian, and Hebrew legends. But the later Hellenes also set up worship centers for her in Cytheria, an island off the coast of the Peloponnese, and still later in the acropolis of Corinth. Although the Maya and Babylonians saw this planet as having dual aspects of love and war, the Greeks saw the corresponding goddess, Aphrodite, simply as a love goddess.

In Greek mythology, there are two basic stories about the origin of Venus. The one most commonly told in Greek myth is that Venus arose from the sea as a result of the castration of Uranus by Saturn. Uranus's genitals fell into the sea and mixed with the sea foam. From that first emerged the three Furies—which can be seen as a shadow side of Venus—followed by Venus floating to shore on a shell. In this version of her origin, Venus is known as Venus Urania, or "celestial" Venus. As a result of this myth, Venus is often characterized as a beautiful young goddess emerging from the ocean, floating on a seashell, as in the poet Hesiod's works (figure 2.7) and later Renaissance artist Sandro Botticelli's well-known painting, *The Birth of Aphrodite* (figure 2.8). The comparison between the Venus Star and seashells was well established in Chapter 1.

Figure 2.5 Terra Cotta Aphrodite

Figure 2.6: Venus de Milo, c. 200 BCE, The Louvre, Paris, France

Figure 2.7 Birth of Aphrodite

39

Figure 2.8: The Birth of Aphrodite, Sandro Botticelli, 1485

One of the fragments left from antiquity that perhaps best embodies the harmony and grace that is said to characterize Venus is the Venus de Milo at the Louvre Museum in Paris, France (figures 2.6 and 2.9). Not unlike the Venus temples of antiquity where worshippers arrived in great numbers to lay their offerings to the Goddess of Love, the Venus de Milo in the Louvre is host to throngs of daily visitors, still worshipping at her feet.

Figure 2.9: Venus de Milo, The Louvre, Paris, France

The other myth of the Greek Aphrodite is that she was sired by Zeus who mated with Dione, an earth goddess. In this form, she is associated with nature, sensuality, and reproduction. Here she is called Aphrodite Pandemos, the "common" goddess, referring to the love of one person for another. The earlier story of her origins from the sea as Aphrodite Urania or the "celestial" goddess reflects the love of the human for the divine.

Several elements in the Pandemos story reveal important aspects about Aphrodite's qualities and symbolism. First, she was forced by Zeus into an arranged marriage to the lame smith god Hephaestus, known as Vulcan in Rome. Aphrodite was the loveliest goddess of the heavenly and earthly realms, yet Zeus married her to the ugliest of gods. However, she took Ares as her lover, essentially ignoring the fact that she was married, causing Hephaestus to be ridiculed before all the gods of Olympus. However, the outrageous act of Aphrodite (Venus in Rome) and Ares (Mars in Rome) gave birth to the goddess Harmonia. Earth is situated between feminine Venus and masculine Mars, and serves to balance the energies of these two primary forces.

Venus's (Aphrodite's) marriage to Vulcan (Hephaestus) in the myth seems to underscore the truth that beauty is in the eyes of the beholder. Hephaestus was considered ugly by the gods of Olympus, yet he forged and crafted the most beautiful objects the eye could behold. Aphrodite was considered the most beautiful goddess to gaze upon, and yet her inner beauty was marred by jealousy and vanity. The Greeks "married" these two gods to reflect the shadow side of beauty. This echoes a basic Jungian concept, merging light and dark, whereby wholeness can be achieved.

Figure 2.10: Venus and Graces, Sandro Botticelli, c. 1484-1486

The myth also demonstrates that Venus is a force of nature that seizes us all at any moment (later pictured as Cupid's arrow), a force that cannot be controlled or suppressed by marriage. Venus arose from earlier, pre-patriarchal, Earth-centered goddess cultures, times before "arranged" marriages became customary. In Greek myth, the "free love" goddess became much less free by virtue of marriage, a patriarchal concept. In more recent times marriage partners have been chosen by virtue of love for one another, rather than arrangements made by their families. In this type of marriage, *hieros gamos*, men and women or same gender couples enter into a union that is based on sacred love, circumstances in which Venus also reigns.

Vulcan and Venus have another interesting connection. There exists severe volcanism on the planet Venus, the word volcano being derived from Vulcan, god of volcanoes. Among other things, these associations suggest that the ancients may have, on some level, linked Venus to the turbulent emotions experienced in love.

Figure 2.11: Venus and Mars, Sandro Botticelli, 1483

Further reminding us that Venus has a dark side are her associations with the tragic side of love told through the ages in literature, song, theater, and opera. Such stories focus on the lack of love, one dying for love, a loved one being inaccessible or betrothed to another. Adonis was a beautiful man with whom Aphrodite became enamored. In the story of Aphrodite's intense love for him, the mortal Adonis died suddenly as the result of a deadly boar hunt. Aphrodite was emotionally torn apart by his death. Though she may rule the kingdom of love, she herself is not immune to its sorrow.

Figure 2.12: Ishtar, c. 2000 BCE
Illustrations by Jaye Oliver

Ancient myths about the Roman goddess Venus and her Greek counterpart, Aphrodite, abound in the literature of mythology (see bibliography). Ean Begg in *The Cult of the Black Virgin*[11] notes that astrology is one of the few fields that has consistently helped keep these pagan goddesses alive during the last two thousand years, with Venus leading the pack.

According to author Michael Baigent[12], the early Greek Olympics, held every eight years, coincided with the eight-year cycle of the Venus Star. Similarly, the Pythia Games in Delphi and the Pan-Hellenic Games throughout Greece coincided with the star of Venus.[13] Later the Olympics were held every four years, perhaps echoing the alternating Venus Star return every four years, between morning and evening phases. It is also possible that the idea of the truce between warring nations as an early component of the games also had something to do with the nature of Venus in her form as the love goddess.

Literature has also played its part in keeping the Venus myth alive. Love stories throughout the ages have portrayed characters that have prayed, sung, danced, and called out to Venus for love in a variety of ways. For example, in the story of Pygmalion, it was Venus who turned stone into living flesh, bringing Pygmalion's marble lover to life. Shakespeare, too, calls upon Venus/Aphrodite, the Morning Star or Evening Star, numerous times when characters implore her to send some of her love charms their way.

A more recent work on Venus that underscores her association with love is C.S. Lewis's *Perelandra*, the second book of a trilogy written in 1943 concerning Venus, Mars, and Earth. Perelandra is the name given to Venus whose environment is a tropical island paradise, a theme linked to Venus as symbolic of passion and love.

The Dual Nature of Venus: Morning Star and Evening Star

Figure 2.13: Venus of Capua
Illustrations by Jaye Oliver

Two observations have led me to conclude that the Venus Star affects Earth and its inhabitants in much greater ways than anyone has yet comprehended. The myths and legends that have come down to us through the ages give Venus two faces—that of the Morning Star and the Evening Star—and the qualities ascribed to Venus in such stories seem correct when observing which star is operating in a person's life based upon when they were born.[14]

The myths point to Venus as both the goddess of love and of war. She does seem to have a firm grip on Earth and its inhabitants, cradling us in her star pattern, keeping humans between the states of love and war. Transcending this duality, so that we can reflect the love that is the core principle of Venus and the universe, is the major challenge currently faced by humanity.

Accepting that Venus has a dual nature—that she is both a love goddess and a warrior goddess—acknowledges the holistic nature of Venus and of love itself. Although we may think of war more as a masculine phenomenon and love as associated with the feminine principle, the ancients saw Venus as female, whether lover (Evening Star) or warrior (Morning Star). This takes in the dual nature of Venus and the dual nature of love, in which the shadow side is fear, anger, jealousy, hatred, rage, and war fueled by a wounded or broken heart.

Astrologer Robert Hand has noted the following:

There are two distinctly different Venuses. <u>All</u> astrological traditions except the modern Western one, and to some extent the Hindu one, recognize this. There is a warrior Venus and a love goddess Venus. They're both female. But one of them is more like Athena. The warrior goddess Venus is Venus as a Morning Star. Phosphorus Lucifer, although it should be "Lucifera." There's nothing satanic about it. It's just a warrior goddess. And the evening one is the soft, squishy love goddess. They actually have different names. In Mesopotamia it was Ishtar Akkad and Ishtar Uruk. One was a Morning Star, the other the Evening Star Venus. The MesoAmericans recognized this phenomenon, the Chinese recognized this phenomenon, so did the Mesopotamians, and there are references to it in Greek astrology as well. If you have a morning Star Venus and it is powerfully placed in your chart and you are a woman, you probably are not as soft and squishy as the modern textbooks would *have you believe. It's a placement that makes a woman very beautiful, but not in a soft, squishy way. Sort of Valkyrian—grand, statuesque, strong. So the ancient Venus embodies two distinctly different types of feminine. And yet, they are both feminine, which is something we should pay a great deal of attention to in modern astrology.*[15]

Various aspects of the dual nature of Venus can be summed up in the following chart:

MORNING STAR	EVENING STAR
Venus Phosphorus Lucifer	Venus Hesperus
Aphrodite Pandemos	Aphrodite Urania
Warrior goddess	Love goddess
Yang	Yin
Closest to Earth: perigee	Farthest from Earth: apogee
Follows retrograde cycle	Follows direct cycle
In the "underworld"	In the "upperworld"
Rules the daytime	Rules the nighttime
Moves slower	Moves faster
Follows inferior conjunction with Sun	Follows superior conjunction with Sun
Ruler of Taurus	Ruler of Libra
Daughter of Zeus and Dione	Daughter of Gaia and Ouranos
Primal, raw sensuality	Refined, social acceptability
Earth goddess	Sky goddess
Ascends rapidly, descends slowly	Ascends slowly, descends rapidly
Visible ~6-8 days following conjunction	Visible ~60 days following conjunction

Table 2.1: Aspects of the dual nature of Venus

As Robert Hand remarks, indeed, there is nothing satanic about the star drawn as a pentagram and named Venus Lucifer, although many people have twisted the image and taken it as a satanic symbol. In the old goddess religions, there were two ways the pentagram was interpreted. If the pentagram pointed upwards, it was seen as a blessing and if it pointed downwards it was seen as a curse or time to focus inward and observe the dark nature of things (see figures 1.20a and b). However, the goddess religions did not negate the dark side but considered it merely a necessary ingredient of life's interplay between light and darkness.

The Venus Star does point in various directions at different times. For example, from 1960 to 1964, when the Venus Star moved across the cusp of Cancer and Gemini, it pointed downward and when the Venus Star transits the cusp of Capricorn to Sagittarius (around

2078), it will point upwards. The only demonic implication of the Venus Star is that when what it represents—light and love—becomes blocked or destroyed by people, its dark side, which is fear, emerges. It is, after all, people's fears that have created demons.

A Psychological Comparison between Morning Star and Evening Star

The Mayan concept of Morning Star/Evening Star that has come down to us refers to the relationship that Venus in the sky had to their decision-making practices concerning policies, politics, weather prediction, and most particularly war. The Maya linked its warrior nature to the Morning Star and its benevolent nature to the Evening Star phase.

A literal interpretation might lead the modern individual to draw an incorrect conclusion about Venus in their chart. What does the modern woman, for instance, as a peace-loving individual, do with the idea that she is a Scorpio (sign of battle) Morning Star (warrior goddess)?

The Morning Star Venus may be instinctually more capable of being a war goddess when the situation arises—that is, expressing her anger or rage, becoming an activist for causes, and fighting for what she feels or believes in—but she is also capable of being a love goddess. The Evening Star Venus may be much more comfortable in surroundings and relationships that are predominantly harmonious, while denying that anger, hostility, and disharmony even exist. But the integrated, self-aware Venus operates from the place that acknowledges both sides as needed at different stages, appropriate to the situation.

If we consider the Greek notion of Venus Pandemos versus Venus Urania, we might glean from their understanding and nomenclature that Pandemos (the Morning Star Venus) was a goddess of the Earth, while Urania (the Evening Star Venus) was a celestial entity. The twelfth century Hebrew astrologer Avraham Ibn Ezra explains how the combination of being light in body and movement, and at the height of its circle above the Earth, makes the planet's influence more subtle and soul-related.

> *It has a less noticeable effect upon earthly events, and in the consideration of temperament and physical description, it describes the body as sensitive and lacking strength; however, there is a greater level of spiritual purity, and the mind is more receptive to inspiration and higher wisdom…as she pulls away from the Sun and descends from apogee to draw closer to the Earth, the strength of her influence upon all mundane matters increases.*[16]

This, I believe, has a fuller and richer psychological implication for the person who possesses the Uranian (Evening Star) Venus versus the Pandemos (Morning Star) Venus. The Pandemos Venus is one who inhabits the earth, is connected to the physical world and the physical sensations of the body, and who is more likely to feel internally complete. The Pandemos Venus is likely to have faith in themselves and what they see in the world of nature. They know how things operate in the physical world, understand the laws of science, accept the mechanical nature of things, are very aware that the needs of the material world (developing skills and resources that are marketable and sustaining) might be driving them and is responsive to their internal drives. Pandemos Venus personalities desire partnership, but because they are complete within themselves, they do not need a partner to validate their ideas, instincts, and actions. The partnerships for Pandemos Venus are driven by desires for companionship, exchange, and for reasons even more basic to the instinctual desires of Pandemos: sexual union, fertility, and reproduction of the species. There is a tendency for the Pandemos Morning Star Venus to see their partnerships realistically rather than idealistically.

The Evening Star, Urania Venus, located on the far side of the Earth, in the heavenly abode, seems to live not only outside the boundaries of the physical body, but often at a great distance from the physical world. Urania Venus, connected to the sky and to the idea of the deity being placed in the cosmic panorama of stars, is where people with this Venus configuration are focused. The Evening Star Venus moves through life as if they float or fly; they have a rich imagination; they are poetry in motion; they are alluring and have a very well formulated "other-worldly" perspective on life. The problem for people born under the influence of this Urania Venus is that they need to be reminded that they do possess a body; they are in human form; they are connected to the earth; and they do have to learn to navigate accordingly. It is more common for them to look outside themselves for approval and validation, and they do this by connecting with a partner, a guru or teacher (or God or the Holy Spirit or the Great Mother Goddess, etc.), or a series of life partners who will seem to offer the completeness they are searching for in life.

Neither of these personalities—Pandemos or Urania—is good or bad; they simply act in accordance with the placement of Venus prior to their birth. Pandemos Venus, the Morning Star, occurs just after Venus and the Sun are in inferior conjunction at their closest point to the Earth. In contrast, the Evening Star, or Urania Venus, occurs when Venus and the Sun are in superior conjunction at their farthest point from the Earth—out there in the heavenly realm—in a world far removed from the physical. There is a different rhythm operating in each of these Venuses as well. The Morning Star Venus shoots rapidly to maximum elongation in about eighty days, then descends quite slowly, while her twin the Evening Star slowly ascends to maximum elongation, then, in about eighty days, quickly descends.[17]

Pandemos Venus, the Morning Star, has been thought of as an initiator, while Urania Venus, the Evening Star, has been considered a receiver. Consequently, it is not surprising that Venus rules two signs in astrology—Pandemos rules Taurus (the earthy one) and Urania rules Libra (the airy one). Both are exalted in Pisces, where Venus becomes one with the oceanic realm from whence she came. In this context, we could say Venus as the Evening Star better fits the nature of Libra in the western part of the zodiacal wheel, reflecting her true western direction as setting after the Sun. Venus as the Morning Star better fits the nature of Taurus, a sign located in the eastern part of the zodiacal wheel, reflecting her position in the eastern sky as rising before the Sun.

Thus, when considering the interpretation of the Venus Star in a person's chart, there are several factors to consider. What house and sign does she occupy? Is she a Morning Star (Pandemos) or an Evening Star (Urania)? And finally, what zodiacal sign does the Venus Star Point occupy at one's birth?

Symbols of Venus and the Medieval Church

Medieval Christianity and its focus on the search for the Holy Grail is a period of history in which a rare interest in Venus turns up. Some intriguing connections exist between ideas associated with both the planet and goddess Venus and iconic religious symbols.

First, the symbol of the rose is linked to both Venus and Christianity in a number of ways. The illustration (figure 1.1) of the orbit of Venus likens her to a flower, particularly a rose. In Rome, the goddess Venus was known by her flower, the rose, which was the emblem of the sacred priestesses in her temples.[18] Later, with the emergence during the Medieval era of the great Gothic cathedrals, especially in France, roses and rose windows became a central focus.

Although these windows were created to honor Mary, who had by then become the main icon of the feminine principle, ancient Venus cult-worship linked the symbol of the rose with the Mary-worship of Medieval Christianity. Another interesting fact is that these rose windows faced west, the direction in which Venus appears in the night sky as the Evening Star, associated with love.

In addition, around this time, the troubadours of southern France, who were known for their songs extolling love, took the rose as their symbol. The word *rose* is an anagram of Eros, the god of erotic love, and the son of Venus in later myths.[19]

Alan Butler makes a comparison between the ancient goddess, the planet Venus, and the rose in his book *The Goddess, The Grail, and the Lodge*[20]. In it he states that the ancient peoples were worshippers of the Goddess, watchers of the planet Venus who were aware of Venus's cycle, and knew of Venus's connection with the rose and five-petaled flowers.[21] This seems to suggest that they were cognizant of the Venus Star the planet draws while orbiting.

Butler also draws convincing associations between Venus and the Christian rosary in which ancient and Christian traditions can be seen as overlapping. The rosary, whose name derives from the word *rose,* is a set of fifty beads separated into units of ten by the inclusion of a larger, extra bead between the groups. Extended from the main section or circle is a string of three beads, marked at each end by a larger bead, and finally at the end of this is a crucifix. Butler then compares the orbital cycle of Venus with the number of beads contained in the rosary[22] to come up with some striking corresponding patterns. One of these patterns, a rosary bead, is shown emulating the shape of the glyph for Venus—a circle of beads with a cross extending out from the circle.[23]

Figure 2.14a: Christian Rosary   Figure 2.14b: Venus Glyph

Venus and the Astrology of the Mayan Calendar

The Moon and Venus cycles described above in Christian symbolism were also of special interest to the Maya, who possessed considerable knowledge about both celestial objects. The Maya were particularly devoted to Venus. They meticulously observed and tracked the planet's orbital cycles of 584 days each and filled their manuscripts and artwork with references to Venus, including the Mayan calendar, which culminates in 2012. As we draw closer to 2012 and explore the meaning of that date, we might conclude that it has a great deal to do with the energy of Venus and the Venus Star.

The wave of love that is sweeping over humankind at this time and the new empowerment of and respect for the voice and way of the feminine seem to be synchronized with the increasing awareness of the Venus Star's power and with the Mayan calendar transitional date of 2012. The fact that astronomical and astrological experts are aware of the Venus pattern and are disseminating information about it through the Internet, combined with the currently changing consciousness and the rising tide of feminine energy, have led me to conclude that the time of the Venus Star has arrived.

The Maya were aware of Venus's 584-day cycle: her appearance first as a Morning Star for 260 days, her disappearance and re-emergence as an Evening Star for 260 days, and finally her forty-day retrograde cycle. Scholars have found it quite remarkable that Mayan calendrics record Venus's orbit as precisely as within one day in 6,000 years[24] and that Venus's 584-day cycle, from one inferior conjunction of Venus with the Sun to the next, may have become the basis for a Mayan calendar of 586 days. They were especially interested in Venus's forward/retrograde cycle and star pattern and the eclipse cycles. Many of these cycles fit into their Long Count, which is an integral part of the Mayan calendar. Especially intriguing is the fact that the Mayan Long Count calendar, which dates from 3114 BCE, ends at the winter solstice in 2012, and six months prior to the winter solstice in 2012 Venus makes a second transit across the Sun, in the sign of Gemini, repeating the one it made in 2004. For the Maya, the beginning of the Venus almanac in *The Dresden Codex* marked the first rising of the planet Venus.[25] While there is no evidence that Venus's second transit of Gemini across the Sun in 2012 is specifically connected to the end of the Mayan calendar, it is one of many astronomical events set to occur at that time. In *Galactic Alignment*, John Major Jenkins[26] explains the astronomical alignment that occurs in 2012—that of the winter solstice Sun aligning precisely with the Center of the Milky Way (the Galactic Center). The more visible and smaller event that simultaneously occurs in 2012 is the rare transit of Venus across the Sun, occurring at the anti-Galactic Center, six months prior, which could be an important marker. It seems reasonable that these transits of Venus were factored into the Long Count and influenced the Mayan awareness of time. However, today's Maya do not use this particular calendar. The elders hold the view that "if our ancestors considered 2012 to be important, it probably is. But it is not a living tradition which we follow today."[27]

It has been widely noted that the ancient Maya recorded the Venus Star cycles in their calendar, particularly *The Dresden Codex*.[28] Furthermore, Mayan researchers consistently observed two astronomical events that were meticulously tracked and recorded—the eclipse cycles and the Venus Star cycles.[29] With this fact in mind, we might take a look at what these two cycles indicate about the important Mayan calendar date of 2012. The Maya might well have noted that in 2012 both solar and lunar eclipses are sandwiched in by the Venus Star at the retrograde cycle (inferior conjunction with the Sun) when Venus emerges as a Morning Star (warrior goddess). Punctuating both of these two carefully observed Mayan events (the rising of the Venus Star and the eclipses), what also occurs in the period from 2010 to 2015, with 2012 dead-center at the heart of it, is the paradigm-shifting Uranus/Pluto square in cardinal signs. This astronomical event would have been completely off the radar screen for the Maya, as neither planet was discovered until recent times (Uranus: eighteenth century, Pluto: twentieth century). Whenever the outer planets (Uranus, Neptune, and Pluto) are aligned, great transformations occur on Earth. Periods of history that involve chaotic times of great change in the world's social, political, and economic institutions are reflections of celestial alignments, a good example of which is the Uranus-Pluto-Venus Star conjunction of the 1960s, a time of great upheaval on earth, a time of uncertainty, chaos, and intense change. During that time, which might give us an indication about changes to come[30], Saturn's entire transit through Pisces opposed both Uranus and Pluto, alongside of which was the Venus Star. Further, the eclipse points squared Saturn, Uranus, Pluto, and the Venus Star, forming a large cross as follows:

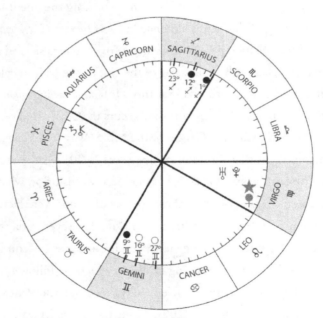

Figure 2.15: 1960s planet/eclipse/Venus Star pattern

Proceeding forward to the timeline of 2012, we note a similar pattern to that which occurred in the 1960's.

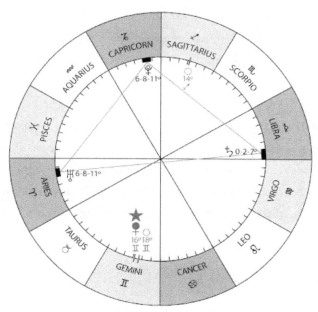

Figure 2.16: The 2012 cycle of Venus and eclipses

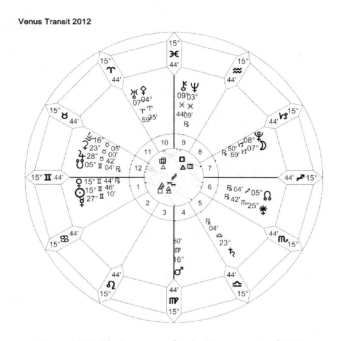

Figure 2.17: The horoscope for the Venus transit of 2012

Figure 2.17 shows the horoscope for the Venus transit through the center of the

51

Sun, positioned at sunrise on the equator, for June 5, 2012. In general, the chart reflects transition to an abrupt end of something and expectation of the birth of something new. The single most important astrological aspect is the Sun/Venus conjunction at 15° Gemini, in an applying square to Mars at 16° Virgo. The male principle represented by Mars at 16° Virgo is being challenged by the female principle, represented by Venus and the Venus Star Point located at 15° Gemini. The feminine perspective is empowered to rise above the horizon when the masculine is at its nadir. Furthermore, when Mars is rising, Venus is culminating.

There also exists a very tight square from Uranus to Pluto that has been in effect for several years and will be for several more. While this aspect is unrelated to the Venus transit, it and the Moon passing through the most critical zone of that orb can leave us feeling poised for some major breakthrough—or breakdown.

Venus Transits Across the Face of the Sun

Figure 2.17 illustrates how Venus passes over the Sun in the unique pair of transits in 2004 and 2012. This transit of Venus is a rare astronomical event, occurring at the following time periods:

December 1631	Venus transits Sun	Sagittarius Morning Star (MS)
December 1639	Venus transits Sun	Sagittarius MS
June 1761	Venus transits Sun	Gemini MS
June 1769	Venus transits Sun	Gemini MS
December 1874	Venus transits Sun	Sagittarius MS
December 1882	Venus transits Sun	Sagittarius MS
June 2004	Venus transits Sun	Gemini MS
June 2012	Venus transits Sun	Gemini MS
December 2117	Venus transits Sun	Sagittarius MS
December 2125	Venus transits Sun	Sagittarius MS

Table 2.2: Venus transits of the Sun

The transit of our time occurs as a twin transit in the sign of Gemini, the twins. The 2012 transit could be a clue left by the Maya, with their numerous references to Venus and to

"Hero Twins" as recorded in their creation epic, the *Popol Vuh*.[31] In fact, Dennis Tedlock's translation of the *Popol Vuh* links the Hero Twins entirely to Venus.

This type of event—the transit of Venus to the Sun—is no different than an eclipse, but is created by a planet rather than the Moon. In this case, both the Sun and Venus occupy the same longitude (degree of the zodiac) and declination north or south of the equator. The Moon can create a total eclipse of the Sun, since from Earth's view both appear to be relatively the same size. Whereas in the Venus transit, the effect is that of a spot moving across the Sun's disc, as shown in Figure 2.18. The historical effects of this transit have not yet been examined in detail, but preliminary signs indicate that they are somewhat epic in terms of both historical events and those who are born during these transits. Both events and individuals that belong to these Venus transits play a large part in subsequently shaping the evolution of new ideas and theories that are transformational to the Earth and its inhabitants.

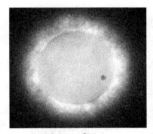

Figure 2.18: Photo of Venus transit 2004

The Mayan Mythos of Venus

In addition to the Mayan knowledge of Venus in connection with their calendar, they had specific myths about Venus. But the myths, stories, renderings, and rituals about Venus by the Maya would take a volume the size of this one to reiterate. It is much too simplistic to think that the Maya had only one story or meaning ascribed to Venus. There were several Mayan periods, several villages and vantage points from which to track her orbit, and thus hundreds of meanings. Among the Maya, who were great astronomers, there is scant information about Mercury, Mars, Jupiter, and Saturn. But about the Sun, Moon, and Venus there exist volumes. Venus had multiple personalities based on the five seasonal risings over the eight-year period, and for each rising a particular face or deity would be ascribed, similar to our Star signs[32].

One of the stories that is linked to Mayan mythology is that when Venus went into retrograde, it went into the underworld. There it encountered the Sun, then became inflamed in the Sun's heart, and emerged as a warrior, dripping with blood and ready for battle. The timing of this correlated to the periods when the Mayan armies prepared for battle. If there was a high degree of tension in the world during the forty-day retrograde periods, such tensions would be accentuated when Venus emerged from the underground as the Morning Star. And there is no hesitation to actions undertaken at this part of the cycle. As mentioned previously, when Venus emerges as the Morning Star, she ascends to maximum elongation in about eighty days—quite rapidly.

Figure 2.19: Photograph of Venus

The Astrology of Venus

In astrology, the consideration of Venus has always related to where it appears in the natal chart, along with the rest of the planets, but there are other contexts in which to consider Venus. The Venus Star transit of the zodiac is unlike any other one because all five points of the Venus Star transit one's chart in any given eight-year cycle. Astrologers will recognize the angular separations of the Venus Star transits from one cycle to the next as the quincunx (150°), the biquintile (144°), and the sesqui-square or tri-octile (135°). These movements have traditionally been considered the minor aspects of astrology, but, looking at all the intricate mechanics that go into creating the Venus Star, a more correct term for these aspects might be "harmonics." Every harmonic aspect is a number equivalent to the circle (360°) divided by the prime numbers, as follows:

360 divided by 2 = 180 = the opposition
360 divided by 3 = 120 = the trine
360 divided by 4 = 90 = the square (quadrature)
360 divided by 5 = 72 = the quintile
360 divided by 6 = 60 = the sextile
360 divided by 7 = 51.4 = the septile
360 divided by 8 = 45 = the octile
360 divided by 9 = 40 = the novile

With the exception of the opposition, every term used to refer to these aspects has been derived from its Latin root. The circle divided by 5 = 72, the 5th harmonic, or quintile.

Thus, five exact quintiles of 72° each would equal a perfect 360° circle. Figure 2.20 illustrates a Venus Star transit over an eight-year period from 1946 to 1954, in which we observe an unequal star pattern. Around the perimeter of this circle, there is, in fact, only one point that measures 72°—the Aries to Aquarius points. Among the astrological aspects that comprise the Venus Star itself, three have been termed "minor" in astrology:

135°– the sesqui-square or tri-octile

144° – the bi-quintile

150° – the quincunx or inconjunct

Figure 2.20: The Venus Star and its astrological aspects

The tri-octile (135°) aspect, (three 45° angles or one and a half squares), occurs once in the Venus Star diagram shown in figure 2.20, while the quincunx (150°) occurs twice, and the bi-quintile of 144° occurs once. The tri-octile of the Venus Star is related to the circle divided by eight (45°) times three. Thus, both the bi-quintile and tri-octile are associated with the harmonics outlined above. But of particular interest is the quincunx (150°) occurring in the Venus Star, an aspect that has confounded students and practitioners of astrology for years. It relates to none of the above stated harmonics, standing alone as a unique, uneven angle as applied to the circle. But because it is a very common angle in creating the Venus Star, I have concluded that the quincunx should be viewed in a revolutionary new manner (discussed later in this chapter under "Finger of the Goddess"). If all five points of the star were 144° from one another, tracing their paths inside the circle, all five points on the perimeter of the circle would measure 72° apiece, creating a perfect star. Thus, the Venus Star, while not quite mathematically equal from each and every star point, is nevertheless a beautifully constructed pentagram, which fulfills its design through aspects that astrology has named as both creative and talented (quintile and biquintile) and as challenging (tri-octile and quincunx).

Measuring the Venus Star

The Venus Star can be measured beginning from any point in the 584-day cycle to any other point in the 584-day cycle. Some astrologers work with it from the stationary <u>retrograde</u> point of one period to the next; others focus on it from the stationary <u>direct</u> point of one period to the next; and still others have chosen to focus on it from the perspective of the <u>heliacal rising</u> (rising with the Sun) from one period to the next. Any of the methods will result in a five-pointed Venus Star.

In much of the ancient literature, use is made of the heliacal rising of Venus from one cycle to the next, that is, its rising when far enough away from the Sun's beams to be seen in the pre-dawn sky. This is discussed by shamanic astrologer Daniel Giamario, especially in regard to how the planet Venus is ritually welcomed to the predawn morning sky after its disappearance into the underworld for many days previous.[33]

However, it is nearly impossible to set your watch by when a heliacal rising will occur. It is always a number of days after inferior conjunction with the Sun (between five and ten), but due to different altitudes and geographical localities, as well as unpredictable weather patterns, it's hard to pin down. Events that are predictable and precise are the two conjunctions of Venus with the Sun, the framework used in this volume to calculate the Venus Star Points.

The dates of these Venus-Sun conjunctions (the Venus Star Points) are listed at the end of Chapter 3. At such times of proximity between Venus and the Sun, the light energy of the Sun merges with the love of Venus, creating unity between the heart of the cosmos and life on Earth. The Venus Star pattern is shaped like a human embryo and Venus takes nine and a half months from one conjunction with the Sun to the next to create the Star Points. In her rotating pattern of Morning Star/Evening Star, the Venus-Sun conjunction transmits to the embryo its life's desire for creation. Consequently, the Venus Star of individuals gives them the particular encoding that determines the mark they will leave on Earth as their legacy.

This is entirely new material in the context of current research. I am observing that if an individual is born very close to a subsequent Venus-Sun conjunction, especially within one to three months of it, at a later period in life the individual will markedly exhibit some of the characteristics of the next star phase, a calculation known to astrologers as a progression. For example, in a horoscope reading, the chart of the individual is progressed forward to their current age where it reveals certain new dynamics that were not present in the birth chart. This can also be done in relation to the Venus Star. This doesn't occur very often, but when a person is born during or near a Venus-Sun conjunction, the change of Star Point will occur in their lifetime. For example, if the next Star Point will occur thirteen days after an individual's birth, it will be at age thirteen that they will experience a new Venus Star Point energy in life. In astrology we are used to using the natal chart as the personal imprint from the stars, meaning that the Venus Star Point before birth affects the life chart, and the Star Point after birth acts more like a progressed influence similar to the way astrologers are accustomed to interpreting those phases in a person's life.

The pattern of Venus's Star rests on the idea that for forty days during every 584-day cycle, Venus is in retrograde from Earth's point of view. This means that Venus, whose orbit never reaches more than 48° away from the Sun, seems to turn backward. Interestingly, the period of forty days figures prominently in many religious and mythological traditions as well as fairy tales and fables. The number forty has special significance in the world's three major monotheistic religions; Christianity, Islam, and Judaism. For example, in all three, the flood lasted forty days and forty nights. Jesus spent forty days in the wilderness, as did Musa Alahi salaam. Lent is celebrated for forty days. In Islam, the Prophet Ilyas spent forty days in the wilderness before God appeared to him. Muhammad prayed and fasted in a cave for forty days, then had forty followers to spread the religion of Islam. In the Greek Orthodox Church, various ceremonies honor the fortieth day of birth and death. The Buddhists also honor a forty-day cycle. Because so many ancient cultures possessed knowledge of the length of time that Venus is in retrograde, it is conceivable that this number became associated with earlier religious practices. The authors of *The Book of Hiram*[34] cite over forty references from both the Old and New Testaments to the number forty as it relates to the greater Venus cycle of forty years (five complete Venus Stars of eight years each).

Astrology defines Venus's forty-day retrograde period as a time when the principles associated with Venus come up for review and evaluation. In all traditional astrological teachings, Venus is associated with substance and worth (both self-worth and net worth), as well as love, relationship, and beauty. During the retrograde phase, it has been observed, we reassess these areas depending upon the house transited by Venus in retrograde for each of us. When planets are in retrograde, they exert more influence upon us than when in direct motion, especially during stationary periods when they pause in their positions, beaming an intensely focused energy to Earth. Each retrograde cycle of Venus over an eight-year period falls in five separate houses of an individual's horoscope; close to the position where she was in retrograde just eight years prior. Thus, every eight years the message of those five houses will be amplified and repeated through a lifetime. For example, by the time an individual is age forty, Venus will have completed five retrograde periods, and by age eighty, ten retrograde periods.

Figure 2.21 shows that for an Aries rising individual, Venus Star Points activate the following five houses in their chart: The first (Aries), the eleventh (Aquarius), the eighth (Scorpio), the sixth (Virgo), and the fourth (Cancer). The same figure shows the Venus Star transit over a 100-year period.

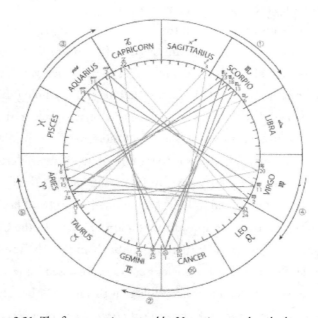

Figure 2.21: The five star points traced by Venus in a one-hundred-year period

Ultimately, Venus's retrograde periods mean that for forty days every twenty months we take stock of our most precious possessions and relationships relative to Venus. For instance, if one of the Venus Star transits falls in our fifth house, a creative intensity centers on the domain of children, investments, and creative pursuits. Those are the areas that need reassessment during this period. As an astrologer, the two most common concerns I hear, especially during a Venus retrograde cycle, are "I'm unhappy with my relationship" and "I'm unhappy with my job but can't afford to quit." Venus's retrograde period is considered an opportunity for positive reevaluation for growth in these areas, as well as growth of a more directly spiritual nature. It is a period in which one gives of oneself or surrenders to the people or circumstances appearing at that time. This type of surrendering of personal will or desire is often what religions require devotees to practice.

People who are aware of Venus' retrograde period or who follow some other kind of religious doctrine that requires observing a forty-day period are resonating to the Venus cycle, but even those who are not aware of Venus's retrograde cycle or are not involved in such practice may sometimes be affected anyway. In any case, the Venus Star transit and Venus retrograde period provide individuals with an opportune time to focus on areas of life associated with Venus for personal development. The forty-day retrograde period every 1.6 years reminds us that the time for such practice has arrived.

The Venus Return

In reference to the natal chart, Venus returns every year to the place it was the previous year. But in reference to the Venus Star, the return occurs every eight years, after moving through all five Venus Star Points. It is during these return periods of one's natal Venus Star Point that an individual may be intensely focused on love, creativity, fertility, and mating. For instance, the age of eight is a time when children begin to come out of their own world to develop social skills and relate to peers in a distinctive way, or, alternately, a time when children can shut down psychically if they are not receiving love. Also around age eight children begin to react to the opposite gender in a polarized way. Boys begin to refuse to be seen with girls, and while girls are more open to associating with boys, they will also succumb to peer pressure. At age sixteen (sweet sixteen), boys and girls are once again relating to each other, but in a distinctly more sexually oriented way. Again at ages twenty-four and thirty-two, a natural Venus Star rhythm, individuals often gravitate toward marriage or serious partnership and parenthood. At age forty, five full Venus star cycles have been completed. This is an age that psychologists, along with most of us, recognize as a period of introspection and reassessment of one's life—fertile ground for the well-known mid-life crisis.

A Double Quincunx—Finger of the Goddess?

According to astrological lore, Venus is linked with three astrological signs: Taurus, her day sign; Libra, her night sign; and Pisces, her sign of exaltation. If drawn in an astrological wheel, the pattern that emerges is a giant yod, also known as the finger of god, a name derived from a golden pencil that points to the Torah in the inner sanctum of orthodox Jewish synagogues. The finger of god created from the placement of orbiting bodies in these signs, and others as well, is the same star pattern that Venus creates. For this reason we could perhaps call this pattern the finger of the goddess, or better, the hand of the goddess, as the Venus Star has five distinct fingers. The astrological basis of this pattern is two quincunxes of 150° each, along with a sextile, joining the two energies at the base of the triangle in a 60°, or sextile, pattern: 150 + 150 + 60 = 360.

Further, remarkably Taurus, Libra, and Pisces are three of the five signs that Venus might transit during a given star period. They are not in effect at present but will be again toward the middle of the twenty-first century. The times when Venus transits all three of her signs bring a much greater orientation towards love, marriage, harmony, and peace. Figure 2.22 illustrates these three Venusian signs as they combine to create the formation of the Venus Star. But it is not just these three Venus-related signs that make up the quincunx. It is routinely an aspect that is formed by the Venus Star in her transit pattern that creates the star, shown in Figure 2.22.

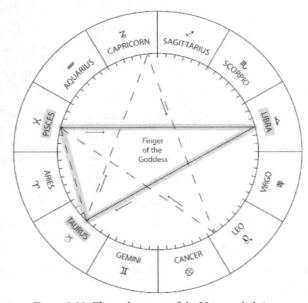

Figure 2.22: The yod pattern of the Venus-ruled signs

The quincunx is difficult for people to analyze and work with because it is the only major aspect not equally divisible by a prime number. It is also a very hard angle to see. In my experience, people who have an abundance of quincunxes in their chart constantly need to let go of old patterns and conditioning to apply their creativity and skills in some different ways. Depending upon where the quincunx is, they may have a hard time fitting into their family, job situation, or the world in general, because they have trouble grasping organizational structures of life. The difficulties associated with the quincunx make sense, however, when one links this aspect to the Venus Star, as the mind-structured approach does not always resonate with the Venus Star's heart-felt urgings and promptings.

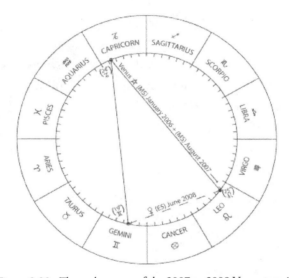

Figure 2.23: The yod pattern of the 2007 to 2008 Venus transit

The Venus Star As Eros

In searching for a way to define the Venus Star as separate from the natal Venus with which astrologers are accustomed to working, I would say the star seems to reflect the concept of Eros. Plato describes Eros thus: "… the madness of love is the greatest of heaven's blessings…"[35]

From the mythology, Eros can be thought of as both the parent to and child of Venus. Eros, a principle of erotic desire and a force of nature, preceded Venus as an energy of creation in the void that existed before anything else. This energy corresponds to a deeply moving, creative life force. In later stories, Eros is the child of Venus, known as Cupid, who shoots arrows into our hearts when we fall in love. We can perhaps grasp the essence of the

Venus Star if we remember that Eros is both the soul of Venus and the child of Venus, acting as a messenger of the principle of love, connecting us to what our own life on Earth is about and how we connect to others in that process. When we are truly in touch with a part of ourselves that is directing us to act in accordance with what we believe to be our reason for living, we are responding to our own Venus Star. To locate your Venus Star Point, see the table in Chapter 3.

Figure 2.24: The Venus Star

The natal position of Venus represents the way we reach out to our environment and to other people to connect ourselves to love, beauty, and friendship. The Venus Star Point represents the manner in which we reach inside of ourselves to reflect the love, beauty, and heart-felt self-expression we innately possess and share with others.

Part II

WORKING WITH THE VENUS STAR POINTS

3. DISCOVERING THE VENUS STAR POINTS

Artists speak in color, shape, texture, and design; linguists resonate with beautiful words. Venus speaks to us through her beautifully constructed five-pointed star pattern. Her cycle around the Sun translates to a giant matrix of five-pointed stars orbiting through the zodiac, affecting people and conditions on Earth in a most unique way.

Working with Venus Star Points is a new way of understanding the power of Venus in the charts and lives of individuals. Part II focuses on the zodiac sign of an individual's Venus Star and offers interpretations of how to focus that energy in life to receive and transmit a higher vibration of Venus as part of their eros, their raison d'etre, the motivating life principle. Even if you do not study or practice astrology, this information will give you sufficient understanding of the Venus Star to experience many benefits. It is beyond the scope of this volume to add the house and aspect pattern information from the Venus Star to charts. However, I recommend doing so if you study or practice astrology, as placing the Venus Star in charts adds additional insights, based on house position, aspect to other planets, and traditional forms of astrological delineation.

Looking at the Venus Star Points through the zodiac reveals what qualities Venus endows to people and how it affects historical eras. We have seen in earlier chapters that Venus and the Sun, moving towards one another from opposite directions at certain intervals, stop at "star gates" or Star Points, where, Venus "kisses" the Sun. The results of this kiss of Venus to the Sun are astounding. Gaining an awareness of how we are affected by our individual Venus Star Point (VSP) and understanding how historical eras are also impacted can help us meet life's challenges both in our personal lives and in our current time frame of history. By synchronizing our minds and bodies to become attuned to the Venus rhythm, we are more attuned with the cosmic energy representing the heart—Venus. When enough people become aligned with their hearts, love spreads like a giant wave around them and peace and healing occurs.

While discovering their Venus Star Point may illuminate a person's potential possibilities and challenges in life, it may also provide a key to fulfilling their heart's desire. For others, it may involve achieving inner peace, living in harmony. And for still others, it may help in healing past wounds, ensuring a more optimistic future.

As an aid in understanding the quality of each VSP, celebrities are listed in the sections on Venus and each of the twelve zodiacal signs. Research was based on examination of approximately 1,400 well-known personalities from the fields of business, entertainment, the arts, politics, and sports to discover how they have achieved their own brand of personal success via their Venus Star Points.

The Twelve Houses of the Zodiac Wheel

In figure 3.1, the numbers one to twelve correspond to the houses of the zodiac wheel, a basic astrological wheel. The wheel also shows the twelve constellations, or signs, of the zodiac, which reflect twelve universal archetypes of life associated with perennial wisdom. In this section, Chapters 4 through 15, the qualities associated with the Venus Star Point in each of the twelve signs of the zodiac are explored. The discussion then proceeds to correlate these various Venus Star Points effect upon an individual's personal and creative expression and the impact these Star Points have on historical, social, economic, and political trends of the Venus Star periods as it passes through each of these signs of the zodiac.

Figure 3.1: The twelve signs and houses of the astrological wheel

The following table gives us the chronological order by star date of the Venus transit to each of the signs. When reading this table, remember to keep in mind that the Venus Star transits five signs simultaneously, entering and leaving a sign at varying times, as illustrated in figure 3.2.

> **VENUS STAR TRANSIT TO THE SIGNS**
> The Taurus/Bull Star Point (1825 to 1934)
> The Sagittarius/Archer Star Point (1830 to 1923)
> The Cancer/Crab Star Point (1852 to 1961)
> The Virgo/Virgin Star Point (1875 to 1984)
> The Aquarius/Cup Bearer Star Point (1890 to 1982)
> The Scorpio/Scorpion Star Point (1926 to 2027)
> The Aries/Ram Star Point (1929 to 2038)
> The Gemini/Twins Star Point (1964 to 2073)
> The Capricorn/Goat Star Point (1986 to 2078)
> The Leo/Lion Star Point (1987 to 2100)
> The Libra/Scales Star Point (2022 to 2131)
> The Pisces/Fishes Star Point (2041 to 2133)

Table 3.1: Venus Star Transit to the Signs

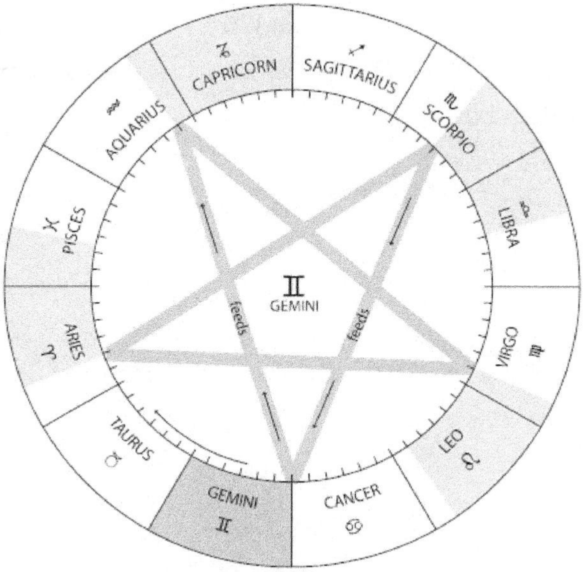

Figure 3.2: The Five Transit Signs of Venus

Figure 3.2 represents the beginning of the transit of the Venus Star through the sign of Gemini (1964). At that time the other points of the star were Aries, Aquarius, Scorpio, and Virgo. The shaded area of Gemini represents the entire 30° of the sign. But notice that the other points do not contain the full signs and are divided between two signs each. When the Gemini Star began, only 10° of the Aries Star had been traversed, leaving two-thirds of the sign to be completed to complement the Gemini Star. The Aquarius Star was nearly finished, having only a few degrees left before the star changed to Capricorn, which would last for the bulk of the Gemini Star's lifetime. The Scorpio Star had about one-half of the sign to complete during Gemini's reign. And finally, Virgo, with only a few degrees remaining, would give the Gemini Star the benefit of the transit through the Leo Star for the majority of its life. These are the important relationships or "Star Mates" to the Gemini Star, which are discussed in detail in Part III. Similarly, each of the other star signs, at their inception, have connections with other signs that are unique to the particular sign.

In reference to the Venus Star, there are two sets of signs that begin and end simultaneously. They have a unique relationship and are what will be referred to as "Life Mates" that feed one another. These are:

Taurus with Sagittarius
Virgo with Aquarius
Scorpio with Aries
Capricorn with Leo
Libra with Pisces

Missing from this list are Cancer and Gemini, which act as mediators, mating with more signs but for shorter periods each.

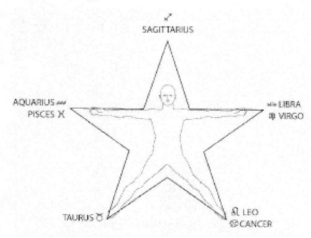

Figure 3.3: The Venus Star Human—As Above, So Below

Figure 3.4: The orbital pattern of Venus as viewed from Earth

The Current Venus Star—Sign of the Times

In figure 3.4, the Venus orbit as viewed from Earth illustrates the retrograde "loops" that Venus draws in the creation of her Star in a given eight-year period. The loops equate to positions on the zodiac wheel or the astrological signs.

 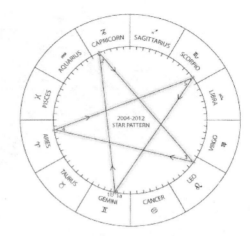

Figure 3.5a: The Venus Star pattern of 1900-1908   Figure 3.5b: The Venus Star pattern of 2004-2012

Observing Figures 3.5a and 3.5b, it is clear that different zodiacal signs are activated by the star pattern at any given time in history. Viewing the two Venus Star patterns a century apart gives us perspective as to which signs are included in various historical periods. In Figure 3.5.a, the activated signs of the Venus Star are: **1-CANCER → 2-AQUARIUS → 3-VIRGO → 4-TAURUS → 5-SAGITTARIUS**. In Figure 3.5b, the signs activated by the Venus Star are: **1-GEMINI → 2-CAPRICORN → 3-LEO → 4-ARIES → 5-SCORPIO**. Each individual sign that is transited by the Venus Star contains its own unique combination of Star sign relationships that are discussed further throughout this volume.

Though both star patterns portrayed in Figures 3.5a and 3.5b created by the orbital path of Venus have almost identical geometry, they incorporate different zodiac sign combinations. Since any possible combination involves five signs and only four astrological elements, there will always be more emphasis on one element. In the first example, the star pattern of 1900 to 1908, the element earth is emphasized, as the zodiac signs of Virgo and Taurus are represented. That period was characterized by many qualities astrologers attribute to earth signs, including practicality, intense focus on materialism, job security, skills development, mechanical inventiveness, groundedness, ambition, health care, and the physical world. In the second example, the star pattern of 2004 to 2012, the element of fire is emphasized, as the zodiac signs of both Aries and Leo are represented. Aptly, this period is characterized by high energy, willful personal expression, bold, dramatic, spontaneous combustion, passion, intense creative urges, and a strong relationship to the spirit world.

Discovering the Venus Star Points

Every generation belongs to a unique star group. The baby boomers' star group includes: Cancer—Aries—Aquarius—Scorpio—Virgo. The millennium babies are: Gemini—Aries—Capricorn—Scorpio—Leo. Those are the two groups most populating the planet in the present time.

Figure 3.6 is the key to deciphering and working with the Venus Star. It illustrates how the Venus Star looks as it transits each Star Point relating to a sign of the zodiac, moving from Morning Star (MS–inferior conjunction with the Sun, always when moving in retrograde and the slowest) to Evening Star (ES–superior conjunction with the Sun, always when direct and moving forward the fastest). Thus, in chronological time, Venus moves rhythmically clockwise around the circle, from MS to ES to MS to ES. The star points, however, are created from MS 1 to MS 2 or ES 1 to ES 2, and so forth, through the heart of the circle.

MS 1	25° Leo	August 2007	
ES 1	19° Gemini	June 2008	
MS 2	07° Aries	March 2009	
ES 2	21° Capricorn	January 2010	
MS 3	05° Scorpio	October 2010	
ES 3	23° Leo	August 2011	four-year star Return of 2007
MS 4	16° Gemini	June 2012	four-year star Return of 2008
ES 4	08° Aries	March 2013	four-year star Return of 2009
MS 5	21° Capricorn	January 2014	four-year star Return of 2010
ES 5	02° Scorpio	October 2014	four-year star Return of 2010

Figure 3.6: The Venus transit from Morning Star to Evening Star along the zodiac

There are several important principles to keep in mind concerning the relationship between the zodiac signs and the orbital movement of Venus that forms the Star. First, each star pattern influences, helps, inspires, or "feeds" the next star pattern, moving clockwise around the circle. That is, when Venus moves from MS 1 to MS 2 (584 days later), she creates the line in the middle of the circle that draws the actual star. In this example from figure 3.6, MS 1 (Leo) feeds MS 2 (Aries). MS 2 (Aries) then feeds MS 3 (Scorpio), which feeds MS 4 (Gemini), which feeds MS 5 (Capricorn), which feeds MS 1 (Leo) and thus completes the five points of the star. This pattern repeats until the zodiac signs change on these points. For example, the next sign change will occur in 2026 when the Venus Star points to Libra instead of Scorpio.

But, notice how two complete stars are drawn in Figure 3.6—one dark star and one light star pattern. The dark star pattern represents the eight-year Evening Star cycle, while the light star pattern illustrates the eight-year Morning Star cycle, both of which operate concurrently in time as an alternating heartbeat of Venus. Thus, the movement of the Venus Star around the circumference of the circle, which is patterned after the actual movement of Venus in the sky, moves from MS 1(Morning Star) to ES 1(Evening Star) to MS 2 (Morning Star) to ES 2 (Evening Star). Understanding these basics of the Venus Star is paramount for discovering the manner in which the Star operates in relationships, the principles of which are discussed in greater detail in Part III, "Relationships on the Venus Star."

When focusing on the specific Star Point of individuals, it is important to keep in mind that no two people with the same Venus Star Point in the same zodiac sign will be exactly alike, just as no two individuals with the same Sun sign are precisely the same. They may share some of the same characteristics, but the fact that their birth may have occurred at different points within the Star cycle allows for many variations in how the Venus Star is linked to the other planets and angles of one's chart. For instance, the Aries Star period encompasses the time span of over a century, beginning in 1929 and ending in 2038. The 1945 Aries Star occurred on April 15, 1945, at 25° Aries, while the 1985 Aries Star took place on April 3, 1985, at 14° Aries. A comparison between individuals born in these two periods would yield many differences in their two birth charts due to the great changes in planetary movement, but the Venus Star sign serves as an archetypal framework to begin to understand certain core desires and urges that an individual will pursue during the course of their life.

Knowledge of the Venus Star is helpful in assessing whether and how people are in synch with prevailing trends and energy forces of a specific period; how they accordingly become motivated to make their mark in life; and how the star provides insights for maximum benefits in partnering.

World/Historical Trends and the Twelve Venus Star Points

On average, the Venus Star will transit through one sign for about 100 years, in effect imprinting the qualities of that particular sign onto humanity. Then it is absent from that sign for approximately 150 years until its next visit. In this context, it becomes clear how the Venus Star impacts historical eras. Two of these signs—Taurus and Sagittarius—have phased out long ago, although a small percentage of people born with these Star Points are still alive. These two star groups are made up of individuals with a very long life span, longer than any other star group preceding or succeeding them. The unique combination of Taurus and Sagittarius operating together on the Star would have the aim of life longevity and extension as a basic motivation. By contrast, the next generation—the Aries and Scorpio Venus Star groups—rather than extend life beyond the body's natural rhythm, will probably leave as their greatest legacy the individual's right to end life peaceably and responsibly. Two other Venus Star groups—Libra and Pisces—will not be activated until 2030 to 2040. As individuals born in that star group lived in the late sixteenth and early seventeenth centuries, none are currently alive, but examples of them are given from past perspective and personal biographies from the last time Venus occupied these zodiac constellations.

Though not all Venus Star Points change zodiac signs at the same time, two Venus Star Points do synchronize their changes, making them "life mates." This creates a unique relationship for them, not just on the Venus Star, but in astrology in general. This is what will occur in the 2020s and 2040s when the Scorpio Star becomes the Libra Star and the Aries Star becomes the Pisces Star. Note that the Venus Star transit moves clockwise around the zodiac wheel, so that Pisces follows Aries rather than Aries following Pisces. Similarly, in the 1980s, the Aquarius Star shifted to Capricorn and the Virgo Star shifted to Leo simultaneously. The change from the Aries Star to the Pisces Star (2038-2041) can be considered quite a bit more significant than the change of the late 1980s, because the Star Point will occur at 0° Aries, the region of the zodiac where everything begins and ends. All we have to do to assess the magnitude of this shift is to observe what happened the last time the Venus Star shifted from Aries to Pisces during the period from 1786 to 1790. This was the turbulent time of the French Revolution, the American Revolution, and the beginning of the Industrial Age. Many of the standards by which the modern world operates were determined by the politics and economics of the last Venus Star shift from Aries to Pisces and Scorpio to Libra. Further, the children we are raising now are the pioneers of that world of tomorrow that begins when the Venus Star changes from Aries to Pisces and from Scorpio to Libra, which will occur from 2022 to 2041. When the Venus Star Points do shift signs, people seem to know without having any tangible evidence, that the times are changing and that the old structures are no longer adequate. Interestingly, Aries Evening Star Bob Dylan penned "The Times They Are A-Changin'"[36] in 1963, just as the 100+/–year cycle of the Cancer Star terminated and Gemini began to rise. This song goes down in history as a prophetic anthem that characterized the people, events, and impulses, as well as the creative, social, and political upheaval of the 1960s.

The last two Venus Star Point signs discussed—Libra and Pisces—are not yet operating. Consequently, discussion of them necessarily entails speculation, although information provided is based on knowledge of the previous Libra VSP and Pisces VSP, which were active from the 1770s to the 1870s. Still, when writing about history that one has not lived firsthand, it may come off sounding like a distant cousin to the actual zeitgeist itself. These chapters should not be read as a Nostradamus quatrain that foretells future events on Earth. However, like Nostradamus, who was challenged to speak in sixteenth-century language about future events radically different from his own time, I speculate in today's limited language by tapping into the archetypes of periods past and looking ahead to the horoscopes of the birth of the new star signs.

The Libra Star Point begins in 2022 and Pisces in 2041. Because those dates are the next major sign shift for the star, major new conditions and laws, lifestyles and industries will begin to take form shaping the future. Venus will leave two signs regulated by Mars (Aries and Scorpio) and enter two signs connected to Venus herself (Libra and Pisces), the meaning of which is discussed throughout this volume in the related sign chapters. This should prove to be a welcome change for the world. Under the influence of double Venus rulership as the Venus Star makes her mark on the world, the implications are that war will become politically incorrect, peace will be seen as a moral obligation to humanity, people will once again be nice to each other, and life lived with two of Venus' signs operating will reinforce the healing power of the feminine.

With the Capricorn VSP still active at this time, even institutions, government, and corporations will be inspired to be people-friendly, compassionate organizations. Furthermore, when the Aries VSP phases out and Pisces begins, humanity will have arrived once again at the all-important equinox of the wheel of life—the zero point of Aries where everything begins and ends. We will be giving birth to more than just two new VSPs in these coming years—we will be entering a completely new era for humanity and Earth.

Referencing Figure 3.2, readers will note that the Venus Star arm of today advances to the next arm in 250 years. Thus, the 1750 Venus Star is identical to the star of 2000.

The five signs of Venus' 1750 transit are:

Aries→Scorpio→Gemini→Capricorn→Leo

The five signs of Venus' 2000 transit are the same:

Aries→Scorpio→ Gemini→Capricorn→Leo

The 1750 period had a similar focus to the current era, especially in relation to fashion, art, and style with the appropriate update for the modern world taken into account. When reference is made to the Venus Star repeating itself in a 250–year period, this means it has rotated from one arm of the five-pointed star to the next inside of two and a half centuries. This causes the zeitgeist of that period to resurface with new voices and faces. Some people from the 1750 era who are still celebrated are John and Abigail Adams (born 1735 and 1744), Marie Antoinette (born 1755), and Wolfgang Amadeus Mozart (born 1756). He and Beethoven (born 1770), two of the geniuses of that era, though born before the Libra/Pisces stars came in, were composing their music in the early days of the last Libra (harmonies)/Pisces (music of the spheres) star. Those Venus Stars are just ahead on our calendar, and it is interesting to speculate what new music might result. Interestingly, Pluto, our outermost planet, also returns cyclically every 250 years, just as Venus does. Pluto is the planet/god of resurrection—death and rebirth—reflecting the cyclical nature of cosmic time, in which souls are reborn after a brief absence from form.

Another important aspect for interpreting the influence of the Venus Star Points in various zodiac signs is the fact that the people born under the first and last sets of each Venus Star group are particularly noteworthy because they are the first and last of a line. Thus, they may be the first or last of their group embodying specific qualities of that Venus Star to influence an era. For example, the elders on our planet now, the Taurus and Sagittarius VSPs, are unique because once they're gone there will not be any more of their kind for another 150 years.

The first of a Venus Star group are pioneers for their group, enjoying an experimental approach to life, while the last of a Venus Star group are highly motivated to ensure that the tradition or message of their star group is carried into the future. Though the message of their Venus Star may clash with their individual natures according to other factors in their personal horoscopes, they are intuitively committed to keeping the flame of their Star eternally burning. Examples of some of these first and last born of a star group may be found in their corresponding sign chapters.

The Venus Star Points of the largest group of people currently alive—the baby-boomers—are the Scorpio and Aries Stars. The chart below shows the current world population categorized according to Venus Stars of zodiac signs. These numbers are approximate, as the first two groups are elderly (eighty to ninety years old) and the last two groups are children.

Current World Population of Venus Star Points

Zodiac Sign of Venus Star	Number of Sets*	Percent of Population
Taurus/Bull	3	2.6
Sagittarius/Archer	2	1.7
Cancer/Crab	11	9.6
Virgo/Virgin	17	14.9
Aquarius/Cup	16	14.0
Scorpio/Scorpion	21	18.4
Aries/Ram	20	17.5
Gemini/Twins	12	10.5
Capricorn/Goat	6	5.2
Leo/Lion	6	5.2
Libra/Scales	0	0
Pisces/Fishes	0	0
Total	114	99.6

*a set is created each time the Venus Star transits a zodiac sign and is comprised of the people born during the transit.

The signs in bold denote the Venus Star of the present cycle (2010).

Table 3.2: 2010 world population of Venus Star Points

Finding Your Venus Star Point

To find your Venus Star Point or that of others, consult the Table of Birth Dates, which ranges from 1900 to 2020 in this chapter or consult the Appendix of Venus Star Dates in the back of the book, which ranges from 1750 to 2050. Once you find your Venus Star date and zodiac sign—using the date prior to your birth date—you can then turn to the chapters on zodiac signs for a detailed explanation of its meaning. For instance, the Virgo Star group spans a timeline that includes 27 sets born between 1875 and 1984. The horoscope for the very first passage of the Venus Star through a sign is included as representative of the entire era, but each set contains its own unique signature. For example, the current group of Gemini Stars runs from June 20, 1964, through May 21, 2072. Within that group are twenty-eight sets, the first of which runs from June 20, 1964, though April 11, 1965; the second from June 20, 1968, through April 7, 1969, etc.

After reviewing the characteristics associated with your Venus Star Point, reflect on how the information applies to your personal traits and life circumstances. For example, do the Venus Star characteristics motivate you? Control you? Do you easily embody its characteristics or resist? If you embody the nature of your Venus Star, it is probably working well in your life. However, if you resist embodying the nature of your Venus Star, you are likely finding life burdensome and will begin to see your physical, mental, or emotional well-being deteriorate. If you resist identifying with the characteristics of your personal Venus Star, but find your personal life populated with people of the same Venus Star sign, there may be an inherent message for you regarding how to take control of your life or discover your authentic self. It may be easier for you to observe another expressing the vibrancy and passion of their Venus Star sign and thereby understand your own Venus Star sign and its relationship to the cosmic order.

The Venus Star Point (VSP) reveals an inherent motivating life principle, a unique talent, an erotic expression of the joie de vivre we possess. People admire us for that particular star quality and how effortlessly that talent is lovingly shared with others. We each possess only one point of the star, but by combining with people in our life that fill in all five star points, we are supported wholeheartedly and strengthened tremendously.

Archetypally, the Venus Star's influence on any sign will bring out the best qualities of the sign. But there are two caveats to keep in mind about that. Sometimes the qualities associated with the sign the Venus Star is in are dramatically overstated by a person. This occurs when they are somewhat insecure about themselves and thus overcompensate. Also, everything in nature possesses a shadow, recognized by the ancients in their mythology of Venus as a goddess of both love and war. Living in a world of duality (yin and yang), humans reflect this double principle. Everyone possesses a Venus Star, even mass murderers and terrorists. When Venus is expressing itself through the dark side of the sign, the individual is operating from fear, lack of love, insecurity, and low self-esteem. In these cases, the continual identification with their self-hatred or pain can create dark, grey matter that prevents the love and healing light of the Venus Star from penetrating. The prevention of this darker manifestation of Venus, even in the most conscious of individuals, is a task undertaken and not easily attained by even the most enlightened of people. It is the embracing and fine-tuning of this star that constitutes human evolution.

Basic information about how the Venus Star functions in your life and the lives of the people with whom you have close relationships is provided in the following chapters, The Venus Star Signs. It is recommended that you read about all five Venus Star Points of your Venus Star era.

Part III focuses on interactive relationships and how the different star signs feed, inspire, and help each other. This knowledge is essential for gaining a broader perspective on the influence and meaning of Venus and her Star—an energy source whose matrix is connected to Earth and all its living organisms.

When a new Venus Star Point is being activated every nine to ten months, both Venus and the Sun are occupying the same degree of the same sign. It is this celestial event—the conjunction of Venus and the Sun—that creates the Venus Star Points referred to in this volume. But for days or even weeks as the two bodies pull either towards or away from one another, they still occupy the same sign. For instance, in 2007 the Venus Star occurred at 25°Leo on August 17th. The Sun remained in Leo for one week following the star date, until August 23rd. But Venus remained in Leo for many weeks, until October 7th, giving individuals a much more pronounced energy of the star. Many such individuals have made exceptional achievements in their various fields and they can be seen as "pure archetypes" of the star's sign, in that the combined energy of Venus and the Sun has provided them with a powerfully focused laser beam of talent at their disposal. This, the triple crown of the Venus Star, is when the Sun, Venus, and the Venus Star are all interacting close together in the sky at a person's birth. Examples are Oprah Winfrey (Aquarius Star); Leonardo DiCaprio (Scorpio Star); Dan Brown (Gemini Star); Tom Hanks (Cancer Star); Venus Williams (Gemini Star); and Jack Nicholson (Aries Star). All of these pure Venus Stars have surpassed the competition in their respective fields. Further, they used their star in bold and dramatic ways in the manner suggested by the sign their star is placed in. If you were born close to a star date, check with someone who can cast the full horoscope of your birth to see if you hold the double or triple crown of your sign: the Sun, Venus, and the Venus Star all in the same sign.

If you work with astrology, you can do much more with the Venus Star in gaining an understanding of how it operates. Be sure to look up the house that the Venus Star occupies in your chart. For instance, if your VSP (Venus Star Point) is in Virgo in the Eighth House, read both the Virgo and Scorpio chapters, as Scorpio is the sign typically associated with the Eighth House. If you are not sure which house corresponds to which sign, consult Figure 3.1 at the start of this section. You can then place the VSP in all the horoscopes you work with to gain deeper insight into the workings of the person's motivating life principle and unique talents and to gather more specifics about their relationships. Even greater understanding is possible by looking at the five houses which the Venus Star will transit for the course of an individual's life. Comparing the VSP and its transits to the outer planet transits is especially illuminating. Begin your journey into Venus Star wisdom by locating your birth date in the following table. It will immediately tell you two things—your Venus Star sign and your Venus Star quality (Morning Star or Evening Star). Astrologers will also take note of the degree and minute of the sign, which are also provided. Then, use chapters 4 through 15 to determine your particular star qualities and chapters 17 through 29 to better understand your star's connections to others.

Finding Your Venus Star Point / Venus Star Dates: 1920 to 2050

To find your particular Venus Star, look up your birthday in the table below. The date listed **<u>preceding</u>** your birthday is your Venus Star. The only exception is if you are born within a week of the next star date, which gives you increased qualities of that star as well. Both Star Points will influence you, but in this case the influence of the star date following one's birth will be more pronounced (especially if the birth occurs just a few days before the next star date). An example of this is Winston Churchill. Though he was born in the Pisces Star period, his birth a mere nine days prior to the Sagittarius Star period gives the latter star a great deal of influence on his life.

MS=MORNING STAR
- A=ARIES
- TA=TAURUS
- GE=GEMINI
- CN=CANCER
- LE=LEO
- VI=VIRGO

ES=EVENING STAR
- LI=LIBRA
- SC=SCORPIO
- SG=SAGITTARIUS
- CP=CAPRICORN
- AQ=AQUARIUS
- PI=PISCES

Date	Phase	Position	Date	Phase	Position
Jul 3 1920	ES	11°Cn34'	Jun 24 1952	ES	03°Cn18'
Apr 22 1921	MS	02°Ta01'	Apr 13 1953	MS	23°A07'
Feb 9 1922	ES	19°Aq46'	Jan 29 1954	ES	09°Aq34'
Nov 24 1922	MS	02°Sg11'	Nov 15 1954	MS	22°Sc24'
Sep 10 1923	ES	16°Vi42'	Sep 1 1955	ES	08°Vi07'
Jul 1 1924	MS	09°Cn22'	Jun 21 1956	MS	00°Cn47'
Apr 23 1925	ES	03°Ta20'	Apr 14 1957	ES	24°A20'
Feb 7 1926	MS	18°Aq06'	Jan 28 1958	MS	08°Aq25'
Nov 21 1926	ES	28°Sc27'	Nov 11 1958	ES	18°Sc37'
Sep 10 1927	MS	17°Vi00'	Aug 31 1959	MS	08°Vi05'
Jul 1 1928	ES	09°Cn31'	Jun 22 1960	ES	01°Cn13'
Apr 20 1929	MS	29°A48'	Apr 10 1961	MS	20°A53'
Feb 6 1930	ES	17°Aq13'	Jan 27 1962	ES	07°Aq00'
Nov 22 1930	MS	29°Sc43'	Nov 12 1962	MS	19°Sc59'
Sep 7 1931	ES	14°Vi33'	Aug 29 1963	ES	05°Vi59'
Jun 28 1932	MS	07°Cn13'	Jun 19 1964	MS	28°Ge37'
Apr 21 1933	ES	01°Ta05'	Apr 11 1965	ES	22°A03'
Feb 4 1934	MS	15°Aq42'	Jan 26 1966	MS	05°Aq57'
Nov 18 1934	ES	25°Sc59'	Nov 8 1966	ES	16°Sc10'
Sep 8 1935	MS	14°Vi46'	Aug 29 1967	MS	05°Vi52'
Jun 29 1936	ES	07°Cn27'	Jun 20 1968	ES	29°Ge08'
Apr 17 1937	MS	27°A35'	Apr 8 1969	MS	18°A37'
Feb 3 1938	ES	14°Aq41'	Jan 24 1970	ES	04°Aq27'
Nov 19 1938	MS	27°Sc16'	Nov 10 1970	MS	17°Sc34'
Sep 5 1939	ES	12°Vi24'	Aug 27 1971	ES	03°Vi51'
Jun 26 1940	MS	05°Cn04'	Jun 17 1972	MS	26°Ge29'
Apr 19 1941	ES	28°A51'	Apr 9 1973	ES	19°A47'
Feb 2 1942	MS	13°Aq16'	Jan 23 1974	MS	03°Aq30'
Nov 16 1942	ES	23°Sc31'	Nov 6 1974	ES	13°Sc45'
Sep 5 1943	MS	12°Vi33'	Aug 27 1975	MS	03°Vi39'
Jun 26 1944	ES	05°Cn22'	Jun 17 1976	ES	27°Ge04'
Apr 15 1945	MS	25°A20'	Apr 5 1977	MS	16°A21'
Feb 1 1946	ES	12°Aq08'	Jan 21 1978	ES	01°Aq52'
Nov 17 1946	MS	24°Sc50'	Nov 7 1978	MS	15°Sc08'
Sep 3 1947	ES	10°Vi14'	Aug 25 1979	ES	01°Vi44'
Jun 24 1948	MS	02°Cn55'	Jun 15 1980	MS	24°Ge20'
Apr 16 1949	ES	26°A36'	Apr 7 1981	ES	17°A28'
Jan 31 1950	MS	10°Aq51'	Jan 21 1982	MS	01°Aq03'
Nov 13 1950	ES	21°Sc03'	Nov 3 1982	ES	11°Sc20'
Sep 3 1951	MS	10°Vi19'	Aug 24 1983	MS	01°Vi25'

Date	Type	Position	Date	Type	Position
Jun 15 1984	ES	24°Ge58'	Mar 25 2017	MS	04°A56'
Apr 3 1985	MS	14°A06'	Jan 9 2018	ES	18°Cp58'
Jan 19 1986	ES	29°Cp18'	Oct 26 2018	MS	03°Sc06'
Nov 5 1986	MS	12°Sc43'	Aug 13 2019	ES	21°Le12'
Aug 22 1987	ES	29°Le37'	Jun 3 2020	MS	13°Ge36'
Jun 12 1988	MS	22°Ge12'	Mar 25 2021	ES	05°A50'
Apr 4 1989	ES	15°A09'	Jan 8 2022	MS	18°Cp42'
Jan 18 1990	MS	28°Cp35'	**Oct 22 2022**	**ES**	**29°Li27'**
Nov 1 1990	ES	08°Sc57'	Aug 13 2023	MS	20°Le28'
Aug 22 1991	MS	29°Le14'	Jun 4 2024	ES	14°Ge30'
Jun 13 1992	ES	22°Ge53'	Mar 22 2025	MS	02°A39'
Apr 1 1993	MS	11°A49'	Jan 6 2026	ES	16°Cp22'
Jan 16 1994	ES	26°Cp44'	**Oct 23 2026**	**MS**	**00°Sc44'**
Nov 2 1994	MS	10°Sc18'	Aug 11 2027	ES	19°Le07'
Aug 20 1995	ES	27°Le29'	Jun 1 2028	MS	11°Ge26'
Jun 10 1996	MS	20°Ge03'	Mar 23 2029	ES	03°A28'
Apr 2 1997	ES	12°A51'	Jan 6 2030	MS	16°Cp16'
Jan 16 1998	MS	26°Cp07'	Oct 20 2030	ES	27°Li07'
Oct 29 1998	ES	06°Sc33'	Aug 10 2031	MS	18°Le18'
Aug 20 1999	MS	27°Le01'	Jun 2 2032	ES	12°Ge23'
Jun 11 2000	ES	20°Ge48'	Mar 20 2033	MS	00°A21'
Mar 29 2001	MS	09°A31'	Jan 3 2034	ES	13°Cp46'
Jan 14 2002	ES	24°Cp07'	Oct 21 2034	MS	28°Li22'
Oct 31 2002	MS	07°Sc53'	Aug 9 2035	ES	17°Le02'
Aug 18 2003	ES	25°Le23'	May 29 2036	MS	09°Ge16'
Jun 8 2004	MS	17°Ge54'	**Mar 21 2037**	**ES**	**01°A05'**
Mar 30 2005	ES	10°A31'	Jan 3 2038	MS	13°Cp46'
Jan 13 2006	MS	23°Cp39'	Oct 17 2038	ES	24°Li47'
Oct 27 2006	ES	04°Sc11'	Aug 8 2039	MS	16°Le07'
Aug 17 2007	MS	24°Le50'	May 30 2040	ES	10°Ge15'
Jun 8 2008	ES	18°Ge43'	**Mar 17 2041**	**MS**	**28°Pi03'**
Mar 27 2009	MS	07°A15'	Jan 1 2042	ES	11°Cp13'
Jan 11 2010	ES	21°Cp32'	Oct 18 2042	MS	26°Li00'
Oct 28 2010	MS	05°Sc30'	Aug 7 2043	ES	14°Le56'
Aug 16 2011	ES	23°Le18'	May 27 2044	MS	07°Ge06'
Jun 5 2012	MS	15°Ge45'	Mar 18 2045	ES	28°Pi43'
Mar 28 2013	ES	08°A10'	Jan 1 2046	MS	11°Cp18'
Jan 11 2014	MS	21°Cp11'	Oct 15 2046	ES	22°Li28'
Oct 25 2014	ES	01°Sc49'	Aug 6 2047	MS	13°Le58'
Aug 15 2015	MS	22°Le38'	May 28 2048	ES	08°Ge09'
Jun 6 2016	ES	16°Ge36'	Mar 15 2049	MS	25°Pi45'
			Dec 29 2049	ES	08°Cp37'

Table 3.3: Finding your Venus Star Point
For a table of Venus Star Point dates from 1750-2050, see Appendix II

> *"Earth provides enough to satisfy every man's need,
> but not every man's greed."*
> –Mahatma Gandhi, Taurus Evening Star

4 THE TAURUS VENUS STAR POINT

The Energy Flow of the Star Is:
Taurus→Capricorn→Leo→Pisces→Libra→Taurus

**The Venus Transit of Taurus began May 19, 1825,
as a Morning Star and ended in 1934 as an Evening Star.**

ELEMENT: EARTH
MODALITY: FIXED

Taurus The astrological glyph for **Taurus** represents a bull's head. Taurus is associated with the bull's strength, determination, sturdiness, grounding, perseverance, and accuracy. It has been said that the bull is an appropriate symbol for both bullheadedness and bull's-eye precision, which characterize this sign. Such traits are implied in common expressions involving the word *bull*, for example, a bull market, in which it is hard to stop stocks from rising once they start, also reflects the perseverance and determination of Taurus.

Some keywords and concepts for Taurus are: supply and demand, commodities, values, natural resources, earthly practicality, Mother Earth, rich in substance, level-headedness, sturdiness, steadiness, financial security, wealth, stubbornness, determination, bull-headedness, materialistic, realistic, earthly sensuality, and lovers and collectors of beautiful and valuable objects and assets.

Of the following well known female and male archetypes of this star, the names in bold below are pure Taurus Star archetypes, having been born on or very close to the inception of the Taurus VSP.

> **Male archetypes:** Pablo Picasso, **Geronimo**, Aristotle Onassis, Franklin D. Roosevelt, D. H. Lawrence, **Henry Fonda**, **Gary Cooper**, Carlo Ponti, and **I.M. Pei**.
>
> **Female archetypes:** Gertrude Stein, Scarlett O'Hara (born with the publication of *Gone With the Wind* in May of 1936, Scarlett is the perfect prototype of a Taurus VSP. She is portrayed beautifully by Vivien Leigh, a Morning Star Taurus VSP), Marlene Dietrich, **Ella Fitzgerald**, Greta Garbo, Nancy Reagan, and **Carol Burnett**.

Greatest Assets: Down-to-earth, no-nonsense practicality; accuracy; the ability to hit the bull's-eye; an instinctive sensual nature that possesses the power of attraction; the ability to remain centered and grounded and to persevere in times of crisis; the desire to create peace and prosperity

Greatest Liabilities: The biggest obstacle to your heart center can be your tendency to devalue something or someone because their value system is not the same as your own. Your self-worth (or another's) does not reside in bankable assets, but more in the depths of one's character and soul.

Are You A Taurus Venus Star Point?

If you were born between the dates listed below, you are a Taurus Venus Star Point (VSP). The Venus Star Point passed through Taurus in ten-month increments, returning to the sign every four years, so it is important to use your exact date of birth to locate your Venus Star Point sign. Don't confuse this Venus Star with your Sun sign or with your Venus sign, even though the Venus Star *can* occur while the Sun is in Taurus at the beginning of each of these four-year periods. If this is the case, you have both Sun and Venus Star Point in Taurus, which creates a very potent expression of Taurus in your life. If you were born *before* or *after* any of the dates listed below, you are *not* a Taurus Venus Star Point individual, though your Sun sign may be Taurus.

```
           MS=MORNING STAR    ES=EVENING STAR       D=VENUS DIRECT
                          Rx=VENUS RETROGRADE
```

MS/ES	DATES OF TAURUS VSP	DEGREE
MS	5/19/1825 – 3/9/1826	28 Taurus 19 Rx
ES	5/20/1829 – 3/6/1830	29 Taurus 30 D
MS	5/17/1833 – 3/7/1834	26 Taurus 09 Rx
ES	5/18/1837 – 3/4/1838	27 Taurus 21 D
MS	5/15/1841 – 3/4/1842	23 Taurus 59 Rx
ES	5/16/1845 – 3/2/1846	25 Taurus 14 D
MS	5/12/1849 – 3/2/1850	21 Taurus 49 Rx
ES	5/14/1853 – 2/27/1854	23 Taurus 04 D
MS	5/10/1857 – 2/27/1858	19 Taurus 39 Rx
ES	5/11/1861 – 2/25/1862	20 Taurus 54 D
MS	5/8 1865 – 2/25/1866	17 Taurus 28 Rx
ES	5/9 1869 – 2/22/1870	18 Taurus 44 D
MS	5/5/1873 – 2/22/1874	15 Taurus 16 Rx
ES	5/7/1877 – 2/20/1878	16 Taurus 34 D
MS	5/3/1881 – 2/20/1882	13 Taurus 05 Rx
ES	5/4/1885 – 2/17/1886	14 Taurus 22 D
MS	5/1/1889 – 2/17/1890	10 Taurus 52 Rx
ES	5/2/1893 – 2/15/1894	12 Taurus 11 D
MS	4/28/1897 – 2/15/1898	08 Taurus 40 Rx
ES	5/1/1901 – 2/15/1902	10 Taurus 00 D
MS	4/27/1905 – 2/13/1906	06 Taurus 27 Rx
ES	4/28/1909 – 2/11/1910	07 Taurus 46 D
MS	4/25/1913 – 2/10/1914	04 Taurus 14 Rx
ES	4/26/1917 – 2/9/1918	05 Taurus 34 D
MS	4/22/1921 – 2/8/1922	02 Taurus 01 Rx
ES	4/24/1925 – 2/6/1926	03 Taurus 20 D
ES	4/21/1933 – 2/4/1934	01 Taurus 06 D

Even if you were not born during these dates, the Taurus VSP affected general behavior patterns on Earth and thus Taurus characteristics prevailed, such as people being motivated to become settled and secure, to emphasize sensuality and beauty in their lives, and to invest their resources in something valuable, solid, and long-lasting.

Venus Star Point's Gift to Taurus

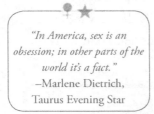

"In America, sex is an obsession; in other parts of the world it's a fact."
–Marlene Dietrich, Taurus Evening Star

A love and heart-centered approach to life is natural for the Taurus VSP individual since Taurus is considered the home base of Venus, a sign in which Venus' nature is expressed to the fullest. Sensuality and practicality go hand-in-hand with Taurus VSP individuals. They are steady and solid, possess the ability to use their charms effectively, and have an eye for beauty and luxury, regardless of budget.

The VSP in Taurus: The Personal Realm

Each of the Venus Star Points has its own special gift, and it's under the sign of your Venus Star Point that the best of yourself is expressed. Of course, as discussed in Chapter 3, the Venus Star, like everything in nature, also has a shadow side. The Taurus VSPs express themselves through the element of earth and are governed by Venus herself.

In the mythology section of Chapter 2, the origins of the Venus archetype were discussed regarding her appearance as either the Morning Star (Pandemos) or Evening Star (Urania). Though one can be either a Taurus Morning Star (MS) or Evening Star (ES), Taurus is more energetically associated with Pandemos. This Venus represents the one who holds court in the earthly realm; i.e., the priestess, the queen, or the mother. Her counterpart is the celestial Urania, whose gaze may be focused in a more heavenly direction. Those who were born with their Venus Star in Taurus carry Pandemos energy in great measure. They take their earthly responsibilities very seriously and are seemingly graced and acknowledged by the fruits of the earth accordingly.

As stated in Chapter 2, the Morning Star Venus is associated more with the Venus rulership of Taurus/Pandemos. So all Taurus VSPs will relate to Pandemos to begin with, but the Evening Star Taurus will also contain a healthy dose of Urania. The MS Taurus Star is queen of her earthly realm. The ES Taurus Star is similarly a queen, but may often look beyond the earthly realm to the sky for her heavenly guidance and direction.

The bull, or more specifically the horns of the bull, are the corresponding image for the constellation of Taurus. These horns bore great mythological fruit, containing such illustrious and diverse stars as the Hyades, the Pleiades, Aldebaran, and Algol. Taurus VSPs reflect some of their mythological counterparts with their varied characteristics. Although the bull is an animal many people regard as aggressive and, when incited, hostile, Taurus is an earth yin (feminine) sign characterized by steadfast determination. Like its animal spirit, it is grounded, needs open space, enjoys a good meal, is very fertile, and loves to mate. Venus adds charm and social graces, making Taurus VSP people both determined and stubborn about achieving their aim, no matter what obstacles appear in their path. However, the preferred method for Taurus, and one which these individuals have mastered, is the art of attracting to them the object of their desire, especially in matters of love, and thus manifesting the dream of Venus.

The wisdom inherent in the Taurus VSP is its connection to mother earth and its ancestry, its roots. If Aries, the first of the astrological signs of the zodiac, indicates the seed germinating in the ground, Taurus, the next sign, establishes its roots. For instance, the author of *Roots*, Alex Haley, was a Taurus VSP who, with the determination its natives possess, undertook the monumental task of tracing his African-American roots back to their source in West Africa.

Further, Taurus VSP individuals possess a talent for making beautiful material things more accessible to everyone. For example, I. M. Pei is one of the most renowned twentieth-century architects. He was born on April 26, 1917, on the day of a Venus (Evening Star) conjunction with the Sun, making him a pure Taurus VSP archetype.

Taurus, the sign so gifted at acquisition, is attested to by billionaire Taurus VSPs Howard Hughes and Aristotle Onassis. This is not to say they didn't work hard for what they achieved and appreciate the value of it to a great degree.

Another major characteristic of Taurus VSP individuals is a stubborn resistance to yielding by digging in their heels. Despite the fact that such stubbornness can test people's patience, in some cases it can be the Taurus Star native's most effective tool for success. For

> *"Get a good idea and stay with it. Dog it, and work at it until it's done right."*
> —Walt Disney, Taurus Evening Star

example, Taurus Evening Star Mahatma Gandhi's refusal to budge on his principles in his resistance to British rule in India ultimately resulted in India's independence. This trait shows up in film stars as well. Fictional character Scarlett O'Hara, brought to life by actress Vivien Leigh (a Taurus Morning Star) in *Gone With the Wind*, also shows the power of stubborn resistance. When in the face of numerous obstacles—the Civil War, unrequited love, the loss of everyone she loved—she held fast to Tara—her roots. One can also observe the quality of unflinching tenacity in two pure Taurus Star archetypes, actors Henry Fonda and Gary Cooper, in the characters they portrayed. Further, Geronimo, a Taurus archetype born very near the star date, held the line for his Apache people as long as humanly possible to preserve their way of life and prevent annihilation.

Another characteristic of Taurus VSP individuals is the ability to calmly remain grounded and hold a steady beat, even if the world around them is in panic. Taurus VSP politicians who were able to impart some semblance of peace and comfort to their people in trying times include Franklin Roosevelt, John and Robert Kennedy, Mahatma Gandhi, Margaret Thatcher, and Gerald Ford.

Further, Taurus VSP individuals tend to surround themselves with lavish possessions, comfort, and beauty. They delight in such things as lovely gardens and surroundings, alluring perfumes, fine vintage wines, and artful and tasteful furnishings and clothes.

While mysticism and spirituality are not the first things that come to mind for Taurus, this star group of individuals was prone to investigate these areas, especially the first half of the group who were born between 1825 and 1893 when the Pisces Star followed Taurus. The second group, born from 1894 to 1922 when the Aquarius Star followed Taurus, instead prefer science, invention, and technology. They also became intrigued with the very newly developed field of aviation technology, as we find three aviators and one astronaut in this group: Howard Hughes, Amelia Earhart, Charles Lindbergh, and John Glenn.

The fact that the Taurus Star is fed by the Libra Star, establishing partnerships, whether for business, pleasure, or creative collaboration, gives the Taurus Star individual the strength and endurance they possess. They honor the institution and ideal of marriage and are persistent about remaining in a marriage—even when it forces both people to compromise with their mates—taking the oath "'till death do us part" to heart. Later in this chapter we will discuss the horoscope for the inception of the 1825 Taurus VSP, which highlights a strong Seventh House (partnership, union).

"No business which depends for its existence on paying less than living wages to its workers has any right to continue in this country."
–Franklin Delano Roosevelt, Taurus Morning Star

The chart for the inception of the Taurus VSP seems to indicate that this group's goal is to enjoy the physical form for as long as possible, and many live into their eighties and nineties. Significantly, Social Security, a program that reflects concepts associated with Taurus such as long-term security, was instituted by Taurus VSP Franklin D. Roosevelt. As the last of their breed dies, the question is whether Social Security will also die, given the current economic and political conditions.

Taurus VSP individuals, the last of whom were born in 1934, comprise only between four and five percent of the world's population, one of the smallest groups of VSPs, along with Sagittarius VSP people. For a list of noteworthy Taurus Star individuals, see Appendix III.

> *"Money is always there but the pockets change."*
> –Gertrude Stein,
> Taurus Morning Star

> *"We are possessed by the things we possess. When I like an object, I always give it to someone. It isn't generosity—it's only because I want others to be enslaved by objects, not me."*
> –Jean Paul Sartre, Taurus Morning Star

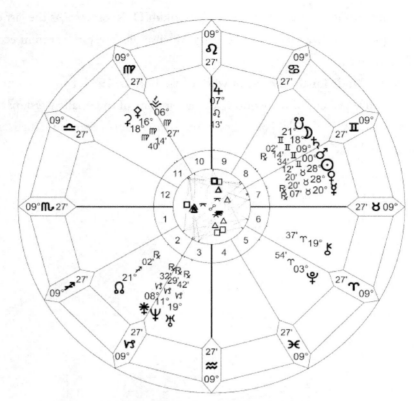

The Horoscope for the Taurus Venus Star Point

The VSP in Taurus: The Historical Realm

The Taurus star was in effect from 1825 to 1934, a time when historical changes translated into an era with numerous new opportunities undreamed of by the generation before, such as the abolishment of slavery and women's suffrage.

Elements of earth and air predominate in this chart with many planets in earth signs placed in air houses. Productivity and progress require forging and sustaining relationships. In this regard, the Taurus VSP era shines. Further, the Taurus Star itself is holding court in the Seventh House of unions. In the chart for the inception of the Taurus VSP, Mars is very close to the Venus Star, Jupiter is the most highly elevated planet, and there is a strong emphasis on Gemini. These combine to indicate enthusiasm, mental agility, and a driving force to attain mastery over the material world, a profitable mastery at that. Call this a bull star charging ahead. Taurus VSP individuals are practical and earthy geniuses with inventive tendencies who possess minds full of ideas (Gemini south node) that quickly become ideals (Sagittarius north node), influencing every corner of the world. The challenge for the world during the course of the Taurus VSP was to mine an abundance of far-reaching ideas and goals and make them attainable.

The period of 1825 to 1934 was a productive period on Earth marked by speculative ventures and inventiveness. Pluto was just beginning a transit through the sign of Aries when the Taurus Star began, unleashing an era of speculators, entrepreneurs, pioneers, and bankers in hundreds of new market enterprises that were opening daily. The link to the Sagittarius Star helped these two stars oversee the laying of a transcontinental railway in America, which expanded commerce and trade beyond any expectations. The Taurus Star linked to the Sagittarius Star ensured progress in Taurus-related fields: money, banking, investments, property acquisition, and the mining of minerals deep inside the earth. Further driving this bullish period was the 1840s Gold Rush in California. Occurring early in the era (1849), this anointed California as the new promised land for numerous other types of speculative ventures that were essentially high-stakes gambling. Interestingly, the New York Stock Exchange (NYSE) was established in 1792 with the Sun, Mercury, and Venus in Taurus. Although the NYSE began a generation earlier than the inception of the Taurus VSP, it surged during the transit of the Venus Star through Taurus before it crashed in 1929, a period when the Taurus VSP was phasing out. The Taurus VSP overlapped with the change from the Victorian era to the Roaring Twenties, a time of excessiveness that resulted in greedy speculation and bullish overconfidence in the stock market. Once the Taurus/Sagittarius Star Points terminated, so did the economic speculation that propelled the stock market and led to the 1929 crash. Then, during the Aries/Scorpio VSP eras, recovery and reconstruction took place.

"The only thing money gives you is the freedom of not worrying about money." –Johnny Carson, Taurus Evening Star

Moreover, the Civil War, which was a conflict over human resources and the control of vast economies, began in 1861 during the Taurus VSP period and ended in 1865 during another Taurus VSP cycle.

In the precessional or greater Age of Taurus (circa 4,000-2,000 BCE) many of the great monuments of Egypt and Crete were erected. Interestingly enough, during the last Venus Star transit of the sign of Taurus (1825-1934) major treasures were unearthed in both regions by Howard Carter (himself a Taurus VSP) and Sir Arthur Evans in Crete. It was also during this era that Heinrich Schliemann's great excavations of Troy took place.

The world will not witness the next a transit of Venus through Taurus until the latter part of the twenty-first century, when the Gemini Star terminates.

"Sometimes I think we're alone. Sometimes I think we're not. In either case, the thought is staggering." –
Buckminster Fuller,
Sagittarius Evening Star

5 THE SAGITTARIUS VENUS STAR POINT

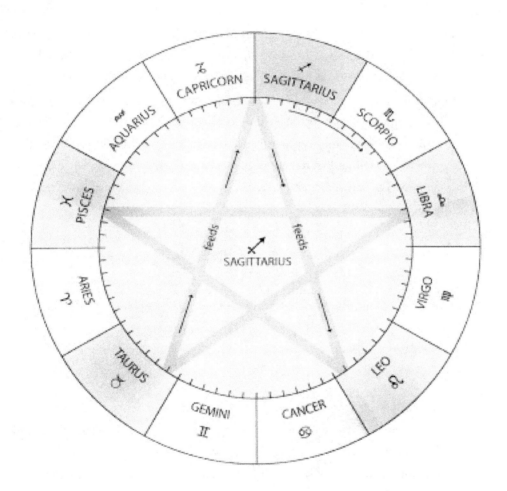

The Energy Flow of the Star is:
Sagittarius→Leo→Pisces→Libra→Taurus→Sagittarius

The Venus Transit of Sagittarius began December 21, 1830, as an Evening Star and ended in 1923 as a Morning Star.

ELEMENT: FIRE
MODALITY: MUTABLE

Sagittarius The glyph for Sagittarius is an arrow shooting up to the sky, representing the high mark for which most Sagittarians aim. It also symbolizes the belief in a spiritual or cosmic order, operating outside earthly concerns. The direction of that order—the center of the galaxy—is where the arrow of the centaur is aimed, located within the constellation of Sagittarius.

Some keywords and concepts for Sagittarius are: aiming high, shooting one's arrow to hit the mark, the spirit of adventure and exploration, the cowboy, the horse, risk-taking and gambling, pilgrimage, foreign countries, languages and studies, institutions of higher learning, immigration and emigration; the courts, judges, and judgments; high-reaching, goal-oriented, the journeyer, the philosopher; the search for truth, justice, and cosmic order; belief in a higher power, magnanimous expansiveness, joviality, and optimism.

Of the following well known female and male archetypes of this star, the names in bold below are pure Sagittarius archetypes, as they were born on or very close to the inception of the Sagittarius VSP.

> **Male archetypes: Giacomo Puccini, C. S. Lewis, Diego Rivera, Sir Ralph Richardson,** Orville and Wilbur Wright, Carl Jung, Jesse James, William Randolph Hearst, Albert Einstein, John Wayne, Ronald Reagan, and Andy Rooney.
>
> **Female archetypes:** Frida Kahlo, Madame Helena Blavatsky, Margaret Sanger, Lucille Ball, Anais Nin, Katharine Hepburn, Eva Peron, and **Madeleine L'Engle**.

Greatest Assets: Willingness to journey to new places, discovering new worlds and ideas; the ability to make one's mark, no matter how challenging; the ability to understand the cosmic order; having a philosophical approach to all things; the ability to keep an eye on the goal; having an aptitude for solutions; and the courage to express viewpoints regardless of what others think.

Greatest Liabilities: The biggest obstacle to your heart center is the inner attitude of superiority you embrace, missing the wisdom that is contained in other points of view. Once you abandon the "high horse" that the Sagittarius rides, and mingle with the masses, great revelations occur—and likewise the heart expands.

Are You A Sagittarius Venus Star Point?

If you were born between the dates listed below, you are a Sagittarius Venus Star Point. The Venus Star Point passed through Sagittarius in ten-month increments, returning to the sign every four years, so it is important to use your exact date of birth to locate your Venus Star Point sign.

MS=MORNING STAR   ES=EVENING STAR   D=VENUS DIRECT
Rx=VENUS RETROGRADE

MS/ES	DATES OF SAGITTARIUS VSP	DEGREE
ES	12/21/1830 – 10/7/1831	28 Sag 54 D
MS	12/21/1834 – 10/4/1835	29 Sag 24 Rx
ES	12/18/1838 – 10/5/1839	26 Sag 21 D
MS	12/19/1842 – 10/1/1843	26 Sag 55 Rx
ES	12/16/1846 – 10/2/1847	23 Sag 46 D
MS	12/16/1850 – 9/30/1851	24 Sag 26 Rx
ES	12/13/1854 – 9/30/1855	21 Sag 11 D
MS	12/14/1858 – 9/27/1859	21 Sag 57 Rx
ES	12/11/1862 – 9/27/1863	18 Sag 39 D
MS	12/11/1866 – 9/24/1867	19 Sag 28 Rx
ES	12/8/1870 – 9/26/1871	16 Sag 05 D
MS	12/9/1874 – 9/23/1875	16 Sag 59 Rx
ES	12/5/1878 – 9/23/1879	13 Sag 33 D
MS	12/6/1882 – 9/20 1883	14 Sag 30 Rx
ES	12/3/1886 – 9/20/1887	11 Sag 01 D
MS	12/4/1890 – 9/17/1891	12 Sag 01 Rx
ES	11/30/1894 – 9/18/1895	08 Sag 29 D
MS	12/1/1898 – 9/15/1899	09 Sag 34 Rx
ES	11/29/1902 – 9/16/1903	05 Sag 57 D
MS	11/30/1906 – 9/14/1907	07 Sag 05 Rx
ES	11/26/1910 – 9/14/1911	03 Sag 27 D
MS	11/27/1914 – 9/11/1915	04 Sag 38 Rx
ES	11/24/1918 – 9/12/1919	00 Sag 57 D
MS	11/25/1922 – 9/9/1923	02 Sag 11 Rx

Don't confuse this Venus Star with your Sun sign or with your Venus sign, even though the Venus Star can occur while the Sun is in Sagittarius at the beginning of each of these four-year periods. If this is the case for you, you have both Sun and the Venus Star in Sagittarius, which creates a very potent expression of Sagittarius in your life. If you were born *before* or *after* any of the dates listed, you are not a Sagittarius Venus Star Point, though your Sun sign may be Sagittarius.

Even if you were not born during these dates, the Sagittarius VSP affected general behavior patterns on Earth nevertheless. During these dates, people were motivated to expand their consciousness, to explore the world or boldly take risks, at times excessively.

Venus Star Point's Gift to Sagittarius

"Throw your dreams into space like a kite, and you do not know what it will bring back: a new life, a new friend, a new love, a new country." –Anais Nin, Sagittarius Evening Star

Love and a heart-centered approach to life come as a result of elevating one's mind and actions to focus on loftier pursuits. The Sagittarius VSP era marked one of the most colorful periods of recent history, and Sagittarius VSP individuals are equally colorful—funny, bold, irreverent, freedom-loving, and high-spirited. The last of the Sagittarius VSPs are still alive but are now in their eighties and nineties.

The VSP in Sagittarius: The Personal Realm

Each of the Venus Star Points has its own special gift, and it's under the sign of your Venus Star Point that the best of yourself is expressed. Of course, as discussed in Chapter 3, the Venus Star, like everything in nature, also has a shadow side. Sagittarius VSPs express themselves through the element of fire and are ruled by the planet Jupiter.

The element of fire associated with the sign of Sagittarius accurately pictures the spirit of a Sagittarian VSP. Like fire, they are a bold, dazzling, bright, hot breed of individuals who aspire to great heights in their chosen pursuit, whether it be politics, sports, cultural achievements, travel, philosophical breakthroughs, social reform, or education. The Sagittarian VSP is a traveler and slips through international borders and boundaries of consciousness adroitly. The Olympic flame, with its torch lit in one city of the world and relayed globally through the cooperative effort of many nations, is a metaphor for the higher aspirations associated with Sagittarius. Significantly, the sign's ruler is the largest planet, Jupiter, which inspires larger than life ideals, plans, and appetites. As Jupiter's nickname Jove implies, this is often done with joviality, which keeps people entertained even if aspirations are not fulfilled.

Sagittarius has two planets that resonate to its sign. Jupiter is only one archetype for the Sagittarian archer, who is literally pictured as a creature: the mythological half man, half horse. The other Sagittarius archetype is Chiron, the comet/centaur, the recently discovered (1977) astronomical object orbiting our solar system, named for the wounded healer centaur god, Chiron, of Greek myths. Thus, we have two distinctly different types of Sagittarius individuals—an extroverted Jupiterian type and an introverted Chiron type. Jupiter resided in the air on Mt. Olympus overseeing the affairs of both the mortals and the immortals. The healing centaur Chiron resided on the earth, in a mountain cave, secluded from the activities and population centers of the masses, but positively dedicated to the treatment and eradication of man's suffering. So the two Sagittarius types reflect the temperaments of these two rulers—an airy, jovial sky individual aspiring to reach beyond the limits of the physical realm and an earthly, part-animal, part-human, part-god individual who concentrates on treating the illnesses and suffering of mankind and the overcoming of their own wounds. Though the arrow of Sagittarius aims to the heavenly realm, Sagittarius experiences life as a journey and may live life to the fullest without concern for the future. Of course, the Venus Star in this sign amplifies the desires and helps the archer reach his or her mark.

> *"Never let the fear of striking out get in your way."* –Babe Ruth, Sagittarius Evening Star

Perhaps the major motivating principle of Sagittarius VSP individuals is their tendency to be explorers in life, whether literally traveling, journeying through reading books, or using their imaginations to pen great adventures. Their ultimate quest is to pierce the veil of what is waiting on "the other side," whether it be the other side of the country, the other side of the ocean, the other side of the galaxy, or the other side of life itself—afterlife.

A Sagittarius VSP individual may have no formal higher education, but regardless holds many opinions about the nature of things and is not shy about expressing their views. Religion has had a profound impact upon them, whether they have totally embraced or rejected it. Whether the Sagittarius VSP believes in God, or has totally rejected any such notion, they are firm about their beliefs. But because the experience of Sagittarius will involve a moral or philosophical dilemma at some point, life forces them to reconcile their view about such issues. If they believe in a strict moral code, life will deal them the situations or people that will challenge them to question that code.

Sagittarius VSP individuals are adventurers not only in the exploration of geography, but also in journeys of the higher mind. Traveling far from their homes to gain a larger worldview is the essential motivating principle of this group. This is evident from the list of prominent Sagittarius VSPs: Ernest Hemingway, who was a sportsman, adventurer, philosopher, lover of foreign culture, writer, and man of excess; Carl Jung, who journeyed beyond the boundaries of the conscious mind to explore vistas of the unconscious and collective unconscious; philosopher, teacher, and fantasy writer C. S. Lewis; and astrological author Dane Rudhyar who pioneered a humanistic, philosophical, and galactic approach to astrology, effectively changing the context of astrological wisdom in the most profound way since the Renaissance.

> *"Show me a sane man and I will cure him for you."*
> –Carl Jung,
> Sagittarius Morning Star

Another major characteristic of Sagittarius VSP individuals, one that sometimes interferes with attaining their goals, is a tendency to overdo things in life. Although this can lead them on courageous quests, like Prometheus's quest for cosmic fire, it can also cause arrogance of the type that inspired the saying, "He's on his high horse."

Sagittarius VSP individuals, the last of whom were born in the 1920s, comprise only between two and three percent of the world population, one of the smallest groups alive on the planet today (along with the Taurus group). For a list of noteworthy Sagittarius Star individuals, see Appendix III.

The VSP in Sagittarius: The Historical Realm

The inception of the Sagittarius Star marked the ending of the Capricorn Star, a change of signs that holds more importance for the world than most sign changes. This is due to the transit of Venus across the solstice point (30° Sagittarius or 0° Capricorn). Indeed, new worlds were opening up due to new and better means of transportation, affecting mass migration patterns globally.

One of the most noticeable features of the horoscope for the birth of the Sagittarius VSP is that its chart pattern is a bucket, with the handle being held by Saturn in the Ninth House in Virgo. This gives strong emphasis to the overwhelming spirit of the times: "work hard and God will reward you" along with the focus on Ninth House issues of immigration, importation, transportation, philosophy, and education. A Neptune/Jupiter conjunction in the productive earth sign of Capricorn, along with Saturn and the Node in the Ninth House of the zodiac (Virgo), indicates the huge wave of immigration that characterized the Sagittarius era. Pluto, Mars, and Vesta in Aries in the Fourth House square Mercury in

The Sagittarius Venus Star Point

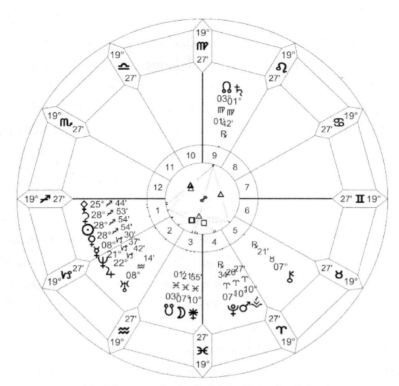

The Horoscope for the Sagittarius Venus Star Point

Capricorn in the First House attests to the enormous transition incurred by the pioneers as they resettled in a foreign territory and replaced their language, culture, religions, and traditions with those of their new home. In the Americas, indigenous peoples were forcibly removed from their homelands by the masses who poured into the New World. This tragedy, as well as the challenges the new settlers endured, are indicated by Saturn in the Ninth House in opposition to the Moon in the Third House. Yet, with the nodes alongside of this pair, it seemed as if destiny had decreed such changes for this time period.

If mass migration to the United States was a defining characteristic of the Sagittarius VSP period, the end of Sagittarius's VSP era coincided with the end of steady immigration. This migratory pattern of Europeans to the New World peaked at the turn of the twentieth century. Further, the Sagittarius VSP era encompassed the era of "manifest destiny," in which settlers went to the West heeding the slogan "Go West, young man" that characterized

> *"In order to write about life, first you must live it!"*
> —Ernest Hemingway,
> Sagittarius Morning Star

99

the mid to late nineteenth century. Europeans crossed the ocean to the New World in great numbers, while those residing east of the Mississippi River continued moving west. Foreign and indigenous cultures both merged and clashed during this era. Asian immigrants came to the West, drawn by the California Gold Rush, or they were brought West to work on the transcontinental railroad. In the South, African slaves provided the labor force for the agriculturally rich economy, increasing racial tensions between blacks and whites, as well as between northern whites and southern whites.

> "We have all, at one time or another, been performers, and many of us still are—politicians, playboys, cardinals and kings."
> –Sir Laurence Olivier,
> Sagittarius Morning Star

During the Sagittarian VSP era, with its symbol of the centaur, a mythological creature half man and half horse, appropriately the relationship between man and horse played a starring role. Cowboys and Indians of the American West rode horses, a motif that has been endlessly portrayed in art, literature, and film. John Wayne and Ronald Reagan are two Sagittarius VSP Evening Stars who represented the cowboy culture in cinema and later in politics.

However, the final years of the Sagittarius VSP brought the demise of the horse (Sagittarius's totem) as the primary mode of transportation, when the industrial world gave birth to the automobile. It was also the time when travel by air began, reflecting the Sagittarian archer's arrow pointing to the sky. Two Sagittarian VSP individuals, Wilbur Wright, a Sagittarius Morning Star and Orville Wright, a Sagittarius Evening Star have been given the credit for invention of the airplane.

Further, the Venus Star in Sagittarius also coincided with the California Gold Rush, which was characterized by adventure, risk taking, and excessiveness. When the Sagittarius VSP period ended, suddenly the excessiveness and over-optimism ended as well. After this, individuals did not so readily leave home and go in search of fortune, and the high spirits that had characterized the Roaring Twenties became more subdued. The lavish lifestyles of the wealthy and privileged classes were then replaced by the sobriety of the Scorpio Star. Once the Scorpio VSP began, people instead undertook inner explorations such as in molecular biology, chemistry, medical research, and psychoanalysis. (See Chapter 9 for more about the Scorpio VSP). Prohibition and the Great Depression sobered people up to a new era. The final transit of Venus's time in Sagittarius occurred at the 1922 to 1923 cycle, the rip- "Roaring Twenties," a true Sagittarian bacchanalia before the onset of the Great Depression.

Finally, spiritualism and occultism became firmly rooted in the late 1800s, when the Theosophical Society was established by the Russian-born immigrant Madame Helena Blavatsky (a Sagittarius Evening Star preceded on the Venus Star wheel by its helpful predecessor, the Pisces Morning Star). The combination of Sagittarius and Pisces is noted for intense spiritual focus and investigation.

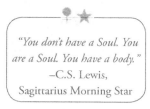

"You don't have a Soul. You are a Soul. You have a body."
–C.S. Lewis,
Sagittarius Morning Star

The early 1920s marked the final days of Venus's stay in Sagittarius until its next entry into that sign in the late twenty-first century.

"If I read a book and it makes my whole body so cold no fire can ever warm me, I know that is poetry. If I feel physically as if the top of my head was taken off, I know that is poetry."
– Emily Dickinson, Sagittarius Evening Star

"Reality is merely an illusion, albeit a very persistent one."
–Albert Einstein, Sagittarius Evening Star

"I'm all in favor of keeping dangerous weapons out of the hands of fools. Let's start with typewriters."
–Frank Lloyd Wright, Sagittarius Morning Star

"Sometimes I wonder if men and women really suit each other. Perhaps they should live next door and just visit now and then."
–Katharine Hepburn, Sagittarius Morning Star

"He who feels it, knows it more."
– Bob Marley,
Cancer Evening Star

6 THE CANCER VENUS STAR POINT

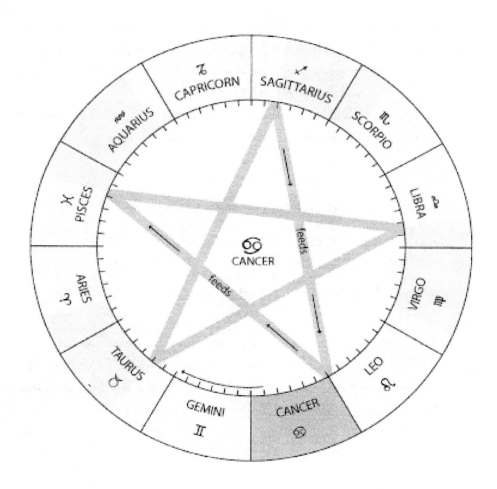

The Energy Flow of the Star Is:
Cancer→Pisces→Libra→Taurus→Sagittarius→Cancer

The Venus Transit of CANCER began July 21, 1852, as a Morning Star and ended in 1961 as an Evening Star.

ELEMENT: WATER
MODALITY: CARDINAL

Cancer The glyph for Cancer represents a crab, an animal that lives in or near the water and carries its home with it as it moves back and forth from land to sea. The glyph also resembles a pair of ovaries or female breasts, associated with the birth and nourishment of infants.

Some keywords and concepts for Cancer are: family, clan, tribe, home; mother, motherhood, matriarchy, family lineage; womb of creation, roots, origins, belonging; food, feeding; nourishing or nurturing others; emotional security, the feminine; intuition; the past; need to be personal and intimate; sensitivity; sentimentality; feelings.

Of the following well known female and male archetypes of this star, the names in bold below are pure Cancer archetypes, having been born on or very close to the inception of the Cancer VSP.

> **Male archetypes:** **George Bernard Shaw, Milton Berle**, Charlie Chaplin, **Pablo Neruda**, Walter Cronkite, **Ringo Starr**, Prince Charles, **Dan Akroyd, Tom Hanks,** and **Montel Williams.**
> **Female archetypes:** Eleanor Roosevelt, Elizabeth the Queen Mother, Helen Hayes, Corazon Aquino, Tipper Gore, **Marianne Williamson**, Rita Wilson, and Katie Couric.

Greatest Assets: A natural, easy-going, down-home demeanor that makes people immediately feel at ease; the ability to nourish others through a capacity for understanding and connecting with people; a preference for living by one's instinctual feelings and intuition.
Greatest Liabilities: The biggest obstacle to the center of your heart is your early childhood wounds and what you didn't get from mommy. Once you get over them, you are embraced by the Divine Mother and comforted by—and comforting to—your beloved.

Are You A Cancer Venus Star Point?

If you were born between the dates listed below, you are a Cancer Venus Star Point (VSP). The Venus Star Point passed through the sign of Cancer in ten-month increments, returning to the sign every four years, so it is important to use your exact date of birth to locate your Venus Star Point sign. Don't confuse this Venus Star with your Sun sign or your Venus sign, even though the Venus Star can occur while the Sun is in Cancer at the beginning of each of these four-year periods. If this is the case for you, you have both Sun and Venus Star Point in Cancer, which creates a very potent expression of Cancer in your life. If you were born *before* or *after* any of the dates listed below, you are not a Cancer Venus Star Point, though your Sun sign may be Cancer.

MS=MORNING STAR   ES=EVENING STAR   D=VENUS DIRECT
Rx=VENUS RETROGRADE

MS/ES	DATES OF CANCER VSP	DEGREE
MS	7/21/1852 – 5/13/1853	28 Cancer 40 Rx
ES	7/20/1856 – 5/9/1857	28 Cancer 05 D
MS	7/19/1860 – 5/10/1861	26 Cancer 31 Rx
ES	7/18/1864 – 5/7/1865	26 Cancer 01 D
MS	7/16/1868 – 5/8/1869	24 Cancer 21 Rx
ES	7/16/1872 – 5/4/1873	23 Cancer 57 D
MS	7/14/1876 – 5/6/1877	22 Cancer 12 Rx
ES	7/14/1880 – 5/2/1881	21 Cancer 54 D
MS	7/12/1884 – 5/4/1885	20 Cancer 04 Rx
ES	7/11/1888 – 4/30/1889	19 Cancer 49 D
MS	7/9/1892 – 5/1/1893	17 Cancer 56 Rx
ES	7/9/1896 – 4/28/1897	17 Cancer 46 D
MS	7/8/1900 – 4/30/1901	15 Cancer 48 Rx
ES	7/8/1904 – 4/26/1905	15 Cancer 42 D
MS	7/6/1908 – 4/28/1909	13 Cancer 39 Rx
ES	7/6/1912 – 4/24/1913	13 Cancer 38 D
MS	7/3/1916 – 4/25/1917	11 Cancer 31 Rx
ES	7/3/1920 – 4/21/1921	11 Cancer 34 D
MS	7/1/1924 – 4/23/1925	09 Cancer 21 Rx
ES	7/1/1928 – 4/19/1929	09 Cancer 31 D
MS	6/29/1932 – 4/20/1933	07 Cancer 12 Rx
ES	6/29/1936 – 4/17/1937	07 Cancer 26 D
MS	6/26/1940 – 4/18/1941	05 Cancer 04 Rx
ES	6/27/1944 – 4/14/1945	05 Cancer 21 D
MS	6/24/1948 – 4/16/1949	02 Cancer 54 Rx
ES	6/25/1952 – 4/12/1953	03 Cancer 18 D
MS	6/22/1956 – 4/13/1957	00 Cancer 46 Rx
ES	6/22/1960 – 4/10/1961	01 Cancer 13 D

Even if you were not born during these dates, the Cancer VSP affected general behavior patterns on Earth and thus Cancer characteristics prevailed. Consequently, you might find that during these periods, people were motivated to spend more time renewing family ties, purchasing a new home, or ensuring that food was readily available for their own family or for poor people of the world.

Venus Star Point's Gift to Cancer

Love and a heart-centered approach to life are expressed through a sweet, warm-hearted nature reflected in a warm and cozy home. Shelter is provided for self and others inside your home or in the willingness to share yourself completely.

The VSP in Cancer: The Personal Realm

Each of the Venus Star Points has its own special gift, and it's under the sign of your Venus Star Point that the best of yourself is expressed. Of course, as discussed in Chapter 3, the Venus Star, like everything in nature, also has a shadow side. The Cancer VSP seeks self-expression through the element of water (feelings). Cancer is ruled by the Moon.

Major principles operating in the lives of Cancer VSP individuals are observation, reflection, and instinctual interactions with the world. The quality of reflection is linked to both water and the Moon. The Moon's light, although bright and beautiful to observe, comes from another source, the Sun. Pools of water are equally reflective. Cancers are instinctive creatures whose behavior mirrors the behavior of the animal that represents Cancer in the zodiac—the crab. Inside its protective shell lives a soft, sensitive creature that has developed both the outer casing and its claws to survive in a world where larger predators could easily swallow it whole. And, because of this extreme sensitivity to larger and more dangerous predators, the instincts of Cancer are razor sharp, allowing them to swim in any direction or to burrow underground and into a safe haven when life outside is too threatening.

> *"My role in society, or any artist's or poet's role, is to try and express what we all feel. Not to tell people how to feel. Not as a preacher, not as a leader, but as a reflection of us all."* – John Lennon, Cancer Morning Star

That may sound like the Cancer VSP is nothing more than a frightened child, retreating from an unsafe and unfriendly world. Perhaps the Cancer VSP experienced these feelings at an early stage of life, but the group of individuals who possess the Cancer VSP are dedicated to providing the kind of shelter, protection, food, warmth, and security to others who are in need of such things.

In the world of Cancer, the mother/child union is experienced as the source and ultimately the quality of their life. Regardless of whether or not they have a history of familial bonding or a sense of community security, they will be motivated to provide this for others—for their offspring, kin, friends, clan, or neighborhood—as the gift of their Venus Star. They are likely to be motivated to become the best mothers in the world and usually succeed. The Cancer VSP needs nothing more than a warm and comfortable home and someone tender with whom they can share it to feel they are living their dream. They do often partner with people who are looking for this type of warm home, mothering, food, or security.

On the Venus Star wheel, the Cancer Star is preceded by the Virgo Star and followed by the Taurus Star, both of which are earth signs. This can give Cancer VSP individuals a tendency to be more grounded and practical, qualities usually associated with earth rather than water. Other common concerns of this group are how to utilize the skills they possess and how to educate themselves and learn new skills to compete in the workplace. All three signs—Cancer, Taurus, Virgo—are very compatible, with emphasis on the use of personal resources to get and keep a good job as well as maintain a home that provides support and safety.

> *"I think someone ought to do a survey as to how many great, important men have quit to spend time with their families who (actually) spent any more time with their family."*
> – Walter Cronkite,
> Cancer Morning Star

The Cancer VSP excels at building or furnishing a stunning environment; a home or business that people will gravitate to and feel the safety and comfort within is one of the gifts of the Cancer VSP.

Cancer VSP individuals carry some part of their mother's lineage forward—as indicated by Cancer VSP Prince Charles. Deep within the souls of such individuals are aspects of their biological mothers, their desire for roles as mothers, or their links to the times of the Great Mother or mother goddess. Interesting in this regard is Cancer VSP Morning Star John Lennon, who was deeply wounded by the separation from his mother early in life. Though labeled the wildest and angriest of the Beatles, he wrote the haunting piece of music "Mother,"[37] the lyrics of which lament his never-to-be relationship with her. Additionally, the sweet song to his wife, Yoko Ono, another Cancer VSP Morning Star, titled "Woman,"[38] remains today one of the best archetypal serenades to women. Lennon also exemplified the major motivating principle of the Cancer VSP when, a few years before his death, he nurtured his young child Sean in a way he had never been able to experience himself as a child. The creative self expression, the development of skills and resources, the forward strides that Cancer VSPs take in their lives may be linked to the healing they have achieved with mom.

The desire to build a family empire or family business is something that the Cancer VSP would strive for, especially for those born in the earlier days of the Cancer Star (1852-1930) when Taurus was its complementary star. For instance, Cancer VSP Joseph P. Kennedy Sr. desired offspring who would become president of the United States. However, only one fulfilled this desire for a short time: his first son, Joseph P. Jr., died before it could become a reality; his second son, John F., did realize his father's dream but was assassinated before the end of his term; his third son, Robert F. was running for president when an assassin's bullet ended his dream; his fourth son, Edward, was in a tragic accident that ended any possibility of being elected president; and finally, his grandson John F. Jr. may have had such a dream but also lost his life at an early age in an airplane crash.

Those Cancer VSPs born at the latter end of the Cancer Star era (1929-1960) would more likely be motivated to draw a heavy line in the sand between themselves and the family. This was when the Aries Star, intent on achieving personal identity and autonomy, was influencing the Cancer Star. It is a more fierce and fiery road that this group of Cancer VSPs would want to choose for themselves, but a necessary one in their evolutionary cycle nonetheless.

"The first gatherings of the garden in May of salads, radishes and herbs made me feel like a mother about her baby— how could anything so beautiful be mine."
– Alice B. Toklas, Cancer Morning Star

Because of their concern for nurturing and providing for the other special relationships in their life, Cancer VSP people must remain aware of how much they are expending—both emotionally and financially—and assess whether this is helping or hurting themselves or various individuals on whose success they are focused. Giving to one's detriment, the textbook definition of codependency, can be a pitfall for Cancer VSP individuals. Still, it is this endless fountain of nurturing that springs from within that motivates the Cancer Star.

The sentimentality, mood swings, and refined instincts possessed by the Cancer VSP allow them to openly express their emotions to others, something they need not feel vulnerable about sharing. Rather, they are highly motivated to share such personal feelings and, in fact, must do so as a way of personal healing and regeneration. They have a highly developed appreciation for music, poetry, and the arts, which further arouses their sentimental nature. Potential partners should be aware that the way to successfully woo a

Cancer VSP is to sing a love song or craft a beautiful object. Then the Cancer VSP is yours forever.

The best choices of professions for Cancer VSP individuals include those involving caring for and nurturing others, providing food, medicine, comfort, security, better homes or habitats for humans and creatures, and better interpersonal connectedness. They are also excellent counselors and therapists for people who are in need of healing family issues. After retiring from politics, Jimmy Carter became actively involved in Habitat for Humanity, bringing the organization to national prominence. Actor Paul Newman introduced a food product line that has earned millions of dollars that have been donated to charities throughout the world, and Prince Charles donates to charities through numerous outlets. Cancer Star people will also be attracted to professions or hobbies involving the housing industry, such as real estate development or sales, or home construction and improvement.

> *"The embarrassing thing is that the salad dressing is out grossing my films."* – Paul Newman, Cancer Morning Star

As well as sharing their homes with others, Cancer VSPs may seem happiest when working from home—whether it be in a home office, kitchen, or garden—or when remodeling their house or improving their environment. Masters at growing food and preparing it beautifully, these people are usually acutely aware of the effect food has on body, mind, and spirit. However, as a result such individuals must take care not to overeat or abuse food, using food intake as a substitute for emotional nurturance and comfort.

Individuals with VSP in Cancer, the last of whom were born in 1961, comprise approximately 9.6 percent of the world's population.

Cancer VSP individuals can seem like a protective parent to their people, such as Eleanor Roosevelt, Elizabeth the Queen Mother, Jacques Chirac, Martin Luther King Jr., and Corazon Aquino.

Among the prominent Cancer VSP individuals, Morning Star Desi Arnaz is an example of someone who focused on the home. During the 1950s and 1960s, Americans were welcomed into the living room of Desi Arnaz and Lucille Ball in *I Love Lucy*. Similarly, today Cancer VSP Alex Trebek is welcomed into people's homes on a daily basis as host of the popular game show *Jeopardy*. And for a short time heavy-metal rock icon Ozzie Osbourne, Cancer VSP Morning Star, and his wife Sharon, Cancer VSP Evening Star, had a reality show called *The Osbournes*, which chronicled their daily lives.

Hollywood figures include Tom Hanks, whose roles have included ones that reflect vulnerability resulting in healing, such as in *Forrest Gump*[39] and *Philadelphia*[40]. He won numerous awards for his sensitive portrayals in both films. His easy-going manner that reminds people of the guy next door, as well as his ability to proudly embrace the feminine side of his nature, have made him one of the most highly acclaimed actors of his era. Even tough guy Sean Penn showed his true Cancer VSP colors in his roles in *I Am Sam*[41] and *Milk*[42]. He won Oscars for each of those performances as well as much critical acclaim. For a list of other noteworthy Cancer Star Individuals, see Appendix III.

> *"My childhood was sad, but now I remember it with nostalgia, like a dream."*
> – Charlie Chaplin,
> Cancer Evening Star

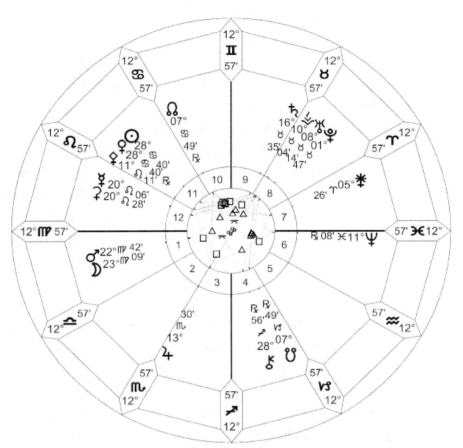

The Horoscope for The Cancer Venus Star Point

The VSP in Cancer: The Historical Realm

During the 108-year Cancer VSP era, historical events focused on issues related to family dynamics, patriotism, national security, and immigration. In the chart for the inception of the Cancer VSP, three of the four elements are represented: fire (Mercury, Ceres, Pallas in Leo, Chiron in Sagittarius, and Juno in Aries); earth (Pluto, Uranus, Vesta, and Saturn in Taurus; and water (the Sun/Venus Star in Cancer, Neptune in Pisces, and Jupiter in Scorpio). Conspicuously lacking is the element of air, associated with detachment, objectivity, and lightness. This indicates an emphasis on some highly flammable emotional engagements, some in the world rivaling the Civil War in America, which occurred during the Cancer Star era. Further, Taurus and Virgo are prominent in this chart. The emphasis is on the element of earth as helpful and friendly mates to the Cancer VSP. Moreover, in the horoscope of the Cancer VSP, Neptune is positioned precisely on the descendant, the gate of marriage. Among this group, marriage or group-partnership was considered a highly respected, sacred union—so much so that such individuals had the impulse to marry and stay married even if circumstances did not support such a view, a practice quickly abandoned once the VSP left Cancer.

Cancer is associated with food, home, family, clan, country, and patriotism. It is also the astrological sign of America. One of the highlights of the Cancer Star period (1901-1913) occurred as Neptune simultaneously transited Cancer. At this time, with both the Venus Star and idealistic and romantic Neptune transiting across America's birth sign Cancer, thousands of immigrants poured out of all parts of the world, especially Europe, into America through Ellis Island off the coast of New York and Angel Island off of San Francisco. Bringing many of their customs with them, they founded dynasties in the New World, providing families with many more opportunities than had been available to them previously. One of the collective values shared during this period was the importance of family and home, particularly the idea of passing skills down the family line. Entrepreneurs thrived and the unwritten law, but highly practical custom imposed on children, was the idea of family unity and continuity through marriage.

When dark and transformational Pluto entered Cancer (1912- 1939), the Venus Star was still transiting Cancer, continuing to support ideas involving the family, clan, home, and patriotism. But this period of Pluto in Cancer was greatly different than the aforementioned idealism of the Neptune period. With Pluto as a punctuation point to the Venus Star's transit though Cancer, the power to transform the ideas and institutions of home, security, family unity, and continuity was achieved.

At the end of World War II in 1945, America enjoyed perhaps its greatest period of power as the Venus Star Point was transiting the third to sixth degrees of Cancer, where America has its Venus, along with Jupiter in her natal horoscope. This was one of the most powerful periods for the United States, both politically and economically. Alliances with former adversaries (the European community and Japan) resulted in America's political leadership and an economic boom. The Venus Star's connection with America's natal Venus and Jupiter produced prosperity beyond people's expectations.

During the last years of the Cancer Star, Cancer was visited by Uranus, the planet affecting both the period itself and the people born within the Cancer Star during those years. The Uranus transit (1948 to 1956) spurred rebellion, sudden change, and liberation from the status quo regarding the stability of the family nucleus, forcing families to become liberated, dissociated, and dispersed. The energy from Uranus gave rise to an explosive birth population, known as the baby-boomers. These boomers, although born in the era of the Cancer Star, would immediately begin to challenge the traditions of family continuation as the Cancer Star phased out. By the last years of the Cancer VSP, the family unit and two-parent nuclear family had been weakened, and a broader spectrum of new types of families had emerged, such as one-parent families and multiple-parent families. The combined influence of Uranus and the Cancer VSP encouraged feelings of universal love that broadened ideas about family systems to include the human family and inspired intermarriage on a more global level. Indeed, the integration of blacks and whites began to progress during this very last phase of the Cancer VSP. Further, family units, once all located in the same village or town, now became more scattered as children began seeking educational, job, and marriage opportunities far from home. Family businesses were now rarely passed down to children. Many daughters sought education rather than marriage as a first priority in life. Food itself changed, becoming poisoned by industrial pesticides and chemical additives and being distributed by food chains rather than the neighborhood family grocer. Prince Charles, born in 1948, serves as the best example of the Venus/Uranus energy of this generation. He is one of that group compelled to break centuries-old family traditions about marriage and relationship, having the Venus Star and Uranus closely interconnected in his chart, with a tension–producing square from Juno, the marriage indicator.

By the early 1960s, when the VSP shifted from Cancer to Gemini, the collective cultural and economic values of the world changed to reflect this. The institutions of home and traditional family, which were an expression of the VSP in Cancer, radically changed. Life would never again be the same, and, as a result, the 1940s and 1950s would later become mythologized as romantic and innocent by people facing a more complex age.

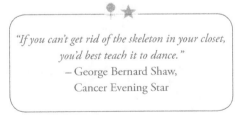

"If you can't get rid of the skeleton in your closet, you'd best teach it to dance."
– George Bernard Shaw,
Cancer Evening Star

> *"Don't confuse having a career with having a life."*
> – Hillary Clinton,
> Virgo Evening Star

7

THE VIRGO VENUS STAR POINT

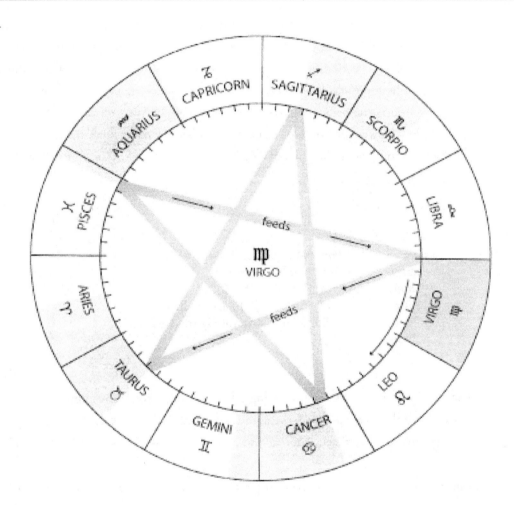

The Energy Flow of the Star Is:
Virgo → Taurus → Sagittarius → Cancer → Pisces → Virgo

The Venus transit of VIRGO began on September 23, 1875, as an Evening Star,
and ended in 1984 as a Morning Star.

ELEMENT: EARTH
MODALITY: MUTABLE

Virgo The astrological glyph for Virgo is reminiscent of the letter "M" with a bundle attached. This is perhaps due to the association with the mother goddess, or Mary in the Christian era, both of whom are seen carrying a newly born infant. She is also earth's harvest goddess, symbolized by the cornucopia.

Some keywords and concepts for Virgo are: harvest and those associated with it, such as the earth mother/goddess, farmers, the labor force of the world; the analytical mind that solves puzzles and problems, including self-analysis; a religion, spiritual path, or career calling devoted to service; skills and tools development; maintaining good health, the digestive system and organs, health, medicine, hygiene and nutrition; service providers.

Of the following well known female and male archetypes of this star, the names in bold below are pure Virgo Star archetypes, having been born very close to or on the day of the Star.

> **Male archetypes:** Sir John Gielgud, Cary Grant, **Paul Muni**, James Stewart, Pope John Paul II, Woody Allen, Bill Gates, **Stephen King** and **David Arquette**.
> **Female archetypes:** Georgia O'Keeffe, Wallis Simpson, **Claudette Colbert**, **Fay Wray**, Hillary Rodham Clinton, Julia Roberts, Celine Dion, **Chrissie Hynde** and **Stella McCartney**.

Greatest Assets: The ability to come up with logical and practical solutions to problems and situations when others are confused; the ability to analyze human behavior; the ability to maintain a systematic and efficient approach to everything; willingness to be a vehicle of divine service.

Greatest Liabilities: The biggest obstacle to the center of your heart is a default program of analysis, judgment, and self-judgment that runs on autopilot. You will always find something in the world that is imperfect and needs improving upon; accept things as they are and put the mind on pause as much as possible through something like yoga, meditation, or music, and just feel. People love you lots for what you can do, but they love you more for just being there and connecting.

Are You A Virgo Venus Star Point?

If you were born between the dates listed below, you are a Virgo Venus Star Point (VSP). The Venus Star Point passed through Virgo in ten-month increments, returning to the sign every four years, so it is important to use your exact date of birth to locate your Venus Star Point sign. Don't confuse this Venus Star with your Sun sign or your Venus sign, even though the Venus Star *can* occur while the Sun is in Virgo at the beginning of each of these four-year periods. If this is the case for you, you have both Sun and Venus Star Point in Virgo, which creates a potent expression of Virgo in your life. If you were born *before* or *after* any of the dates listed below, you are *not* a Virgo Star Point individual, though your Sun sign may be Virgo.

MS=MORNING STAR   ES=EVENING STAR   D= VENUS DIRECT
Rx= VENUS RETROGRADE

MS/ES	DATES OF VIRGO VSP	DEGREE
ES	9/23/1875 – 7/13/1876	29 Virgo 52 D
ES	9/21/1883 – 7/11/1884	27 Virgo 40 D
MS	9/21/1887 – 7/10/1888	28 Virgo 19 Rx
ES	9/18/1891 – 7/8/1892	25 Virgo 27 D
MS	9/19/1895 – 7/8/1896	26 Virgo 03 Rx
ES	9/16/1899 – 7/7/1900	23 Virgo 15 D
MS	9/17/1903 – 7/7/1904	23 Virgo 46 Rx
ES	9/15/1907 – 7/5/1908	21 Virgo 04 D
MS	9/15/1911 – 7/15/1912	21 Virgo 30 Rx
ES	9/12/1915 – 7/2/1916	18 Virgo 54 D
MS	9/13/1919 – 7/2/1920	19 Virgo 16 Rx
ES	9/10/1923 – 6/30/1924	16 Virgo 43 D
MS	9/10/1927 – 6/30/1928	17 Virgo 01 Rx
ES	9/3/1931 – 6/28/1932	14 Virgo 34 D
MS	9/8/1935 – 6/28/1936	14 Virgo 47 Rx
ES	9/6/1939 – 6/25/1940	12 Virgo 24 D
MS	9/6/1943 – 6/26/1944	12 Virgo 33 Rx
ES	9/13/1947 – 6/23/1948	10 Virgo 14 D
MS	9/3/1951 – 6/24/1952	10 Virgo 19 Rx
ES	9/1/1955 – 6/21/1956	08 Virgo 07 D
MS	9/1/1959 – 6/21/1960	08 Virgo 05 Rx
ES	8/30/1963 – 6/19/1964	05 Virgo 59 D
MS	8/30/1967 – 6/19/1968	05 Virgo 51 Rx
ES	8/27/1971 – 6/16/1972	03 Virgo 51 D
MS	8/27/1975 – 6/17/1976	03 Virgo 38 Rx
ES	8/25/1979 – 6/14/1980	01 Virgo 43 D
MS	8/25/1983 – 6/15/1984	01 Virgo 25 Rx

Even if you were not born during these dates, the Virgo VSP affected general behavior patterns on Earth and Virgo characteristics prevailed, such as people being motivated to invest personal resources in education, skills development, training, or apprenticeship programs; people being called to be of service; or people being inclined to learn more about staying healthy physically and mentally.

Venus Star Point's Gift to Virgo

Love and a heart-centered approach to life come through serving or providing for others by doing what the Virgo VSP does best.

The VSP in Virgo: The Personal Realm

Each of the Venus Star Points has its own special gift, and it's under the sign of your Venus Star Point that the best of yourself is expressed. Of course, as discussed in Chapter 3, the Venus Star, like everything in nature, also has a shadow side. In the case of Virgo VSP individuals, the wish to share the best of themselves is expressed through the element of earth, ruled by the planets Mercury and Ceres, the influence of which will be discussed forthwith. Virgo VSP individuals are thus privy to two types of tendencies derived from two bodies of the solar system, which combine to give Virgo its qualities. One is the youthful, sprightly, ever so flighty Mercury. The other is the grounded, practical, and sometimes hysterical earth mother, Ceres. The Virgo VSP can go either way, or sometimes both ways at different times. Two examples are Virgo VSP Salvador Dali, whose flights of fancy took shape on the canvas, and Virgo VSP Adelle Davis, whose pioneering works on health, nutrition, food production, and insights into Mother Earth informed millions.

> *"People are always asking me when I'm going to retire. Why should I? I've got it two ways— I'm still making movies, and I'm a senior citizen, so I can see myself at half price."* – George Burns, Virgo Morning Star

The gifted Virgo VSP has numerous bankable talents and skills. They also have an endless capacity to share their resourcefulness and service, sometimes without asking for nearly as much compensation as their skills are worth. This may well be the Virgo VSP's shining aspect: serving the world without the need of equal recompense. The reward is the ultimate feeling of pleasure that the Virgo VSP receives from sharing their finely crafted services and products in a seemingly effortless way.

The Virgo VSP individuals have sharp minds and excel in devising strategies others cannot comprehend. The Virgo VSP individual possesses exceptional analytical and problem-solving capabilities and lives life in a grounded, level-headed way, effortlessly handling challenges until a major glitch occurs, causing them to become temporarily judgmental. Such people also possess unsurpassed dexterity in working with their hands, allowing them to craft finely detailed objects. Virgo VSP individuals demonstrate a willingness to take care of people, land, or animals, even risking their lives in such service, if necessary.

"Songwriting is a kind of therapy for both the writer and the listener if you choose to use it that way. When you see that stuff help other people that's great and wonderful confirmation that you're doing the right thing."
– Sting, Virgo Morning Star

Though not every Virgo VSP individual is motivated to serve their loved ones, the song "Gotta Serve Somebody" by Bob Dylan [43] hints at their plight. They will wind up serving someone—"it may be the Devil, it may be the Lord, but you're going to serve somebody". Thus the Virgo VSP individual develops a loving and fulfilling relationship to the service they choose. The Venus Star in Virgo has endowed them with the necessary talents for service. All they have to do is figure out what that talent is and how and when to use it. One talent that the Virgo VSP possesses is a sharpened faculty of discrimination and discernment, making them great editors, illustrators, and designers.

The Virgo Star Point sits one turn away from the Cancer Star Point and in the creative relationship that these two stars make with one another, service often comes in the form of serving the family, one's spouse, or more likely, one's offspring. In fact, the Virgo VSP often faces a huge dilemma when the family member they were serving so diligently passes on or moves away, removing their anchor of service. At such times, it is essential for them to find new ways to feel needed. Likewise, when Virgo VSP persons face retirement or old age, they must seek ways to remain useful in order to maintain health and vitality.

Virgo VSP individuals place considerable focus on skills enhancement. An old astrological saying is, "If you want the job done correctly, hire a Virgo." One of the Virgo VSP individuals' biggest fears is that they won't be able to complete a job perfectly or know the solution to a problem immediately. This causes undue job stress and personal stress affecting the vital organs. They are highly motivated to invest in the acquisition of training and skills for maximum self improvement, and often build superior résumés that can open opportunities for them anywhere. They make especially good human resources managers, as they have the knack of knowing which people can do jobs most efficiently. They also excel at informing others how to increase job performance and thus marketability. And, because their ultimate reward is satisfaction at doing a great job, they may "marry" the job and focus on little else.

Because Virgo Star individuals love to keep their brains sharpened, they can easily become overwhelmed by their cognitive powers. Comic relief is essential and one of their best therapies, on the job or off. There are a surprising number of Virgo VSPs who have used comedy to parody human frailties, delivered with dry wit, razor-sharp precision, and a remarkable sense of timing. Unlike the slapstick humor of Sagittarius VSP comedians such as Lucille Ball, the humor of Virgo star comedians, such as George Burns, Woody Allen, Billy Crystal, Steven Wright, Jamie Foxx, Whoopi Goldberg, Bill Maher, and Stephen Colbert are usually deadpan and dead on!

However, pleasure and relaxation may not come easily for Virgo VSP individuals since they are always striving to be at the top of their game. The Virgo VSP individual's idea of vacation may often be a working vacation, so they do not feel like they are wasting time. Wasting time is something they avoid, realizing that there is much to do all the time. One solution to their tendency to dismiss vacation time is for them to work at jobs that require travel and R&R, which they need to remain healthy and vital.

There is a somewhat hysterical side of the Virgo VSP, when its ruling archetype, Ceres, is receiving stress. In the mythology, when Ceres was experiencing shock and mourning, her physical organs collapsed. Virgo Morning Star Woody Allen is the perfect archetype for illustrating how annoying and troublesome life can be for the Virgo VSP individuals—especially when the heart of Venus is controlled by the analytical process rather than feelings. He has done what is typical of the behavior of Virgo VSP individuals—made a career out of pointing the finger at everyone, including himself, continually analyzing and parodying his and other people's neuroses, complexes, and chronic fears. Allen's medium of the cinema is reflected in his chart by Neptune (planet of film) being closely linked to his Venus Star Point.

"I'm astounded by people who want to 'know' the universe when it's hard enough to find your way around Chinatown." – Woody Allen, Virgo Morning Star

In the seasonal round of life (in the northern hemisphere), the Sun peaks at the summer solstice in Cancer. By the time it reaches the end of Virgo, poised at the equinoctial gate, its light is beginning to wane. This gives Virgo VSP individuals a sense of mortality, an understanding of frugality, a budget-conscious mind that abhors waste, an inability to discard anything that might be useful someday, and an awareness of recycling and restoring. If the environment of Virgo VSP people is cluttered and chaotic, it is usually due to their need to save everything, a quality they share with Cancer VSP people.

Healthy living in body, mind, and spirit may be the lifelong pursuits of a Virgo VSP—to refine each of these parts as best as possible. Some Virgo VSPs, still caught up in the details of Virgo, strive for just one part of this equation, but when they have transcended the separateness, they will observe the necessary unity of all the components and dedicate themselves to this integration process. The Virgo VSP can invest small fortunes in health products that advertise rejuvenation and anti-aging qualities or in a health guru, program, or body practice, and nutritional routine. In the process, they can develop skills at marketing their services to others—coaching, counseling, yoga, energetic healing, bodywork, etc.—to keep others on a healthy routine. But these services that they provide to others serve the Virgo VSP best when they themselves are taking the treatments and giving self-care in as large a dose as they are advocating. In fact, it is essential to their survival. Stress factors in life, especially around a job situation, will cause hyperactive nervous responses and indigestion to which the Virgo VSP is no stranger. Virgo VSP Woody Allen, who performs the perpetual hypochondriac, when asked in the film *Scoop* how he could possibly eat nothing but bread for a meal and never gain a pound, responded: "My highly nervous condition creates an aerobic like response in my intestines."[44]

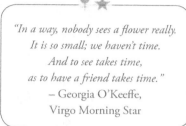

"In a way, nobody sees a flower really. It is so small; we haven't time. And to see takes time, as to have a friend takes time."
– Georgia O'Keeffe,
Virgo Morning Star

The influence of Venus in Virgo has given the Virgo VSP individual the ability to integrate mind and body holistically, key to the Virgo VSP individual's success and longevity. Once they have dedicated themselves to self-improvement, they set their sights to larger goals of improvement, focusing on the health and well-being of the planet.

Virgo VSP individuals, the last of whom were born in the first half of 1984, belong to a group of people who comprise approximately 15 percent of the world's population.

Among prominent Virgo VSP individuals, artist Georgia O'Keeffe, a Virgo Morning Star, possessed the technical ability to paint with great detail, making her one of the finest artists of the twentieth century. Tiger Woods, another Virgo Morning Star, has broken many golf records using his precision and focus, and Virgo VSP Dr. Ruth has made a career out of approaching the subject of sexual intimacy with concrete facts and razor-sharp pointedness. Horror author Stephen King's chart contains the triple crown of Venus: the Sun, Venus, and the Venus Star closely aligned in his Third House, which is story-telling and writing.

Further, many members of the Joseph Kennedy Sr. (born 1888) family are Virgo VSP individuals. One son (Edward), three daughters (Jean Ann, Kathleen and Patricia), two daughters-in-law (Ethel and Joan), and a grandson (Joseph Patrick II) of his are Virgo VSPs who have dedicated the better part of their lives to public service. President John F. Kennedy's famous statement "Ask not what your country can do for you, ask what you can do for your country" suggests how he was influenced by his Virgo VSP father.

People who share the same star sign seem to "know" the other person very well, and identify extremely well with many of their ideas, a phenomenon known as "twin stars" (see Section III). For example, Virgo VSP filmmaker George Lucas (13° Virgo) has publicly stated that his films were greatly influenced by friend, mentor, and fellow Virgo VSP mythologist and teacher Joseph Campbell (24° Virgo). Finally, Julia Roberts, a Virgo VSP Morning Star, possesses the quick-witted reflexes and responses of Virgo's ruling planet Mercury. Her Venus Star is flanked by five planets in Virgo, including Venus. This combination has helped make her one of the world's favorite and most talented actresses, as well as one of the cutest and most successful! For a list of other noteworthy Virgo Star Individuals, see Appendix III.

> "I think the person who takes a job in order to live—that is to say, (just) for the money —has turned himself into a slave."
> – Joseph Campbell,
> Virgo Morning Star

The Virgo Venus Star Point

The Horoscope for the Virgo Venus Star Point

The VSP in Virgo: The Historical Realm

Astrologically the inception of the Virgo VSP era marks one of the smaller paradigm-shifting periods of the world, as it follows the Libra Star in the Venus transit across an important equinoctial point of the wheel. This period occurred during the 1870s, when one world was collapsing and a new one emerging. In America, it was called Reconstruction, after the war between the north and south. Around the world it produced similar urges towards the mechanization and industrialization of life and an abrupt ending to a time-honored agricultural way of life. The inventions and production of machinery and manufacturing at a heretofore unprecedented pace and volume suddenly revealed that the tedious toil of human hands would decrease substantially. The Virgo Star era also brought progress on many fronts

> *"Everything that used to be a sin is now a disease."* – Bill Maher, Virgo Evening Star

in health, hygiene, and social welfare, mating for life as it does with its Aquarius Star. The Virgo Star is fed by the Aquarius Star, and together this pair is associated with the ability to master the laws of physics and develop technology accordingly. Consequently, this period can be called the golden age of science, technology, and medicine.

During this era, many medical advances were made and medicines developed to extend human life. The pharmaceutical industry also gained prominence in the corporate world. Ironically, at the same time life was being extended, technology was inventing potential ways of shortening it as well, including nuclear weapons and industrial devices causing environmental threats to people and animals. In fact, the biggest dilemma during the one hundred years of the Virgo VSP was how to keep ourselves and our planet healthy in the face of rapid deterioration.

One of the ways this conundrum manifested was through changes in agriculture around the world. Farming became increasingly more corporate. Efficient machinery replaced human hands, allowing for greater profits and producing food in ways that poisoned the soil and the people who consumed it through the use of pesticides, herbicides, and fertilizers. Although many new drugs were produced, still many more illnesses and diseases appeared.

During this time advances in technology and communication made the world much smaller and allowed many types of work to be done more efficiently. In many situations, the use of machines surpassed human efforts at a fraction of the cost. The mechanization of societies in such a short time resulted in "future shock."

During the Virgo Star era, an era where devotion is both emphasized and redefined, science and industry became the new god, prompting the existentialist question: "Is God dead?" in the twentieth century. On the one hand discoveries in science and technology made it more difficult for fundamentalists to defend the old religions. On the other hand, the charismatic Pope John Paul II, a Virgo VSP, defended the greatest challenge yet and saved millions from turning their backs on the Catholic church.

> *"Talent is cheaper than table salt. What separates the talented individual from the successful one is a lot of hard work."* – Stephen King, Virgo Evening Star

The Great Depression of the 1930s occurred during a Virgo Star era, an economically difficult time in which the Virgo proficiency at budgeting and knowing how to live with less were the means of survival.

From 1928 to 1942, Neptune (god of spirits)

graced Virgo while the VSP transited as well. This was reflected in the sobriety instituted by law during the Prohibition years. However, this may have actually produced the opposite effect—a generation of people born with VSP in Virgo and Neptune in Virgo who became alcohol abusers later in life. Disease centers of the world are still coping with this illness fifty to nearly one hundred years later.

During the 1960s, both Uranus and Pluto transited Virgo, while the VSP was in Virgo as well. This undermined the order associated with Virgo and resulted in the spirit of rebellion prevalent in the times, which brought to public attention such important issues as workers' rights, labor unions, health care, and animal rights—all Virgo issues.

In the 1990s, the traditional laws of physics were supplanted by quantum physics, metaphysics, and other phenomena that science was powerless to explain fully, and newfound aspects of the universe beyond comprehension were discovered.

Additionally, in this era the stewards of planet Earth began to gather en masse all around the globe to proclaim the need for environmentally friendly attitudes and action. The last Virgo VSPs, born in the early 1980s, were born to carry on the spirit of eco-friendliness that began in the 1960s, especially the ones who also have Uranus and Pluto in Virgo. If it is possible to save Earth, this last group of Virgo VSPs will implement the necessary process. The leaders of any movement devoted to this goal must either be inspired by or themselves be Virgo VSPs, such as Al Gore who is a Virgo Evening Star.

> *"I get to play golf for a living.*
> *What more can you ask for—*
> *getting paid for doing what you love."*
> – Tiger Woods,
> Virgo Morning Star

> *"I am my own experiment.*
> *I am my own work of art."*
> – Madonna Ciccone,
> Aquarius Morning Star

8 THE AQUARIUS VENUS STAR POINT

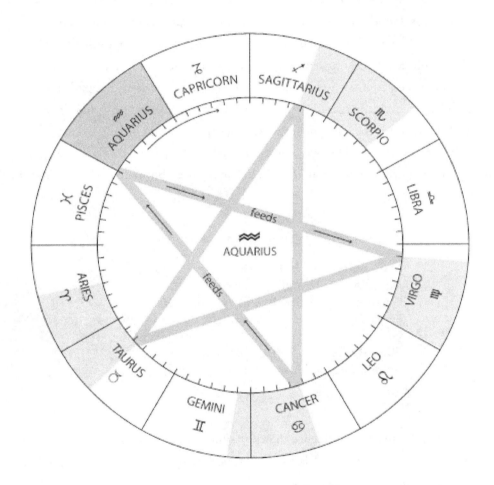

The Energy Flow of the Star Is:
Aquarius→Virgo→Taurus→Sagittarius→Cancer→Aquarius

The Venus transit of Aquarius began February 18, 1890,
as an Evening Star and ended in 1982 as a Morning Star.

ELEMENT: AIR
MODALITY: FIXED

Aquarius The astrological glyph for Aquarius represents not waves of water but waves of energy that animate Earth, the stars, the galaxies, and, at the subatomic level, the human body. Although Aquarius has been depicted as the water pourer, Aquarius is not a water sign but an air sign.

Some keywords and concepts for **Aquarius** are: circulation—of products, information, ideas, blood; futuristic, group-oriented, humanistic, universal, visionary, intelligent, scientific, inventive, activist, eclectic, eccentric, detached, idealistic, freedom, social reform, collectives, steering committees, co-ops, people who speak for the masses, socialism, communes, communities, believers in social justice, legislatures, parliaments, reaching for the stars; the merger of man with machine (in the early part) and the merger of human and star man (in the later part); the new age or new world order.

Of the following well known female and male archetypes of this star, the names in bold below are pure Aquarius Star archetypes, having been born on or very close to the inception of the Aquarius VSP.

> **Male archetypes:** Nelson Mandela, Bill Moyers, Bill Clinton, Dr. Phil McGraw, Prince William, **Garth Brooks**, **Chris Rock** and **Ashton Kutcher**.
> **Female archetypes:** Mother Teresa, Queen Elizabeth II, Gloria Steinem, Shirley MacLaine, **Oprah Winfrey**, **Ellen De Generis**, **Helen Gurley Brown**, **Natalie Cole** and **Carole King**.

Greatest Assets: the ability to influence the viewpoints of many, potentially changing the world; the ability to act as role models and leaders; a detached nonemotional response to other people's criticisms and judgments.

Greatest Liabilities: The greatest obstacle to your heart-centered self is the vast amount of resources you have invested in mental and intellectual pursuits, closing you off or potentially blocking the feelings and affections of others. Even though you are usually right and your point will eventually be accepted, give in to someone else's point of view.

Are You An Aquarius Venus Star Point?

If you were born between the dates listed below, you are an Aquarius Venus Star Point. The Venus Star Point passed through Aquarius in ten-month increments, returning to the sign every four years, so it is important to use your exact date of birth to locate your Venus Star Point sign. Don't confuse this Venus Star with your Sun sign or with your Venus sign, even though the Venus Star *can* occur while the Sun is in Aquarius at the beginning of each of these four-year periods. If this is the case for you, you have both Sun and Venus Star Point in Aquarius, which creates a very potent expression of Aquarius in your life. If you were born *before* or *after* any of the dates listed below you are *not* an Aquarius Venus Star Point individual, though your Sun may be Aquarius.

MS=MORNING STAR   ES=EVENING STAR   D= VENUS DIRECT
Rx= VENUS RETROGRADE

MS/ES	DATES OF AQUARIUS VSP	DEGREE
ES	2/18/1890 – 12/3/1890	29 Aquarius 49 D
MS	2/16/1894 – 11/29/1894	27 Aquarius 43 Rx
ES	2/16/1898 – 11/30/1898	27 Aquarius 19 D
MS	2/15/1902 – 11/28/1902	25 Aquarius 20 Rx
ES	2/14/1906 – 11/29/1906	24 Aquarius 48 D
MS	2/12/1910 – 11/25/1910	22 Aquarius 56 Rx
ES	2/11/1914 – 11/26/1914	22 Aquarius 18 D
MS	2/10/1918 – 11/23/1918	20 Aquarius 32 Rx
ES	2/9/1922 – 11/24/1922	19 Aquarius 46 D
MS	2/7/1926 – 11/20/1926	18 Aquarius 07 Rx
ES	2/6/1930 – 11/21/1930	17 Aquarius 13 D
MS	2/5/1934 – 11/18/1934	15 Aquarius 42 Rx
ES	2/4/1938 – 11/19/1938	14 Aquarius 42 D
MS	2/2/1942 – 11/15/1942	13 Aquarius 16 Rx
ES	2/1/1946 – 11/16/1946	12 Aquarius 08 D
MS	1/31/1950 – 11/13/1950	10 Aquarius 50 Rx
ES	1/30/1954 – 11/14/1954	09 Aquarius 35 D
MS	1/28/1958 – 11/10/1958	08 Aquarius 24 Rx
ES	1/27/1962 – 11/11/1962	07 Aquarius 00 D
MS	1/26/1966 – 11/8/1966	05 Aquarius 57 Rx
ES	1/24/1970 – 11/9/1970	04 Aquarius 27 D
MS	1/24/1974 – 11/5/1974	03 Aquarius 30 Rx
ES	1/22/1978 – 11/7/1978	01 Aquarius 52 D
MS	1/21/1982 – 11/3/1982	01 Aquarius 02 Rx

Even if you were not born during these dates, the Aquarius VSP affected general behavior patterns on Earth nevertheless, and thus Aquarius characteristics prevailed, such as people being motivated to break loose from their roots and try new things like networking for a cause or becoming more socially active.

Venus Star Point's Gift to Aquarius

Love and a heart-centered approach to life come through demanding egalitarian relationships and focusing on, and combining energies with, a special friend/life mate as the source of your life's meaning and abundance.

The VSP in Aquarius: The Personal Realm

Each of the Venus Star Points has its own special gift, and it's under the sign of your Venus Star Point that the best of yourself is expressed. Of course, as discussed in Chapter 3, the Venus Star, like everything in nature, also has a shadow side. Aquarius is an air sign, ruled by two planets: Saturn in traditional astrology and Uranus in contemporary astrology. Thus, the Aquarius VSP will embody important elements of both these planetary rulers, seen as principles of physical and metaphysical realities that the Aquarius VSP has at its command.

The element of air symbolizes the circulation of energy, and for Aquarius VSP individuals, the principle of circulation is emphasized, whether it is connected with the circles in which they move, the network of operations they oversee, the ways in which they conduct energy, or the information airwaves that they use to generate and receive ideas. People admire their mix of creativity, eccentricity, and style, and often choose them to advocate for people or advertise a product.

Aquarius VSP individuals can be rigid or innovative, depending on the conditions of the ruling planets operating in their charts. They are people endowed with the gift of seeing the future and are challenged to share that vision with the world. The way they express their worldview to others is key to how their message is received. Aquarians are usually twenty-five to fifty years ahead of their time, and this seems true for the Aquarius VSP group as well. They're already living in the future while most people around them are still living in the present or past. But as time passes, Aquarius VSP individuals are not only

> *"All human beings are also dream beings. Dreaming ties all mankind together."*
> – Jack Kerouac,
> Aquarius Evening Star

vindicated for their point of view but also celebrated.

Uranus and Saturn are the two ruling planets of Aquarius. In mythology, these two are related: they are a father/son pair that were locked in struggle until the son forcibly removed his father from power. If the Aquarius VSP finds themselves torn between the past and the future, or battling an overpowering parental tradition in order to fulfill their own destiny, they are reflecting the tense dynamic at play in this sign. When Saturn is more influential in the Aquarius Star's chart, Aquarius VSP individuals can become stuck in a pattern of life that seems better suited to their parents' dream rather than living the liberated, self-engineered, visionary life they seek. So the nature of the Aquarius Star with its two ruling planets—Saturn (the past) and Uranus (the future)—is the choice they are faced with in life. When Uranus is the guiding spirit, they are attuned to their own voices and visions. But even if they are aligned with Saturn, the Aquarius VSP is likely to have experienced times when they were forced to summon courage and break from parental influences and generations-old traditions and values. Aquarius VSP individuals rival only Aries VSP people in wasting no time in leaving home in search of their own destinies.

Aquarius VSP individuals are artists, geniuses, or visionaries who express themselves best within a social context. They seem born to lead, whether they want to or not. People elect them, and as role models for the masses, they often generate a cult following. For instance, among the many pop/rock stars with many fans, the ones that make it to superstardom tend to be Aquarius VSP individuals. It doesn't always mean they are more talented than others in their field but that they possess a charisma that makes them especially appealing to their generation. Some examples of this phenomenon include Paul McCartney, Brian Wilson, Barbara Streisand, Elvis Presley, Marilyn Monroe, Madonna, Prince, and Michael Jackson. These particular Aquarius VSP individuals, as well as most of the group, send influential messages to the masses through what they think, say, buy, wear, or do. The trap they can easily fall into is playing the part so well that they can't escape from it. For an Aquarius VSP individual being trapped with no escape is like death. Such people absolutely need to be free to live their own way.

> "I used to think that anyone doing anything weird was weird. I suddenly realized that anyone doing anything weird wasn't weird at all and it was the people saying they were weird that were weird."
> – Paul McCartney,
> Aquarius Morning Star

Aquarius VSP people are excited by the new technologies currently being advanced and they are often among those helping to invent them. They come up with ingenious ideas and inventions quickly and easily—whether it's a computer game, a kitchen tool, a car part, or a new type of clothing. However, many are not motivated enough to market them, nor do they need to. They simply enjoy the pleasure of having created something really wild.

For Aquarius VSP individuals, social senses and graces are instinctual. As a result, they often become involved in community affairs and networking for a great part of their lives. Whether it's family or friends, *people* are the key ingredient in making Aquarius VSP individuals successful in life. However, Aquarius VSP individuals are best suited to relating to people in a community rather than in one-to-one relationships, and thus many from this group also feel estranged from people. Although they inspire people with their dazzling intellect and charismatic personality, they often really long for someone to ground them and support them. A very high percentage (75 percent) of Aquarius VSP individuals are fed by the Cancer VSPs, and thus an instinctual yearning is to create for themselves their own family dynasty. Aquarius VSP individuals can take or leave marriage, which is not something they *need* as much as something they *desire*. If they decide not to marry, they are likely to choose peers as life companions or partners.

> *"Lots of people want to ride with you in the limo, but what you want is someone who will take the bus with you when the limo breaks down."*
> – Oprah Winfrey,
> Aquarius Evening Star

Although many Aquarius VSP individuals come from loving families, they may wonder why they were born to a particular family since they often feel like black sheep as they are free-thinking nonconformists. For them, transcending their early roots and upbringing is a commonplace occurrence and can even be necessary to fulfilling their personal destiny. Often they create a new family consisting of people who are completely outside their birth-family nucleus. As they separate from their family of origin, peers often constitute their adopted families, and they enjoy establishing communities of like-minded individuals. Their sense of fulfillment in relationships comes through groups with which they identify, such as peer groups, political action groups, church groups, or high school or college groups, with which they are often connected for their entire lives.

Since social systems and ideologies come under the sign of Aquarius, social and political ideals are what fuel the life passions of Aquarius VSP individuals. Thoughts about what kind of world they'd like to see for their children and what changes need to be made are frequently their motivating principle. They often have an intuitive understanding of what's wrong with the system and how to make it right. Whether they are on the left (the majority) or on the right, very few identify themselves as "middle of the road." For instance, former presidents Bill Clinton and George W. Bush are both Aquarius Evening Stars, although they have totally different beliefs and visions and have amassed a large number of followers who support those visions. Their positions on both the left and the right reflect the ruling of Aquarius by both Saturn and Uranus.

With the Aquarius VSP pointing toward or feeding the Virgo VSP, Aquarius VSPs may find themselves struggling to come down to earth from their broad, airy perch and focus on the minute details of life. But this talent is often applied to the workplace, whereby advocating for a more humanitarian and dignified interchange with the workers, greater efficiency is produced, and the yearnings of the Venus Star's influence in Aquarius—a happy and peaceful heart—are thereby achieved. They take great pride when they have been successful at implementing changes in the workplace that make employees feel their work environment is safer, fairer, and better supports their needs.

Keeping their pulse on social concerns is the right kind of public service for the Aquarius VSP and may force them to become involved in politics or policy-making at their work place, becoming the community's "voice," a role they are well equipped to take on. Even when they don't formally enter politics, the Aquarius VSP has their eye on what's going on and is a strong voice for or against much proposed legislation.

The Aquarius VSP has command of the airwaves with the media coming to them just as often as they try to influence the media. Especially strong examples are Aquarius VSP individuals who have provided a voice to a particular group: for compassion for people who are suffering (Mother Teresa); for people's freedom and dignity (Nelson Mandela and Evita Peron); for laborers (Cesar Chavez); for restless youth (Elvis Presley, Paul McCartney); for feminism (Gloria Steinem); for old-fashioned radio entertainment in *A Prairie Home Companion* (Garrison Keillor); for marine life (Jacques Cousteau); for late-night television (Jay Leno); for the primates (Jane Goodall); for right-wing radio in America (Rush Limbaugh); for the new age (Shirley MacLaine). But of all these Aquarius VSP voices who gained their own massive followings, perhaps the most effective voice of our time that influences culture and marketing is Oprah Winfrey, an Aquarius Evening Star, who expresses herself especially effortlessly and powerfully, because she was born on the day of the Aquarius VSP's inception, a true living archetype of the Aquarius Star.

> On things she had to pack before leaving her home in advance of a forest fire, in 1996: *"Childhood pictures and pictures of my life. Do you know how many pictures that is? Not just this life; I have pictures from 13,000 lives."* – Shirley MacLaine, Aquarius Morning Star

If you are an Aquarius VSP individual, the last of whom were born in 1982, you belong to a group comprising approximately 15 percent of the world population.

Among prominent Aquarius VSP individuals are Prince William, future heir to the British throne, born during Venus' last transit through Aquarius for one hundred years; and his younger brother Harry who was born during Venus' last transit through Virgo for one hundred years. This may suggest that these young men are the last of a line, or at least a hierarchy, that will terminate with them. Moreover, since the present reigning monarch, Queen Elizabeth II, is an Aquarius VSP individual like her grandson Prince William, there is a good chance that he will be the voice of his people and be one of the more popular monarchs of his century.

As discussed previously, each of the individual star periods of a sign contains its own unique qualities. For the 1958 Venus Star transit to Aquarius, the Pandemos Morning Star was both conjunct Chiron and opposite Uranus. Three notable and highly marketable pop stars were born with this signature: Michael Jackson, Prince, and Madonna, all of whom rode their Venus Star/Uranus connection to the heights of celebrity popularity. Chiron in Aquarius brings the alien-like earth visitor, a wounded healer archetype who heals the masses while enduring his own private suffering. Uranus in Leo, illuminated by the Venus Star, gave these individuals the ability to transmit to each adoring fan the feeling that they were personally connecting to them, fans whose adoration produced in many cases, a type of spontaneous healing through the music of their master. For a list of other noteworthy Aquarius Star Individuals, see Appendix III.

> *"People like to label you. I've never liked being labeled. I can't take it because I'm never going to do the same thing over and over and over. I hate being limited. I hate being put in a box."*
> – Queen Latifah,
> Aquarius Evening Star

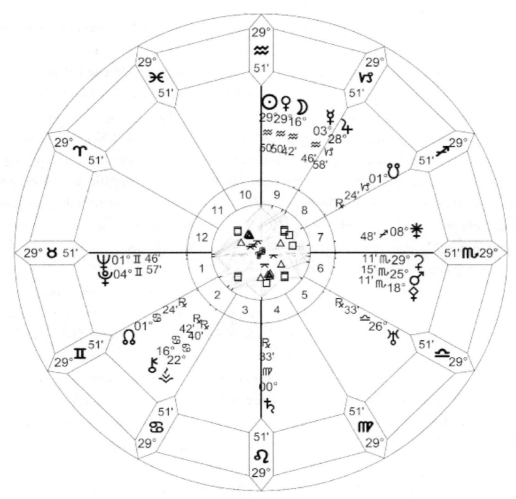

The Horoscope for the Aquarius Venus Star Point

The VSP in Aquarius – The Historical Realm

The beginning of Venus' transit through Aquarius, with seven planets in air signs, was marked by a call for changes in outdated laws and customs, as well as human rights in general. The major innovations in the world involved health, women's rights, and societal and marital roles. In the fields of health care and healing, Aquarius VSP individuals were always up on the latest breakthroughs and were willing to experiment with them. Progress in many areas of health was announced. Global distribution of new vaccines began in order to keep up with the parade of stronger viruses appearing on a global scale. Organ transplants and the discovery of DNA also emerged during this period.

When the VSP began transiting Aquarius in 1890, the world was emerging from the Victorian age, and the industrial age was in full swing. It was during this era that the works of Thomas Edison, Nikola Tesla, Alexander Graham Bell, and Albert Einstein became known to the world, helping mankind to make a giant leap from an agriculturally based society to an electronically based one. Telecommunication systems advanced greatly, especially from 1960 to 1982 when the Aquarius VSP (air sign) was being fed by the Gemini VSP (another air sign) at the phasing out of the Aquarius Star and the birth of the Gemini Star. Consequently, during this transition period where two air signs were in focus, the broadcast media also took on increased importance. The 1980s film *Broadcast News*[45] depicted the state of the television media, which had such an elevated place in life that it not only reported the news but also determined it. Moreover, even more miraculous innovations in the field of communications systems may occur in the future, because the Gemini VSP will last until 2073.

The Aquarius VSP era produced numerous ideologies and social systems that people blindly followed. During this period, the occurrence of the rare Neptune/Pluto conjunction (1891-92), peaking simultaneously with the birth of the VSP in the Aquarius Star, created a fertile environment for free thinkers and experimenters who focused on social orders. Alternative societies, such as communes and communities based on specific ideologies like democracy, fascism, and communism, were established during the era. Such political and social orders gained as much power and influence as at any other time in the history of the world, giving rise to global tensions due to contrasting belief systems. For instance, communism was established at the height of the Aquarius VSP period. In 1916–1917, the Russian Revolution took place, and thirty years later communism came to China. Then for seventy years, the super power nations of the world were in conflict over the ideologies of communism and capitalism. However, just as the VSP exited Aquarius, the Iron Curtain dissolved in Europe with the Berlin Wall coming down in 1989 and the USSR being dissolved in 1991.

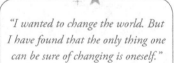

"I wanted to change the world. But I have found that the only thing one can be sure of changing is oneself."
– Aldous Huxley,
Aquarius Morning Star

But free thinking also flourished in spite of the establishment of groups based on ideologies. It was as if the VSP transit through Aquarius was giving people a choice: maintain freedom of thought or be swept up by a mass movement that controls your life, i.e., let others do the thinking. Considering that Aquarius is a sign oriented towards the collective, joining a group, being influenced by a cause, and devoting one's life to supporting an ideology seem appropriate.

While the VSP was in the air sign, the Aquarius VSP appropriately gave media better access to the airwaves for evolution of the information age. Television, video, and satellite systems made it possible to send information seemingly at the speed of light. It was an appropriate time, cosmically, for inventions of machines that transmitted people's voices, and then finally their images around the world—whether a pope, president, dictator, guru, sports hero, or rock star. There was an emphasis on innovative use of the airwaves, as well as flight in the air. Historic achievements with flight occurred; Orville and Wilbur Wright launched their first flight in 1903 and Charles Lindbergh flew "The Spirit of St. Louis" from New York to Paris in 1927. One of the hallmarks of the Aquarius VSP era was the industry of "air" travel.

Further, before the VSP in Aquarius ended in 1982, man began to explore space. During the last thirty years of this era, super-powers were in a race to see who could launch the most successful missions into outer space. The United States triumphed in 1968 to 1969 with the lunar landing that was seen

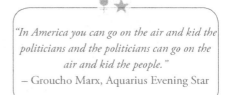

"In America you can go on the air and kid the politicians and the politicians can go on the air and kid the people."
– Groucho Marx, Aquarius Evening Star

as "one small step for man, one giant leap for mankind." For inhabitants of Earth, this event was also a reminder of man's origin in connection to the stars. This new perspective of human merging with star-man was expressed through numerous ideas, technologies, films, books, and videos of the era that either welcomed space visitors to become friends with earthlings, such as ET, or emphasized the potentially more sinister side of such encounters, as in *Star Wars*.

In connection with Aquarius as an air sign, depicted by a figure pouring stars from the sky out of an urn, star children began to be born while the VSP transited Aquarius. The theme of the "age of Aquarius," which was immortalized in a popular 1960s song, accurately expressed how this era focused on the attainment of higher consciousness and increased awareness of man's relationship to the cosmos. One of the extraordinary features of the chart for the Aquarius VSP is the conjunction of Neptune and Pluto, which occurs only every four to five hundred years. These two planets are rising in the Aquarius VSP cycle, bringing forth a planetary spiritual transformation that has challenged just about every sacred law and institution of the previous era.

Aquarius VSP individuals born during the 1940s and 1950s experienced a tense relationship with Pluto's transit through Leo that expressed itself as "free love" during the

1960s and 1970s. The Venus Star Point representing outpouring of love to humanity, and Pluto, representing death and regeneration, gave that generation roller-coaster rides both to the heavenly realms and down to Hades. This group, upon reaching maturity, experimented with the most Aquarian manifestation of love (group love, free love, love-ins) and the most Plutonian expression of love (intense sexual desire and possession by love), collectively celebrating their perspective at Woodstock and becoming known as the Woodstock Generation. Highlighting the era of the Woodstock Generation was the transit of Neptune, representing idealistic longings and romanticism, or escapism, through Libra (partnership) during this period. The era was sharply defined by the combination of the Venus Star Point passing through Aquarius, Neptune in Libra, and Pluto in Leo. The resulting influences produced an entire generation of individuals who were idealistic concerning love and romance, experimental, and unstable with regard to the institution of marriage.

During the last twenty years of the Aquarius Star (1964-1982), the Gemini Star fed the Aquarius VSP, a unique time in which individuals were endowed with keen vision and powerful voices and minds that inspired and led millions to adopt their visions. Since that rare alignment of the young and robust Gemini Star feeding the last rays of the Aquarius Star, there has to date not been a time when the collective voice for change was as amplified as it was by that special group of souls born in the 1960s, 70s, and 80s. Will they be able to maintain their ideological and visionary voices into their later years? Only time will tell.

That period of history contained the same star alignment as the period 250 years prior (1713-1733), which was also a time when the collective voice for change was powerful and spawned a philosophical revolution. The early 1700s saw the beginning of the Age of Enlightenment, a term used to describe a new philosophy in Europe and the American colonies that was a revolution in thought. Writers from this period used the phrase to indicate their belief that humanity was coming out of centuries of ignorance and into a new age defined by reason, science, and respect for humanity. The period is also referred to as the Age of Reason. The new belief system saw the established church, especially the Roman Catholic church, as the principal force that enslaved the human mind. Though they generally didn't dismiss a belief in God and the afterlife, the movement's proponents insisted that human aspirations should be centered on improving this life and not on a reward gained only in Heaven. They believed that through proper education and guided by reason, humanity itself could be altered, and its nature changed for the better. The Age of Enlightenment led directly to the American Revolution and French Revolution and strongly influenced the Industrial Revolution.[46]

The Aquarius Venus Star Point

This is precisely the kind of thinking that would gain a wide acceptance during times when two air signs rule the world. The image portrayed by the constellations Gemini and Aquarius depict humans rather than animals. The human's finest hour—and greatest glory—is his gift of humanity to his fellow beings. It is also true, that since the Aquarius Star follows the Pisces Star, it is a naturally occurring progression to find humanity devoutly influenced by religion during a Pisces Star period, followed by a period of the Aquarius Star where men and women of science and intellect would overthrow such notions, advocating reason, free-thinking, and the devotion to fellow human beings in favor of a deity.

> *"Basically, everything I try to do is to present an alternative to what somebody else is doing."*
> – Matt Groening,
> Aquarius Evening Star

"That is the exploration that awaits you! Not mapping stars and studying nebulae, but charting the unknown possibilities of existence." – Leonard Nimoy, Scorpio Morning Star

9 THE SCORPIO VENUS STAR POINT

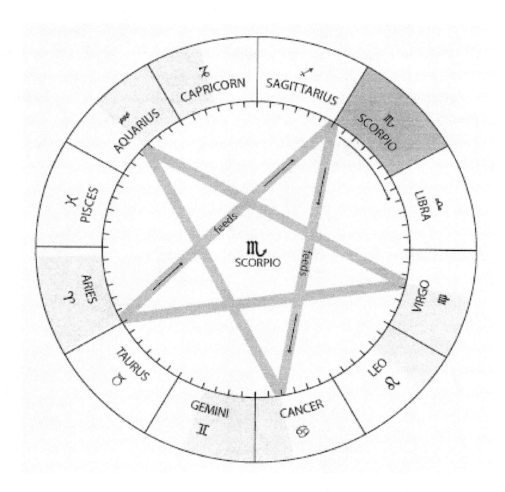

The Energy Flow of the Star is:
Scorpio→Cancer→Aquarius→Virgo→Aries→Scorpio

The Venus transit of Scorpio began November 21, 1926, as an Evening Star and will end in 2027 as a Morning Star.

ELEMENT: WATER
MODALITY: FIXED

Scorpio   The astrological glyph for Scorpio is similar to the glyph for Virgo. They both resemble the letter *M*, but in Scorpio's case, there is a tail pointing upward, which some say is the stinger the scorpion uses for self-protection. It also resembles the movement of a snake, reflecting Scorpio's long tradition of association with the serpent or caduceus (double serpent), from which is derived the modern medical symbol.

Some keywords and concepts for Scorpio are: transformation; alchemy, regeneration, recycling, purification; the psyche's strength; alliances with great power, wealth, and sexuality, secret motives or hidden agendas, shared power; death as a natural consequence of life; the serpent energy of death, rebirth, and healing; inheritance—emotional, psychic, financial, or karmic; feminine power and strength.

Of the following well known female and male archetypes of this star, the names in bold below are pure Scorpio Star archetypes, having been born on or very close to the inception of the Venus Star Point.

> **Female Archetypes: Marie Antoinette, Condoleeza Rice,** Janis Joplin, Camilla Parker Bowles, **Demi Moore, Linda Evans, Jodie Foster, Anne Hathaway** and Angelina Jolie.
> **Male Archetypes: Sai Baba, Martin Scorsese, Ted Turner,** James Dean, Fidel Castro, Mick Jagger, Steven Spielberg, David Bowie, Elton John, Karl Rove, **Leonardo DiCaprio,** and **Yanni**.

Greatest Assets: A desire to grasp the deepest mysteries of life; ability to empathize with others; ability to resonate with the shadow side, mystery, and the unconscious—realms that frighten others.

Greatest Liabilities: The biggest obstacle to your heart centered self is the many layers of protection you build to keep people away from the innermost depths of your heart. You desire relationships for the shared power it brings, but you can easily overstep the line and possess others. Once you release the hold on that which needs to be free, love will embrace you fully.

The Scorpio Venus Star Point

Are You A Scorpio Venus Star Point?

If you were born between the dates listed below, you are a Scorpio Venus Star Point (VSP). The Venus Star Point passed through Scorpio in ten-month increments, returning to the sign every four years, so it is important to use your exact date of birth to locate your Venus Star Point sign. Don't confuse this Venus Star with your Sun sign or with your Venus sign, even though the Venus Star *can* occur while the Sun is in Scorpio at the beginning of each of these four-year periods. If this is the case for you, you have both Sun and Venus Star Point in Scorpio, which creates a very potent expression of Scorpio in your life. If you were born *before* or *after* the dates listed below, you are *not* a Scorpio Venus Star Point individual, though your Sun sign may be Scorpio.

MS=MORNING STAR   ES=EVENING STAR   D= VENUS DIRECT
Rx= VENUS RETROGRADE

MS/ES	DATES OF SCORPIO VSP	DEGREE
ES	11/21/1926 – 9/9/1927	28 Scorpio 27 D
MS	11/22/1930 – 9/7/1931	29 Scorpio 44 Rx
ES	11/19/1934 – 9/7/1935	26 Scorpio 00 D
MS	11/20/1938 – 9/5/1939	27 Scorpio 17 Rx
ES	11/16/1942 – 9/5/1943	23 Scorpio 31 D
MS	11/17/1946 – 9/2/1947	24 Scorpio 51 Rx
ES	11/14/1950 – 9/2/1951	21 Scorpio 03 D
MS	11/15/1954 – 8/31/1955	22 Scorpio 25 Rx
ES	11/11/1958 – 8/31/1959	18 Scorpio 37 D
MS	11/11/1962 – 8/29/1963	19 Scorpio 58 Rx
ES	11/9/1966 – 8/29/1967	16 Scorpio 10 D
MS	11/10/1970 – 8/26/1971	17 Scorpio 33 Rx
ES	11/6/1974 – 8/26/1975	13 Scorpio 45 D
MS	11/8/1978 – 8/24/1979	15 Scorpio 07 Rx
ES	11/4/1982 – 8/24/1983	11 Scorpio 20 D
MS	11/5/1986 – 8/22/1987	12 Scorpio 42 Rx
ES	11/1/1990 – 8/21/1991	08 Scorpio 57 D
MS	11/3/1994 – 8/20/1995	10 Scorpio 18 Rx
ES	10/30/1998 – 8/19/1999	06 Scorpio 33 D
MS	10/31/2002 – 8/17/2003	07 Scorpio 53 Rx
ES	10/27/2006 – 8/17/2007	04 Scorpio 10 D
MS	10/29/2010 – 8/15/2011	05 Scorpio 30 Rx
ES	10/25/2014 – 8/14 2015	01 Scorpio 49 D
MS	10/26/2018 – 8/13/2019	03 Scorpio 06 Rx
MS	10/24/2026 – 8/11/2027	00 Scorpio 45 Rx

Even if you were not born during these dates, the Scorpio VSP affected general behavior patterns on Earth nevertheless, and thus Scorpio characteristics prevailed, such as people being inclined to marry or join forces with another, invest jointly, fund some particular kind of research or institution, or explore the less-known, more mysterious realms of life.

Venus Star Point's Gift to Scorpio

Love and a heart-centered approach to life comes through the Scorpio VSP individual's ability to transform their own lives as well as the lives of others. They make the most of life's devastating storms, possessing the ability to greet the new day with hope, renewal and rebirth. Using their reliable and powerful instincts, they are masterfully skilled at making good use of their own and other's resources. The Scorpio VSP may be an alluring, sexy, flirtatious tease who attracts the affections and resources of others to them easily. But that's their special magic—things come to them.

The VSP in Scorpio: The Personal Realm

Each of the Venus Star Points has its own special gift, and it's under the sign of your Venus Star Point that the best of yourself is expressed. Of course, there's a shadow side to everything in nature, and also in the Venus Star Point. The Scorpio VSP expresses itself through the element of water (feelings) and is ruled by Pluto (contemporary astrology) and Mars (traditional and Vedic astrology). The contrasting emotions of Scorpio VSP individuals are associated with the planets ruling Scorpio. Like other signs, Scorpios possess two natures, one that resonates more closely with Mars, and one that identifies more fully with Pluto.

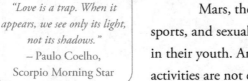

"Love is a trap. When it appears, we see only its light, not its shadows."
– Paulo Coelho, Scorpio Morning Star

Mars, the youthful god of action, boundless energy, sports, and sexuality, typically will influence the Scorpio VSP in their youth. And, because Scorpio is a sign of extremes, these activities are not engaged in lightly. By middle age, however, Pluto, god of the underworld, comes to visit the Scorpio VSP. The penetrating knock on the door beckons the Scorpio VSP to Pluto's underworld where, deep below the surface, one may examine what's lurking in the invisible realms. What might lie hidden in these unseen places? Secrets about one's past? The truth about someone you loved and trusted? The secrets of nature, of the cosmos, of someone's hidden motives? This underworld is a good place for detective work, whether you're looking at your own health or history, or if you're looking into mysteries such as molecular biology, archeology, cosmology, or the numerous unseen worlds that make up a good part of life.

The Venus Star's appearance in Scorpio every four years for a brief period of about ten months each signals a time for all of us to turn our attention inward, focusing on our psychological well being, as contrasted to the physical world and all its attendant drama. While the Venus Star itself can be either the love goddess or the war goddess as mentioned earlier in this text, the sign of Scorpio clearly is a sign of war that spends time on the battlefield. But it is the inner battlefield, one's inner landscape rather than the outer battlefield where this war is being waged to slay one's ego, one's emotions, and attachment to the material world. Thus, those who have been born with the Venus Star passing through the gate of Scorpio may live in this condition perpetually. This is home to them and this is the realm they seek to master.

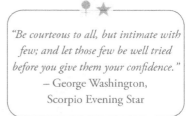

"Be courteous to all, but intimate with few; and let those few be well tried before you give them your confidence."
– George Washington,
Scorpio Evening Star

Scorpio VSP individuals can experience extreme contrasting feelings, although such shifts can go undetected by others. The Scorpio VSP, ruled by the shadowy Pluto, can easily slip in and out of the underworld, mostly undetected by others. This VSP carries a deep secret that they can manage to conceal from others. However, they are greatly relieved when they can actually unburden themselves and let it go. The animals associated with Scorpio reflect its contradictory moods—the scorpion and the snake—and two that soar to the heavenly heights—the eagle and the mythical phoenix.

Scorpio has always been associated with healing, mystery, esoteric teachings, and piercing the veils that conceal people's appearances and secret motives. Consequently, Scorpio VSP individuals have a keenly developed sixth sense. This can make people nervous that their inner motives will be exposed, but it makes Scorpio VSP individuals perfect for detective work. Driven by the Mars/Pluto rulership, Scorpio VSP people have the courage and inclination to plunge into the depths of the human psyche, arriving at the crossroads where the physical and nonphysical aspects of life intersect. This same instinct gives them a keen awareness of people's ailments and the ability to provide insights into treatments and cures.

Some of the most critical issues for Scorpio VSP individuals involve joint ventures and partnerships. The Scorpio VSP, fueled by the Venus Star, loves to dive into the fire of dangerous liaisons, ones that may appear safe at the onset, but become increasingly more intolerable.

Mars and Pluto are two of Scorpio's ruling planets. Mars and Pluto were both gods who took what they wanted. The Scorpio VSP must be careful of an innate tendency to take over others or to be taken over by another's enchanting and seductive powers. This also includes their possessions or assets.

Scorpio VSP individuals are fed by the Aries VSP (who is also their life mate), altering the mantra "I can do anything" so that it becomes "I can change things at will." This ability to craft oneself into a model work of art necessarily entails releasing emotional or psychological baggage that has been collected or inherited. If they do not constantly let go of such baggage, Scorpio VSP people are likely to feel toxic. By contrast, they feel healthiest and most alive when they are fasting, cleansing, and thus transforming their own biochemistry or guiding others in doing so.

Scorpio VSP individuals are drawn to the shadow side of everything as a butterfly is drawn to a flower. Once drawn to dark realms, they may realize they're in over their heads and become anxious. Yet no individuals are more capable of walking through the valley of the shadow of death than Scorpio VSP people. They came equipped at birth with special lenses—instincts—that can navigate through dark, uncharted terrain.

A recurring theme in the life of Scorpio VSP individuals is the cycle of life, death, and rebirth, a metaphor for the process that Scorpio is achieving mastery over—alchemy. The Scorpio VSP may recognize that they have a death wish, in fact, there may actually be a near-death experience in their life, a time when they are given the choice to stay or go. Because regenerations is the constant underlying reality of their lifetime, a certain proficiency at understanding the dying process can become their greatest skill and talent.

All mythologies about Scorpio and its planetary rulers speak about the change of seasons, the journey to the underworld or the unconscious, the transitions between two phases of life, and the power to transform one substance or emotional entity into another. The Scorpio VSP is clearly here for a life of transformation, of mapping the depths of the unconscious and the soul, of living in the nether-world or the underworld where the understanding of the movie behind the movie becomes apparent, illuminating the hidden motives and urges of self and others. For the Scorpio VSP, it is a lifetime of shedding one's skin like a snake and ultimately regenerating. With each cycle of transformation, the Scorpio VSP discovers the true self in the deep inner core and is successful at differentiating it from the illusion or mask of self that is so apparent in the exterior world.

Thus, Scorpio VSP individuals have the ability to face a changed future. Having the strength and courage to navigate through the dark night of the soul is what gives them the power to maintain equilibrium in an impermanent world. For example, they can accept that where there was once a field of sunlit flowers and a beloved's smiling face, there is now dark emptiness. If tragedy visits the lives of Scorpio VSP individuals more frequently than the lives of others, they are also more able to gain knowledge and wisdom from the experience.

The youngsters of the Scorpio VSP will continue to be born until the 2030s. They are highly perceptive and have a great capacity to see and understand unseen realms and trust implicitly in magic, characteristics reflected in the Harry Potter series, created during the Scorpio VSP cycle. Such children may shock or surprise parents who are not of that group with their inquisitiveness about topics beyond their years. Such precocious preoccupation with sex has been afflicting society ever since the Scorpio/Gemini line of energy became activated after 1964. It now has become even stronger, with the other sign of youth, Leo, involved in the Venus Star Point since the early 1990s. A dark societal manifestation of this trend has been the rising tide of the child porn industry.

Since Scorpio is a feminine sign associated with deep feelings and the psyche, female Scorpio VSP individuals may be more comfortable handling this energy than their male counterparts, even though the sign is co-ruled by Mars. This may give Scorpio VSP women the upper hand in partnerships. The intensity of feminine power associated with Scorpio VSP individuals harkens back to the era of 1500 to 1250 BCE when the feminine principle was a ruling force. It was at this time that the Sumerian goddess Inanna journeyed to the underworld and returned stripped of wealth, power, and freedom—assets that, since the inception of the VSP in Scorpio in 1926, are now being re-examined and reclaimed by women. Many women today who have experienced such loss of wealth, power, and freedom, actually or symbolically, are on a life-long campaign to keep this from happening again to themselves or others.

> "I like to hide behind the characters I play. Despite the public perception, I am a very private person who has a hard time with the fame thing."
> – Angelina Jolie,
> Scorpio Evening Star

Scorpio VSP men are attracted to this powerful feminine principle but can also be fearful of becoming enslaved by it. They often seek to marry women who embody it but can become frightened by its dark undercurrents linked to the psyche and the unconscious. Scorpio VSP men who have a healthy relationship with the feminine principle usually enjoy good relationships with powerful women, beginning with their mothers. They can also become fixated by and seek to marry the inner feminine or destroy her in adult relationships. This is especially true of the first generation of Scorpio VSP individuals (1926–1960) born during the time when the Scorpio VSP was feeding the Cancer VSP. By contrast, the second generation of Scorpio VSP men (1964–2027), born while Scorpio is feeding Gemini, are oriented less toward their mothers and more toward relationships with peers and siblings.

Scorpio VSP individuals, the last of whom will be born through the 2020s, comprise approximately 18 percent of the world population, one of the largest population groups on Earth.

The Scorpio VSP includes numerous prominent film stars or directors who have portrayed the shadow side of characters lurking within dark, mysterious, or occult realms: David Bowie, Steven Spielberg, Andrew Lloyd Weber, Janet Leigh, Jamie Lee Curtis, James Dean, Martin Scorsese, Francis Ford Coppola, Bruce Willis, Nicole Kidman, Leonardo DiCaprio, Robert De Niro, Johnny Depp, Ewan McGregor, Angelina Jolie, Kurt Cobain, and Heath Ledger. For a list of other noteworthy Scorpio Star Individuals, see Appendix III.

> *"I look inside myself and see my heart is black."*
> – Mick Jagger, Scorpio Evening Star

The VSP in Scorpio: The Historical Realm

At about the time Venus began as a Morning Star in Scorpio in 1926, Pluto was discovered (1930), in effect, doubling the influence of Scorpio and emphasizing forces of the underworld. Not long after this, plutonium was developed for use in nuclear projects that remain a threat to the existence of life on Earth. The collective fear of living with the possibility of nuclear extinction has subconsciously affected everyone during this era, as if a dark veil had descended on earth and its population was powerless to remove it.

At the beginning of the Scorpio VSP era, the world was experiencing an unprecedented economic crisis, which was realized with the stock market crash of 1929 and subsequent Great Depression. This great financial collapse, the most horrifying one of the 20th century, is foretold in the horoscope for the inception of the Venus Star in Scorpio. The chart for November, 21, 1926, finds the entry of the VSP into Scorpio, a sign dealing with power, wealth, and other people's resources, coming into a face-to-face planetary conjunction with Saturn, the planet symbolizing limits, restriction, and recession. Both the VSP and Saturn are in conflict with Neptune, a planet symbolizing ideals, dreams, and false hopes and promises. With Neptune's square to Saturn in the chart for the Scorpio VSP, many people's dreams of great wealth and prosperity were shattered. The underworld forces rose to power at this time. All over the world, there were headlines about power-hungry dictators, politicians, and serial killers. The mobsters and bootleggers of the 1920s and '30s were prime examples.

The Scorpio Venus Star Point

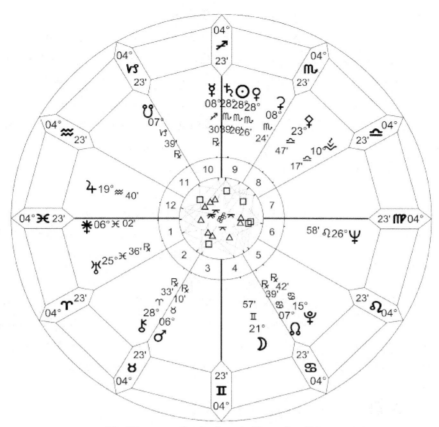

The Horoscope for the Scorpio Venus Star Point

The chart for this period is not limited solely to economic crisis but also contains empowering forces for positive change, fueled by new knowledge, human ingenuity, and the will to succeed. Some industries and groups that actually benefited from the VSP/Saturn square to Neptune were photography, the film industry, the drug industry, the oil industry, and the government regulators who controlled the flow of such commodities.

Moreover, this period is characterized by the reemergence of the feminine principle, linked with Juno rising on the Scorpio VSP. Suppressed for centuries, the feminine principle associated with Juno (Hera), the Great Goddess of ancient times, was poised to regain power during this era. This brings power, wealth, sovereignty, and strength to women and feminine values, as well as to men who resonate with the feminine principle, whether as supporters of feminine causes or in connection with a gay lifestyle.

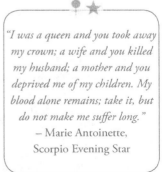

"I was a queen and you took away my crown; a wife and you killed my husband; a mother and you deprived me of my children. My blood alone remains; take it, but do not make me suffer long."
– Marie Antoinette,
Scorpio Evening Star

149

Concurrent with the empowerment of the feminine principle, there was a renewed interest in mythological and historical icons of the feminine principle, such as the Great Goddess and the Christian Black Madonna, or Black Virgin, prayed to as the Holy Mother by millions of worshippers around the world. During the current Scorpio VSP transit, there has been a resurrection of numerous legends, myths, and stories about the sacred feminine in all religions, particularly those intent on uncovering the truth about Mary Magdalene's relationship with Christ and her role in the evolution of Christianity.

An overarching theme of this era was an interest in the contrasting forces of good and evil, especially how they play out in spiritual and occult realms, whether for physical healing or psychic or spiritual transformation. The Scorpio VSP, symbolic of healing, transformation, resurrection, and rebirth, has brought the world numerous healing schools and techniques, mystery schools and teachers, and leaders who perform shamanic journeys. Accompanying the phenomenon is a fascination with excavation of ancient sacred relics and the search for hidden treasure, another activity associated with the Scorpio VSP. Many of the healing techniques now in vogue were associated with the Greek god of healing Asklepius, whose cult involving dreams and altered states of consciousness flourished for nearly a millennium. Asklepius's emblem—a serpent entwined around a staff, indicating healing and rebirth—reflects the Scorpio mysteries.

Regarding healing of the mind, depth psychology and mapping of the human psyche have been pursued with fervor during the Scorpio VSP era. By the 1920s and 1930s, Freud was already a household word and the field of psychoanalysis was flourishing, with other great analysts, including Carl Jung, acquiring cult followers.

During the era of the Scorpio VSP, popular culture also focuses on dark, mysterious, occult, or science fiction themes. For example, the beginning of the Scorpio VSP during the 1930s and 1940s gave rise to *film noir* and to Batman comic books, which later became the wildly successful *Batman* movie series. The most recent *Batman* movie starred the late Scorpio Morning Star Heath Ledger in *The Dark Knight*[47] in what critics have deemed one of the darkest roles to date. In the movies, perhaps the most dramatic metaphor for the conflict between forces of darkness and light is in George Lucas's *Star Wars* when Darth Vader and his dark armies march into the light, symbolized by the Jedi of the "good" world.

Further, in popular cultures of the era, the color black assumed new significance and importance. Though the phrase "black is beautiful" was meant as a political statement of pride of black people, black is a color associated with Scorpio, and during the Scorpio VSP era black did indeed become beautiful, particularly in the fashion world, as verified by the numerous noted Scorpio VSPs for whom wearing black is a personal trademark, including Johnny Cash, James Dean, Carlos Santana, David Bowie, Johnny Depp, and Ricky Martin. In power center cities like San Francisco and New York, black is especially fashionable.

The sexual revolution is associated with the ideas and free-thinking lifestyles of the 1960s and 1970s when sexuality was beginning its liberation, but sexual researcher Alfred Kinsey's findings on human sexuality in the 1940s may have been the start of the phenomenon. By the 1980s when Pluto joined the Venus Star in Scorpio, it became a commercially viable industry. This combination of Pluto and Venus together in Scorpio (1980s and 1990s) was a time of more explicit sexuality than had occurred before in the world, influencing entire subcultures of young people.

As the Scorpio VSP era progressed, secrets of a once-taboo subject—people's sexual preferences and practices—filled books, journals, newspapers, and videos that fed a hungry public. Further, pornography Web sites boasted increasingly more hits, creating serious new addictions. Children were exploited as valuable commodities in these enterprises, being wooed by wealth and power. The positive side of the horrific revelations of childhood sexual abuse and incest was that it could no longer be kept in the dark underworld. Advocates for child victims forced public awareness campaigns, funding, and legislation to identify and expose perpetrators and pedophiles.

Perhaps the three most critical issues that emerged during this current Scorpio VSP era were the proliferation of nuclear materials, abuse or overuse of Earth's resources, and the right of individuals to choose a humane way to die in situations of chronic illness and suffering. One could view the historical period of the transit of the Venus Star through Scorpio as one where the greatest transformation occurs for people on the planet and for Earth itself. Purging and purification in the final years of the Scorpio VSP are surely meant to punctuate this point. Thus, we will observe that the "time of change" will arrive just preceding the end days of the Scorpio Star. This brings us to the present moment in time (2010), a mere two decades before the Scorpio Star phases out and becomes the Libra Star. We are in that transition period now, with only three passes of the Scorpio Morning Star to go. By the time we reach the Libra Star, we will have witnessed great changes in many of our industries, our ways of doing business, and our motivations: the result being that the Sun rises on a new and better humanity on a renewed and healthier planet.

> "My therapist told me the way to achieve true inner peace is to finish what I start. So far today, I have finished two bags of M&M's and a chocolate cake. I feel better already."
> – Dave Barry, Scorpio Morning Star

> *"Instant gratification is not soon enough."*
> – Meryl Streep,
> Aries Evening Star

10 THE ARIES VENUS STAR POINT

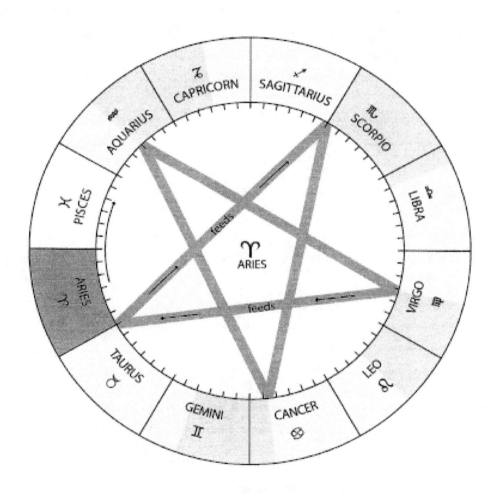

The Energy Flow of the Star is:
Aries→Scorpio→Cancer→Aquarius→Virgo→Aries

The Venus transit of Aries began April 20, 1929, as a Morning Star
and will end in 2038 as an Evening Star.

ELEMENT: FIRE
MODALITY: CARDINAL

Aries The astrological glyph for Aries represents the horns of the ram, an animal associated with springtime and rapid growth, but it also resembles a young plant shooting out of the ground. Aries is gifted with and challenged by its inner rhythm of swift progression.

Some keywords and concepts for Aries are: the age of the ram; "I am;" the quest for personal identity or the hero's journey; self-propulsion, self-awareness, self-discovery, and self-direction; precociousness, new beginnings, growth, birth or rebirth; leadership abilities; catalyst; pioneering; adventure-seeking; head strong; intelligent; intuitive; impulsive; and impatient.

Of the following well known female and male archetypes of this star, the names in bold below are pure Aries Star archetypes, having been born on or very close to the inception of the Aries VSP.

> **Female archetypes:** Audrey Hepburn, Princess Grace of Monaco, Jacqueline Kennedy Onassis, Jane Fonda, **Hannah Marks**, **Ann-Margret**, **Jessica Lange**, Princess Diana and J. K. Rowling.
>
> **Male archetypes: William Wordsworth**, Bill Cosby, Dustin Hoffman, **Jack Nicholson**, **Ryan O'Neal**, Bob Dylan, Muhammed Ali, Barack Obama, **Adrien Brody**, Daniel Radcliffe, **Gerard Way** and **Hayden Christensen**.

Greatest Assets: The Aries VSP is predominantly self-made, self-confident, and self-directed, capable of rising to the occasion when leadership is needed; able to act quickly; in possession of a pioneering spirit; able to recover quickly from personal injuries and trials; tendency to be full of wonder and hope, as if seeing the world with the eyes of a child.

Greatest Liabilities: The biggest obstacle to your heart center is your impatient and impulsive nature, which often doesn't give others the chance to prove themselves. You like to direct or lead, for fear of not getting there quickly enough. When you slow down and smell the roses, love's most pleasurable attributes will grace your life.

Are You An Aries Venus Star Point?

If you were born between the dates listed below, you are an Aries Venus Star Point (VSP). The Venus Star Point passed through Aries in ten-month increments, returning to the sign every four years, so it is important to use your exact date of birth to locate your Venus Star Point sign. Don't confuse this Venus Star with your Sun sign or your Venus sign, even though the Venus Star *can* occur while the Sun is in Aries at the beginning of each of these four-year periods. If this is the case, you have both Sun and Venus Star Point in Aries, which creates a very potent expression of Aries in your life. If you were born *before* or *after* any of the dates listed below, you are *not* an Aries Venus Star Point individual, though your Sun sign may be Aries.

MS=MORNING STAR   ES=EVENING STAR   D= VENUS DIRECT
Rx= VENUS RETROGRADE

MS/ES	DATES OF ARIES VSP	DEGREE
MS	4/20/1929 – 2/5/1930	29 Aries 48 Rx
MS	4/18/1937 – 2/3/1938	27 Aries 36 Rx
ES	4/19/1941 – 2/1/1942	28 Aries 51 D
MS	4/15/1945 – 1/31/1946	25 Aries 21 Rx
ES	4/17/1949 – 1/30/1950	26 Aries 36 D
MS	3/13/1953 – 1/29/1954	23 Aries 07 Rx
ES	4/14/1957 – 1/27/1958	24 Aries 20 D
MS	4/11/1961 – 1/26/1962	20 Aries 52 Rx
ES	4/12/1965 – 1/25/1966	22 Aries 03 D
MS	4/8/1969 – 1/23/1970	18 Aries 36 Rx
ES	4/9/1973 – 1/23/1974	19 Aries 47 D
MS	4/6/1977 – 1/21/1978	16 Aries 20 Rx
ES	4/7/1981 – 1/21/1982	17 Aries 28 D
MS	4/4/1985 – 1/18/1986	14 Aries 05 Rx
ES	4/5/1989 – 1/18/1990	15 Aries 09 D
MS	4/1/1993 – 1/16/1994	11 Aries 48 Rx
ES	4/2/1997 – 1/15/1998	12 Aries 51 D
MS	3/30/2001 – 1/13/2002	09 Aries 31 Rx
ES	3/31/2005 – 1/13/2006	10 Aries 31 D
MS	3/27/2009 – 1/11/2010	07 Aries 15 Rx
ES	3/28/2013 – 1/10/2014	08 Aries 10 D
MS	3/25/2017 – 1/8/2018	04 Aries 57 Rx
ES	3/26/2021 – 1/8/2022	05 Aries 50 D
MS	3/23/2025 – 1/5/2026	02 Aries 40 Rx
ES	3/23/2029 – 1/5/2030	03 Aries 29 D
MS	3/20/2033 – 1/3/2034	00 Aries 23 Rx
ES	3/21/2037 – 1/3/2038	01 Aries 06 D

Even if you were not born during these dates, the Aries VSP affected general behavior patterns on Earth nevertheless, and thus Aries characteristics prevailed, such as people being motivated to begin a journey, launch an enterprise, or take a risk to make a giant leap forward in life.

Venus Star Point's Gift to Aries

Love and a heart-centered approach to life come through a profound belief in oneself. Aries VSPs, early on, assume the driver's seat in life. They are what they make of themselves, and Aries VSP endows them with the good fortune to experiment, take risks, and do things most others just dream about. Their intuition is strong, and they act quickly. They are born to lead, not follow.

The VSP in Aries: The Personal Realm

> "Change will not come if we wait for some other person or some other time. We are the ones we've been waiting for. We are the change that we seek."
> – Barack Obama, Aries Morning Star

Each of the Venus Star Points has its own special gift, and it's under the sign of your Venus Star Point that the best of yourself is expressed. Of course, like everything in nature, there's a shadow side that can assert its own authority. Aries expresses itself through the element of fire and is ruled by Mars.

Aries is a masculine, cardinal, fire sign in which the Sun is exalted and Mars rules. Aries is associated with the ram, or lamb, and spring, a time of birth, new growth, and exuberant child-like energy. The Aries VSP possesses an optimistic belief in the potential for endless future possibilities. The Aries VSP individuals, likewise, possess a boundless spirit, a radiant youthfulness and so much energy that people can't quite keep up with them. Take Aries VSP Barack Obama, for example. All along his life course, people remarked that he was too young, too inexperienced, too black, etc., to accomplish the goals he'd set for himself. His mantra, "yes, we can," became "yes, we will" and then, as history demonstrates, "yes, we did" (elect the first African American president).

The archetype of the Aries VSP individual is a young lad or hero who sets out to make his own way in the world, eager to leave his family and establish his own identity and destiny in his own, very unique way. Aries VSP people need no instruction, and, in fact, often resent being directed, preferring to use their great gifts of intuitive spontaneity—or to simply just do it their way. Aries VSP individuals live their lives like a great adventure story, and, as a result, Aries VSPs often make good subjects for biographies or action-adventure drama. Not only are they independent but they pursue great life quests, not unlike the heroes of the classical era (actually the age of Aries) such as Theseus, Perseus, Jason, and Hercules. The current Aries VSP era has also given us powerful mythic heroes like Superman, Batman, and Spider Man, who originated as comic book characters and became film heroes with an enormous impact on popular culture. These larger than life heroes, like their human Aries VSP counterparts, seem indefatigable and indestructible.

Aries is the first sign in the zodiac, and its corresponding First House asks: "Who Am I?" A retrospective of one's life becomes the answer. The VSP gives that life story some adventure, heat, passion, daring, drama, and sparkle. Aries VSP individuals are on a mission to build a distinctive identity. Almost all Aries VSPs make something of themselves, and at Aries speed, steadily and quickly, knowing they can't forestall their inevitable death.

> "I don't know the key to success, but the key to failure is to try to please everyone."
> – Bill Cosby, Aries Morning Star

Aries VSP individuals are often chosen as leaders, despite the fact that they are really only children themselves. Yet they are equipped to lead in many ways because of their strength, courage, and ability to quickly take charge of a situation, whether they know what they're doing or not. Aries VSP people can be likened to the classical hero Achilles, who was a strong, courageous, and seemingly indestructible warrior, except for his one vulnerability—his heel. Enemies or competitors of Aries VSP individuals will attempt to use their vulnerability, their Achilles' heel, to bring about their downfall. But the Aries VSP does not go down for long, if at all.

Aries VSP individuals come into a new life in search of individuality (what Jung called the individuation process) with the innocence and eagerness, albeit impatience, of a child. Despite their innocence, they generally know what they want from life early.

The peer group and friendships of the Aries VSP, rather than their parents, are their role models in life. They are likely to identify with that moment of shining youth and retain it for their entire lives. If they are on the immature side, the Aries VSPs will remain children forever.

The Aries VSP individuals have distinctive personalities that can either inspire or repel people due perhaps to the Aries/Libra polarity at play. An example is the Aries VSP archetype Jack Nicholson—a well-defined character who has made an art out of portraying roles that people find both compelling and disgusting at the same time. Another good example is Aries VSP pop star Britney Spears. People either love her or hate her.

The Aries VSP possesses a certain kind of defiance, passing through a period in life where they can fully embrace being a "bad" boy or girl. Artists such as Aries VSPs Bob Dylan, Billy Joel, and Bruce Springsteen poured that angst into their creative process and received the adoration of millions who could relate. Media personalities such as Aries VSP Bill O'Reilly similarly find audiences hungry to hear him vent his rage. Then there are the Aries VSPs who are so highly accomplished, it makes people who aren't Martha Stewart ask "is there anything she can't do?" or about Meryl Streep, "any part she can't play?" or J.K. Rowling, "any book she can fail at?"

> *"I catnap now and then, but I think while I nap, so it's not a waste of time."*
> – Martha Stewart, Aries Evening Star

Because Aries VSP individuals have heightened masculine energy, an Aries VSP woman can possess this in greater quantity than many non-Aries VSP men. For women, the Aries VSP meant (especially during the early years of feminism) and means: "I am the leader of my life, my relations, my group." The feminine voice and feminist voice is strong in Aries VSP women. They often spend their lives repairing, reconciling, and fine-tuning a key life relationship, such as that of a mother or daughter. If family relationships in general seem to be a constant source of Aries VSP attention, it is because the first born Aries Star group (1929-1961) has the Cancer VSP in close relationship to them and they are working out the tension of a cardinal square, i.e., "If I am to follow my own destiny, and not what my family carved out for me, why do I feel like I can't fully embrace and enjoy it without disappointing them?" The younger generation of Aries VSP (1964-2037) will not have this issue to deal with.

The male and female planet rulerships for Aries are Mars and Athena, both warrior dieties themselves, though Mars was clearly the lover of the two (Athena was asexual). In this regard, the Aries VSP draws more from its Martian rulership, possessing a healthy and vital libido.

The Aries VSP's ability to command attention can either be a gift or a curse. As with the Aquarius VSP, the Aries VSP often becomes a role model for others who want their strength and courage. But the Aries VSP doesn't really want to lead others as much as he wants to follow his own course, regardless of whether others follow along or not. In rare cases (such as Barack Obama) they become leaders, but the other overwhelming signature to the horoscope will reveal this.

Self-renewal and beginning new chapters of life are a key part of the Aries VSP experience. Because the entire life cycle of the Aries VSP individual is linked with that of the Scorpio VSP person, this Star Point gives birth to people who are constantly reinventing themselves. This could mean quick starts and abrupt endings followed by new beginnings, making such individuals feel that they have lived many lives inside of their current one.

If the Aries VSP makes choices in life that involve risk and danger, and their loved ones are aghast at such moves, they will encounter a pause, a detour, or a temporary change of course, but they will usually get back to where they were originally headed, regardless of others.

Finally, the Aries VSP is one for whom "been there, done that" is likely true. Their passion, driven by the Venus Star, is to stay on the path of adventure, self-discovery, and renewal. If it comes down to a choice—such as the job that pays well and offers hard-to-resist perks, but isn't what ultimately satisfies their deep passion—they will typically choose the path of uncertainty, the road they've never driven down before or the mountain they haven't quite scaled, as long as their energy holds up. How will the Aries VSP do in old age? As of this writing, the first-born of that group are nearly ninety.

Aries VSP individuals, who will continue to be born until 2037, comprise 17.5 percent of the world population, the largest group on the planet, along with the Scorpio VSP group. Aries VSP individuals currently alive include the large population of baby boomers, an eternally youthful high spirited, visionary, and fiercely independent group.

Among prominent Aries VSPs are men who reflect the sign's trait of remaining youthfully feisty: Bill Cosby, Dustin Hoffman, Jack Nicholson, Steve Martin, Tim Allen, Michael J. Fox, Bob Dylan, Bruce Springsteen, Ray Romano, and Ben Stiller. Aries VSP women who reflect the typical Aries VSP independence and leadership qualities are Barbara Walters, Jane Fonda, Goldie Hawn, Diane Keaton, Jennifer Lopez, Cate Blanchett, Gwen Stefani, J. K. Rowling, and Beyonce. Some examples of Aries VSP women who in their marriages demonstrated characteristic strong identity and a well-defined character performing their perfunctory duties in a very individualistic way include Jacqueline Kennedy, Princess Grace of Monaco, and Diana, Princess of Wales. These three women married not just men but family dynasties, which required certain protocol and impeccable behavior in order to survive. Their spark and style allowed them to shape a never-ending series of seemingly routine, dutiful public appearances into something out of the ordinary. In Aries style, they originated fashion styles and cultural trends that millions sought to emulate. For a list of other noteworthy Aries Star Individuals, see Appendix III.

> *"He not busy being born is busy dying."* – Bob Dylan, Aries Evening Star

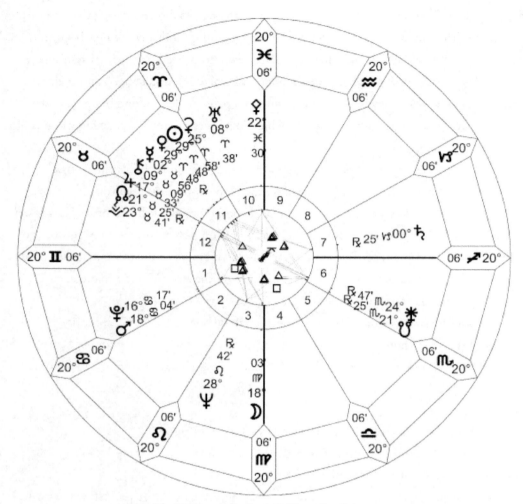

The Horoscope for the Aries Venus Star Point

The VSP in Aries: The Historical Realm

The fact that Venus began its transit of Aries nearly simultaneously with its transit of Scorpio (1920s and 1930s) resulted in rapid, dramatic changes in the world related to political and social conflicts, social institutions, warfare, economic turmoil, and the altering of traditions, as indicated also by the horoscope for the Aries VSP inception. Political and social conflicts during the early years of the Aries VSP era led to the European Holocaust in the quest to achieve a "pure" and supreme Aryan race. In the horoscope of the Aries VSP the war god Mars, planetary ruler of Aries, is in close proximity to Pluto, (god of death, rebirth, and secret motives). Both are in Cancer, which is the sign of family, clans, and homeland.

The breaking up of these family clans and seizing of their homes was a primary motive of the warfare that ensued.

Further, the chart for Aries VSP warfare was reflected by fierce competition among nations, significant military buildup, development of bigger and more efficient weaponry, and the invention of mega-defense systems. Gangsters and bullies, whether in school, the family, or the political or military arenas, commanded power and caused massive destruction, and in many cases were getting away with it. Regarding the economic turmoil, the beginning of the Aries VSP era coincided with the stock market crash of 1929 to 1930, the onset of the Great Depression in America, and economic crisis worldwide. Ironically, the Sabian symbol[48] for the first point of Aries that was touched by the Venus 1929 transit reads: "A Duck Pond and Its Brood." Ducks and their broods imply moving through life as a unit rather than as an individual, but it can also mean that if you are following others, like ducks, you might wind up falling in a pond and getting drowned. This reflects the idea of the masses being led to invest on Wall Street and subsequently becoming victims of the crash and perhaps also the notion of others being led astray by charismatic leaders of fascism and Nazi Germany who gained power seemingly effortlessly during this time.

The Venus Star and Uranus, together in Aries in the 1930s, gave rise to a breed of world leaders, such as Winston Churchill in Britain and Franklin Delano Roosevelt in America, who challenged people to take charge and refuse to submissively accept the tyranny of fascist leaders like Adolf Hitler and Benito Mussolini. This was also the era of the "War of the Worlds," when a simulated invasion by Martians was broadcast live over the radio, causing considerable panic until the public learned it was simply a radio drama.

Later in the Aries VSP era, a more positive image of heroism emerged in popular culture when two notable Aries VSP individuals—J. K. Rowling and Daniel Radcliffe—created and portrayed the adventures of Harry Potter, a tale about a young boy's magical encounters. The story underscores aspects of the nature of the Aries/Scorpio VSP period—the childlike quality of the Aries VSP person, the loss of innocence, the realization of the forces of good and evil ever at play in the world of "magic"—all certainly mirroring the politics of good and evil that exist side by side in the world.

> *If you're going to be crazy, you have to get paid for it or else you're going to be locked up.*
> – Hunter S. Thompson, Aries Morning Star

Regarding the realm of social relations and institutions, the horoscope for the inception of the Aries VSP does not prognosticate a very favorable outcome for the institution of marriage. First, Saturn is in the Seventh House of partnership and union, squaring rebellious, separatist Uranus in the Tenth House. Second, the archetypal couple of marriage, Jupiter and Juno, are sitting in exact opposition on the wheel, flanked by the lunar nodes. Finally, the virgin goddess Athena, another ruling archetype for Aries, sets the example for women to resist the loss of personal power through marriage. She boldly and prominently stands on the Midheaven, opposing traditional female roles, represented by the Moon in Virgo in the lower hemisphere of the chart.

If traditions concerning marriage suffered during the VSP of Aries, what was gained was deemed more crucial to the time: the liberation of women. Aries is a pioneering sign with a voice that is powered by outrage and certain action when people are not given their life and liberty. Such movements as feminism and the Civil Rights Movement owe the success they achieved in those early days of the struggle to the Aries VSP.

The Aries VSP era experienced a particularly challenging period for relationships during the early 1950s, when both Saturn (form) and Neptune (dissolution) were in Libra, opposite the Venus Star Point. At the start of the Aries VSP era, female/male roles were still fairly traditional. But by its halfway point, in the 1970s and 1980s, gender roles had become less differentiated, jobs were no longer gender exclusive, and women had gained power. Same-sex marriages occurred in record numbers, with brave Aries VSP pioneers leading the battles to enact legislation giving them the same rights as other married couples. The gender discrimination legislation, though hotly contested, is a human rights issue and not something that should require legislation.

Twice in the course of the Venus Star transit to Aries, the planet Uranus graced the sign for seven years each time. The first time occurred in the early days of the Aries Star period (1935-42) when the world was in upheaval. The second visit occurs in the latter days of the Aries Star period (2010-2018), when Uranus may once again help turn the world on its side, but also lead the world to achieve enlightening new breakthroughs of consciousness that will result in birth pangs of a new kind of human behavior.

When the Aries and Scorpio Stars phase out (2027-2038), once again a new era begins. At that time the Libra Star (partnership, cooperation) and the Pisces Star (awareness of suffering, universal compassion) begin their reign. The hundred years or so during which Scorpio and Aries are activated by the Venus Star Point perhaps might later be seen, metaphorically, as a time when the individual young hero or soldier (Aries) must face the enemy, fight the battle, die, and be reborn (Scorpio) as an individual who henceforth is disgusted by war and renounces it, thus resulting in a period of peace and increased enlightenment.

"I think computer viruses should count as life. I think it says something about human nature that the only form of life we have created so far is purely destructive. We've created life in our own image."
– Stephen Hawking,
Aries Evening Star

> *"If you're really a rapper,
> you can't stop rapping."*
> – Ice T, Gemini Morning Star

11 THE GEMINI VENUS STAR POINT

The Energy Flow of the Star Is:
Gemini→Aquarius→Virgo→Aries→Scorpio→Gemini

The Venus transit of Gemini began June 20, 1964, as a Morning Star and will end in 2073 as an Evening Star.

ELEMENT: AIR
MODALITY: MUTABLE

Gemini   The astrological glyph for Gemini resembles two vertical columns contained by a horizontal foundation and ceiling or the Roman numeral two. This is a fitting representation for Gemini, which, unlike other zodiac signs symbolized by animals, is represented by the mythical twin brothers Castor and Pollux, after which the two bright stars in the constellation of Gemini are named. The Gemini experience supports two realities.

Some keywords and concepts for Gemini are: the twins; duality; mobility; flexibility; changeability; movement; strong intellect; curiosity; inquisitive mind; avid reader; quick thinker; agile; fast; gift of gab; charming.

Of the following well known female and male archetypes of this star, the names in bold below are pure Gemini archetypes, having been born on or very close to the inception of the Gemini VSP.

> **Male archetypes: Brigham Young, Dan Brown, Michael Cera,** Prince Harry of Wales, Ben Affleck, Elijah Wood, Macaulay Culkin, Will Smith, and Eminem.
>
> **Female archetypes: Venus Williams,** Gwyneth Paltrow, Halle Berry, Jennifer Anniston, Paris Hilton, and Scarlett Johannsen.

Greatest Assets: Tendency to be multi-talented multi-taskers, and thus are never bored or boring to others; ability to be agile and react quickly; success in games and sports; capacity to exchange viewpoints and engage in lively conversations using a storehouse of information on almost any topic; tendency to seek a partner who is the "straight man" to their fun-loving, comedic style.

Greatest Liabilities: The biggest obstacle to your heart's desire is not aiming your arrow in a straightforward direction, being distracted by the myriad of possibilities for fulfillment that lie behind every door. Once you tire of your many minds and tune into your heart channel, you're there.

The Gemini Venus Star Point

Are You a Gemini Venus Star Point?

If you were born between the dates listed below, you are a Gemini Venus Star Point. The Venus Star Point passed through Gemini in ten-month increments, returning to the sign every four years, so it is important to use your exact date of birth to locate your Venus Star Point sign. Don't confuse this Venus Star with your Sun sign, even though the Venus Star *can* occur while the Sun is in Gemini at the beginning of each of these four-year periods. If this is the case, you have both Sun and Venus Star Point in Gemini, which creates a very potent expression of Gemini in your life. If you were born *before* or *after* any of the dates listed below, you are *not* a Gemini Venus Star Point individual, though your Sun sign may be Gemini.

MS=MORNING STAR   ES=EVENING STAR   D= VENUS DIRECT
Rx= VENUS RETROGRADE

MS/ES	DATES OF GEMINI VSP	DEGREE
MS	6/20/1964 – 4/11/1965	28 Gemini 38 Rx
ES	6/20/1968 – 4/7/1969	29 Gemini 08 D
MS	6/17/1972 – 4/8/1973	26 Gemini 30 Rx
ES	6/18/1976 – 4/5/1977	27 Gemini 04 D
MS	6/15/1980 – 4/6/1981	24 Gemini 21 Rx
ES	6/16/1984 – 4/3/1985	24 Gemini 58 D
MS	6/13/1988 – 4/5/1989	22 Gemini 13 Rx
ES	6/13/1992 – 3/31/1993	22 Gemini 54 D
MS	6/10/1996 – 4/1/1997	20 Gemini 03 Rx
ES	6/11/2000 – 3/29/2001	20 Gemini 48 D
MS	6/8/2004 – 3/30/2005	17 Gemini 54 Rx
ES	6/9/2008 – 3/26/2009	18 Gemini 42 D
MS	6/6/2012 – 3/27/2013	15 Gemini 45 Rx
ES	6/7/2016 – 3/24/2017	16 Gemini 35 D
MS	6/3/2020 – 3/25/2021	13 Gemini 35 Rx
ES	6/4/2024 – 3/22/2025	14 Gemini 29 D
MS	6/1/2028 – 3/22/2029	11 Gemini 25 Rx
ES	6/2/2032 – 3/19/2033	12 Gemini 23 D
MS	5/30/2036 – 3/20/2037	09 Gemini 16 Rx
ES	5/31/2040 – 3/17/2041	10 Gemini 15 D
MS	5/27/2044 – 3/18/2045	07 Gemini 06 Rx
ES	5/28/2048 – 3/15/2049	08 Gemini 09 D
MS	5/25/2052 – 3/15/2053	04 Gemini 57 R
ES	5/26/2056 – 3/12/2057	06 Gemini 02 D
MS	5/22/2060 – 3/12/2061	02 Gemini 47 Rx
ES	5/23/2064 – 3/9/2065	03 Gemini 54 D
MS	5/20/2068 – 3/10/2069	00 Gemini 38 Rx
ES	5/21/2072 – 3/7/2073	01 Gemini 45 D

Even if you were not born during these dates, the Gemini VSP affected general behavior patterns on Earth nevertheless, and thus Gemini characteristics prevailed, such as people being motivated to invest personal resources in education, travel, and writing to satisfy their insatiable curiosity for new experiences, partnerships, or lifestyles.

Venus Star Point's Gift to Gemini

Love and a heart-centered approach to life comes through as charm, wit, and playfulness. Gemini VSP individuals engage people easily and can cause laughter instantly. They are great storytellers with wide appeal. Whether they use their voice for alerting people to global concerns or expressing their own views, they know how to get their point across. Due to their ability to imagine and create multiple realities in which to live, their partners never get bored with them.

The VSP in Gemini: The Personal Realm

Each of the Venus Star Points has its own special gift, and it's under the sign of your Venus Star Point that the best of yourself is expressed. Of course, as discussed in Chapter 3, the Venus Star, like everything in nature, also has a shadow side. Gemini expresses itself through the element of air and is ruled by the planet Mercury.

The motif of Gemini is that of twins, based on the two bright stars of its constellation, Castor and Pollux. These dual identities may either compete for one's attention or guide the Gemini VSP into balanced oneness. If these dual stars are in harmony, there is quite a bit that can be accomplished. If, on the other hand, they are competing with one another, there will be conflict and duality plaguing the Gemini Star's life. The Venus Star's influence supports the integration process, and that of importing the heart into the mind before any action is ever taken.

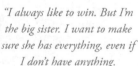

"I always like to win. But I'm the big sister. I want to make sure she has everything, even if I don't have anything. It's hard. I love her too much. That's what counts.
– Venus Williams, Gemini Morning Star

A major aspect of Gemini VSP individuals, one that relates to its planetary ruler Mercury, is their ability to transmit information. Mercury's image is the messenger archetype, adorned with winged helmet and sandals, bearing a message that must be delivered. It is the idea of the message bearer that the Gemini VSP animates best, executed with wit and style. In this regard, it is the Gemini VSP individuals who live their lives as travelers, writers, teachers, coaches, or broadcasters—people who deliver messages in various ways to help or advise others whether as a vocation or avocation. Physically, Gemini VSP individuals reflect this; they are usually youthful in appearance and behavior; lean, fit, and fast.

The use of language is of paramount interest to Gemini VSP individuals. Whether they write or speak one language with nuance and style, or are bi- or trilingual, they are motivated to discover new ways to communicate with others. Consequently, they are often attracted to and suitable for jobs in which the use of language plays a significant role. Technical languages are included in the diversification of the Gemini VSP mind. Gemini VSP individuals can communicate with even the most sophisticated computer network, something that can be very advantageous in their lives. This group consists of perpetual students of life. They are proficient in playing a variety of different roles: the stand-up comic or comedic writer, actor, or rapper are all areas where a Gemini VSP can really stand out among the crowd.

> *"One thought fills immensity."*
> – William Blake, Gemini Evening Star

What has become more and more prominent in journalism since the inception of the Gemini VSP are sound bites of information: news briefs, pop-ups, and video clips. Three forms of communication—instant messaging, text messaging, and tweeting—are all characteristic of the current age of the Gemini Star and individuals born under this star. Seeking ways to communicate powerfully but briefly is a most appropriate Gemini trait.

Rap is an art form born in the age of the Gemini Star and aptly so, for the Gemini individual is bursting to tell their story or give their rap. The Venus Star's influence graces the Gemini Star individual with a purpose in life—to bind this information together in a book or to package their tools, techniques, and strategies for success. Those Gemini VSPs who are stronger in the earth element and excel at marketing will easily succeed at this. Those without the earth element are simply content to pass the information on, but might be attracted to VSPs who do excel at marketing, such as the Scorpio or Capricorn VSP, who can successfully partner with them towards that end.

Gemini VSP individuals have a youthful, free-spirited manner and love to play. Generally, they are the goofballs of the family, keeping everyone laughing or keeping everyone entertained in some manner. If they are raised in a strict environment that limits their creative expression, they will escape as soon as possible. Once free, they will need to maintain a playful and fun-filled atmosphere for at least a decade before they can truly feel their spirit unbound. The youthful, free-spirited manner that seizes the Gemini VSP may be the result of major changes that were taking place in the world at the inception of the

Gemini Star. These individuals seem to have been born ready for the new world that was unfolding. All over the world the voice of a new generation was heard, characteristic of the revolutionary upheaval that was taking place in the 1960s.

The Gemini Star feeds the Capricorn VSP, uniting the sign of youth with the sign of age and complementing each sign with the other's influence. By honoring the traditions and wisdom of their elders, their ancestors or the past, the Gemini VSP advances forward in their evolutionary cycle.

In contrast to the Cancer Star whose motivation is to partner in a mother-child relationship, Gemini Stars are motivated toward partnering with peer groups. However, those born when the two cycles were overlapping and changing (1956–1972) may be motivated by both types of relationships. Further, Gemini VSP individuals may regard same-sex relationships as being of equal significance as opposite-sex relationships—the twins archetype suggests same-gender twins, based on the myth of Castor and Pollux. Gemini has inspired twin boy or twin girl stories in every culture, with some of the more notable ones being Osiris and Seth, Enlil and Enki, Castor and Pollux, Cain and Abel, and Romulus and Remus. In many of these stories, one sibling dies or is defeated by the twin. In the life of the Gemini VSP, there is a real or imaginary twin (sibling) with whom they must grapple. When one succeeds while the other is suffering, both are adversely affected. As in the myths, jealousy can rear its head—to the point of one twin strongly desiring to extinguish the other twin. The evolved and aware Gemini VSP is cognizant that the suffering of one twin causes suffering to both, and seeks nothing greater in life than to heal the rift.

"Life is like a roller coaster, live it, be happy, enjoy life." - Avril Lavigne, Gemini Evening Star

Several pairs of twins and siblings among notable Gemini VSP individuals include British royals Prince Harry, a Gemini Evening Star, and older brother Prince William; sports stars Venus Williams, a Gemini Morning Star, and sister Serena; Dutch royals Princess Beatrice, a Gemini Morning Star, and sister Princess Eugenie; celebrity model Paris Hilton, a Gemini Morning Star, and sister Nicky Hilton; film star Haylie Duff, a Gemini Evening Star, and sister Hillary; and Gemini Evening Star twins and film stars Amanda and Rachel Pace, and Cole and Dylan Sprouse.

At the inception of the Gemini VSP in the 1960s, new kinds of partnerships became acceptable among this generation. Gemini VSP individuals are suited to living with partners who don't believe in marriage, being in serial marriages, or having sibling-type relationships with friends and lovers. Though they can get bored and feel the need to move on, it is quite possible for a Gemini Star to remain with one partner forever. For this to happen, there must be a steady movement forward in the relationship.

These people are also chameleons; they shift roles as circumstance necessitates, and seem to have endless possibilities. Like the Aries Star (see Chapter 10), the Gemini Star child is eager to move on very quickly once an experience is achieved or a certain type of information is gained. Perpetual students, the Gemini VSP will go to the ends of the earth seeking out the next bit of information they need for a book, a degree, a resume, or a spiritual quest.

The Gemini VSP belongs to a group of people who comprise approximately nine percent of the world population. Births in this group began about 1970, and around 2060 they will be among the most populous star groups on the Earth.

Among prominent individuals from the previous Gemini VSP era are gifted writers Victor Hugo, Lord Alfred Tennyson, and Henry David Thoreau (Gemini Morning Stars), William Blake, Daniel Webster, Mary Shelley, Elizabeth Barrett Browning, Johann Von Goethe, and Fyodor Dostoevsky (Gemini Evening Stars). Among this group, the efforts of three authors that especially reflect Gemini VSP characteristics are Goethe's poetic drama *Faust*, about a hero's struggle for his soul, involving God and the devil; Shelley's novel *Frankenstein* about man and his shadow side; and Daniel Webster's writings, which are characterized by a mastery of language.

Among individuals from the current Gemini VSP era, two born at the inception of the Gemini Star strongly embodying Gemini VSP traits are Dan Brown and Venus Williams. Brown's book, record-breaking seller *The DaVinci Code*[49], illustrates his talent at crafting a great story that actually incorporates the Venus five-pointed star symbolism and its connection to the worship of the sacred feminine. Venus Williams's record-breaking achievements in tennis can be associated symbolically with the image of swift Mercury in his winged victory sandals. One might wonder if whoever is responsible for giving Venus Ebony Starr Williams her name was aware that she was born at the actual star date of the Venus Gemini Point. For a list of other noteworthy Gemini Star Individuals, see Appendix III.

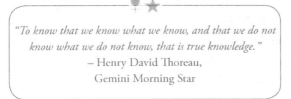

"To know that we know what we know, and that we do not know what we do not know, that is true knowledge."
– Henry David Thoreau,
Gemini Morning Star

The Horoscope for the Gemini Venus Star Point

VSP in Gemini: The Historical Realm

The inception of the Gemini Star is one of the four star changes that are historically more meaningful than most and often signal tremendous shifts in the world. This is due to those four stars' location at the cardinal axis of the signs (the other three are Pisces, Virgo, and Sagittarius). The Venus Star transited the summer solstice point through the cusp of Cancer and into Gemini in the 1960s, an era historically documented as one of massive social movements toward change all around the world.

The Gemini Venus Star Point

The horoscope for the Gemini Star Point reflects the great transformations that characterize the era: Mars, Saturn, Uranus, and Pluto are locked into a tension-filled T-square in mutable signs on the cardinal axis. Saturn (law, authority, tradition) is rising squared by Mars (impetuous youth eager for new direction) and opposed by Uranus (widespread rebellion) in conjunction with Pluto (collective transformation). The Gemini VSP transit began in the mid-1960s when revolution and change were brewing around the world and old values were questioned. As referenced earlier, the tendency of the tumultuous 1960s was aptly expressed by Bob Dylan in his classic lyric line written in 1963 and released in 1964 just as the Gemini Star was born: "*The Times They Are A-Changin.*"[50] Even if not everyone born in the Gemini VSP group experienced radical change, many people at least maintained individualism and resistance to authority that reflected the times.

The early Gemini VSP era (1964 to 1983) was a period when the swift transference of information via communication systems became a major factor in societal transformations. During this time when the Gemini Star fed the Aquarius Star, vast amounts of information from around the world flooded the airwaves, the medium of the two prominent air signs. There was a loss of innocence for America and Americans. In 1963 President Kennedy was assassinated in front of adoring Americans around the country. Since that time, television has remained a focal point of global news reflecting the hunger for information during the Gemini VSP period. After 1988, when the Gemini VSP began to feed the Capricorn VSP (a sign of government, order, and stability) instead of the Aquarius VSP (a sign of the masses hungering to circulate information), corporations began to increasingly control the media, influencing programming to increase profits.

> "Beauty is mysterious as well as terrible. God and devil are fighting there, and the battlefield is the heart of man."
> – Fyodor Dostoevsky, Gemini Evening Star

Further, the women's movement was especially influenced by the Venus Star Point leaving Cancer and moving into Gemini in the early 1960s. Traditional female roles as wife, mother, and housekeeper changed, and women began to have increased choices in domestic and work situations. As a result, they could more easily pursue education and travel, and enter professions that had previously been closed to them. But, in keeping with the dual nature of Gemini, many women wanted both a career and a family, and in this time period societal customs and new laws supported their expanded vision. Traditional family roles began to take a back seat and marriage and children were no longer the primary goal. People didn't just automatically come home after their educations and run family businesses, as they had so often done during the era of the Cancer Star. Instead, education increasingly became a springboard to success in the larger world.

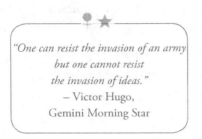

"One can resist the invasion of an army but one cannot resist the invasion of ideas."
– Victor Hugo,
Gemini Morning Star

Moreover, with the Gemini Star connected to and feeding the Capricorn Star, young consumers, with their rapidly changing interests in games and communication devices, began to dominate the marketplace. New technologies—ranging from cell phones to the Internet and iPods, e-mail and text messaging—exemplify the Gemini VSP era with its emphasis on language and communications systems. Youth still commands attention from corporate industry executives, who try to predict market trends for future sales. Indeed, the Capricorn–Gemini VSP union accounts for a large percentage of corporate profits at this time.

Regarding the world of politics, the Gemini VSP has affected U.S. presidential elections since 1964. But, up to the 1960 election, it was the Cancer Star that characterized U.S. elections and influenced who was deemed electable. When Venus transited Cancer (1852 to 1961), in the United States we elected national leaders based on a different set of values than after 1964, when the Gemini VSP became activated. During the Cancer VSP, people chose leaders who, regardless of their age, possessed a fatherly demeanor, a "family man" to reinforce domestic security and prosperity, while during the Gemini VSP period they selected candidates with more youthful personalities, ones who possessed charm, as well as good debate and communications skills. In the last decades there have also been candidates with the dual nature characteristics of Gemini who have had the tendency to change their minds on issues. Further, the opposition from Pluto to the Gemini VSP was in effect for both the 2000 and 2004 elections, which resulted in justified outrage about questionable votes and, in keeping with characteristics of Gemini, a divided country of red and blue regions. In this period the United States and much of the world remained ideologically polarized due to terrorism and emphasis on religious conflicts in contrast to more peaceful and hopeful past eras.

These circumstances reflect the Venus Star transit in direct conjunction and opposition with the Pluto (collective transformation and fear) transit through the middle degrees of Sagittarius (foreign countries, culture, religion, air travel). Remembering that Gemini is an air sign, we can understand how restrictive air travel in the United States and the world has become during this time.

The transit involving the Venus Star in Gemini opposite Pluto in Sagittarius has had a divisive effect on personal relationships and marriage as well as politics and religion. In the period from 1995 to 2008, Pluto transited Sagittarius while the Venus Star transited Gemini. Both signs, Gemini and Sagittarius, are mutable. They are searchers. The relationships that would survive this unstable period and be better for it would be those who focused on developing and improving communications skills, those who share a similar philosophical view, and those who are careful to not "possess" their partner, allowing both plenty of space to grow.

> *"When ideas fail, words come in very handy."*
> – Johann Wolfgang von Goethe,
> Gemini Evening Star

"Power is not revealed by striking hard or often, but by striking true." –
Honore de Balzac,
Capricorn Evening Star

12 THE CAPRICORN VENUS STAR POINT

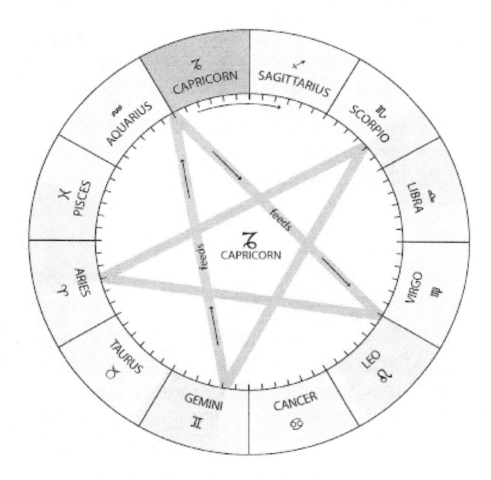

The Energy Flow of the Star Is:
Capricorn→Leo→Aries→Scorpio→Gemini→Capricorn

The Venus transit of Capricorn began on January 19, 1986, as an Evening Star,
and will end in 2078 as a Morning Star.

ELEMENT: EARTH
MODALITY: CARDINAL

Capricorn   The astrological glyph for Capricorn represents the sea goat, an animal capable of living on both land and in the sea. However, contemporary astrologers associate it more with the mountain goat, a land animal that can climb the craggy, barren peaks with agility. Because it is a sign connected with the winter solstice, it is also linked with survival and the ability to carefully manage resources.

Some keywords and concepts for Capricorn are: authority figures and institutions—teachers, the parents, the executives or CEOs, governments, corporations; overcoming physical obstacles, ascent to the heights; laws, traditions, obeying laws; conservation and management of personal and Earth's resources; ancestral voices from the past.

Of the following well known female and male archetypes of this star, the names in bold below are pure Capricorn Star archetypes, having been born on or very close to the inception of the Capricorn VSP.

> **Male archetypes:** Prince Albert, **Robert Burns**, John Adams, John Quincy Adams, Thomas Jefferson, Andrew Jackson, and **Boo Boo Stewart**.
>
> **Female archetypes:** Harriet Beecher Stowe, Queen Victoria, Empress Josephine, **Mischa Barton**, and Dakota Fanning.

Greatest Assets: Steadiness and sure-footedness, especially in challenging times; ability to take command of situations and implement practical and efficient solutions to problems; tendency to be level-headed and cautious, refraining from taking foolish risks, opting for quick fixes, or jumping on bandwagons promoted by others; laying groundwork and steadily working toward goals.

Greatest Liabilities: The obstacle that can stand in the way of the direct channel to your heart is your commitment to duty over all else. You expect of others what you expect of yourself and become disappointed or angry when they don't match up. What your beloved is looking for from you are your soft but strong shoulders. Ratchet your responsibility quotient down a few notches and learn that heart-felt companionship is your true ambition.

Are You a Capricorn Venus Star Point?

If you were born between the dates listed below, you are a Capricorn Venus Star Point. The Venus Star Point passed through Capricorn in ten-month increments, returning to the sign every four years, so it is important to use your exact date of birth to locate your Venus Star Point sign. Don't confuse this Venus Star with your Sun sign, even though the Venus Star *can* occur while the Sun is in Capricorn at the beginning of each of these four-year periods. If this is the case, you have both Sun and Venus Star Point in Capricorn, which creates a very potent expression of Capricorn in your life. If you were born *before* or *after* any of the dates listed below, you are *not* a Capricorn Venus Star Point individual, though your Sun sign may be Capricorn.

MS=MORNING STAR   ES=EVENING STAR   D= VENUS DIRECT
Rx= VENUS RETROGRADE

MS/ES	DATES OF CAPRICORN VSP	DEGREE
ES	1/19/1986 – 11/4/1986	29 Cap 17 D
MS	1/19/1990 – 10/31/1990	28 Cap 34 Rx
ES	1/17/1994 – 11/2/1994	26 Cap 44 D
MS	1/16/1998 – 10/29/1998	26 Cap 09 Rx
ES	1/14/2002 – 10/30/2002	24 Cap 09 D
MS	1/14/2006 – 10/26/2006	23 Cap 40 Rx
ES	1/12/2010 – 10/28/2010	21 Cap 32 D
MS	1/11/2014 – 10/24/2014	21 Cap 12 Rx
ES	1/9/2018 – 10/25/2018	18 Cap 58 D
MS	1/9/2022 – 10/22/2022	18 Cap 44 Rx
ES	1/6/2026 – 10/23/2026	16 Cap 22 D
MS	1/6/2030 – 10/19/2030	16 Cap 17 Rx
ES	1/4/2034 – 10/20/2034	13 Cap 46 D
MS	1/4/2038 – 10/17/2038	13 Cap 47 Rx
ES	1/1/2042 – 10/18/2042	11 Cap 13 D
MS	1/1/2046 – 10/14/2046	11 Cap 17 Rx
ES	12/29/2049–10/15/2050	08 Cap 34 D
MS	12/30/2053–10/12/2054	08 Cap 49 Rx
ES	12/27/2057–10/13/2058	06 Cap 01 D
MS	12/27/2061 – 10/9/2062	06 Cap 20 Rx
ES	12/24/2065–10/10/2066	03 Cap 28 D
MS	12/25/2069 – 10/7/2070	03 Cap 52 Rx
ES	12/22/2073 - 10/8/2074	00 Cap 53 D
MS	12/22/2077 – 10/5/2078	01 Cap 24 Rx

Even if you were not born during these dates, the Capricorn VSP affected general behavior patterns on Earth. Thus, Capricorn characteristics prevailed, creating interest in investigation of historical events, research into and celebration of one's ancestry, investing in education, on the job training, and skills enhancement that secure one's future.

Venus Star Point's Gift to Capricorn

"We are not interested in the possibilities of defeat. They do not exist."
– Queen Victoria of England, Capricorn Morning Star

Love and a heart-centered approach to life is expressed through a modest, dignified, traditional type of beauty, as illustrated by the fashion and decorating statement of the last Capricorn VSP era, the Victorian era, inspired by Queen Victoria and Prince Albert, Twin Stars of Capricorn. Capricorn VSP individuals possess a natural ability to command respect. Whether or not they are the eldest born, their role is looking after others and managing enterprises, qualities that are inherent in the Capricorn Star.

The VSP in Capricorn: The Personal Realm

Each of the Venus Star Points has its own special gift, and it's under the sign of your Venus Star Point that the best of yourself is expressed. Of course, as discussed in Chapter 3, the Venus Star, like everything in nature, also has a shadow side. The Capricorn VSP expresses itself through the element of earth and is ruled by the planet Saturn.

Signs that contain the element of earth tend to be practical and realistic, in tune with nature, and concerned with protecting Earth's resources. Further, affected by their ruling planet Saturn, Capricorn VSP individuals prefer to live within a certain set of limits. Moreover, the ability of the mountain goat to climb barren, rocky heights with agility reflects the Capricorn VSP's steadfastness and dependability in the face of challenges. The ambitious and productive nature of Capricorn is linked to the image of the mountain goat traversing sharp and steep terrain in a seemingly effortless way. The Capricorn VSP does not need the accelerator on high speed the way the Aries VSP does. They know how to maintain a safe and reliable pace and still get to their destination.

Responsibility and maturity are part of Capricorn VSP individuals from childhood. Often such infants and children seem older than their years and more serious than their siblings. They are typically the ones elected to take care of not just themselves but also family members even from an early age. Because they are so mature for their age, they are perceived

The Capricorn Venus Star Point

as older and as qualified to take on adult responsibilities very early in life. The children of this sign tend to experience early loss of innocence, as is evident from the chart for the inception of the Capricorn VSP with the south lunar node conjunct Pluto with nearby Mars, all in Scorpio.

Capricorn VSP individuals may have teachers, mentors, and role models as guides, but in the end it is their father who has the greatest influence on their character. Capricorn VSP people may take the commandment to honor and obey the father very seriously. But in their cases, honoring and obeying the father can take the form of service in the military, or religious or civil institutions. In cases where a Capricorn VSP's father is absent, the mother fills that role, although the Capricorn VSP person is likely to still search for their father in a variety of ways throughout life.

However, this doesn't mean that Capricorn VSP individuals necessarily agree with or want to submit to such authority figures. Rather, many of them, governed by Saturn who in myth swallowed his children, rebel against such authority figures. Capricorn clearly is a sign of executive authority and tends to form relationships with people who are looking for them to take charge and be administrators of life. Some of these Capricorn VSP partners are perpetual children hiding in adult bodies. This occurs due to the Gemini Star linked directly to the Capricorn Star, suggesting a unique partnership that establishes itself between the youthful Gemini and the wise elder Capricorn. In this regard it is interesting to note that the young would-be nation of America possessed many Capricorn VSPs, who in term became founding fathers of America after successfully commandeering a rebellion against father, King George of England. They achieved the goals of a collective Capricorn VSP vision in becoming autonomous and self-governing, while learning the politics of forging important alliances with other nations to insure continued strength and security.

Lest one forget that Capricorn is focused on achieving what it sets out to accomplish, their ruler Saturn (old father time, Cronus) continues to remind them of how precious time is and consequently how to avoid wasting it. In this context, another way to interpret the myth of Saturn swallowing his children is that time swallows us all, a fact of which the Capricorn VSP is instinctually aware.

Fed by the Gemini VSP, a youthful air sign, the Capricorn VSP person appears as mature and wise but inside is harboring a life-long teenager, who on occasion performs outrageous acts that express an inherent wildness. But because Capricorn VSP individuals have

> *"Men are what their mothers made them."* – Ralph Waldo Emerson, Capricorn Morning Star

the outward appearance of maturity and wisdom, in youth most are attracted to older, more mature people as role models, even though in adulthood much younger people seek them out as mentors.

As youngsters, Capricorn VSPs are drawn to form meaningful, life-long relationships with their grandparents' generation. This is not only because of Capricorn's innate attraction to eldership and mentorship, but also because many of the star signs of these elders are Taurus and Virgo—the two other earth signs besides Capricorn—that together create beautiful harmonies. Mapping their family genealogy is one way for the Capricorn VSP to connect with the elders in their lives and to become deeply involved in the history of their people and their planet. This satisfies them on two levels: first, they are keeping their own history alive; and second, they are motivated to pass it down to the succeeding generation.

Capricorn VSP individuals also have the task of passing religious and cultural traditions on to the next generation. The structure of their VSP—that they are feeding the Leo VSP—suggests that they are talented at illuminating things from a former era in new and creative ways, like playing a classic repeatedly but each time giving it a new interpretation.

For the Capricorn VSP, beauty is streamlined, budget conscious, classic and elegant, and there are many ways for them to bring such style into their lives. Professions such as engineering, architectural design, landscape design, or professions related to the crisis of sustainable resources will be inspiring to them. In the era of the Capricorn Star, the world is facing a huge deficit in its resources, a challenge tailor-made for the instincts and abilities of the Capricorn VSP individuals to address and resolve.

One striking phenomenon that occurred at the inception of the simultaneously occurring Capricorn and Leo Venus Star Points, aided by the helpful star mates of Aries and Gemini, was power accorded to youth, especially celebrity youth, creating fame that can also have a shadow side. Leo VSP individuals can handle such fame more gracefully because of their extroverted nature, while Capricorn VSP people have an unsteady relationship with the media and the public, often performing ghastly and outrageous acts because they think that's what the public expects of them. Aries, Gemini, and Leo Star celebrities can get away with such extreme behavior and are often adored even more for it. But the Capricorn VSP, born of a sign that aligns itself with political correctness and manners, suffers great loss of reputation and fame when they misbehave.

The "limelight" for the Capricorn Star often involves an elevated status in the pursuit of one's career to a position in human resources management, executive leadership, political office, corporate office, or religious leadership, more often than the celebrity limelight. Training, teaching, working with children, organizing field trips, and research and development undertakings are all worthy enterprises in which the Capricorn VSP can invest time and energy.

Capricorn VSP individuals comprise approximately five percent of the world's population. By 2080 it will be among the biggest star groups.

Among prominent Capricorn VSP child prodigies are the following: Dakota Fanning, acclaimed actress and recipient of multiple young actor awards, and her younger sibling, Elle Fanning; the Olsen twins, Mary Kate and Ashley; Charlotte Church; and the late Jon Benet Ramsey. Stars of the Twilight Trilogy, Kristen Stewart and Robert Pattinson are also graced with the Capricorn Venus Star. For a list of other noteworthy Capricorn Star Individuals, see Appendix III.

> *"In this broad earth of ours,*
> *Amid the measureless grossness and the slag,*
> *Enclosed and safe within its central heart,*
> *Nestles the seed of perfection."*
> – Walt Whitman,
> Capricorn Morning Star

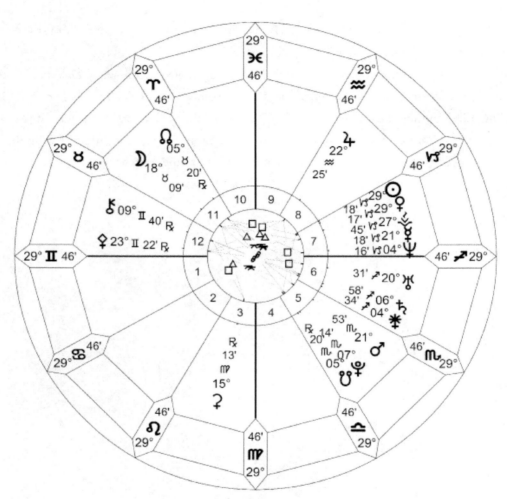

The Horoscope for the Capricorn Venus Star Point

The VSP in Capricorn : The Historical Realm

Tendencies of renewed power and authority within all the stratospheres of human activity can be seen in the horoscope for the Capricorn Venus Star Point. Positioned within less than one-twelfth or 30° of the circle are Saturn, Uranus, and Neptune forming their rare triple conjunction in Capricorn just a few years after the inception of the Capricorn VSP. This new era of law and order in the 1980s and 1990s, symbolized by the power and strength of the collection of planets occupying Capricorn, gave immense power to laws supporting politics and big business as one giant world conglomerate was being forged. The high technology industries, symbolized by Uranus and the quest to control the world's supply of oil (Neptune), were a part of this equation. Exchange of assets, trade, and commerce, indicated by Moon in Taurus opposite Mars in Scorpio, were not in such areas as textiles or grains. They involved more dangerous and scandalous commodities: arms, narcotics, human trafficking, and human harvesting.

On a personal level, although the concept of traditional marriage was undermined in the earlier years of the Scorpio and Aries VSPs, during the Capricorn VSP era it looked as if it was in high demand once again. This is attested to in the horoscope for the Capricorn VSP by the crowded Seventh House of marriage and partnership. The combined influences of Neptune, Mercury, Vesta, Venus, and the Sun suggest the dream of and active pursuit of partnering as a primary goal. Neptune and Vesta seek spiritual union through a partner, while Mercury, the ruler of this Gemini rising star chart, trines the Moon in Taurus, where it finds identity, security, and wholeness in partnership. This is further echoed by Juno, the marriage and partnership asteroid closely conjunct Saturn, Capricorn's ruler and the planet of tradition and law. Their union in the sign of Sagittarius in the Sixth House suggests a belief in traditional marriage, along with ample opportunities to fine tune the intricate workings of the partnership throughout the course of such unions.

During the opening years of the Capricorn VSP, rulers of nations as well as their countries' political boundaries were in the midst of a radical shift. Perhaps the greatest ones included the collapse of the Berlin Wall, a Saturn boundary that suddenly eroded and subsequently shattered due to the presence of both Neptune and Uranus in Capricorn. Dictatorships perpetrated human rights abuses in the Middle East, Africa, Latin America, and China, notably Tiananmen Square. Although the outcome for Tiananmen Square was not as successful as the collapse of communism in Europe, it was an appropriate time for several of China's brave citizens to push forward and make a statement as outlined by the combined influence of Saturn, Uranus, and Neptune. Similar outcries around the world began to be heard in support of Tibet's plight of occupation by China, to no avail, other than to increase awareness of the human rights work still needed in those parts of the world.

But the Venus Star in Capricorn did smile favorably upon suppressed peoples in other parts of the world. For instance: in 1990 Nelson Mandela was released from prison in South Africa and in 1994 was elected the first black president in the country's first multiracial elections; the Cold War ended in 1989; the Soviet empire collapsed in 1991; in 1989 the nonviolent Velvet Revolution overthrew the communist government in Czechoslovakia; also in 1989, a popular uprising in Romania ended the repressive and corrupt regime of communist dictator, Nicolae Ceausescu. These events, along with a youthful and forward-looking Clinton presidency, seemed to add a spiritual dimension to the politics and policies of the era.

In the early stages of the Capricorn VSP, there was a trend towards focus on issues of retirement, healthcare requirements, and future assisted living possibilities for the elderly. The development and maintenance of assisted living facilities and healthcare for the elderly remain key issues for the Capricorn VSP era.

Leo and Capricorn, two of the primary Star Points activated in the chart of this era, indicate self-direction, focus, and the guiding role of the father, both in families and in institutions. For example, it was during this era that Pope John Paul II reigned as a highly charismatic Holy Father to a world of devotional followers, a leader who brought untold numbers of lapsed Catholics back to the church. Similarly, the humble and charismatic Dalai Lama remains an icon of peace and hope to millions of followers worldwide during this Capricorn VSP era.

In addition to a renewed emphasis on the role of the father in society, since Capricorn is the most patristic sign in the scheme of astrology, paternal and fraternal orders and societies such as the Freemasons have also emerged or resurfaced in the Capricorn VSP period.

The business trend in the era of the Capricorn VSP is globalization, which has increased significantly since the beginning of the Venus Star Point transit through Capricorn in the early 1980s. While this trend may be characteristic of the entire Capricorn VSP one-hundred-year period, there should be a more balanced partnership model after 2022, when the star fed by Capricorn becomes Libra rather than Scorpio.

Several key principles of Capricorn—economizing, taking responsibility, and ensuring the future—have become fundamental aspects of businesses and inventions that will prosper during the Capricorn VSP era. These principles, combined with a new awareness about Earth's disappearing resources and the impending consequences of global warming, will be crucial to finding solutions to problems and ensuring a positive future. In addition, Capricorn VSP individuals will also be resourceful in creating new alternative forms of energy necessary for conservation.

The Venus Star cycle of 1986-1987 constituted another turning point on the wheel of the Venus Star, affecting the world in new ways. The Harmonic Convergence[51] occurred at this time, pegged by many historians and journalists as the birth of the New Age. Though termed the New Age, much of its teachings and philosophies were new renderings of old traditions and practices of Earth's ancestors from eras long forgotten. In this context, the Capricorn VSP's desire to connect with the wisdom of ancestral voices and elders was initiated with fervor by many New Age seekers. The New Age bible of the time penned by James Redfield, *The Celestine Prophecy*,[52] concerned the search for an ancient scroll high in the Andes of Peru. Crystals and gems with their magical powers of healing became the newly anointed objects of power for the children of the New Age. Ancient scrolls, high mountaintops, crystals, rocks, and minerals—all belong to the kingdom of Capricorn.

The Gemini and Leo Stars, companions to the Capricorn Star, were hungry for such voices, journeying to foreign lands in search of ancient knowledge and reading books about ancient beliefs and practices, and speculating about the characteristics of a new age. That initial frenzy has subsided, but the Venus Star Point will still energize Capricorn for a long time, continuing to unearth ancient wisdom and teachings with the intent of saving and healing a world in need of such wisdom.

Another development of the era that occurred during the relatively short period that the first degree of Capricorn was transited (the 29th degree of Capricorn in 1990) was mass marketing aimed at a public hungry for metaphysical tools and New Age concepts, especially for psychic and Tarot hot-lines, represented by the Sabian

> *"Never give up, for that is just the place and time that the tide will turn."*
> – Harriet Beecher Stowe,
> Capricorn Morning Star

symbol for that degree, the image of "A Woman Reading Tea Leaves." Two things emerged from this. First, it became clear that any type of enterprise was fair game if it entailed corporate profitability. Second, such types of enterprises could be made available to a wider public that had no previous involvement with such services. This was undoubtedly helped by the Uranus/Neptune conjunction that was transiting the middle degrees of Capricorn during the same period.

Capricorn's wisdom is attained from practical life experience, by learning from one's elders, and from history. In this context, a look back to the last transit period of the Venus Star through Capricorn (1735-1827) is revealing.

That period coincided with the birth of America and many of its future leaders. It was the period of both the French and American revolutions, as well as the birth of the U.S. Constitution, crafted by many Capricorn VSP Evening Stars. A repeat of those exact Capricorn VSP degrees occurs from 1986 to 2022. If this pattern manifests as it did before, we might speculate that the founders of a new world order are being born and/or are currently developing their vision. For the founding fathers of America in the previous era, the term was "Novus Ordo Seclorum" (new order of the ages), often mistranslated as new world order. The United States was shaped during that era, with five of the first seven U.S. presidents born in the Aries MS/Capricorn ES Venus cycle, as follows:

U.S. Presidential Sequence:	VSP Cycle
2. John Adams, born 1735	Capricorn ES
3. Thomas Jefferson, born 1743	Capricorn ES
5. James Monroe, born 1758	Capricorn ES
6. John Quincy Adams, born 1767	Capricorn ES
7. Andrew Jackson, born 1767	Capricorn ES

Interestingly, many of the founding fathers were bonded by the brotherhood of Freemasonry[53] and were aware of the Venus pentagram and its eight-year cycle.

Since the Venus Star Point pattern is repeated in 250-year periods, and thus the year 2026 corresponds to the year 1776, one wonders what fresh new ideas might emerge from the end of the Aries VSP transit, that will materialize during the Capricorn VSP era, and how many future leaders have been or will be born to determine the course of any new age. The changing of the Venus Star Points (2022-2041) practically insures that there will be a new order of the ages, once again as before; that much is clear. But until enough people can agree on a unified vision and steer a course there steadily, all we have is dissention and separateness. History has time and again demonstrated that new governments and orders arise out of old ones that have outlived their purpose. This is a key concept of the Capricorn era and star, especially from 1986 to 2026, the first half of the Capricorn Star when the Aries Star is also in effect and pushes forward for new life, growth, and assertive action.

> *"Remember, democracy never lasts long. It soon wastes, exhausts, and murders itself. There never was a democracy yet that did not commit suicide."*
> – John Adams,
> Capricorn Evening Star

> *"Life begets life. Energy creates energy.
> It is by spending oneself that one
> becomes rich."*
> – Sarah Bernhardt,
> Leo Morning Star

13 THE LEO VENUS STAR POINT

The Energy Flow of the Star Is:
Leo→Aries→Scorpio→Gemini→Capricorn→Leo

The Venus transit of Leo began August 23, 1987, as an Evening Star,
and will end in 2100 as an Evening Star.

ELEMENT: FIRE
MODALITY: FIXED

Leo The astrological glyph for Leo, the lion, resembles a lion's mane. Though considered a masculine, or yang, sign, the glyph possesses a feminine curvaceousness emphasizing Leo's movement and style.

Some keywords and concepts for Leo are: sunshine, light; the stage, celebrity, fame; children; investments; gambling; sports; recreation; creativity, color, and flair; brightness; the lion, the Lion King; leadership, royalty; pomp and parade; ego, will; the heart.

Of the following well known female and male archetypes of this star, the names in bold below are pure Leo Star archetypes, having been born on or very close to the inception of the Leo Star.

> **Male archetypes: Pope Pius VII, Tsar Ivan VI of Russia, Percy Byssche Shelley, Adolph Bandelier,** Hans Christian Andersen, Claude Monet, and Sir Richard Francis Burton.
>
> **Female archetypes:** Abigail Adams, Sarah Bernhardt, Jenny Lind, Louisa May Alcott, Abigail Breslin.

Greatest Assets: Ability to radiate energy like the Sun, inspiring others with luminescence and leadership; the power of attraction and tendency to fame; bravery; ageless beauty; style and sophistication; ability for romance and creativity.

Greatest Liabilities: The pathway or channel to your heart is of utmost importance, Leo Star, for your sign "rules" the heart. Obstacles that keep you from getting there are the tendency to need constant attention and pampering. Once you embrace the equality of all people and can assess and serve the needs of those around you, your heart opens wide and the world is at your command.

Are You a Leo Venus Star Point?

If you were born between the dates listed below, you are a Leo Venus Star Point individual. The Venus Star Point passed through Leo in ten-month increments, returning to the sign every four years, so it is important to use your exact date of birth to locate your

Venus Star Point sign. Don't confuse this Venus Star with your Sun sign, even though the Venus Star *can* occur while the Sun is in Leo at the beginning of each of these four-year periods. If this is the case, you have both Sun and Venus Star Point in Leo, which creates a very potent expression of Leo in your life. If you were born *before* or *after* the dates listed below, you are *not* a Leo Venus Star Point individual, though your Sun sign may be Leo.

MS=MORNING STAR   ES=EVENING STAR   D= VENUS DIRECT
Rx= VENUS RETROGRADE

MS/ES	DATES OF LEO VSP	DEGREE
ES	8/23/1987 – 6/12/1988	29 Leo 37 D
MS	8/22/1991 – 6/12/1992	29 Leo 14 Rx
ES	8/21/1995 – 6/9/1996	27 Leo 30 D
MS	8/20/1999 – 6/10/2000	27 Leo 01 Rx
ES	8/18/2003 – 6/7/2004	25 Leo 23 D
MS	8/18/2007 – 6/8/2008	24 Leo 51 Rx
ES	8/16/2011 – 6/5/2012	23 Leo 18 D
MS	8/15/2015 – 6/6/2016	22 Leo 39 Rx
ES	8/14/2019 – 6/2/2020	21 Leo 12 D
MS	8/13/2023 – 6/3/2024	20 Leo 29 Rx
ES	8/12/2027 – 5/31/2028	19 Leo 07 D
MS	8/11/2031 – 6/1/2032	18 Leo 18 Rx
ES	8/9/2035 – 5/29/2036	17 Leo 02 D
MS	8/8/2039 – 5/30/2040	16 Leo 07 Rx
ES	8/7/2043 – 5/26/2044	14 Leo 56 D
MS	8/6/2047 – 5/27/2048	13 Leo 57 Rx
ES	8/4/2051 – 5/24/2052	12 Leo 51 D
MS	8/4/2055 – 5/25/2056	11 Leo 46 Rx
ES	8/3/2059 – 5/22/2060	10 Leo 47 D
MS	8/1/2063 – 5/23/2064	09 Leo 36 Rx
ES	7/31/2067 – 5/19/2068	08 Leo 43 D
MS	7/30/2071 – 5/20/2072	07 Leo 28 Rx
ES	7/29/2075 – 5/17/2076	06 Leo 37 D
MS	7/28/2079 – 5/18/2080	05 Leo 17 Rx
ES	7/27/2083 – 5/15/2084	04 Leo 35 D
MS	7/25/2087 – 5/16/2088	03 Leo 08 Rx
ES	7/24/2091 – 5/12/2092	02 Leo 30 D
MS	7/23/2095 – 5/14/2096	00 Leo 59 Rx
ES	7/22/2099 – 5/11/2100	00 Leo 26 D

Even if you were not born during these dates, the Leo VSP affected general behavior patterns on Earth and thus Leo characteristics prevailed, such as the passionate pursuit of creativity and romance, as well as playing, rather than working, at life.

Venus Star Point's Gift to Leo

Love and a heart-centered approach to life come through a burning desire to live life in a proud, passionate, and creative way, to shine like a beacon of strength and leadership to others.

The VSP in Leo: The Personal Realm

Each of the Venus Star Points has its own special gift, and it's under the sign of your Venus Star Point that the best of yourself is expressed. Of course, as discussed in Chapter 3, the Venus Star, like everything in nature, also has a shadow side. The Leo VSP expresses itself through the element of fire and is ruled by the Sun.

The Venus Star age of Leo arrived in 1987, so the birth of Leo VSPs has only occurred since then. While we can only speculate about what contributions will be made by these highly creative, strong-willed, adorable, and talented youngsters, one thing is clear: children are stars again. Youth rules! We're still in the early days of this star period and have predominantly observed this group as youths, but it seems obvious that these talented Leo VSPs, with their inherent star power, are in their element in our celebrity culture. The creative urge burns strong in both the Morning Star and Evening Star of this sign, with the Morning Star Leo more driven to produce progeny. Its Evening Star counterparts express their creative urges in the fields of art, fashion design, literature, or film. From the previous Leo VSP era, Claude Monet, Pierre Renoir, Auguste Rodin, and Percy Bysshe Shelley are all examples of such highly focused and well-executed Leo Evening Star creative urges. Leo VSP children like the Aquarius VSP, possess a magnetic attraction that causes them to be noticed and adored. Due to this adulation, their style, dress, and appearance will also be watched and copied by many. The peacock with its bright fan of feathers fully open, a beautifully flowering tree, a colorful kite or hot air balloon, a fiery multi-colored sunrise or sunset: these are all head-turning, show-stopping images. Likewise, the Leo VSP has the ability to turn heads and inspire awe. Knowing that they possess this kind of magnetic star-quality can be dangerous for these Leo children and can give them an over-inflated sense of self. The Venus Star quality added to the star presence that Leo already possesses might be fine for them, but can be a detriment to the relationships they form with the people around them.

Among Leo VSP adolescents, this star quality can result in mega-celebrity status in the pop youth culture. In the lives of Leo VSP children, there may be a stage mother urging them into the spotlight, while for other children there can be a jealous mother, or sibling, doing everything they can to undermine their zest for life and tendency to succeed. Two notable divas were born in the last era of the Leo Star, shining examples of the Leo VSP's mega-celebrity star power—19th century opera singer Jenny Lind and actress Sarah Bernhardt, both Leo Morning Stars.

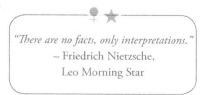

"There are no facts, only interpretations."
– Friedrich Nietzsche,
Leo Morning Star

Born in 1820 in Stockholm, Sweden, Jenny Lind was admitted to the Royal Theatre School at the age of nine, began singing on stage when she was ten and, by the age of 17, was a favorite in the Royal Swedish Opera. Among her many suitors were composers Felix Mendelssohn and Frederic Chopin. At Mendelssohn's death, he was composing his unfinished opera *Lorelei* for her. Hans Christian Anderson also fell in love with Lind, who inspired three of his fairytales: *The Ugly Duckling*, *The Angel*, and *The Nightingale*. Even contemporary rock star Elvis Costello announced in 2005 that he was writing an opera about her called *The Secret Arias*.

Born in Paris in 1844, Sarah Bernhardt began her acting career at the age of thirteen. Sometimes heralded as the "mother of all divas," she became the most famous actress of her time and has even been called the most famous of all time. Among her many lovers were Victor Hugo and Albert Edward, the Prince of Wales. British playwright Oscar Wilde wrote his play *Salome* for her. The Puccini opera *Tosca* was based on a play written for her as well. A lithograph poster for a new play featuring Bernhardt was created by Alphonse Mucha and launched a new style of art, initially called the Mucha Style, but later known as Art Nouveau. Attesting to her continued appeal is the fact that an excerpt from *Queen Elizabeth*[54], a silent film from 1912, can be viewed today on You Tube.

The heart is the centerpiece of the Leo universe. Ruled by the longings of the heart, they live for love, without which they would be nothing. The moment they perceive that the well of love has dried up, they search for new fountains. Further, Leo VSP individuals are always reaching for the light, and, as they grow, they become increasingly aware that cultivating inner light is the way to experience inner security and true love.

Leo is the mama lion and the Leo Star is passionate about children. These individuals also adore animals, especially any animal in the cat family. Leo VSP women tend to display a strong mothering instinct with animals and may be gifted at taming wild ones. Such a scenario is expressed by the Strength card in the Tarot deck, which is associated with the sign Leo and depicts a beautiful lady gently wrapping her hands around a lion's mouth, soothing the wild beast. In the symbolic language of the soul, wild animals have often been correlated to the ego. In this regard, Leo VSP individuals have no problem letting their ego assert itself; it's the tempering of it that they must work at. Parents of the current crop of Leo VSP children, while encouraging their inborn creativity, will also need to set boundaries to keep their children's wills in check. Although they may be the star of the family or the classroom, they must recognize that their star quality can diminish people around them, making others the supporting players in their own life's drama.

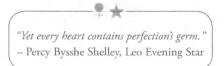

"Yet every heart contains perfection's germ."
– Percy Bysshe Shelley, Leo Evening Star

The Leo Star's mates are Capricorn and Aries; Capricorn for the entire cycle and Aries for the first third. With these three signs feeding and being fed by one another, there are super-human expectations placed upon them, such as becoming an Olympic gold medalist. They are capable of becoming strong, bold leaders who can achieve whatever they truly desire, and this is the key to their success. They will not excel at projects or tasks they have been assigned to by others. They must be able to carve out their own personal destiny as they see fit.

Notably in Elizabethan England, the Leo Star era of two cycles previous to the current one (500 years ago) gave birth to the daughter of Henry VIII and Ann Boleyn, a Leo Evening Star, named Elizabeth. At young Elizabeth's birth, the odds were stacked against her ever becoming an heir to the English throne. Not only did she achieve the throne, but she is the rare female who is remembered from five centuries ago. This grand monarch's status is not only remembered, but she continues to be one of the most popular female leaders of all time.

Since 1990 Leo has been feeding the Aries VSP—one fire sign feeding another, creating a highly charged field of combustible energy with sparks flying everywhere. The youthful group of souls belonging to these two star groups has been more interested in play than work, or at least following career paths where performance, personal self-expression, and play is a good part of it. Industries that flourish as a result of this pairing are the entertainment field, recreation, sports, games, pleasure, and vacation travel. Leo and Aries VSP individuals are children at heart, no matter how old. This combination has resulted in a large population that doesn't want to hold down a job for any long-term security but is more focused on lucrative salaries. Such people want fast money, fast food, fast cars. They tend to be self-employed, self-made individuals. An especially lucrative industry in this Aries/Leo Star period has been the music business, more for its celebrity pop culture and entertainment value than its brilliance in delivering intricately crafted musical geniuses. Entertainment values will shift when the Leo Star is linked to the Pisces Star, between 2030 and 2040. Then, creative self–expression for the Leo VSP will become less about them and more about the vehicle of the divine that they are bringing forth.

Leo VSP people are recipients of the Capricorn VSP individuals' focus on progeny and are aware of the importance of making their parents proud of them. In turn, the biggest humiliation in life for Leo VSP individuals is when their loved ones, especially children, fail or embarrass them.

Because both Leo and Venus rule the heart, Leo VSP people repeatedly fall in love with people and experiences. Romance lights their fire and keeps them inspired, uplifted, and vibrating at a high frequency. In turn, this contagious energy is passed on to everyone around them.

The Leo VSP individuals possess courage and will not shy away from trying anything. If Leo VSP individuals lack courage they become depressed or suicidal, as depicted by the cowardly lion from the *Wizard of Oz*[55]. What's a lion without the courage to be who it strives to be, to do what it was born to do?

If you are a Leo VSP you belong to a group of people who comprised approximately four percent of the world population in 2010, but this will drastically change over time. The current Leo VSP has just begun, and the last of the Leo VSP individuals will not appear until the onset of the twenty-second century. For a list of noteworthy Leo Star Individuals, see Appendix III.

> *"I cannot say that I think you very generous to the Ladies, for whilst you are proclaiming peace and good will to Men, emancipating all Nations, you insist upon retaining an absolute power over Wives."*
> – Abigail Smith Adams,
> Leo Evening Star

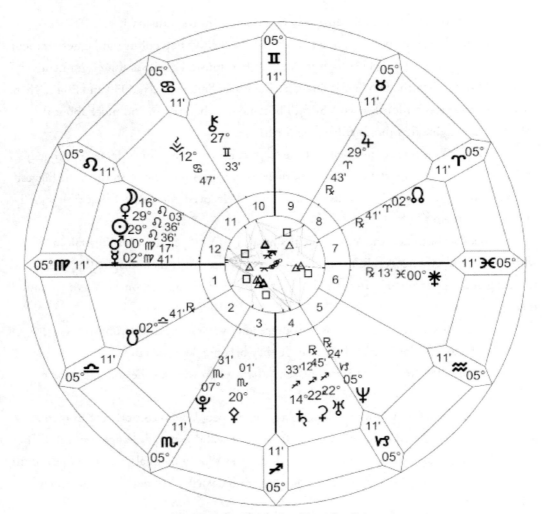

The Horoscope for the Leo Venus Star Point

The VSP in Leo: The Historical Realm

The Leo Star was born during the period known as the "Harmonic Convergence," August 1987. The Harmonic Convergence symbolized the start of a twenty-five-year period that culminated in 2012, presumably inspired by Mayan elders centuries ago. The Leo Star called to spiritual seekers around the globe whose beliefs and practices brought forth the New Age. This and the Capricorn Star, Leo's life mate born two years prior, were the two signs designed to prepare people for the widespread spiritual awakening and revolution that would take place just a few years later in the 1990s. Such spiritual visions seem to be reflected in the horoscope for the Leo VSP. Five inner planets (Sun, Moon, Mercury, Venus, and Mars) in the Twelfth House of the chart for the Leo Star implies a strong spiritual voice from the past echoing into the present, emphasized by the late waning Moon in Leo. This balsamic Leo Moon urges the people born of this star and born into this star period to bring forth a reservoir of talent and, above all, to keep the world laughing, singing, dancing, and moving. It further indicates the echoes of ancient voices of the past bleeding into the present to fulfill a specific mission. Thus people born during the Leo VSP are old souls with a destiny influenced by a former time period.

The horoscope also shows that the element of fire is boldly stated: the Venus Star Point and the Moon are in Leo, with Jupiter, Saturn, and Uranus in other fire signs. That this was the beginning of the era of fire, both symbolically and literally, is further implied by the fact that the element of fire is doubly represented by Aries and Leo. At the beginning of this Leo star era, the world was beginning to see the implications of widespread fire as both personally creative and collectively destructive.

The prior Leo VSP age from 1744 to 1849 similarly gave birth to a bright new colorful era. It was during that 104-year period that the French and American Revolutions and the founding of America as a nation occurred. Just prior to the French Revolution, the royal families and their privileged guests partied to excess in their gilded palaces, while throngs of people on the streets searched for any scrap of food. The Napoleonic era reflects the commanding solar presence of the Leo VSP, and its emphasis on riches was not confined to Europe. The prior Leo VSP coincided with the California Gold Rush, appropriate since Leo is the sign associated with gold.

Although the current Leo VSP era has just begun, some trends are already evident. In this Leo VSP era, the quest for riches is linked to other substances such as oil. There is no shortage of entrepreneurial individuals, corporations, and governments around the world seeking wealth through the discovery and control of oil reserves. The quest for oil, found in Neptune's domain—the sea—is shown by a prominently placed Neptune in the current Leo VSP horoscope. It falls in Capricorn's sign, in Leo's House, and is powerfully supported by aspects from the ascendant, Mars, Mercury, and Pluto.

Many world leaders of the Leo Star period, such as U.S. President Bill Clinton and South African President Nelson Mandela, exemplify the heart-centered solar steadiness of the era. The Leo Sun of President Clinton, who related to the public through a heart-centered approach, is positioned very close to the degree of the then-active Leo VSP.

> *"The love for all living creatures is the most noble attribute of man."* – Charles Darwin, Leo Evening Star

The current focus on celebrity culture and related enterprises seems to be the prevailing theme of the Leo Star era. Entertainment values have soared, competition is fierce, and the rewards do lead to a pot of gold, witnessed by such shows as *American Idol*. People who would have been considered ordinary in any other era have suddenly been catapulted to celebrity status and previously unheard-of salaries—with a sports star making enough money per year to feed a small country in Africa or a pop star making enough money from one CD to do likewise in a Latin American nation. This is the new royalty—not of blood lines and elected heads of state—but crowned by adoring crowds of the celebrity culture that drives the current of the modern time. The bright and hopeful side of this Leo Star era is that many of these iconic, youthful role models are using their star power and celebrity status to influence political and social causes, fund charitable drives, and inspire great humanitarian efforts around the globe. With Leo representing sports and games, the same can be said about that industry, its celebrities, their salaries, and their overwhelming influence on the masses.

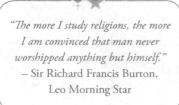

"The more I study religions, the more I am convinced that man never worshipped anything but himself."
– Sir Richard Francis Burton, Leo Morning Star

When Leo is the star, it is not surprising that a renewed focus on royalty was evidenced. During the previous one-hundred-year Aquarius era, which ended in the 1980s, royalty had been relegated to a subordinate position as the Russian Revolution eliminated their royals and parliamentary governing bodies superseded royalty in Europe. In addition, one future king, Edward, Duke of Windsor, abdicated his throne to marry the woman of his choice. But under the new Leo VSP, with the marriage of Prince Charles and Princess Diana, attention was once again given to royalty, as the fairytale-like prince and princess captivated a world-wide audience hungry for some Leo color, splash, adornment, and style.

Meanwhile, Hollywood returned to an era in which celebrity status again became dominant. Not since the 1930s and 1940s have such huge blockbusters captivated audiences—the enterprising spirit of the Capricorn VSP is alive. They range from commando-type heroes, such as those played by Sylvester Stallone, Arnold Schwarzenegger, and VanDamme, to animated heroes such as the lion in *The Lion King*[56], a film that can be seen as an apt metaphor for the Leo VSP period. It is also an example of the creative spirit reflected by the link of the Capricorn VSP with the Leo VSP. Compare this to the Leo Star of two periods ago when live theater was the rage of the day. This was due to the brilliant playwrights and actors of the Elizabethan stages of England; notably Shakespeare, whose appearance on the London stage in the 1580s, 1590s, and early 1600s corresponds to the Leo

Star period of two cycles ago, featuring most prominently, Queen Elizabeth I, herself a Leo Evening Star.

The Capricorn-Leo link also has given rise to young stars endorsing many products. Product visibility has become a key in marketing, with the celebrity culture (Leo) successfully having an influential voice (Gemini). Child stars earn large sums of money, and parents and society support this development. For example, the young actress, Abigail Breslin, who is herself born of the Leo Star, plays a child star in *Little Miss Sunshine*[57] who commandeers her entire family to join in her quest for fame, a parody of the celebrity youth culture and the exploitation of children prevalent during the Leo VSP era. Another related phenomenon is the rise of the child-centered household, where children are given enormous attention and decision-making power in the family.

Yet another current fashion connected to the Leo Star era are youth-oriented internet sites such as YouTube, Facebook, and MySpace, where individuals can become instant overnight celebrities of their own life, witnessed by millions around the world.

In addition, the Leo VSP era is associated with investments, artistic creations, bold self-expression, recreation, and sports. The accelerated growth of both the vacation industry and the gaming industry are examples of the type of preferred investments under the Leo VSP. The vacation industry now includes a proliferation of everything from motor homes and parks to time-share units and five-star resort properties. The gaming industry, formerly limited to specific destinations such as Las Vegas, Atlantic City, and Monte Carlo, has spread to Indian lands all over North America. Additionally, state lotteries became the new way to raise capital.

Real estate, which before the Leo VSP era was usually a simple family necessity, now became a driving force in economies all over the world, with investors buying up multiple houses for quick profits. Further, increased risk-taking by ordinary people, businesses, and institutions contributed to a recession in the first decade of the twenty-first century. The real estate industry alone, when on the verge of collapse in the early twenty-first century, was a strong enough force to bring down enough other industries and economies as to cause a catastrophic crisis.

These are some of the influences of the age of Leo as seen through the Venus Star lens, and as this age still has several decades to complete, we can only imagine what new types of creativity and progeny will be created by the lives of billions of people on the planet.

"I do not want the peace which passeth understanding, I want the understanding which bringeth peace." – Helen Keller, Libra Morning Star

14 THE LIBRA VENUS STAR POINT

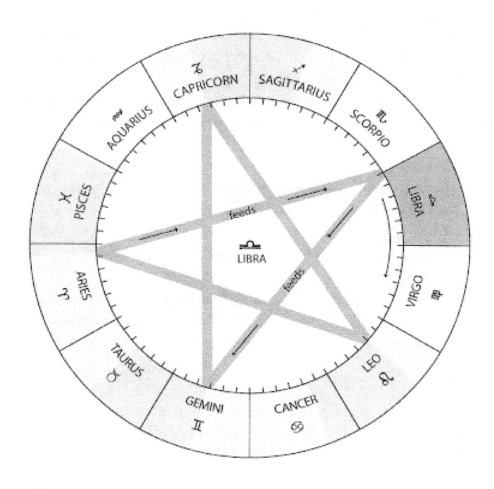

The Energy Flow of the Star Is:
Libra→Gemini→Capricorn→Leo→Pisces→Libra

The Venus transit of Libra begins October 22, 2022, as an Evening Star, and ends in 2131 as a Morning Star.

ELEMENT: AIR
MODALITY: CARDINAL

Libra The astrological glyph for Libra represents scales and is associated with the balance between summer and winter, day and night. It is a sign signaling the equinox when the day and night are of equal length and nature achieves a perfect balance between yin and yang.

Some keywords and concepts for Libra are: Balancing the scales, weighing and measuring, the reconciliation of opposites; give and take; attraction to partnering, objective analysis, and reflection, mediation; seeking equality and fairness in relationships, a desire to obtain harmony, peace, beauty, and aesthetics.

Of the following well known female and male archetypes of this star, the names in bold below are pure Libra Star archetypes, having been born on or very close to the inception of the Libra VSP.

> **Male archetypes: John Keats, Franz Liszt,** Mark Twain, Paul Gauguin, Lewis Carroll, and Dante Gabriel Rossetti.
>
> **Female archetypes:** Elizabeth Cady Stanton, Susan B. Anthony, Marie Curie, George Sand, and **Annie Besant**.

Greatest Assets: Your natural charm and grace easily attract people, as does your easy-going manner, which does not threaten others; your sense of aesthetics draws you to harmonious environmental settings, especially nature; you strive for peace, objectivity, and equality in relationships.

Greatest Liabilities: Trying to find the perfect partner, the pathway to your heart can be blocked by your mind's cool and objective analysis of others, luring you into dangerous relationships conceived of by your mind and not your heart. Once you allow the heart to override the default pattern of the mind's rule, love will be yours.

Are You A Libra Venus Star Point?

People born between the dates listed below, the previous Libra Venus Star Point, are Libra Venus Star individuals. Although none are living today, it may be helpful to use the dates to refer to historical individuals who exemplify the archetypal characteristics of the

The Libra Venus Star Point

Libra VSP. This will also provide information about the traits of the next Libra VSP period and its individuals. The Venus Star Point passed through Libra in ten-month increments, returning to the sign every four years, so it is important to use exact birth dates to locate the Venus Star Point sign of individuals. The first and last in a group are noteworthy since they represent the first and last in a line.

The previous Venus transit of Libra began on October 22, 1771, as an Evening Star, and ended on July 12, 1880, as a Morning Star.

MS=MORNING STAR	ES=EVENING STAR	D= VENUS DIRECT
	Rx= VENUS RETROGRADE	
MS/ES	DATES OF LIBRA VSP	DEGREE
ES	10/22/1771 – 8/11/1772	29 Libra 40 D
ES	10/20/1779 – 8/9/1780	27 Libra 18 D
MS	10/21/1783 – 8/7/1784	28 Libra 39 Rx
ES	10/18/1787 – 8/6/1788	24 Libra 58 D
MS	10/19/1791 – 8/5/1792	26 Libra 15 Rx
ES	10/15/1795 – 8/4/1796	22 Libra 36 D
MS	10/16/1799 – 8/4/1800	23 Libra 53 Rx
ES	10/14/1803 – 8/4/1804	20 Libra 18 D
MS	10/15/1807 – 8/1/1808	21 Libra 31 Rx
ES	10/11/1811 – 7/31/1812	17 Libra 58 D
MS	10/13/1815 – 7/30/1816	19 Libra 10 Rx
ES	10/9/1819 – 7/29/1820	15 Libra 40 D
MS	10/10/1823 – 7/28/1824	16 Libra 49 Rx
ES	10/7/1827 – 7/27/1828	13 Libra 23 D
MS	10/8/1831 – 7/26/1832	14 Libra 29 Rx
ES	10/4/1835 – 7/24/1836	11 Libra 07 D
MS	10/5/1839 – 7/23/1840	12 Libra 10 Rx
ES	10/2/1843 – 7/22/1844	08 Libra 51 D
MS	10/3/1847 – 7/21/1848	09 Libra 51 Rx
ES	9/30/1851 – 7/21/1852	06 Libra 35 D
MS	9/29/1855 – 7/19/1856	07 Libra 31 Rx
ES	7/27/1859 – 7/17/1860	04 Libra 21 D
MS	9/28/1863 – 7/171864	05 Libra 14 Rx
ES	9/25/1867 – 7/15/1868	02 Libra 06 D
MS	9/26/1871 – 7/15/1872	02 Libra 55 Rx
MS	9/23/1879 – 7/12/1880	00 Libra 38 Rx

Since the Libra VSP also affects general behavior patterns on Earth during these dates, they were likely to be periods when principles of fairness and balance were in operation and when balance between genders was emphasized through new laws, social movements, or writings.

Venus Star Point's Gift to Libra

Love and a heart-centered approach to life come with double blessings for the Libra VSP under Venus' influence, which gives them a magnetic attraction and the ability to harmonize nicely with others. The Libra VSP strives to bring peace to partnerships, their environment, and the world.

The VSP in Libra: The Personal Realm

Each of the Venus Star Points has its own special gift, and it's under the sign of your Venus Star Point that the best of yourself is expressed. Of course, as discussed in Chapter 3, the Venus Star, like everything in nature, also has a shadow side. The Libra VSP expresses itself through the element of air and is ruled by the planet Venus.

The Libra glyph represents the setting of the sun, defining its primary role as the boundary between day and night. Likewise, winter and summer, north and south are also in perfect balance at the onset of Libra. All this and gender balance, too, are sought by the Libra VSP individual. The saying "everything in moderation," as well as Apollo's famous dictum at Delphi, "nothing in excess," express well Libra's role in the zodiac. Apollo is a fitting archetype for Libra as his rulership is over music, mathematics, archery, and law-giving. Similarly, science, harmony in nature, world peace, and the balance of polarities are some main concepts associated with the Libra VSP.

In Chapter 2 (mythology), a comparison was made of the two types of Venus that make up her characteristics and motivations, based on Pandemos Venus, the Morning Star, and Urania Venus, the Evening Star. The Venus belonging to Libra corresponds to the latter, a celestial sea figure born of sky god Uranus and sea god Neptune. This strange union produced the fairest of the fair, Aphrodite/Venus, a more reflective and perfected one than earthy Venus Pandemos, associated with Taurus. Of course, as impossible as such perfection and beauty are for any earthly Venus inhabitant to achieve, the Libra Star will not stop trying.

A good example of the blend of Pandemos and Urania sprang forth from Pyotr Illich

Tchaikovsky, a Taurus Sun who was a Libra Morning Star. With a double dose of Pandemos (Taurus and the Morning Star) and a dose of Urania in the Libra VSP, works such as "The Nutcracker Suite" and "The Overture of 1812" evoke both the fine, delicate nuances of Libra and the powerfully majestic earthiness of Taurus expressed in a beautiful and harmonious manner.

The emphasis on living in a peaceful and orderly world in the Libra VSP era is no doubt a severe reaction to the one hundred-year Aries VSP period that directly preceded Libra. That era gave birth to individuals who valued fast action, possessing mannerisms not nearly so refined as Libra's. People tend to be more pleasant with one another in a Libra period. A criticism that the Libra can sit on the fence weighing the options on both sides for so long that they simply cannot choose is always a potential. But the thoughtful reflection of the Libra always insists that the picture of both sides be illustrated. An appropriate example is the opening sentence in Libra VSP Charles Dickens' *A Tale of Two Cities*[58]: "It was the best of times, it was the worst of times."

> "No amount of ability is of the slightest avail without honor."
> – Andrew Carnegie, Libra Evening Star

Libra VSP individuals, so enhanced by the rulership of Venus and her muses, tend to reflect beauty, grace, dignity, charm, and etiquette. Raucous behavior or name-calling does not suit them unless they possess a double dose of Mars. An example of an individual who would seem out of place among Libra VSP people is comedian W. C. Fields, who exemplified some of the raunchier sides of human behavior. Fields' horoscope reveals he was born with a very tight conjunction of Mars and Pluto in Taurus (Venus's sign), which explains his obsession with the darker side of humanity.

Typically the Libra VSP yearns for a peaceful, beautiful world and gets easily rattled by loud offensive voices or noises. They are supported by enthusiastic children who have similar values, in contrast to current youth with their love of racing motorcycles, loud, angry music, and boisterous activity. The dignity and grace of Libra VSP people make others seem somewhat unrefined, abrasive, and distasteful by contrast. But if Libra VSP individuals are too adamant about rejecting the brassier side of human nature, they run the risk of attracting such elements instead.

Considering the characteristics of the preceding Libra VSP cycle, it's likely that the people born in the coming Libra VSP cycle will dedicate their lives to reassessing laws and reversing many injustices of previous times since Libra VSP people see injustices as not just reprehensible but also intolerable. Consider the lives of two Libra VSPs of the previous cycle:

Elizabeth Cady Stanton and Susan B. Anthony, who worked tirelessly for gender equality and the right of the female voice to count.

The great steel magnate and philanthropist Andrew Carnegie, a Libra Evening Star, also exemplified the Libra VSP's belief in peace, equality, and fairness. Andrew and his family arrived in the U.S. from Scotland in 1848 when Andrew was thirteen years old. He immediately got his first job in a cotton mill at a wage of $1.20 a week. The classic American Dream come to life, Carnegie went on to become the richest man in the world at that time. At age 65, he sold his Carnegie Steel Company for $480 million then dedicated the rest of his years to giving his money away. Carnegie was perhaps the first to state publicly that the rich have a moral obligation to give away their fortunes. He asserted that all personal wealth beyond that required to supply the needs of one's family should be regarded as a trust fund to be administered for the benefit of the community. Toward this end, Carnegie created seven philanthropic and educational organizations in the United States and Europe and spent over $56 million to build 2,509 libraries around the world.[59] In 1904 he established the Carnegie Institute of Technology in Pittsburgh, now known as Carnegie-Mellon University. He also formed the Carnegie Endowment for International Peace in 1910. For a list of other noteworthy Libra Star Individuals, see Appendix III.

"The greatest question that has never been answered and which I have not yet been able to answer, despite my thirty years of research into the feminine soul, is "What does a woman want?" – Sigmund Freud,
Libra Morning Star

"Liberty, Humanity, Justice, Equality"
– Susan B. Anthony, Libra Evening Star

The Libra Venus Star Point

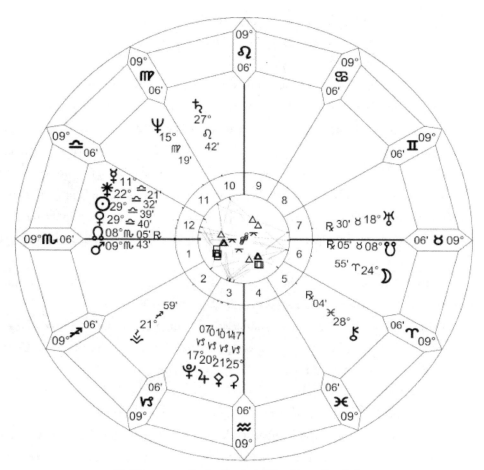

The Horoscope for the Previous Libra Venus Star Point

The VSP in Libra: The Historical Realm

Libra is the sign of reflection in its natural position on the zodiac wheel. At the onset of the Libra Star, for a very brief period the Aries Star feeds Libra before quickly changing to Pisces. The Pisces Star then becomes Libra's much longer life mate. For this brief moment in history, when Aries and Libra are present simultaneously, the extreme polarization will be felt.

Among the defining features of the horoscope for the previous Libra Star are a collection of planets in signs and houses dedicated to fulfilling a deep desire to partner and taking aggressive action to do so. The horoscope calls people to correct karmic mistakes from a previous era, even embracing enemies in the process. Adding even more emphasis to this tendency is a full moon where the Sun/Venus Star rises and the Moon sets (awareness and fulfillment, partnership and reflection). Two grand trines indicating ease and flow in this horoscope—one in the element of earth (practicality, groundedness) and the other in the element of fire (spontaneous passion and action)—show a period of great vision supported by practicality and productivity. There are not very many moments in history when all three outer planets (Uranus, Neptune, and Pluto) are forming an exact trine such as this one in the element of earth. The earth signs emphasize the material success of this period, due in great measure to the extraordinary breakthroughs (Uranus), vision and imagination (Neptune), and transformation (Pluto) that were occurring in nearly every field. Finally, notice the power and force of Mars (individual drive) in its own House (Aries) and its own sign (Scorpio)—a call to action and the numerous wars fought to correct serious imbalances of power and wealth in the world at the time, including both the French and American Revolutions and the American Civil War.

Perhaps the greatest gifts of the Libra VSP to the history of the world were events crucial to developing equality, including class, racial, and gender equality.

During the last Libra VSP cycle, gender equality emerged as one of the period's major causes. Two Libra VSP individuals who represented this cause were Elizabeth Cady Stanton, a Libra Morning Star, and Susan B. Anthony, a Libra Evening Star. This steady partnership of two fixed Sun signs, one Scorpio, one Aquarius, shook the roots of gender inequality and supported the cause of feminine rights. Though they were not alive to witness all the fruits of their efforts, they made great strides in the cause, paving the way for others to follow. Consequently, with the arrival of the next Libra VSP, it seems likely that we can look forward to a world reminded once again of the importance and value of such causes as justice and equality.

In the last Libra Star period there was an extraordinary musical and artistic renaissance in Europe. The courts of Europe were filled with great music, and included such Libra VSP individuals as Franz Liszt (1811), Pyotr Ilich Tchaikovsky (1840), and Gustav Mahler (1860). Ludwig von Beethoven (1770), was an Aries VSP born just at the start of the last Libra VSP (1771). He composed and performed his great works at the height of the Libra VSP era. During the era there was also an explosion of art and writing both in Europe and the United States. Artists such as Dante Gabriel Rossetti (1828), Mary Cassatt (1844), Henri Rousseau (1844), Paul Gauguin (1848), and Paul Klee (1879) also flourished. Libra VSP writers who influenced the culture included Mark Twain

> *"Whenever you find yourself on the side of the majority, it's time to pause and reflect."*
> – Mark Twain, Libra Evening Star

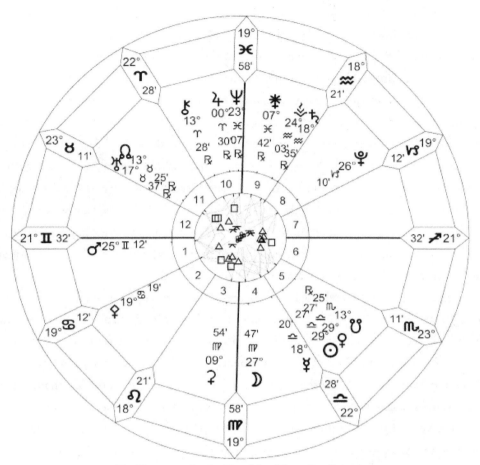

The Horoscope for the Next Libra Venus Star Point

(1835), Charles Dickens (1812), and Jules Verne (1828). We can probably expect a similar musical and artistic renaissance to prevail in the coming Libra VSP cycle.

As in the last Libra Star era, Mars is rising again in the coming one. This asserts the need to be an activist for an ideal; in this case, Mars in Gemini will assert the pursuit of freedom of speech and expression. The onset of the Venus transit to Libra is a bit unusual in that the Libra VSP will be phasing in before the Scorpio VSP is fully phased out, during the period between 2022 and 2030. Libra VSP individuals who will be born between 2022 and 2030 will be Evening Stars, while the intervening Morning Star of 2026 will occur in Scorpio. This time will be an eight-year period of tumult and uncertainty, such as those that often occur when there is a major shift. Punctuating this point is the 2022 Libra VSP itself squaring Pluto (Scorpio's planet), the mastermind of transformation (death and rebirth).

Perhaps the T-square in mutable Virgo, Pisces, and Gemini gives us a clue to the direction of the world at that time: Mars in Gemini stressing a Moon/Neptune opposition. If the Moon/Neptune opposition is struggling to give voice to the underlying feelings that are provoking such struggle, certainly Mars in Gemini is the remedy.

Libra VSP individuals born to serve humanitarian causes will tap knowledge that is ageless in their effort to keep themselves, their families, and the planet moving forward in *its own evolutionary cycle*. Many people seek to understand the New Age. The age they are referring to has to do with the Age of Pisces ending and the Age of Aquarius beginning, which is a more than two-thousand-year cycle. It also is an age that has sparked a wide array of opinions about precisely when it does change. With the Venus Star, we can glimpse another type of age change much more precisely. It is with this in mind that we will bear witness to two Venus Star Point cycles ending and beginning, which is akin to a minor age change. This occurs in the years between 2022 and 2041.

In spite of the somewhat Martial nature of the horoscope for the new Libra Star that begins in 2022, it is good to keep in mind that the astrological ruler of Libra is Venus. Other signs that Venus is linked to are Taurus and Pisces. When the Libra VSP becomes activated, the Taurus and Pisces VSPs will similarly be activated—Pisces just a few years later in 2041 and Taurus in 2076—ushering in a time when Venus plays a predominant role in people's value systems. In the coming era, the Venus Star Point will then contain three signs over which Venus has great influence. When Venus rises, so to speak, Mars will retreat, as both Aries and Scorpio are retired. The temporary retreat of Mars-ruled signs occurring simultaneously with an outpouring of Venus-ruled signs will no doubt be experienced as a world that is ready for peace and perceived as a safer, more beautiful, and healthier planet on which to live.

The Libra Venus Star Point

*"Men judge us by the success of our efforts.
God looks at the efforts themselves."*
– Charlotte Bronte, Libra Morning Star

*It was the best of times, it was the worst of times...
we were all going direct to Heaven,
we were all going direct the other way..."*
– Charles Dickens,
Libra Evening Star

> *"I can believe anything, provided it is quite incredible."*
> – Oscar Wilde,
> Pisces Morning Star

15   THE PISCES VENUS STAR POINT

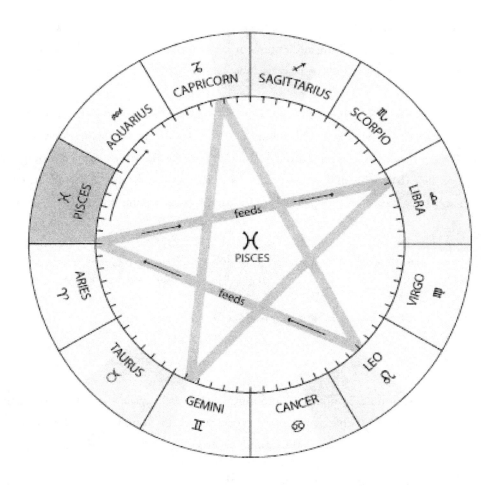

The Energy Flow of the Star Is:
Pisces→Libra→Gemini→Capricorn→Leo→Pisces

The Venus transit to Pisces will begin March 18, 2041, as a Morning Star and will end in 2133 as an Evening Star.

ELEMENT: WATER
MODALITY: MUTABLE

Pisces The astrological glyph for Pisces represents two fish swimming apart from each other in opposite directions but bound together by a cord. One fish lives in the spiritual dimension, the other fish resides on Earth, representing the dual nature of the Pisces seeking integration.

Some keywords and concepts for Pisces are: ocean currents, a boat on the sea, sea life and sea climates, the beginning and ending or the completion of life's cycle; spiritual dimensions, dreams, visions, and the unconscious; faith in a higher power, compassion, sensitivity.

As with Libra VSP people, Pisces VSP individuals will not begin to be born until 2041. However, in the prior Pisces VSP period (1790 to 1886), the following Pisces VSP individuals are noteworthy and all showed a distinct talent for the Pisces gift of keeping their imaginations alive, balancing and reconciling the physical and spiritual realms and bringing the vision and imagination of the spiritual realm into physical manifestation.

> **Male archetypes:** Maxfield Parrish, Alexander Graham Bell, George Eastman, Robert Louis Stevenson, Oscar Wilde, H. G. Wells, and Harry Houdini.
>
> **Female archetypes:** Emily Bronte, Isadora Duncan, and Anne Sullivan.

Greatest Assets: Kindness, compassion, and humility that helps others greatly; a spiritual focus and psychic sensitivity that provides the capacity to feel and understand things that others do not; an inclination towards music and the arts.

Greatest Liabilities: The blockage to the center of the heart is not usually a problem for you. Your heart is so open that you're in danger of diving into deep waters and drowning, lured by the Siren's sweet songs. Once you overcome the urge to take the plunge without first looking clearly at what you're diving into, you are able to love everyone without suffering.

Are You a Pisces Venus Star Point?

The dates below are derived from the last cycle of the Pisces VSP, from which we can draw some very strong archetypal characteristics of the Pisces period and its natives. Although all of these people have long passed on, their legacies and devotion to their life's causes reveal much about the nature of the Pisces Star and its inhabitants. Their lives can also give us clues about the people to be born in the next Pisces VSP period. The first and last in a group are always noteworthy, since they represent the first and last of a line.

The previous Venus transit to Pisces began on March 18, 1790, as a Morning Star, and ended on December 1, 1886, as a Morning Star.

MS=MORNING STAR   ES=EVENING STAR   D= VENUS DIRECT
Rx= VENUS RETROGRADE

MS/ES	DATES OF PISCES VSP	DEGREE
MS	3/18/1790 – 12/31/1790	28 Pisces 14 Rx
ES	3/19/1794 – 12/31/1794	29 Pisces 02 D
MS	3/15/1798 - 12/29/1798	25 Pisces 54 Rx
ES	3/17/1802 – 12/30/1802	26 Pisces 39 D
MS	3/14/1806 – 12/27/1806	23 Pisces 37 Rx
ES	3/15/1810 – 12/27/1810	24 Pisces 16 D
MS	3/12/1814 – 12/25/1814	21 Pisces 17 Rx
ES	3/12/1818 – 12/25/1818	21 Pisces 53 D
MS	3/9/1822 – 12/22/1822	18 Pisces 57 Rx
ES	3/10/1826 – 12/22/1826	19 Pisces 29 D
MS	3/7/1830 – 12/19/1830	16 Pisces 40 Rx
ES	3/7/1834 – 12/20/1834	17 Pisces 02 D
MS	3/5/1838 – 12/17/1838	14 Pisces 19 Rx
ES	3/5/1842 – 12/171842	14 Pisces 38 D
MS	3/2/1846 – 12/141846	11 Pisces 58 Rx
ES	3/2/1850 – 12/15/1850	12 Pisces 11 D
MS	2/28/1854 – 12/12/1854	09 Pisces 36 Rx
ES	2/28/1858 – 12/12/1858	09 Pisces 44 D
MS	2/25/1862 – 12/9/1862	07 Pisces 15 Rx
ES	2/25/1866 – 12/10/1866	07 Pisces 17 D
MS	2/23/1870 – 12/7/1870	04 Pisces 52 Rx
ES	2/23/1874 – 12/7/1874	04 Pisces 48 D
MS	2/20/1878 – 12/4/1878	02 Pisces 30 Rx
ES	2/20/1882 – 12/5/1882	02 Pisces 19 D
MS	2/18/1886 – 12/1/1886	00 Pisces 07 Rx

Since the Pisces VSP also affected general behavior patterns on Earth during these dates, they were likely times when events related to water were dramatized and spirituality was emphasized. With impeccable timing, the planet Neptune (Greek sea god Poseidon) was discovered during this period. Neptune is known as a higher octave or expression of Venus; Venus herself is exalted in the sign of Pisces, and the discovery of Neptune occurred during a Pisces Star era. These correlations combine to give a very romantic and dreamy quality to the Pisces VSP, who is governed by both Venus and Neptune.

Venus Star Point's Gift to Pisces

Love and a heart-centered approach to life is expressed with the fluidity of a flowing stream of imagination with Pisces VSP individuals sensitive to even the most subtle energies.

The VSP in Pisces: The Personal Realm

Each of the Venus Star Points has its own special gift, and it's under the sign of your Venus Star Point that the best of yourself is expressed. Of course, as discussed in Chapter 3, the Venus Star, like everything in nature, also has a shadow side. The Pisces VSP expresses itself through the element of water and is ruled by the planet Neptune.

Pisces VSP individuals are likely to be great dreamers, poets, and mystics due to the influence of water, which is the element of the emotions and reflection. The fact that Venus, goddess of love, is said to have been born of the sea further enhances these tendencies. Water dissolves everything and the Pisces soul is attuned to this dissolution process in their quest to merge with everyone and eliminate boundaries between themselves and their beloved.

These people tend to be drawn to watery environments as both the romance and turbulence of the sea stirs the Piscean soul. They can be imaginative, creative people but can also live in an illusionary world of their own, which may leave them vulnerable to deceit and betrayal. Full of imagination and wonder, Pisces VSP individuals are wizened old souls living life through the eyes of a child. And like a child, they are innocent and trusting of everyone to such a degree that they can be forcibly thrown overboard and swept, windblown and battered, to the shore by the romantic interludes they engage in.

> *"Keep your eyes on the stars, keep your feet on the ground."*
> – Theodore Roosevelt, Pisces Evening Star

The Pisces point on the wheel is the Alpha and the Omega—the beginning and the end points. It is here where reunion, reflection, and reconciliation take place in an individual's life. The mysteries or voyages of discovery they embark upon easily take them around the world and through the star-filled galaxy.

Pisces VSP individuals are able to tap into intuition, imagination, and creativity and are adept at storytelling that comes from the collective unconscious. The gift of fluidity is alive and flourishing inside the Pisces VSP. The myriad ways this is expressed are poetry in motion, through story, song, dance, or film. The Pisces VSP can easily access the spiritual realm and may choose to reside there in favor of the material realm. But there are two fish in Pisces, and thus the challenge is to maintain balance between the two fish in their separate domains. They achieve this through the medium of water, easily soaking up the other fish's energy as if it were their own.

Pisces VSP individuals' quest for the reconciliation of the physical and spiritual realms—the reason for their existence—leads them to engage in religious or spiritual practices throughout their lifetime. Here too, they can go overboard, swimming through dangerous waters where the bigger fish swallows them. They believe so much in a

> *"There's a sucker born every minute."*
> – Phineas T. Barnum, Pisces Evening Star

higher spiritual reality that they become blinded to the physical one right in front of them and much too easily submit their personal will to some cause or belief system.

The Venus Star gives the Pisces individual the ability to rise above the three-dimensional world and see it as but a microcosm of the universe. To them, the human plight of being trapped in three-dimensional bodies, occupying time and space, engenders compassion towards their fellow earthlings who have a limited perspective. Because they are so comfortable in the spiritual dimension, Pisces VSP individuals have the capacity to laugh at this earth-bound existence and transform it through fanciful science fiction stories, which may seem like children's animated tales of adventure.

Psychic sensitivity to nonphysical realms and an unflinching faith in unseen forces give a Pisces VSP an acute vulnerability to everything around them. This can lead to irrational fears that lead to depression and in some cases suicide.

Pisces VSPs are easily able to satisfy their longings for romance because their creativity and sensitivity attract others. If, however, they are blocked from achieving the love they seek, it is all too easy for Pisces VSP people to escape from the real world into substance abuse—often through prescription drugs, illegal drugs, or alcohol—which provides a preferable alternative to a loveless life.

Although for the Pisces VSP love and romance are high on the list of attainments in life, it is not the stage where they want to stop. They are partnered, practically for life, with the Libra VSP who is motivated to form partnerships and marry. The other VSPs that are partnered with Pisces are the Leo and Cancer Stars, indicating a further dream of parenting.

The gift of the Pisces VSP—a spiritual perspective, heightened sensitivity, a keen imagination, and compassion for others—are all qualities that will be contained in the grandchildren of today's children. This is a breed of individuals we are looking forward to welcoming to the world. For a list of noteworthy Pisces Star Individuals from the previous era, see Appendix III.

"No wonder the hills and groves were God's first temples, and the more they are cut down and hewn into cathedrals and churches, the farther off and dimmer seems the Lord himself."
– John Muir, Pisces Morning Star

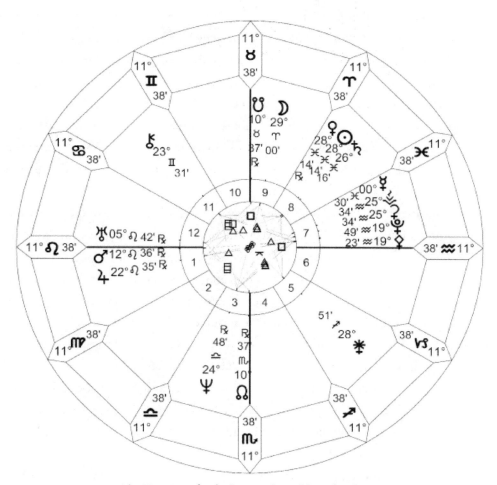

The Horoscope for the Previous Pisces Venus Star Point

The VSP in Pisces: The Historical Realm

The previous Pisces Venus Star Point era opened with a strong dose of fire and air, added to its already strong water theme. Conspicuously absent in this horoscope is earth. This added to the times the dimension of spiritual dreaminess, theater and the arts, magic and masters of illusion, and intelligent discourse and debate, even if it all seemed somewhat impractical and ungrounded. What was revealed beneath the veils of Pisces were hidden dimensions that people were compelled to explore and seemingly powerless to avoid.

Saturn sitting alongside the Venus Star in Pisces tested the limits of the church authorities and their doctrines. It pushed them to update their view and interpretation to keep abreast of all the scientific advancements and revelations that were occurring almost daily. Oppositions to religion by science are dramatically shown by the potent quartet of planets in Aquarius (Pallas, Pluto, Ceres, Vesta) challenging the heavyweights rising in Leo (Mars, Jupiter, Uranus). The heavy Leo and Aquarius provided drama and intensity to the debates. This was accompanied by a questioning of old systems of religious leadership and the church's laws. The work of Charles Darwin (a Leo VSP), who was born during the Pisces VSP era, took center-stage in a battle that is still raging some two hundred years later. During the last Pisces VSP era, radical new scientific views emerged, but there were still many people around the world who preferred holding on to their religious views, despite evidence to the contrary.

The impact of the heated opposition between Uranus and Pluto in the horoscope for the opening of the Pisces Star is reflected by the spirit of revolution and social change that characterized the era. This opposition was fueled by the fiery Mars/Uranus/Jupiter conjunction rising in Leo (catalyst for swift action and heated rebellion) in the Pisces VSP chart, indicating a very rare planetary alignment that opens the flood gates for social change. The French Revolution of the 1790s inspired an upsurge of democracy that spread to other areas of the world. In 1810, one of the early years of the Pisces VSP, Mexican revolutionary Padre Miguel Hidalgo sounded the bells of the village of Dolores and led the poor in revolt against the aristocracy in the Mexican War of Independence. In Latin America, Haiti was the first to gain independence from European (French) rule. Many other Latin American countries quickly followed suit, and under the leadership of Simon Bolivar, achieved liberation from Spanish overlords.

With Capricorn and Sagittarius as two successive Evening Stars for the Pisces VSP, age-old belief systems were challenged in two different arenas during this era. During the first part of the Pisces VSP cycle, with Capricorn as a partner, the challenge was to government and society's laws, as in France and the Americas. By the time the Pisces/Sagittarius phase arrived, unprecedented exploration and colonization of the rest of the globe by Europe's seafaring nations was underway. The tragic side of these explorations were the cargos of slaves brought, shackled and beaten, to the New World as a labor force. Shown in the Pisces VSP chart by the Venus Star conjunct Saturn in the Eighth House squaring Chiron and Juno, it would require the passage of the Venus Star through the entire sign of Pisces for the issue of slavery to be reconciled.

During the last half of the nineteenth century when the Sagittarius Star was interacting with the Pisces Star, exploration turned inward as prominent researchers of the

The Pisces Venus Star Point

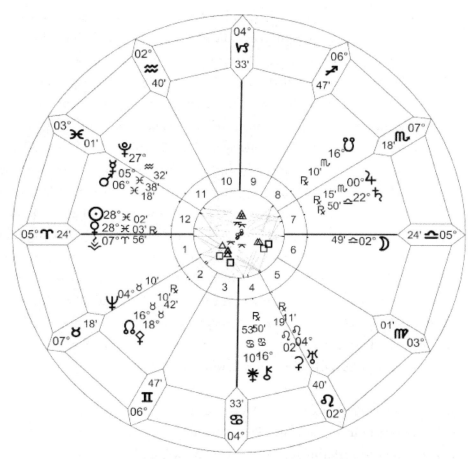

The Horoscope for the Next Pisces Venus Star Point

time explored the psyche. This was a profound period, unlike any since, which gave birth to spiritual and philosophical concepts such as the mapping of the unconscious, the scientific exploration of dreams, and the uncovering of secrets of the universe by such advanced thinkers as Sigmund Freud, Carl Jung, Charles Darwin, Albert Einstein, Helena Blavatsky, and George Orwell.

Further, during the last era of the Pisces VSP, there was a fascination with the discovery of treasures from ancient civilizations and speculation about the existence of lost cultures. Buried treasures from sunken ancient worlds were discovered, and people speculated on the existence and location of the lost continent of Atlantis. Ignatius Donnelly authored the most comprehensive work on the subject since Plato's rendering in classical times.[60] Since Donnelly's work, explorers and divers have been searching the seven seas for evidence of the existence of Atlantis.

The horoscope for the onset of the next Pisces VSP indicates the need for new values and radical changes in the areas of economic stability in the world. Both Pisces's rulers—Neptune the new and Jupiter the old—are standing in a direct opposition to each other, challenged further by revolutionary Uranus in Leo. Maybe we can expect new types of monetary exchange impacting global trade during this era. Perhaps shares of stock or real estate will be traded differently. Sales might well be offered on other orbiting bodies besides Earth, as Earth's resources could be nearly used up. Speculators will likely focus on newly invented products providing alternative forms of energy to sustain Earth in a new era. Whatever the commodity, it seems as if there will be an aggressive and enthusiastic surge toward speculation due to the three-way meeting of both of Pisces's rulers, Jupiter and Neptune, as well as unpredictable Uranus. In addition, impassioned activism by the disenfranchised is indicated by the Mercury/Mars conjunction in Pisces. Discoveries made toward the end of the Pisces VSP era may be a catalyst for rethinking how information is transmitted. This could include new technologies that send information in ways we cannot currently conceive of or discoveries from ancient times that might cause history to be rewritten.

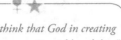

"I sometimes think that God in creating man somewhat overestimated his ability."
– Oscar Wilde, Pisces Morning Star

A renewed interest in marriage, including marriage customs from around the world, is indicated by Pisces's primary star mate Libra containing Saturn and the Moon. Along with this trend, religious doctrine forbidding priests to marry will likely be challenged.

The Pisces VSP paired with the Libra VSP promises new integrations of the feminine principle in organized religion, indicated by not only Uranus (rebellion and change) squaring both rulers of Pisces, but also the Moon and Saturn in Libra. During the last pairing of Pisces and Libra, feminists Elizabeth Cady Stanton and Susan B. Anthony worked for women's suffrage. In the new Pisces VSP era, the world's religious organizations that still keep women as second-class citizens, forbidden to enter the holiest of holies or the priesthood, will be challenged. These restrictions will be viewed as obsolete and religious organizations that want to continue to flourish may well be forced to give women such rights.

When women are no longer viewed as divine feminine icons such as the Virgin Mother, but can also be acknowledged as flesh and blood humans who are capable of performing the most sacred and holy of rites, religious institutions of the time will survive and perhaps even thrive. If there is a new wave of religious followers, it will no doubt be due to the updated views of the religions that are in power at the time. This is shown in the horoscope of the new Pisces VSP era by the enormous amount of energy in the sign of Pisces as well as its two ruling bodies Neptune and Jupiter locked in a three-way square with Uranus, planet of sweeping reforms. A question that might be considered now, in the decades before the inception of the Pisces Star, is this: religions and belief systems that are intricately linked to Pisces will thrive, but what kind of religions, what kind of beliefs? Humanity, during a Pisces Star era is easily drawn to devotion under the spell of Pisces, but what new evidence will emerge, what new ideas will take shape that alter beliefs and cause a kind of religious fervor we haven't yet dreamed of?

In the last Pisces Star era, 1790-1886, the earth was navigated by seagoing vessels that brought people and products across the seven seas. During the next Pisces Star era, beginning in 2041, we might see space navigated in a similar manner.

> *"Religion is the sigh of the oppressed creature...*
> *It is the opium of the people. ."*
> – Karl Marx, Pisces Evening Star

226

Part III

RELATIONSHIPS ON THE VENUS STAR

How the Venus Star Defines Relationships

In this part of the book the Venus Star Point pattern indicates links between people, particularly exploring the possible effects on love and relationships. We shall consider several points in this matter.

After observing hundreds of family relationships, partnerships, and love triangles, I concluded that the impact of the Venus Star Point on relationships cannot be ignored. First, I undertook an investigation of many couples in connection with the Venus Star (see results later in this section). After examining the data that emerged, it was clear that uniting friends, couples, business partners, creative collaborators, and even family groups and teams on a five-pointed star pattern of Venus produced some very convincing results.

The Venus Star has five points continually operating to produce one full star. The first idea to clearly emerge was that in groups of five or more, all of the points of the star need to be represented by a member for maximum harmony and success. In this way, each group member carries equal weight and has some influence in the outcome of the venture. Furthermore, the success of the group as a whole is insured, as this five pointed star is designed in harmony with the principle of attraction and growth. More about group dynamics and the Star is contained in Chapter 30.

STAR SIGN	YIN	YANG
ARIES		*
TAURUS	*	
GEMINI		*
CANCER	*	
LEO		*
VIRGO	*	
LIBRA		*
SCORPIO	*	
SAGITTARIUS		*
CAPRICORN	*	
AQUARIUS		*
PISCES	*	

Table 16.1: Star sign yin or yang energy

Another factor to consider in determining how each of the Venus Star Points influences relationships is to determine which members carry yin or yang energy and how that influences the rest of the group. For instance, yin is receptive energy while yang is active energy. The zodiacal wheel is perfectly balanced by six yang signs alternating with six yin signs. The fire (Aries, Leo, Sagittarius) and air signs (Gemini, Libra, Aquarius) are yang; the earth (Taurus, Virgo, Capricorn) and water signs (Cancer, Scorpio, Pisces) are yin. The Morning Star carries a yang energy, while the Evening Star possesses a yin energy. Thus, if you're an Aries Morning Star, you are carrying double yang energy, because Aries is yang, and the Morning Star is yang. If you're an Aries Evening Star, you possess yang/yin energy, because Aries is yang and the Evening Star is yin. If you're a Taurus Morning Star, you possess yin/yang energy, but if you're a Taurus Evening Star you are double yin energy, and so forth throughout the signs, as illustrated in the table above.

In analyzing a couple, if one partner is double yin and the other is double yang, they are complementary opposites and highly polarized. In group dynamics, if there is a majority of one type of energy over another, it will definitely influence the group expression and potentially the outcome of any venture undertaken.

Chinese Medicine, Feng Shui, and the Venus Star

To further understand how the Venus Star Points may influence relationships, it is also useful to know more about the significance of the number five and the five-pointed star in cultural traditions. This information is provided to illuminate how ancient systems have made use of the energy contained in the five-pointed star, rather than to suggest that education about these disciplines is needed to receive the benefits of using the Venus Star.

A good example of how the configuration of five aspects has been used for thousands of years in a very practical and healing way is the star pattern that makes up the five-element Chinese medical model[61], a model now also used by many practitioners of Western medicine—physicians, nurses, and other healers. Chinese medicine looks at five distinct organs that correlate to the seasons, to five elements, five colors, five metals, five senses, and five sounds. Each of these five points in Oriental medicine possesses energy flows that feed one star point and receive from another point, possessing an essential body of wisdom that defines each point's purpose in the overall design of the star. This theory and practice can well be used to assess the Venus Star Point's relationships in understanding how one star point feeds another.

Another related ancient Oriental practice that has been enthusiastically received in the West and illustrates the application of the energy of five elements to achieve harmony is a practice known as *Feng Shui*. It also employs the five elements of Chinese medicine to achieve harmony in the environment around an eight-sided *bagua*. Intriguing is the use of the numbers five and eight as in Venus's special star point cycle (it takes eight years to complete one full five-pointed star) and how the practice in Oriental medicine concerns achieving harmony in the body and the environment—distinctly Venusian principles.

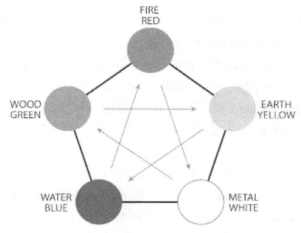

Figure 16.1: The Chinese five-element theory

Contained in the five-element Chinese medical model is what is called the *ko* (destruction) or *sheng* (creation) relationship. For instance, moving clockwise around the circle from point to point is the *sheng* creation relationship, while moving through the heart of the star from point to point (which is how the Venus Star is formed) is called the *ko* (destruction) relationship.[62] In this sense, the word destruction does not mean destroying, but rather a yielding or giving way to the next sign on its star-making path.

Figure 16.2: The energy flow of the star

Interestingly, this system, which has been practiced for centuries, provides a practical working model to understand the operation and energy flow of the Venus Star Points and ultimately how they influence relationships.

Elson M. Haas, M.D., states that the *ko* sequence in Chinese medicine can be thought of as a control relationship.[63] For the purposes of Venus, what Haas terms the destruction relationship might better be termed a control relationship, because moving this way around the star, one point is eliminated by the next. But it is Venus's control and, done with the loving aspects of Venus, this might be interpreted as the first point "feeding" the next point. In the Venus Star relationship between two people, one's point feeds the next. The choice is whether the feeding is done in a dominating way or in a nurturing way.

Another way to look at the control relationship cycle with regard to star points is to compare it to the relationship between parent and child. The child is dependent upon the parent for feeding, but the parent who feeds the child can also easily control or destroy the child as in the myth of Saturn (Greek Cronus), swallowing his children.

The *sheng* (creation) relationship of the five-element Chinese model can also be applied to the Venus Star. In the Chinese model, this is a straightforward clockwise progression of the seasons. When applied to the Venus Star Point, the clockwise progression around the circle is: the Morning Star (yang) of one relationship creates the Evening Star (yin) of the next relationship, which creates the Morning Star (yang) of the next relationship and so forth.

How the Venus Star Defines Relationships

Relationships of the Venus Star

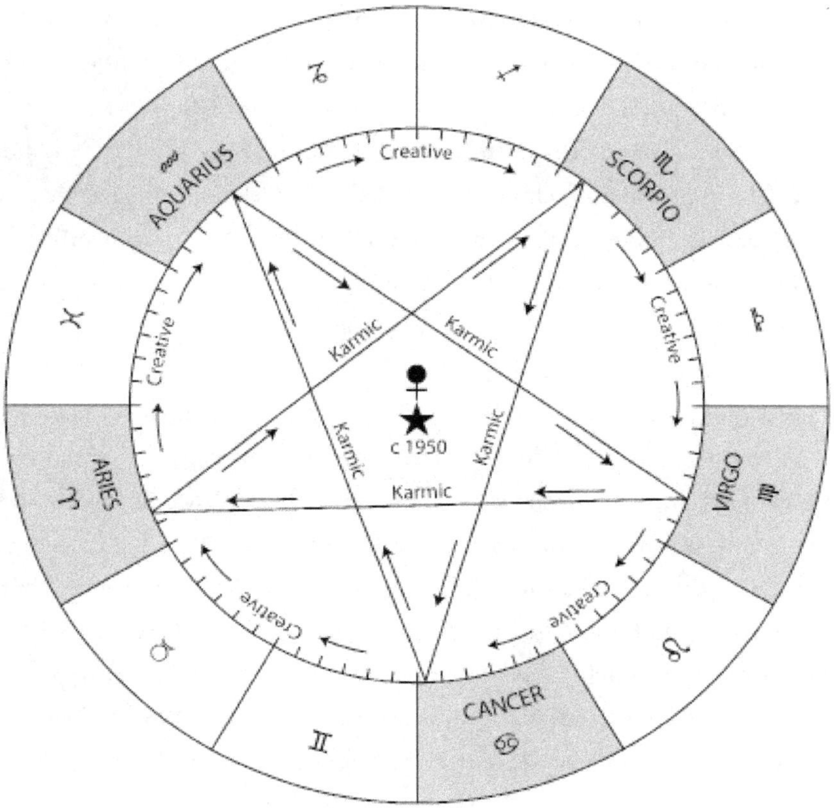

Figure 16.3: The Venus Star relationship principles

Using the Venus Star Relationship Data

The Venus Star brings people together in compelling and erotic ways. We can use this important information about its cycles to better understand the relationship dynamics of well-known people from past and present as well as to comprehend our own relationships.

The assumptions in this section are based on an examination of over five hundred couples who are currently married or have been in partnership for a minimum of five years. Of these couples, two hundred couples are relatively well-known personalities, while three hundred are people whose data was from private sources. The data base is composed of people who were born in different locations around the world over a period of two centuries. Most of the data, however, is comprised of North American and European births in the twentieth century.

Further, we can examine our own relationships in connection with the Venus Star Point theory in the following ways.

Without the use of the birth chart: We can simply identify our Venus Star and that of our friends and partners to obtain information about relationship qualities as described earlier in this section.

With the use of the birth chart: The addition of planets, asteroids, and houses that the Venus Star falls in provides much more information for relationship analysis regarding personal needs, and the influence of partners on each other. Perhaps not surprisingly, in marriages or relationships that lasted for a long time many of the Venus Star contacts were to the partner's Juno, the asteroid of long-term mating. The other planets' natures were also revealed by how significantly they influenced the Venus Star. For example, when Uranus was present, the relationship was magnetic and exciting but also involved long separations; when the nodes were involved, it seemed doubly karmic; when Venus herself was involved, a high level of sensuality, romance, and intimacy were present; when the Moon was involved, family, children, home, and security were primary dynamics; when the Sun was involved, there was a desire for leadership, fame, self-awareness, and light; and when Saturn was present, there was a need for a parent (father) figure offering long-term stability. Many of the celebrity examples did not have accurately timed births, so the ASC/DSC and other important axes could not be taken into consideration, but if timed birth data is available for the individuals in question, there is much more evidence that the Venus Star Point affects relationships in significant ways.

What follows are basic assumptions derived from this Venus Star Point couples research about relationships, which reveal which VSP combinations are likely to result in successful long-term relationships. An understanding of these dynamics is necessary for comprehending how relationships are influenced by the Venus Star Point.

THE THREE RELATIONSHIPS OF THE VENUS STAR

THE KARMIC STAR whereby one person's VSP feeds the other person's VSP through the <u>inner</u> heart of the circle.

THE TWIN STAR whereby two people possess the same VSP.

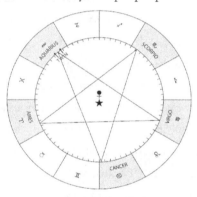

THE CREATIVE STAR whereby one person's VSP helps the other person's VSP through the very next point of the star on the <u>outer</u> circle.

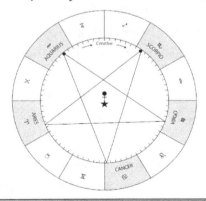

Figure 16.4: The three relationships of the Venus Star

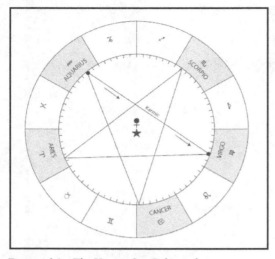

Figure 16.5: The Karmic Star Relationship

The Karmic Star relationship is the relationship formed between one Venus Star Point and the next, taking 584 days to complete. It is an evolutionary relationship and also implies an attraction from one person to the next based on the very crucial concept of "feeding". It is called the karmic cycle as it is a predestined Venus path in its eight-year creation cycle of one star. The name also underscores the fact that relationships worth cultivating allow us to clear any past debts, or karma, so that we can progress to the next level.

In this type of relationship, an individual's Venus Star Point can be seen as the head, while the two possible Karmic Star points would be the legs that support the body. People consciously or unconsciously chose such mates, two to one over the next largest group (the Twin Star relationships), and three or four to one over the Creative Star relationships. The Venus Star relationship principles help us understand why. Couples in a Karmic Star relationship are bound together by laws more powerful than matrimonial contracts due to the energy dynamics of the Venus Star where one star point feeds another. The principle of one star point feeding the next may seem to imply that only one person in the partnership benefits. But both parties benefit greatly because when one partner is fed in a relationship they automatically provide support so that there is great benefit for the other as well. In this relationship, there is giving and receiving. In our hypothetical model, the star point that symbolizes the head is feeding the leg that in turn supports the body, providing a positive reciprocal energy exchange. Always in the karmic relationship star, when one person represents the head, the other is the leg and vice-versa. However, only one of those points feeds the other on the Venus Star energy flow.

The Karmic Star relationship occurs with people we are most compelled to be with, either in a positive or negative way. Of the couples researched, these were partners who were greatly desired by each other—or almost completely repulsed but whose soul needed the relationship for some psychological or karmic reasons. And, like karmic relationships, people attracted to this type of relationship need each other for the essential missing ingredient that the partner can provide. Referring to the Chinese five-pointed star theory, we must keep in mind that there is control operating within such relationships, suggesting that if one person is feeding the other, they are also controlling and in the worst possible case destroying the other.

> **THE ASTROLOGICAL ASPECTS OF THE KARMIC STAR**
> BiQuintile (144°) – talent, creativity
> TriOctile (135°) – stress, leading to tension
> Quincunx (150°) – adjustment, reorganization, surrender

In Karmic Star relationships, there is a point of completion when the two parties have exchanged what was needed and the relationship is ready to terminate. When one partner's feeding of the other becomes controlling or destructive, the negative implications of the star emerge. Too much control by such a person of their mate can result in a love-hate dynamic and dissolve a union. Sometimes, though, such parties realize later that they really did need one another and regret what occurred. In such surrender comes healing. Astrologers will recognize the astrological aspects that are formed by the Venus Star in this particular type of relationship. Two of these aspects involve tension and discomfort, while the other one supports healing. You are in a Karmic Star relationship if you and your partner have the following Venus Stars:

Aquarius → Virgo
Aries → Scorpio
Cancer → Aquarius
Cancer → Pisces
Capricorn → Leo
Gemini → Aquarius
Gemini → Capricorn
Leo → Aries
Leo → Pisces
Libra → Taurus
Libra → Gemini
Pisces → Libra
Sagittarius → Cancer
Scorpio → Cancer
Scorpio → Gemini
Taurus → Sagittarius
Virgo → Aries
Virgo → Taurus

Additional investigation into the Venus Star's time lines indicates that certain signs are companions for life. There is an especially compelling connection between these Venus Star signs to also consider:

Libra and Pisces
Leo and Capricorn
Virgo and Aquarius

Aries and Scorpio
Taurus and Sagittarius

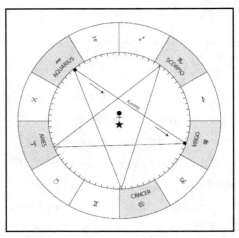

Figure 16.6: The Twin Star Relationship

In the relationship data analyzed, the second most common type of relationship that occurred was the Twin Star relationship, in which both individuals were born under the same Venus Star sign. In this type of relationship, partners mirror each other's characteristics. Further, the data showed a particularly large number of Gemini VSP and Aquarius VSP individuals, which makes sense, as both signs tend to focus on the development of sibling-type (Gemini) and close-friend-type (Aquarius) relationships. Yet despite having twin souls, such partners can and do have personality differences based on other factors in their charts. They can certainly see their own reflection in their mate. Typically, people of Twin Stars see the other as a double, a side kick, a twin. There is a greater ability to relax, be oneself, and enjoy all the shared interests.

This type of Venus Star relationship emerges in many parent/child pairings. This reflects, on a biological level, the Venus Star's impetus to reproduce itself through subsequent generations. The principle of the Venus Star at work here is seeing one's partner be who you would like to be or affirm who you already are, which is especially true of parent and child. The shadow side of such relationships occurs when they foster competition and jealousy, as in sibling rivalry. The astrological aspect related to this Twin Star is the conjunction (0-12°), signifying union, the merging of two into one. There are two types of Twin Star relationships as follows:

The reflecting Twin Star relationship, consisting of individuals born under the same Venus Star Point. Both are either Morning Stars or Evening Stars.

The harmonizing Twin Star relationship, consisting of two persons born on the same Venus Star Point. One is a Morning Star and the other an Evening Star.

You are in a *Twin Star* relationship if you and your partner have the following Venus Stars:

Aries Star – Aries Star
Gemini Star – Gemini Star
Leo Star – Leo Star
Capricorn Star – Capricorn Star
Scorpio Star – Scorpio Star
and so forth

> **ASTROLOGICAL ASPECT OF THE TWIN STAR**
> Conjunction (0-10°) merging, togetherness

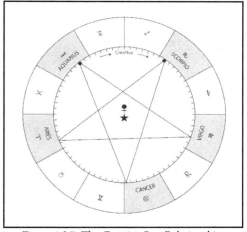

Figure 16.7: The Creative Star Relationship

The third type of relationship that can occur on the Venus Star is called the Creative Star relationship. Such a relationship is formed when Venus moves around the perimeter of the circle sequentially from one conjunction with the Sun to the next. Among such pairings are many successful artistic, musical, and business partnerships. Such partners have no karmic debt to each other and their relationships generally reflect romance, play, and freedom. Both parties encourage each other's personal self-expression and offer stimulus to their creativity. This Venus Star relationship is formed in such a way that when one person's star is the head, the other person's star is the arm (or hand) and vice versa. Such a relationship can be thought of as each other's "helping hand." There is not as much long term security or transformation in this pairing, but there is also less control and more freedom. These couples see each other as comfort food, with neither partner bent on forcing the other to comply to a particular agenda. People feel free to come and go from this relationship with no strings attached. Of the two possible kinds of Creative Star relationships, the MS with an ES comprised 60 percent, indicating a slightly stronger attraction to one's opposite quality. This matches the pattern of Venus's own rotating rhythm: Morning Star -- Evening Star – Morning Star – Evening Star, clockwise around the zodiac wheel. In this Creative Star, the individuals help or inspire each other, rather than "feed" each other as in the Karmic Star.

On the star pattern the flow is clockwise around the circle, possessing an alternating rhythm between MS and ES, as follows:

The Aquarius/Capricorn MS helps the Sagittarius/Scorpio ES
The Sagittarius/Scorpio MS helps the Virgo/Leo ES
The Virgo/Leo MS helps the Cancer/Gemini ES
The Cancer/Gemini MS helps the Taurus/Aries ES
The Taurus/Aries MS helps the Aquarius/Capricorn ES
The Aquarius/Capricorn ES helps the Sagittarius/Scorpio MS
The Sagittarius/Scorpio ES helps the Virgo/Leo MS
The Virgo/Leo ES helps the Cancer/Gemini MS
The Cancer/Gemini ES helps the Taurus/Aries MS
The Taurus/Aries ES helps the Aquarius/Capricorn MS

ASTROLOGICAL ASPECTS OF THE CREATIVE STAR
Quintile (72°)—creativity and talent
Sextile (60°)—opportunity and flow

The symbol in the charts ahead for the Venus Star Point is:

Venus Star Point Connections in the Horoscope

In summary, to evaluate any relationship on the Venus Star, take note of the following:

1. VSP → VSP: Examine the five points of the Venus Star of your birth era. How are the relationships of your life being fed by you? How are you being fed by them?
2. Are you in a Karmic Star relationship, a Creative Star relationship, or a Twin Star relationship?
3. Are you and your partner balanced by star sign and energy output, i.e., is yours a yang star and your partner's a yin? Are you the same or are you mixed?
4. For astrologers to consider: What is the role of your VSP in your partner's horoscope? What is the role of your partner's VSP in your horoscope? What are the house connections?
5. What are the planet to Venus Star Point (VSP) connections?
    - VSP to Moon—desire for nurturing and comfort; safety; for food, family and home
    - VSP to Sun—desire for self-awareness and light; for leadership, fame; for procreation and self-expression
    - VSP to Mercury—desire for communications; for education and travel; for playfulness
    - VSP to Venus—desire for love and romance; artistic self-expression; for harmony, beautiful surroundings, and sensual pleasures
    - VSP to Mars—desire for action, strength, courage, and victory; for sexual union
    - VSP to Jupiter—desire for expansion, growth, adventure, and optimism; for hope
    - VSP to Saturn—desire for father; building a support system or structure, something enduring and stabilizing
    - VSP to Uranus—desire for living outside the boundaries, for change and excitement, space, social causes, freedom and free-thinking
    - VSP to Neptune—desire for spiritual union and mystical states; for fantasy, escape, and living a dream; for creative, artistic stimulation and partnership

- VSP to Pluto—desire for power, to effect transformation and change; for depth and intensity in relationship
- VSP to Chiron—desire for healing and health awareness; compassion, kindness and awareness of suffering
- VSP to Vesta—desire for inner focus and strength; for devotion, sacrifice
- VSP to Juno—desire for long-term mating and for equality in relationship
- VSP to Ceres—desire for home, food, nourishment, and children
- VSP to Pallas—desire for wisdom and skills
- VSP to Nodes—desire to know each other again, to replay the past; to reunite and reconcile
- VSP to Ascendant/Descendant—desire to mate for life; for energy exchange to help balance one's extremes
- VSP to Midheaven/Imum Coeli—desire for a role model, teacher, leader; to live together and build something together—a family, a home, a business, an institution; for publicity

17 Marriage and partnerships on the venus star

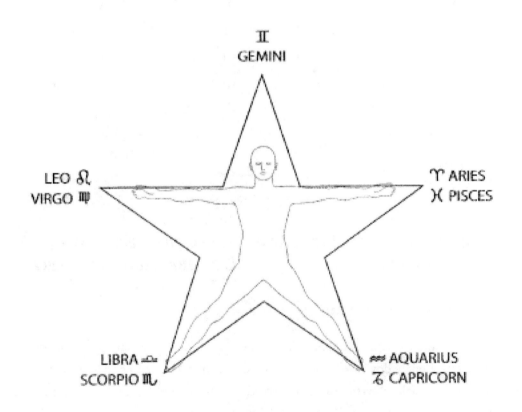

243

Connections to Our Star Partners

Previously we have shown how the flow of the Venus Star occurs. In the Scorpio Star, the relationship is:

SCORPIO IS THE HEAD

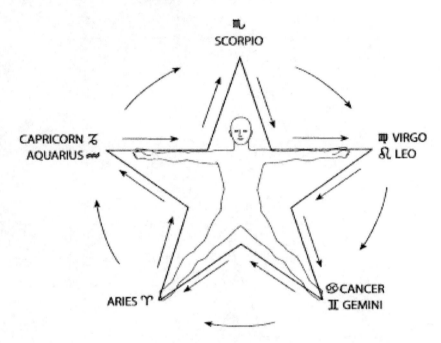

Figure 17.1: The flow of the Scorpio Venus Star

AQUARIUS/CAPRICORN IS THE ARM   **VIRGO/LEO IS THE ARM**
ARIES IS THE LEG   **CANCER/GEMINI IS THE LEG**

How the Venus Star Gives and Receives

Giving and receiving is the principle according to which the Venus Star operates in relationships. Energy flows well when it is circulated correctly, leading to harmony, endurance, and growth in partnerships. The concept of the karmic dynamic is that giving is usually balanced with receiving. The Scorpio VSP gives to (feeds) the Cancer/Gemini VSP, which in turn feeds the Aquarius/Capricorn VSP. Using the Scorpio Star example above, it is the Aries Star that gives to (feeds) the Scorpio Star, and it is the Cancer/Gemini Star that receives from (and is fed by) the Scorpio Star.

If there is a lack of reciprocity between giving and receiving in the relationship of the two individuals being examined, it leads to stagnation and a diminished relationship and is more likely due to character flaws rather than a lack of energy flow in the Venus Star. Note also that in the Creative Star dynamic, the helping hands to the Scorpio VSP are the Virgo/Leo Star, to which Scorpio gives help and inspiration, and the Aquarius/Capricorn Star, from which Scorpio receives help and inspiration. Tables 17.1 and 17.2 indicate how a Venus Star Point gives and receives within the Karmic and Creative Star dynamics.

How Your Venus Star Point Feeds and is Fed by: The Karmic Star

Using the first column, find your Venus Star Point; then using the other columns determine how it feeds and is fed from the other Venus Star Points.

This STAR	feeds this STAR	and is fed by this STAR
TAURUS	CAPRICORN	LIBRA
TAURUS	SAGITTARIUS	VIRGO
SAGITTARIUS	LEO	TAURUS
SAGITTARIUS	CANCER	
CANCER	PISCES	SAGITTARIUS
CANCER	AQUARIUS	SCORPIO
VIRGO	TAURUS	AQUARIUS
VIRGO	ARIES	
AQUARIUS	VIRGO	CANCER
AQUARIUS		GEMINI
SCORPIO	CANCER	ARIES
SCORPIO	GEMINI	
ARIES	SCORPIO	VIRGO
ARIES	SAGITTARIUS	LEO
GEMINI	AQUARIUS	SCORPIO
GEMINI	CAPRICORN	LIBRA
CAPRICORN	LEO	GEMINI
CAPRICORN		TAURUS
LEO	ARIES	CAPRICORN
LEO	PISCES	SAGITTARIUS
LIBRA	GEMINI	PISCES
LIBRA	TAURUS	AQUARIUS
PISCES	LIBRA	LEO
PISCES		CANCER

Table 17.1: The feeding relationships on the Karmic Star

How Your Venus Star Point Gives and Receives: The Creative Star

Using the first column, find your Venus Star Point; then using the other columns determine how it gives to and receives from the other Venus Star Points.

THIS STAR	Gives to THIS STAR and	Receives from THIS STAR
TAURUS	PISCES/AQUARIUS	LEO/CANCER
SAGITTARIUS	LIBRA/VIRGO	PISCES/AQUARIUS
CANCER	TAURUS/ARIES	LIBRA/VIRGO
VIRGO	CANCER/GEMINI	SAGITTAR/SCORPIO
AQUARIUS	SAGITTAR/SCORPIO	TAURUS/ARIES
SCORPIO	VIRGO/LEO	AQUARIUS/CAPRI
ARIES	AQUARIUS/CAPRI	CANCER/GEMINI
GEMINI	ARIES/PISCES	VIRGO/LEO
CAPRICORN	SCORPIO/LIBRA	ARIES/PISCES
LEO	GEMINI/TAURUS	SCORPIO/LIBRA
LIBRA	LEO/CANCER	CAPRI/SAGITTAR
PISCES	CAPRI/SAGITTAR	GEMINI/TAURUS

Table 17.2: Giving and receiving on the Venus Star

It is helpful to take an inventory of the relationships in your life which have been most vital and life-changing. In this review, an assessment can be made of where these people will be placed on your own Venus Star. Which people are your foundational support (legs) and who are your helping hands? Who are your twins?

Start with your family, then extend your review to friends, co-workers, teachers, and lovers. If your Venus Star connects to too many people to whom you are feeding (on the Karmic Star) and helping to inspire (on the Creative Star) with little or no reciprocation, you will very quickly feel depleted. If, on the other hand, you are helped and fed by the other people's Venus Stars without being able to feed or give to them, while you are well supported, you are also "hungry" for someone in your life whom you can feed. This is particularly evident when the one star mate you were feeding is the child that has left home or the spouse that has passed on.

The concept of "feeding" should be considered without a value judgment placed upon it. For instance, the Virgo Venus Star Point feeds the Aries Venus Star Point as a natural occurrence in the construction of the five-pointed star of Venus. Thus, the principles of Virgo energetically feed the principles of the sign Aries; Aries then moves on to energetically feed Scorpio and so on. Simply put, it is Aries Star energy feeding Scorpio Star energy, based on the Star of Venus. Whether that Star Point is fed person to person, or time period to person, or persons and events of a totally different era feeding that person, it is the energetic feed of the two signs in operation. And while we can then be tempted to conclude that an Aries Star individual will thus feed its Scorpio Star partners and friends in a good way, this isn't always the case. Nevertheless they are being fed, whether the recipient judges it as a helpful and nourishing feeding or a controlling and demanding feeding.

There are many combined astrological factors at work that add to the understanding of relationships, including the position of Sun, Moon, Ascendant, Nodes, etc. The Venus Star is one more factor to add to this understanding, itself providing revelations concerning the principles of attraction and connectedness between people that cannot be seen in any other way.

The following chapters on the relationships of the individual star signs provide more detailed information on how the Venus Star influences relationships.

18 Taurus Venus Star Relationships

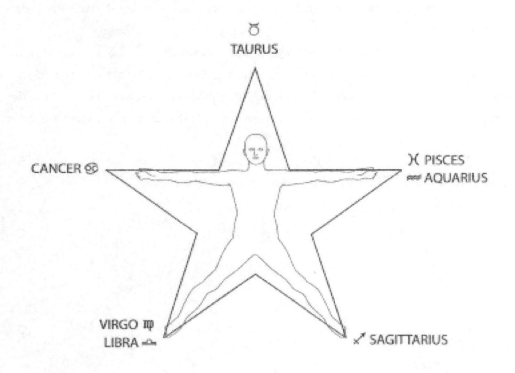

From the human star above, we observe that the Taurus Star interacts with seven other star signs as its arms and legs over the course of its lifetime. They are:

    Feet of Taurus: Virgo & Libra; Sagittarius & Scorpio[64]
    Hands of Taurus: Cancer; Aquarius & Pisces

Since only five signs are active on the Venus Star at any given time period, we can break these different star sign relationships into the following periods for the course of the Taurus Star:

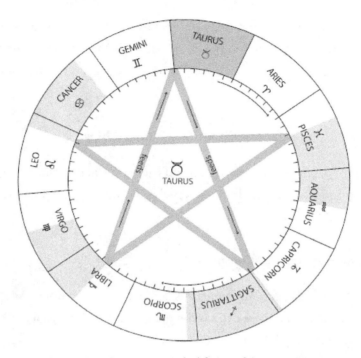

Figure 18.1: Interactions in the lifetime of the Taurus Star

FEET on the Karmic Star:

Taurus-Libra:	(1825-1881)	56 years
Taurus-Virgo:	(1875-1933)	58 years
Taurus-Sagittarius:	(1830-1922)	92 years LIFE MATES

HANDS on the Creative Star:

Taurus-Pisces:	(1825-1886)	61 years
Taurus-Aquarius:	(1890-1934)	44 years
Taurus-Cancer:	(1852-1933)	81 years

In relationships, Taurus VSP individuals are motivated to marry and remain married, even in challenging circumstances. That's not to say they won't succumb to amorous tendencies wherever they occur, as Taurus was the favorite sign of the goddess Venus. But in general Taurus VSP individuals remain loyal to their mates and are not prone to divorce, even when given ample opportunity to consider it. If divorced or separated, the Taurus VSP will likely keep trying to establish a relationship that will produce the longevity and security they are seeking. The Taurus VSP individuals born between 1825 and 1933 were the most elderly on the planet at the turn of the twenty-first century. Notable natives of this group include Nancy Reagan, Prince Philip, Barbara Bush, B.B. King, Larry King, and Willie Nelson.

Taurus Karmic Star Relationships

For most of the cycle, the Taurus Star and Sagittarius Star are life mates, phasing in and phasing out together. Only briefly, at the very beginning and end, does the Taurus Star link to Capricorn and Scorpio.

Taurus Star-Sagittarius Star Relationships

Taurus is a fixed sign feeding Sagittarius, a mutable sign. Taurus is also an earth sign, feeding Sagittarius, a fire sign. These contrasting natures serve to complement one another and provide the necessary ingredient the other requires. And since these two signs are life-mates on the Venus Star, there is a compelling attraction of the heart between these two, even if there are distinct differences in how they approach life and love. And because they are life-mates on the Venus Star, the challenges they encounter in a relationship to one another serve a higher purpose—that of loving each other unconditionally.

Taurus VSP people possess a steady, earthy focus and a determination to achieve their desired aim, and this is how they feed their Sagittarius Star mates. It is the Taurus Star that controls the Sagittarius Star and would necessarily set limits on the wandering tendencies of their high-spirited, flirtatious mates. If the Sagittarius Star wanders too far afield from the Taurus Star's bull-pen, the bull may get feisty and full of rage, but is forgiving nonetheless. The Taurus Star loves the Sagittarius Star's sense of adventure and fun loving nature, which contrasts sharply or harmonizes well with the steady, practical, and even-tempered Taurus VSP. Additionally, the Taurus VSP person provides earthy grounding and a foundation for the many creative fires of a Sagittarius VSP type, as well as the bullseye toward which the Sagittarius VSP can aim its arrow.

Taurus VSP individuals remind Sagittarius VSP people that long-term planning and careful investment will ultimately help them reach their goals. The Sagittarius Star possesses a large appetite for adventure, education, exploration, and travel. Sagittarius is also the sign of gambling and risk-taking and will not hesitate to gamble on an opportunity if presented with one. In the process they can and do incur enormous debt, which their Taurus Star mate may find intolerable. The Taurus VSP tends to be much more aware of the financial implications involved in any undertaking, reining in the budget and temporarily grounding the high aims of its partner. The more reserved nature of Taurus VSP individuals complements the more outgoing character of Sagittarius VSP people. Some celebrity relationships pairing Taurus with Sagittarius on the Karmic Star include:

Dorothy W. Bush	**Taurus ES**	**Prescott Bush**	**Sagittarius ES**
Johnny Carson	**Taurus ES**	**Ed McMahon**	**Sagittarius MS**
D.H. Lawrence	**Taurus ES**	**Frieda Lawrence**	**Sagittarius ES**
Vivien Leigh	**Taurus MS**	**Sir Laurence Olivier**	**Sagittarius MS**
Nancy Reagan	**Taurus MS**	**Ronald Reagan**	**Sagittarius ES**
Jessica Tandy	**Taurus ES**	**Hume Cronyn**	**Sagittarius ES**

Taurus Star-Capricorn Star Relationships

The birth dates of this combination occurred from 1825 to 1827 at the inception of the Taurus Star and the phasing out of the Capricorn Star. Since both signs are associated with earth elements, we might surmise that such partners are practical, security-oriented, and industrious.

In the current star cycle, the last of the Taurus Star births occurred in 1933, while the first of the Capricorn Stars occurred in 1986. This more than fifty-year age difference pairs someone of the Taurus group with their grandchild or great-grandchild. Because they are both earth signs, the influence on each other is profoundly comforting and nurturing. In this case it is the elder Taurus Star that feeds the younger Capricorn Star.

Taurus Star-Scorpio Star Relationships

The Venus Star dates of this combination occurred from 1925 to 1927 at the moment of the inception of the Scorpio Star and the termination of the Taurus Star. But there are many examples of this pairing with people born before and after these dates. Because Taurus feeds Scorpio on the Karmic Star and because these two signs form an opposition or polarity relationship to one another, it is not the easiest of relationships, no matter how compelling. However, it is one of the Venus Star's evolutionary relationships that forces the two opposites to find a compromise or balance point in order to keep the love alive. If trouble arises it often involves a contract dispute. In oppositions such as this, neither partner is prone to enter into compromise or negotiation willingly. The partner who makes the first step towards this end is the winner in this case, even if it seems like they have lost something in the process. By being the one to act first, they will have inspired their partner to follow along. Some examples of this star pairing are as follows:

Tony Curtis	**Taurus ES**	**Janet Leigh**	**Scorpio ES**
Tony Curtis	**Taurus ES**	**Jamie Lee Curtis**	**Scorpio ES**
Roman Polanski	**Taurus ES**	**Sharon Tate**	**Scorpio ES**
Gene Roddenberry	**Taurus MS**	**William Shatner**	**Scorpio MS**
Gene Roddenberry	**Taurus MS**	**Leonard Nimoy**	**Scorpio MS**

Taurus Star-Libra Star Relationships

See the Libra Star Relationship section, Chapter 28.

Taurus Star-Virgo Star Relationships

See the Virgo Star Relationship section, Chapter 21.

Taurus Creative Star Relationships

The hands of Taurus on the Creative Star are divided almost equally into two separate star signs: Pisces (born from 1825 to 1886) and Aquarius (born from 1890 to 1934). The hand that helps Taurus is the Cancer Star and will be discussed in the Cancer Venus Star Relationship, Chapter 20.

The first group (Taurus: Pisces) results in a relatively easy relationship as earthy Taurus and watery Pisces complement each other. The second group (Taurus: Aquarius) produces relationships that contain the endurance factor found in these two fixed signs. The earth element found in Taurus is moist and solid, while the air element of Aquarius is dry and light. There are distinct contrasts in temperament between these two, but because they are linked on the helpful Creative Star of Venus, this combination tends to be successful and inspired. When resistance is a problem for the Taurus Star, the Aquarius Star helps them break through. Aquarius is outgoing and gravitates to the public or to publicity, while the

Taurus Star is concerned less with people and more with material substance.
Taurus Star/Aquarius Star pairs in the relationship data include:

Gerald Ford	Taurus MS	**Betty Ford**	Aquarius MS
Lillian Hellman	Taurus MS	**Dashiell Hammett**	Aquarius MS
Rock Hudson	Taurus ES	**Doris Day**	Aquarius ES
Charles Lindbergh	Taurus ES	**Anne M. Lindbergh**	Aquarius ES
Dean Martin	Taurus ES	**Jerry Lewis**	Aquarius MS
Harriet Nelson	Taurus ES	**Ozzie Nelson**	Aquarius ES
Prince Philip	Taurus MS	**Queen Elizabeth**	Aquarius MS
Carlo Ponti	Taurus MS	**Sophia Loren**	Aquarius MS
Gene Wilder	Taurus ES	**Gilda Radner**	Aquarius ES

Taurus Twin Star Reationships

The Taurus Star, ruled by talented and lovely Venus herself, presents a glittering example of two Taurus Twin Stars: that of Evening Star Louis Armstrong and Evening Star Ella Fitzgerald, united in musical harmony. Not only are they united by twin Venus Stars, but her Sun, natal Venus, Mercury, and Jupiter are also in Taurus, making her one of the pure Taurus archetypes. Twin Taurus Stars include:

Louis Armstrong	Taurus ES	**Ella Fitzgerald**	Taurus ES
John F. Kennedy	Taurus ES	**Robert F. Kennedy**	Taurus ES

Once the Taurus Star phased out between 1929 and 1933, the Aries Star began. Technically they are twins (from the same star point), but this pattern can be described as Aries being the next generation of the Taurus Star. Many couples from just before and after this time period are united by Venus, as follows:

John F. Kennedy	Taurus ES	**Jacqueline Kennedy**	Aries MS
Aristotle Onassis	Taurus MS	**Jacqueline K. Onassis**	Aries MS
Ferdinand Marcos	Taurus ES	**Imelda Marcos**	Aries MS

Jacqueline Kennedy Onassis, one of the first-born Aries Stars of the 100-year period of the star, married two Taurus Stars. John F. Kennedy was a Taurus Evening Star and

Aristotle Onassis was a Taurus Morning Star. Here it might help to know that her astrological chart places the sign Taurus in her Seventh House of marriage. In JFK's chart, his Seventh House of marriage is dominated by the sign of Aries, where her Venus Star resides. In Jacqueline's chart, her Seventh House of marriage is dominated by Taurus, where both JFK's and Onassis' Venus Stars reside. Furthermore, JFK has Mars, Mercury, and Jupiter in Taurus as well.

The first marriage might seem probable, but when the widow of the former U.S. President became involved with a foreign businessman a generation her senior, many people asked: what is the connection? Not only are their two Venus Stars in close proximity (an out-of-sign conjunction), but his Venus Star connected with numerous other points in her chart as shown in the chart below. In a case such as this, it is the elder Taurus Star that is said to give energy to or feed its younger star sign, Aries. Because it is the parent or elder, it also has the capacity to control and/or withdraw when necessary. Onassis' Venus Star Point feeds and supports Kennedy's three Scorpio points, including Juno, one of the primary indicators of marriage.

But what is even more noteworthy than the presence of Juno, the marriage asteroid, in aspect to the Venus Star Points of both her spouses, is the involvement of Chiron, the wounded healer. Jacqueline's Chiron sits in proximity to the VSPs of both men, directly opposite her Juno in Scorpio. The tragic loss of JFK and the subsequent mourning period that the world shared with Jacqueline speaks to the Juno/Chiron opposition. The same aspect illuminates a pre-destined karmic pattern embedded in her horoscope by the appearance of the Nodes nearby. Thus, the starring role of the mourning widow of a dearly beloved national leader provided her the script to enact Chiron for a nation and a world. And further, the healing, comfort, and feeling of safety that was offered by her new spouse also gave Chiron a starring role. Jacqueline's Aries Star, located on the same point as both Taurus Star men, clearly shows the heart connection she would have with both of them, even if the Star Points were in different signs, signifying "different generations." Jackie O was always in possession of her own fiery Aries Star, Leo Sun spirit and, in the best of cases with both gentlemen, was nourished by the security and stability that their Taurus Star provided. In the worst cases, she may have also been suffocated by them, as earth smothers fire that burns too hotly and too freely.

Taurus Venus Star Relationships

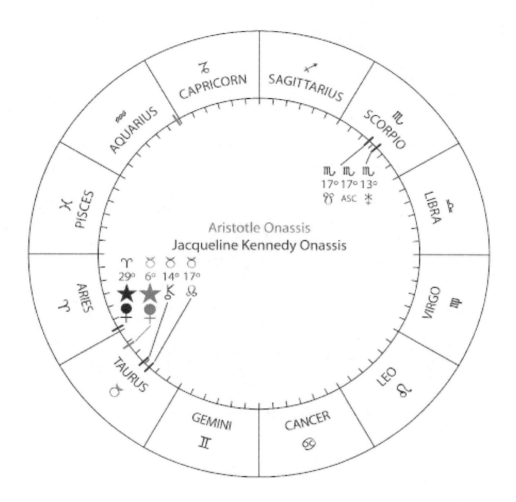

Figure 18.2: THE ARISTOTLE and JACQUELINE KENNEDY ONASSIS
RELATIONSHIP STAR CHART

Jacqueline Kennedy: 29° Aries Morning Star (yang/yang)

Aristotle: 6° Taurus Morning Star (yin/yang)

TWIN STARS of a DIFFERENT GENERATION

Aristotle's desire (VSP) for healing and care-giving (Jacqueline Kennedy's Chiron)

Aristotle's desire (VSP) to know again, to replay the past (Jacqueline Kennedy's Nodes)

Aristotle's desire (VSP) for marriage, long-term union (Jacqueline Kennedy's Juno)

Aristotle's desire (VSP) for a mate, energy exchange, to help balance extremes
(her ASC/DSC)

19 SAGITTARIUS VENUS STAR RELATIONSHIPS

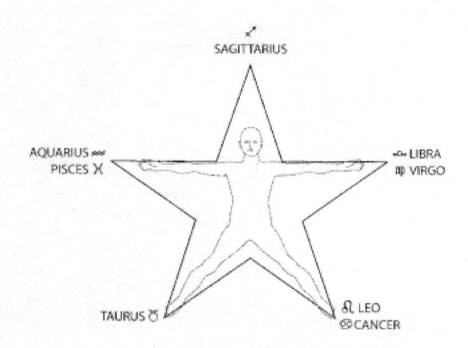

In the star human above, we observe the Sagittarius Star interacting with many signs to make up its hands and feet. They are as follows:

Feet of Sagittarius: Taurus; Leo & Cancer
Hands of Sagittarius: Aquarius & Pisces; Libra & Virgo

Since only five signs of the Venus Star are active at any given moment in time, we can break these signs into the different time lines as follows:

Figure 19.1: Interactions in the lifetime of the Sagittarius Star

FEET on the Karmic Star:

Sagittarius-Leo:	(1830-1849)	19 years
Sagittarius-Cancer:	(1852-1923)	71 years
Sagittarius-Taurus:	(1830-1922)	92 years LIFE MATES

HANDS on the Creative Star:

Sagittarius-Libra:	(1830 to 1871)	41 years
Sagittarius-Virgo:	(1875 to 1924)	49 years

Sagittarius Karmic Star Relationships

The fiery temperament of the Sagittarius VSP individuals give them humor, charisma, spunk, and restlessness. These characteristics make them irresistible to other signs, and most especially to Taurus, since they are life-mates on the Venus Star (detailed in Chapter 18). The other Karmic Star relationships for Sagittarius are the signs that it feeds,

Leo and Cancer. The Leo Star was briefly fed by the Sagittarius Star at the inception of the cycle. But it is the relationship between the Sagittarius Star and Cancer Star that occurs more often and, when successful, constitutes the evolutionary progress for both stars.

Sagittarius Star-Leo Star Relationships

From the previous era of the Leo Star there is one example that turned up to demonstrate the relationship dynamics of this pair. That is:

| **Helena Blavatsky** | **Sagittarius ES** | **Henry Steel Olcott** | **Leo ES** |

In the current era of the Leo Star there exists a more than sixty-year age difference between these two star signs. The last of the Sagittarius Stars were born in 1923 and the first of the Leo Stars were born in 1987. The relationships most likely to occur, then, would be an elder grandparent or teacher engaging with their grandchild or young student. Since both signs are of the element of fire, we can surmise that such a relationship would be energetic and vibrant, with the elder Sagittarius being the dominant or controlling one of this pair.

Sagittarius Star-Cancer Star Relationships

The much longer period of engagement for the Sagittarius VSP to the sign that it feeds is the Cancer Star. Sagittarius VSP individuals are idealistic, extroverted, and goal-oriented; they help sensitive, introverted Cancer VSP people to interface with the world in a broader way through travel, greater perspective, philosophical vision, and a more playful approach. Some with this combination are:

Lucille Ball	**Sagittarius ES**	**Desi Arnaz**	**Cancer MS**
Humphrey Bogart	**Sagittarius MS**	**Lauren Bacall**	**Cancer MS**
Douglas Fairbanks	**Sagittarius MS**	**Mary Pickford**	**Cancer MS**
William R. Hearst	**Sagittarius ES**	**Marion Davies**	**Cancer ES**
Carl Jung	**Sagittarius MS**	**Toni Wolff**	**Cancer ES**
Joseph Kennedy Jr.	**Sagittarius MS**	**Joseph Kennedy Sr.**	**Cancer ES**
Les Paul	**Sagittarius MS**	**Mary Ford**	**Cancer MS**

Sagittarius Creative Star Relationships

Sagittarius Star-Libra Star Relationships

For a period of approximately forty years, the Sagittarius VSP/Libra VSP relationship existed on the Venus Star. This relationship is primarily a harmonious one, due to the compatible elements of fire and air at work and play here. The Libra VSP likes to maintain balance and can help the Sagittarius VSP recognize or curtail its excesses. In this partnership it is Sagittarius' fire or vision that helps to inspire Libra's air or ideas. Some examples of this pairing are:

Pierre Curie	**Sagittarius MS**	**Marie Curie**	**Libra ES**
Carl Jung	**Sagittarius MS**	**Sigmund Freud**	**Libra MS**

An example of this combination is Pierre Curie, a Sagittarius MS, and wife and coworker Marie Curie, a Libra ES. It is worth noting that it was Pierre's vision that fueled Marie's ideas, but in the case of Jung and Freud, it was Freud who was initially Jung's mentor. However, because the feeding was in reverse, it was Jung who eventually had to fuel his own fire, and separate from Freud's influence.

Sagittarius Star-Virgo Star Relationships

When the Libra Star phased out, the Virgo Star took its place as the help-mate receiving the beneficial creative input from Sagittarius. Sometimes in relationships one partner is the dreamer and the other is the realistic one, far too practical for dreams. In this relationship combination, the extroverted Sagittarius VSP individual is the dreamer who has a broad perspective, looking towards distant horizons. The more introspective and grounded Virgo VSP, concerned with the reality of here and now, serves to provide a more practical framework. Both are mutable signs given to the quality of understanding. This gives them common ground, but the frustration of the square that characterizes this relationship can provide a source of ongoing tension nevertheless. Typically the Sagittarius VSP provides the inspiration for the Virgo VSP to execute its visions with a high degree of perfection. For this pair to excel at their highest level they must truly embody their philosophy of "walking their talk" rather than just expecting it to happen. Examples of this combination are as follows:

Lydia Clarke	**Sagittarius MS**	**Charlton Heston**	**Virgo ES**
Ava Gardner	**Sagittarius MS**	**Frank Sinatra**	**Virgo ES**
Katharine Hepburn	**Sagittarius MS**	**Spencer Tracy**	**Virgo ES**
Anais Nin	**Sagittarius ES**	**Henry Miller**	**Virgo ES**
Les Paul	**Sagittarius MS**	**Gene Autry**	**Virgo ES**
Eva Peron	**Sagittarius ES**	**Juan Peron**	**Virgo MS**
Florenz Ziegfeld	**Sagittarius MS**	**Fanny Brice**	**Virgo ES**

Sagittarius Star-Pisces Star Relationships

See Pisces Star Relationship, Chapter 29.

Sagittarius Star-Aquarius Star Relationships

See Aquarius Star Relationship, Chapter 22.

Sagittarius Twin Star Relationships

The following pairs among this group all reflect the vivacious, adventuresome, and high-spirited nature that typifies this sign:

Frida Kahlo	**Sagittarius MS**	**Diego Rivera**	**Sagittarius ES**
Wilbur Wright	**Sagittarius MS**	**Orville Wright**	**Sagittarius ES**
Fred Astaire	**Sagittarius MS**	**Ginger Rogers**	**Sagittarius ES**
Bob Hope	**Sagittarius ES**	**Bing Crosby**	**Sagittarius ES**

Twin Stars are harmonizing or reflecting doubles or side kicks to one another. It is interesting to note that all of the celebrity examples in this category were unified by a common purpose. In the case of Kahlo and Rivera it was artistic pursuit; for the Wright brothers it was to make aviation history; for Astaire and Rogers it was dance; and for Hope and Crosby it was comedic film-making, in which their most successful collaborations detailed their "road" trips, a fitting Sagittarius pursuit. Twin stars are often united by a common theme, but because their other signs are different, there are distinct character differences. This is well depicted by the reflecting Twin Star relationship of Sagittarian VSP Morning Star Frida Kahlo and Sagittarius VSP Evening Star Diego Rivera. The fact that they were well matched energetically and twins on the Venus Star (their hearts were united) kept this couple together for the better part of their lives. Their individual signs (she a Cancer, he a Sagittarius) further united them on the Venus Star by virtue of that pair's Karmic Star relationship. In this case, Kahlo has a Cancer Sun and five other planets in that sign, indicating how well fed she was by her own Sagittarius Star and by Rivera's Sagittarius VSP, as well as his Sun, Venus, and Mercury also in Sagittarius.

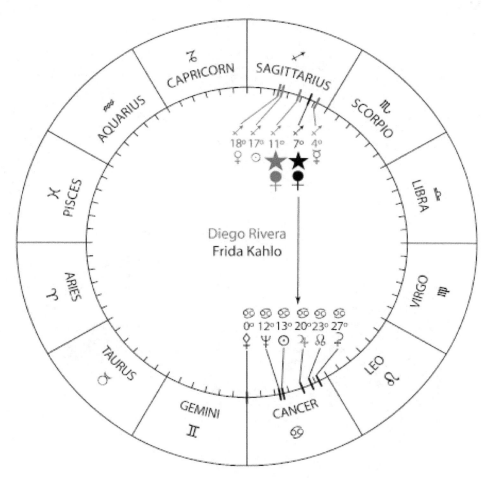

Figure 19.2: THE FRIDA KAHLO and DIEGO RIVERA
RELATIONSHIP STAR CHART

Kahlo's VSP: 7° Sagittarius Morning Star (yang/yang)

Rivera's VSP: 11° Sagittarius Evening Star (yang/yin)

Rivera's Mercury – 4° Sagittarius

Rivera's Sun – 17° Sagittarius

Rivera's Venus – 18° Sagittarius

Kahlo's desire (VSP) for: communications, travel, education, and playfulness (Mercury)

Kahlo's desire (VSP) for: love, romance, art, beautiful surroundings, intimacy (Venus)

Kahlo's desire (VSP) for: self-awareness, leadership, light, fame, offspring (Sun)

CANCER VENUS STAR RELATIONSHIPS

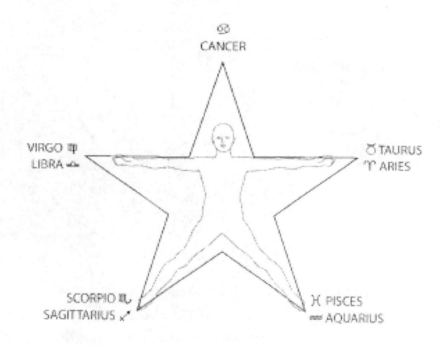

In the Venus Star universe, Cancer is partnered with many other relationship stars to fulfill its need of settling into a warm and comfortable relationship in an intimate and cozy setting. From the star human above, we observe Cancer's star mates as follows:

Feet of Cancer: Scorpio & Sagittarius; Aquarius & Pisces
Hands of Cancer: Virgo & Libra; Aries & Taurus

Since only five signs are active at any given time period, these relationship periods break down as follows:

Figure 20.1: Interactions in the lifetime of the Cancer Star

FEET on the Karmic Star:

Cancer-Sagittarius:	1852-1924	72 years
Cancer-Scorpio:	1926-1961	35 years
Cancer-Pisces:	1852-1886	34 years
Cancer-Aquarius:	1890-1962	72 years

HANDS on the Creative Star:

Cancer-Libra:	1852-1880	28 years
Cancer-Virgo:	1875-1961	86 years
Cancer-Taurus:	1852-1933	81 years
Cancer-Aries:	1929-1961	32 years

The Cancer VSP individual is highly motivated to marry, create offspring, and would love nothing more than one life-long soul mate. But this is not always the case for Cancer. In searching for that one life partner, the Cancer VSP individual initiates dozens of relationships hoping each time that it is the ONE, but also initiates just as many separation proceedings when it becomes clear that it isn't the ONE. Many of their former partners will remain in the inner circle of Cancer's family throughout their lifetime.

Cancer Karmic Star Relationships

Cancer is fed on the Karmic Star by both Sagittarius and Scorpio, and in turn feeds Karmic Star mates Pisces and Aquarius.

Cancer Star-Pisces Star Relationships

For the first third of the Cancer Star and the final third of the Pisces Star, these two signs are linked together on the Karmic Star of Venus. This might be perceived as a match made in heaven as the two have the feeling element of water, quenching each other's thirst for soulful, healing, and intimate exchanges with a partner.

Cancer Star-Aquarius Star Relationships

When the Pisces Star terminated, Cancer began feeding the Aquarius Star for the duration of its life. This seventy-two-year period gave Aquarius VSP individuals more traits associated with Cancer, including the tendency to seek a cozy home, an intimate partnership, good food, emotional connections, and a family life or some sense of belonging. In turn, it gave Cancer VSP people more characteristics associated with Aquarius, such as a broad world perspective; a levelheaded, more detached and less emotional approach; and the tendency to entertain new ideas and possibilities to offset the Cancer VSP tendency to get stuck in situations and focus on past wounds.

Aquarius VSP individuals tend to be "orphans," feeling they don't belong even if they have a family. Cancer VSP individuals provide their Aquarius VSP mates care, intimacy, and a home base, all characteristics sought by Aquarius people. Cancer is a yin sign and Cancer VSP people tend to be more introverted than their extroverted Aquarius VSP partners, who exemplify a yang sign. Motivated by very different principles and extremely different characteristics, it is nonetheless an evolutionary relationship on the Venus Star.

Cancer Venus Star Relationships

This pair is united by the Venus Star in a passion-filled, heartfelt connection for one another, while simultaneously working towards shifting out of their comfort zone to meet the needs of their partner. Some examples with this connection are:

Clyde Barrow	Cancer MS	**Bonnie Parker**	Aquarius MS
Warren Beatty	Cancer ES	**Annette Bening**	Aquarius MS
James Brolin	Cancer MS	**Barbara Streisand**	Aquarius MS
Laura Bush	Cancer MS	**George W. Bush**	Aquarius ES
Prince Charles	Cancer MS	**Queen Elizabeth II**	Aquarius MS
Dick Cheney	Cancer MS	**George W. Bush**	Aquarius ES
Imogene Coca	Cancer MS	**Sid Caesar**	Aquarius ES
Bo Derek	Cancer MS	**John Derek**	Aquarius MS
Mamie Eisenhower	Cancer ES	**Dwight Eisenhower**	Aquarius ES
Eliz. Queen Mother	Cancer MS	**Queen Elizabeth II**	Aquarius MS
Joseph Kennedy Sr.	Cancer ES	**Rose Kennedy**	Aquarius ES
Joan Kroc	Cancer ES	**Ray Kroc**	Aquarius MS
John Lennon	Cancer MS	**Paul McCartney**	Aquarius MS
Mike Love	Cancer MS	**Brian Wilson**	Aquarius MS
Marcello Mastroianni	Cancer MS	**Sophia Loren**	Aquarius MS
John McCain	Cancer ES	**Cindy McCain**	Aquarius ES
Paul Newman	Cancer MS	**Joanne Woodward**	Aquarius ES
Richard Nixon	Cancer ES	**Spiro Agnew**	Aquarius MS
John Oates	Cancer MS	**Daryl Hall**	Aquarius ES
Mickey Rooney	Cancer ES	**Judy Garland**	Aquarius ES
Ivana Trump	Cancer MS	**Donald Trump**	Aquarius ES

One of the most successful partnerships of this type was formed in the early 1960s between John Lennon and Paul McCartney of the Beatles. Their collaboration lasted one full Venus Star period—eight years—from 1962 to 1970, but the results of that union will live in eternity. Lennon's Cancer Morning Star VSP fed McCartney's Aquarius Morning Star and was closely aligned with McCartney's Jupiter and Sun. McCartney's Sun is in 27° Gemini, within the orb of Lennon's 5° Cancer VSP. McCartney's Aquarius VSP, the recipient of Lennon's Cancer VSP, was closely aligned with Lennon's Moon, as can be seen in the following chart.

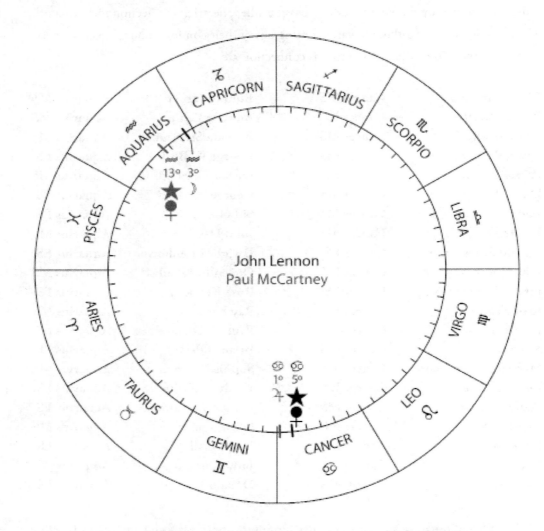

Figure 20.2: THE JOHN LENNON and PAUL McCARTNEY
RELATIONSHIP STAR CHART
McCARTNEY: 13° AQUARIUS MS (yang/yang)
LENNON: 5° CANCER MS (yin/yang)
LENNON FED McCARTNEY ON THE KARMIC STAR
Lennon's desire (VSP) for: expansion and hope, gain and growth (McCartney's Jupiter)
McCartney's desire (VSP) for: nurturing, comfort, mother, children (Lennon's Moon)

Cancer Star-Capricorn Star Relationships

This is most likely to occur among people of at least one generation apart. The Cancer Star terminated in 1961 and the Capricorn Star began in 1986. The two signs form an opposition or polarity relationship, and because it is also a karmic relationship on the Venus Star, there are serious adjustments required by both individuals to ensure harmony and stability.

Cancer Star-Sagittarius Star Relationships

See the Sagittarius Star Relationship, Chapter 19.

Cancer Star-Scorpio Star Relationships

See the Scorpio Star Relationship, Chapter 23.

Cancer Star Creative Relationships

On Cancer's Creative Star, there are two signs that it gives help and inspiration to: the Taurus Star from 1852 to 1933 and the Aries Star from 1929 to 1961.

Cancer Star-Taurus Star Relationships

These two signs, Cancer and Taurus, have always been viewed as complementary since both signs are associated with elements (earth and water) that mix well. It may also have to do with the long-term creative relationship they enjoy on the Venus Stars for a period of eighty-one years. The Taurus VSP can be likened to a plant or flower, firmly rooted in the earth element, but absolutely needing Cancer's frequent watering to grow and thrive. In viewing the pairs that represent these two stars, it can be seen how creative inspiration was a key factor in enhancing the dynamics of the relationship. Representatives include:

Eric Clapton	**Cancer ES**	**B.B. King**	**Taurus ES**
Clark Gable	**Cancer MS**	**Vivien Leigh**	**Taurus MS**
Jayne Meadows	**Cancer ES**	**Steve Allen**	**Taurus MS**
Mary Tyler Moore	**Cancer ES**	**Dick Van Dyke**	**Taurus ES**
Eleanor Roosevelt	**Cancer MS**	**Franklin Roosevelt**	**Taurus MS**
Alice B. Toklas	**Cancer MS**	**Gertrude Stein**	**Taurus MS**

Cancer Star-Aries Star Relationships

In 1929 when the Taurus VSP phased out, Aries became Cancer's Evening Star, lasting for the remainder of the Cancer VSP. This is a very different breed of Cancer Star than in the previous group, Cancer and Taurus. The relationship between Aries and Cancer can create an environment of highly charged emotional outbursts, fireworks that possess an explosive dynamic when least expected. These individuals are dealing with a cardinal square, which has been described by astrology as a crisis in action. For these individuals, relationships can be challenging and their endurance depends on partners having sufficient self-confidence and emotional maturity. On the one hand, Cancer seeks a mate who can provide a home base and security, while the Aries Star seeks to individuate by breaking away from relationships that are characterized by too much dependency. It is often the Cancer VSP individual who is equipped to provide a home, family, security, and a type of mothering for the Aries VSP, while the Aries Star person gives the Cancer VSP a fresh direction, more activity, and some experimentation in life. In this case, it is the Cancer Star that helps and inspires, but may also be the one in control. The Aries Star will appreciate the warm and homey nurturing and sense of belonging to a family that a Cancer Star provides, but will resist the Cancer Star's tendency to direct and control what they (Cancer Stars) may perceive as an immature and sometimes irresponsible Aries. If this relationship is to succeed, the Cancer Star will cease its over-protecting, loosen the reins, and lighten up, allowing the Aries Star some room for personal expression and self-direction. Further, the Aries Star will cool its engines, resist the temptation for defiance, and allow its Cancer Star mate to soothe its ruffled feathers. It can certainly be a steamy relationship, but is it steam that fuels the engine, or steam that blows a gasket?

A couple who falls into this pairing is the late Princess Diana and Prince Charles, whose Venus Star connections did not provide the harmony they sought to keep their relationship growing. In the Scorpio relationship star section just ahead, the Venus Stars of Prince Charles and Camilla Parker Bowles are provided, demonstrating how the Venus Star of Camilla (Scorpio) does feed Charles (Cancer). Celebrity couples representing Cancer-Aries stars include:

Prince Charles	Cancer MS	**Princess Diana**	Aries MS
John F. Kennedy Jr.	Cancer ES	**Carolyn Bessette Kennedy**	Aries ES
Michael Douglas	Cancer ES	**Catherine Zeta Jones**	Aries MS
Antonio Banderas	Cancer ES	**Melanie Griffith**	Aries ES
James Carville	Cancer ES	**Mary Matalin**	Aries MS

Cancer Star-Libra Star Relationships

See the Libra Star Relationship, Chapter 28.

Cancer Star-Virgo Star Relationships

See the Virgo Star Relationship, Chapter 21.

Cancer Twin Star Relationships

Twin star relationships possess a profound sense of familiarity with one another, even at their first meeting. It's as if a psychic bond is present, whereby the two people recognize each other's souls. Furthermore, because the Cancer Star is an intuitively based water sign to begin with, the instant knowing may be even more pronounced in this particular VSP. Because the Cancer Star possesses the qualities of expressing innate desires through establishing a home and family, there is a life-long sense of bonding that will occur for twin Cancer Stars, even after years of separation.

Earlier in this chapter the Karmic Star relationship of Cancer Star John Lennon and Aquarius Star Paul McCartney was discussed. In that relationship, Cancer (John) fed Aquarius (Paul). What seemingly ended their very karmic and creative relationship was the introduction of Yoko Ono (Cancer Star) to John Lennon. Born one full eight-year Venus Star cycle apart, John Lennon and Yoko Ono reflect the Twin Star dynamic of becoming each other's double. Even their honeymoon reflected the Cancer Star tendency toward a relaxed, homey style as they lounged in bed in their pajamas in a hotel suite with the media filming and the world watching the first reality show, a full generation before reality shows became the craze.

Among the next generation, in the true era of reality shows, is another pair of Cancer Twin Stars, Ozzie and Sharon Osborn, pioneers of the reality TV era, who likewise openly invited camera crews to film their most personal and intimate moments of domestic elation and crisis. Twin Cancer VSPs in the celebrity group are:

John Belushi	**Cancer MS**	**Dan Akroyd**	**Cancer ES**
Kirk Douglas	**Cancer MS**	**Michael Douglas**	**Cancer ES**
Zelda Fitzgerald	**Cancer MS**	**F. Scott Fitzgerald**	**Cancer ES**
Tom Hanks	**Cancer MS**	**Rita Wilson**	**Cancer MS**
Lyndon Johnson	**Cancer MS**	**Lady Bird Johnson**	**Cancer ES**
Jack Lemmon	**Cancer MS**	**Walter Matthau**	**Cancer ES**
John Lennon	**Cancer MS**	**Yoko Ono**	**Cancer MS**
Paul Newman	**Cancer MS**	**Robert Redford**	**Cancer ES**
Ozzie Osborn	**Cancer MS**	**Sharon Osborn**	**Cancer ES**
Christopher Reeve	**Cancer ES**	**Dana Reeve**	**Cancer ES**
Vincent van Gogh	**Cancer MS**	**Theodore van Gogh**	**Cancer ES**

21 Virgo Venus Star Relationships

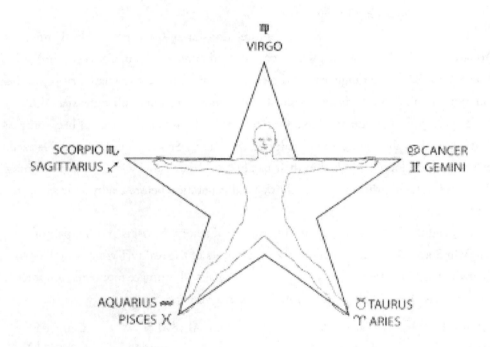

From the star human above, it is easy to see that the Virgo Star interacts with eight other star signs as its arms and legs over the course of its lifetime. They are:

        Feet of Virgo: Aquarius & Pisces; Aries & Taurus
        Hands Virgo: Scorpio & Sagittarius; Gemini & Cancer

Since only five signs are active at any given moment, we can break these different star sign relationships into different periods in the life span of the Virgo Star, as follows:

Figure 21.1: Interactions in the lifetime of the Virgo Star

FEET on the Karmic Star:

Virgo-Taurus:	(1875-1933)	58 years
Virgo-Aries:	(1929-1985)	56 years
Virgo-Pisces:	(1875-1886)	11 years
Virgo-Aquarius:	(1890-1984)	94 years LIFE MATES

HANDS on the Creative Star:

Virgo-Cancer:	(1875-1961)	86 years
Virgo-Gemini:	(1964-1984)	20 years
Virgo-Sagittarius:	(1875-1928)	53 years
Virgo-Scorpio:	(1926-1984)	58 years

At the inception of the Virgo Star in 1875, its legs were Pisces and Taurus, both elementally and energetically compatible signs for Virgo. The link from Virgo to Taurus in the first half of the Virgo Star era allowed the Virgo VSPs born then to be somewhat more steady and sure about their goals and aspirations. But, by the termination of the Virgo Star in 1984, Virgo's legs were Aries, a wilder but faster-acting combination of energies and Aquarius, an innovative sign. In this chapter, we will discuss the relationships that Virgo feeds on the Karmic Star and helps on the Creative Star. For signs that feed and help Virgo, please refer to the appropriate chapters.

Virgo Karmic Star Relationships

The Aries VSP became activated in the late 1920s while simultaneously the Taurus VSP was phasing out in the early 1930s. Therefore, the 1920s-1930s were decades of change and readjustment as the world witnessed and reacted to one of the five star points of Venus changing signs, bringing in new ideas and energies. The common denominator that unified the transition was the Virgo Star.

The 1980s was again a decade of change and readjustment as the Venus Star was shifting signs once again. One of these changes was the termination of the Virgo Star, after a 100-year run. The Virgo VSPs born in the last twenty years of its era are the last of its line, and therefore are interested in making a huge impact on those around them by reinforcing the qualities of their star sign. This also reflects how the Virgo VSP individual is governed or influenced by the star signs that feed it and the star signs that it feeds, dependent upon at what part of the cycle the Virgo VSP was born. For instance, the people of the baby-boomer generation have the Virgo-Aries link, not the Virgo-Taurus link, as was the case for the Virgo VSP born in the early twentieth century. This influences them in entirely different ways than their predecessor Virgo VSPs.

Virgo Star-Taurus Star Relationships

This Venus Star relationship covered the first half of the Virgo Star period, the late nineteenth and early twentieth century. Because it is a karmic feed, there is a highly magnetic and irresistible quality to these two star signs that will usually result in a penetrating and powerful life-long connection. And, because they are both earth signs, no matter the personality differences, they can usually find common ground.

The Taurus VSP individuals emanate an earthy sensuality and, because they also possess Venus' magnetic abilities to attract to them whatever they most desire, they are a force to be reckoned with. Virgo VSP individuals are a great match for people with such sensuality and are themselves very attractive and charismatic. The double dose of earth gives compatibility in matters relating to the physical and the sensual, the body, the material realm, and practical solutions to life's challenges. This would be a pair focused on productivity, working towards achieving security, and providing services, products, or contributions to each other, one's family, or one's community. Further, they are both yin signs. The challenge that is presented here is that the Virgo VSP is a natural-born editor and problem solver, and the Taurus VSP is head-strong or stubborn about their point of view, resisting change and criticism, even when the facts support the Virgo VSP's point of view.

Some of the celebrity pairings for this combination are:

Burt Bacharach	**Virgo MS**	**Hal David**	**Taurus MS**
Philip Berrigan	**Virgo ES**	**Daniel Berrigan**	**Taurus MS**
George H. W. Bush	**Virgo ES**	**Barbara Bush**	**Taurus MS**
Maria Callas	**Virgo ES**	**Aristotle Onassis**	**Taurus MS**
Simone de Beauvoir	**Virgo ES**	**John Paul Sartre**	**Taurus MS**
Ethel Kennedy	**Virgo MS**	**Robert F. Kennedy**	**Taurus ES**
Frances Seymour	**Virgo ES**	**Henry Fonda**	**Taurus MS**
R. Sargent Shriver	**Virgo ES**	**Eunice Kennedy Shriver**	**Taurus MS**
Frank Sinatra	**Virgo ES**	**Dean Martin**	**Taurus ES**
Elizabeth Taylor	**Virgo ES**	**Richard Burton**	**Taurus ES**

Virgo Star-Aries Star Relationships

This relationship between Virgo and Aries is highly charismatic and enchanting, because they are linked as mates on the karmic relationship star of Venus. But, because their natural rhythms are quite different from one another, they are learning to appreciate the other's uniqueness, and must avoid trying to change the other one into being more like themselves. The Aries VSP appreciates the Virgo VSP's ability to do the homework and research so that the Aries partner can take action armed with facts and information. But what the Aries VSP does not like about the feed from Virgo is too much information, too much editing, too much input, and especially too much control.

The Virgo VSP individuals feed Aries VSP people by offering practical solutions and attention to detail and by remaining calm through the storms. Virgo's ability to statistically analyze and evaluate a number of probable outcomes helps the high-adrenalin Aries Star, who is in constant motion, to slow down, become organized, and better focused before venturing forth. The Virgo VSP's innate sense of groundedness, attention to the physical world and the physical body provides the Aries Star with the quality it generally lacks itself and appreciates or seeks out in a mate.

In turn, Aries VSP individuals provide Virgo VSP people with courage, leadership, and that dazzling spark of fire that lights the flame under Virgo's pot of slow-cooked soup. Aries VSP people also help Virgo VSP individuals overcome self-doubt and believe in themselves. The Aries VSP normally does not hesitate in taking action on its inner promptings, while the Virgo VSP is prone to analyzing those inner messages to death before risking themselves or taking the leap. Some celebrity pairings in this group are:

Woody Allen	Virgo MS	**Diane Keaton**	Aries MS
Johnny Cash	Virgo ES	**June Carter Cash**	Aries MS
Camille Cosby	Virgo MS	**Bill Cosby**	Aries MS
Celine Dion	Virgo MS	**Rene Angelil**	Aries ES
Wynona Judd	Virgo ES	**Naomi Judd**	Aries MS
John Kerry	Virgo MS	**John Edwards**	Aries MS
Royston Langdon	Virgo ES	**Liv Tyler**	Aries MS
Stevie Nicks	Virgo ES	**Lindsey Buckingham**	Aries ES
Michelle Obama	Virgo ES	**Barack Obama**	Aries MS
Marie Osmond	Virgo MS	**Donny Osmond**	Aries ES
Lisa Marie Presley	Virgo MS	**Priscilla Presley**	Aries MS
Diana Ross	Virgo MS	**Berry Gordy Jr.**	Aries MS
Gavin Rossdale	Virgo MS	**Gwen Stefani**	Aries MS
Sam Shepard	Virgo MS	**Jessica Lange**	Aries ES

Among the numerous celebrity pairings that turned up for the Aries-Virgo Star relationship, a stunning example is Celine Dion, a Virgo Morning Star who feeds Rene Angelil, an Aries Evening Star. Her Star, at 6° Virgo, feeds his 29° Aries Star in a 127° separation. Although considered quincunx by sign, this is much closer to the trine of 120°. Having been married since 1994, this pair continues to have an enduring, highly prosperous, and loving relationship, even though there is a twenty-six-year age difference between them. This partnership reflects how it can be the dream of a Virgo VSP to have a life-long mate, friend, mentor, coach, and business manager all in one, as seen in the following chart.

Virgo Venus Star Relationships

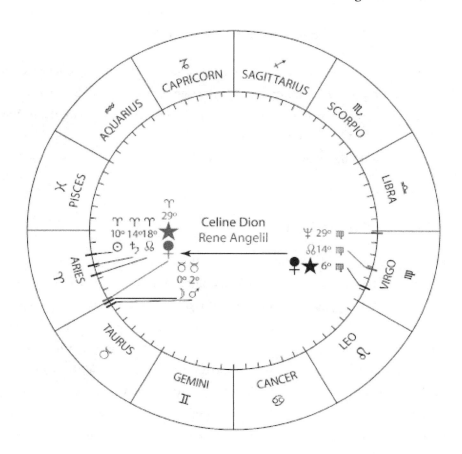

Figure 21.2: THE CELINE DION and RENE ANGELIL RELATIONSHIP STAR CHART
DION: 6° VIRGO MS (yin/yang)
ANGELIL: 29° ARIES ES (yang/yin)
DION FEEDS ANGELIL ON THE KARMIC STAR

Dion's desire (VSP): to replay the past (Angelil's Nodes)

Dion's desire (VSP): for soul union, spiritual companionship, fulfillment of dreams
(Angelil's Neptune)

Angelil's desire (VSP): for self-awareness, leadership, light, fame, procreation, self-expression
(Dion's Sun)

Angelil's desire (VSP) to be a father, a support system, to build something solid and long-lasting
(Dion's Saturn)

Angelil's desire (VSP) to know again, to replay the past (Dion's Nodes)

Angelil's desire (VSP) for nurturing, for comfort, food, mothering and children (Dion's Moon)

Angelil's desire (VSP) for action, strength, courage, sexual union, victory (Dion's Mars)

275

Virgo Creative Star Relationships

Like the feet of Virgo, the hands of Virgo are also divided into separate eras. The early generation is composed of helping hands in the signs of Cancer and Sagittarius, while the more recently born Virgo Stars are helped and inspired by both the Gemini and Scorpio Venus Star Points. In this chapter, we will examine the signs that Virgo inspires: Cancer and Gemini. For relationships between the Sagittarius and Scorpio Stars with Virgo, see Chapters 19 and 23.

Virgo Star-Cancer Star Relationships

The pairing of Virgo and Cancer on the Venus Star occurred from 1875 to 1961, a period of eighty-six years, by far one of the longer, more enduring relationships on the Venus Creative Star. From an astrological point of view, Virgo and Cancer are signs that are quite well matched—both are yin and one is earth, the other water, a compatible mix. Although these two stars are linked on the Creative Star and they have such a long lasting link, there is a compelling attraction that is characteristic of the Karmic Star mates. With an almost sacred view of marriage and family, the Cancer VSP attracts partners that are looking to move into their comfortable and cozy nest. Both signs are naturally geared toward an abnormal interest in food: growing it, preparing it, analyzing its nutritional content, and, of course enjoying the consumption.

It is the Virgo VSP who is here to assist the Cancer VSP, and can do this in a rational and level-headed manner. Often the Virgo VSP assists the Cancer VSP in healing its family wounds or helping them develop healthy disciplines for body or mind practices. The Virgo VSP approaches solutions to problems with logic and rational thought rather than emotion. In this manner, the Virgo VSP can help the over-stimulated and moody Cancer VSP remain calm, reassured, and steady in a crisis. Challenges to the long-term success of these star mates are the Virgo VSP's overly analytical and sometimes critical nature to the Cancer VSP's extreme sensitivity about being analyzed. Another challenge is that the Virgo VSP is drawn by its need to "serve" through the community or world work. The Cancer VSP wants more personal and family time. The Cancer VSP appreciates the Virgo VSP's finely tuned analytical skills when it comes to perfecting a product or service, rather than when it is applied to the person they are involved with. Cancer VSP people receive skills from Virgo VSP individuals that can help them become more competitive in their work environment. In turn, Virgo VSP people receive from Cancer VSPs the emotionally secure component in the comfort of a home and family that the Virgo VSP seeks. Some examples from this pairing are:

Woody Allen	Virgo MS	Mia Farrow	Cancer ES
Burt Bacharach	Virgo MS	Dionne Warwick	Cancer MS
Dorothy Bridges	Virgo ES	Lloyd Bridges	Cancer ES
Al Gore	Virgo ES	Tipper Gore	Cancer MS
James Ivory	Virgo MS	Ishmael Merchant	Cancer ES
Edward Kennedy	Virgo ES	Joan Kennedy	Cancer ES
Patricia Nixon	Virgo MS	Richard Nixon	Cancer ES
Rhea Perlman	Virgo ES	Danny DeVito	Cancer ES
John Ramsey	Virgo MS	Patsy Ramsey	Cancer MS
Debbie Reynolds	Virgo ES	Eddie Fisher	Cancer ES
Dick Smothers	Virgo ES	Tom Smothers	Cancer ES
Harry Truman	Virgo ES	Bess Truman	Cancer MS
Andrew Lloyd Weber	Virgo ES	Tim Rice	Cancer ES

The comedy of the Smothers Brothers exemplified the high sensitivity of Tom's Cancer Star: "Mom always liked you best," to Dick's Virgo Star straight-man role.

Virgo Star-Gemini Star Relationships

The pairing of the Virgo Star with the Gemini Star occurred for a much briefer period (twenty years) from 1964 to 1984. These two Venus Star signs are united by the planet Mercury as their primary ruler, giving both the Virgo and Gemini VSPs born in these decades the ability to prove what talent Mercury possesses when hosting two star signs. It is this period of history that is credited with the development of both the personal computer and the Internet. This talent is exemplified by the relationship of Bill and Melinda Gates in which mutability, adaptability, and high-speed productivity are reigning qualities. It is Bill, a Virgo ES, who helps and inspires Melinda, a Gemini MS. His Virgo Star skill at developing a vast computer language and network and her Gemini Star talent as a personable public relations and communications agent make a formidable pair. The angle of their Stars falls at the 72° (quintile) relationship, indicating an abundant flow of creative energy. Furthermore, Uranus, a planet that has associations with technology and the information age, appears in the Venus VSP pattern of this couple. Placed at 9° Virgo, Melinda's Uranus sits alongside of Bill's VSP at 8° Virgo.

This pair is linked on the Creative Star of Venus and they are united by the rulership of Mercury and the quality of mutability. With all this common ground, there is much potential for partnership. However, the two elements occupy completely different domains, with Virgo's strong focus on the material realm and the body while Gemini is clearly in the air. Of course, this forces Virgo, the more naturally grounded one, to provide even more grounding for the Gemini Star. This steadiness helps Gemini, whose nature is light and breezy, charming and playful, focus its numerous ideas in something tangible and meaningful. The Virgo Star can also be the more serious of the two, while the Gemini Star can offer needed comic relief in a sometimes constrained atmosphere. Although the Virgo Star loves and needs their work, they may feel taken advantage of or perceive that they are carrying the bulk of the load while all the Gemini Star wants to do is play. This is especially true in the pairings of an older Virgo Star with a younger Gemini Star, as exists in many parent/child connections. Celebrity pairings of these signs are:

Prince Edward	Virgo ES	**Countess Sophie**	Gemini MS
Jennifer Garner	Virgo ES	**Ben Affleck**	Gemini MS
Bill Gates	Virgo ES	**Melinda Gates**	Gemini MS
Jada Pinkett Smith	Virgo ES	**Will Smith**	Gemini ES
Brad Pitt	Virgo ES	**Jennifer Anniston**	Gemini ES
Julia Roberts	Virgo MS	**Danny Moder**	Gemini ES

Virgo Twin Star Relationships

Many of the celebrity and private examples of this combination acknowledged that their relationship was based on a work-related component, as well as a feeling of some similar quality or interest they chose to channel their life's energy into. This was certainly the case of Virgo Twin Stars Ike and Tina Turner. The bonding adhesive that brought them together to begin with was both of their Neptunes (planet of music and of dreams) residing in Virgo alongside of their Venus Stars.

When Virgo Star relationships fail to achieve their intended fulfillment, they may find that developing tolerance, understanding, and forgiveness for their own imperfections, as well as their mate's, plays a major role. Celebrities of the Twin Stars of Virgo include:

Prince Andrew	Virgo MS	**Sarah Ferguson**	Virgo MS
Joseph Campbell	Virgo MS	**George Lucas**	Virgo MS
Hillary Clinton	Virgo ES	**Chelsea Clinton**	Virgo ES
Courtney Cox	Virgo ES	**David Arquette**	Virgo ES
Francis Crick	Virgo ES	**James D. Watson**	Virgo MS

Virgo Venus Star Relationships

Wynona Judd	**Virgo ES**	**Ashley Judd**	**Virgo MS**
Georgia O'Keeffe	**Virgo MS**	**Alfred Stieglitz**	**Libra MS***
Burt Reynolds	**Virgo MS**	**Dinah Shore**	**Virgo ES**
Tina Turner	**Virgo ES**	**Ike Turner**	**Virgo ES**
Tiger Woods	**Virgo MS**	**Elin Nordegren**	**Virgo ES**

In cases of Twin Stars who share the same Star Point, there is not a feeding such as we have seen when the flow is from one angle of the Star to another. The Twin Stars are in relationship with one another to reinforce important concepts of their star sign's heart felt expression. Twin Stars, though very different in personality, emotional expression, and outward appearance, share something basic and fundamental in the heart center and are in relationship with one another to be reminded of that. Besides reinforcing that quality for each other, they double their effectiveness when interacting with others as a pair as marketing reps for their sign's most alluring attributes. In cases where there are Twin Stars occupying different signs, the reinforcement of the same quality diminishes greatly, but they still possess, in most cases, the two Venus Stars in a close enough proximity to one another, serving to bind the heart-mind together.

In the case of artist Georgia O'Keeffe (Virgo VSP) and photographer Alfred Stieglitz (Libra VSP) noted above, the Venus Star Points are closely aligned with one another by a talent and passion for artistic excellence. But the signs in which they are placed give each a unique expression. Stieglitz' Libra Star allowed him to shine in the public eye, hosting and sponsoring many artists in his American Gallery in New York in an era when European (most notably French) artists were stealing the scene. His ability for public relations and social media (of the time) profited both artists. O'Keeffe, on the other hand, being the Virgo VSP, notably chose her workspace environment over the relationship dynamic, trading the multi-relational, bustling marketplace of New York City and a life at her husband's side, for the mystical qualities of isolated northern New Mexico for her canvas.

* born on the same star point, with just a few degrees of separation, but different signs

AQUARIUS VENUS STAR RELATIONSHIPS

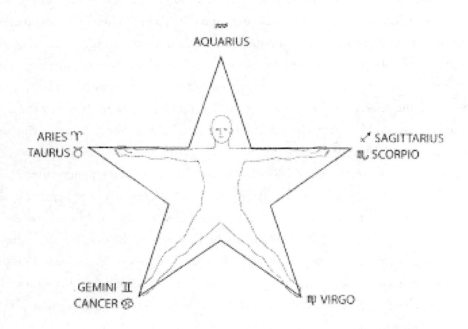

From the star human above, we observe that when the Aquarius Star is the head, it interacts with many different star signs through the course of its life. They are:

Feet of Aquarius: Gemini & Cancer; Virgo
Hands of Aquarius: Aries & Taurus; Scorpio & Sagittarius

Since only five signs are active on the Venus Star at any given time period, we can break these different star sign relationships into time periods for the course of the Aquarius Star, as follows:

Figure 22.1: Interactions in the lifetime of the Aquarius Star

FEET on the Karmic Star:

Aquarius-Cancer:	1890-1962	72 years
Aquarius-Gemini:	1964-1982	18 years
Aquarius-Virgo:	1890-1983	93 years LIFE MATES

HANDS on the Creative Star:

Aquarius-Taurus:	1890-1934	44 years
Aquarius-Aries:	1929-1982	53 years
Aquarius-Sagittarius:	1890 to 1923	33 years
Aquarius-Scorpio:	1926 to 1982	56 years

Aquarius Karmic Star Relationships

Aquarius Star/Virgo Star Relationships

For most of the life of the Aquarius VSP, it feeds the Virgo Star as life mates in a ninety-three-year Venus Star relationship. Among the baby boomer generation, two of the five points of the Venus Star are Virgo and Aquarius. As is always the case with the Venus Star, where the feeding occurs in a clockwise direction around the wheel, it is Aquarius who feeds Virgo. As noted in the history section of both stars, theirs was an era that catapulted medicine, science, and technology to iconic status. The individuals born of these two stars will most likely find at least one of these endeavors a life-long fascination, glue that serves the purpose of binding the two stars together in an intellectually satisfying union.

The Aquarius VSP works in harmony with the Virgo VSP, but as its parent, can also control it. Aquarius VSP people are highly charismatic, easily attracting a crowd of envious onlookers, but they can be spacey and sometimes adrift in the masses. So, even though the Aquarius VSP is in the parental role, the Virgo Star acts as the organizer and quality control department. They keep Aquarius on track, reminding them of life's responsibilities and commitments, as well as of its vast playing field of pleasures. Celebrity examples of this type of relationship include:

Gracie Allen	Aquarius MS	George Burns	Virgo MS
Tammy Fae Bakker	Aquarius MS	Jim Bakker	Virgo ES
George W. Bush	Aquarius ES	George H.W. Bush	Virgo ES
Bill Clinton	Aquarius ES	Al Gore	Virgo ES
Bill Clinton	Aquarius ES	Hillary Rodham Clinton	Virgo ES
Sean Connery	Aquarius ES	Ian Fleming	Virgo ES
Sandra Dee	Aquarius MS	Bobby Darin	Virgo MS
Roger Ebert	Aquarius MS	Richard Roeper	Virgo MS
Edward VIII	Aquarius MS	Wallis Simpson	Virgo MS
Harrison Ford	Aquarius MS	George Lucas	Virgo MS
Gloria Hatrick	Aquarius MS	James Stewart	Virgo ES
Michael Jackson	Aquarius MS	Lisa Marie Presley	Virgo MS
Victoria Kennedy	Aquarius ES	Edward F. Kennedy	Virgo ES
Stan Laurel	Aquarius ES	Oliver Hardy	Virgo ES
Lotte Lenya	Aquarius ES	Kurt Weill	Virgo ES
Federico G. Lorca	Aquarius ES	Salvadore Dali	Virgo MS

Audrey Meadows	Aquarius ES	Jackie Gleason	Virgo ES
Marilyn Monroe	Aquarius ES	Arthur Miller	Virgo ES
Michelle Pfeiffer	Aquarius MS	David Kelley	Virgo ES
Ryan Phillippe	Aquarius MS	Reese Witherspoon	Virgo MS
Kelly Ripa	Aquarius ES	Regis Philbin	Virgo ES
Donald Trump	Aquarius ES	Marla Maples	Virgo ES

An example of such partnership is the relationship between Aquarius Evening Star Bill Clinton and Virgo Morning Star Hillary Rodham Clinton, who withstood penetrating media scrutiny of them when he was president and when she was a candidate for the presidency. In view of this intense media publicity and the troublesome events that have plagued their marriage, the two are united on the Venus Karmic Star, with Hillary, a Virgo ES fed by Bill, an Aquarius ES.

Aquarius Star/Cancer Star Relationships

See the Cancer Star Relationship, Chapter 20.

Aquarius Star/Gemini Star Relationships

(See the Gemini Star Relationship, Chapter 25.

Aquarius Creative Star Relationships

Aquarius Star/Sagittarius Star Relationships

This first generation of "helping hands" that is inspired by the Aquarius Star is the Sagittarius Star. Located two signs apart from each other on the astrological wheel, they form a complementary relationship, the 60° or sextile aspect. In their Venus Star relationship, the distance between them averages 78°. Moving clockwise around the wheel, as the Venus Star does, it is the Aquarius Star that helps or inspires the Sagittarius Star. Some celebrity examples of such relationships are:

Natalie Cole	Aquarius MS	Nat "King" Cole	Sagittarius ES
Henry Luce	Aquarius ES	Clair Booth Luce	Sagittarius ES
Richard Rogers	Aquarius MS	Oscar Hammerstein	Sagittarius ES

Aquarius Star/Scorpio Star Relationships

When the Sagittarius Star phased out, it was replaced by the Scorpio Star as the helping hand of Aquarius. Their Star relationship ran from 1926 to 1982, and comprised two points on the Star that encompass the baby boomer generation. Though the two signs form a tense 90° aspect, the square, their Venus Star relationship, approximates 78°-80°, loosening up the tension of the square somewhat. In any case, these two signs constitute a highly charismatic pair who are compelled to be together by forces stronger than their own rational judgments that might say otherwise. Because both signs are fixed, these individuals are prone to having their way and resist yielding to the point of view of others. Aquarius VSP individuals embody the element of air, an extroverted and publicity-oriented energy, while Scorpio VSP people reside in the element of water, making them introverted and better suited to intimate, one-to-one encounters. Aquarius is the crowd pleaser, the role model, the "people who need people" people, as so well sung by Aquarius Star Barbra Streisand. They help to inspire these qualities in the Scorpio Star, with whom they have a highly creative and stimulating relationship. But though the Scorpio VSP can itself be charismatic and alluring, they tend to be more private and even secretive. The Scorpio Star, forever focused inward, can and does help the Aquarius Star, forever looking outward, achieve depth, power, and the ability to find answers inside their own eternal wellspring of inner truth. Examples of celebrity pairings in this group include:

Victoria Beckham	Aquarius MS	David Beckham	Scorpio ES
Ingmar Bergman	Aquarius MS	Liv Ullman	Scorpio MS
George W. Bush	Aquarius ES	Karl Rove	Scorpio ES
Cher	Aquarius ES	Sonny Bono	Scorpio ES
Tom Cruise	Aquarius ES	Nicole Kidman	Scorpio ES
Tom Cruise	Aquarius ES	Katie Holmes	Scorpio MS
Kirsten Dunst	Aquarius MS	Tobey Maguire	Scorpio ES
Harrison Ford	Aquarius MS	Steven Spielberg	Scorpio MS
David Furnish	Aquarius ES	Elton John	Scorpio MS
Ashton Kutcher	Aquarius ES	Demi Moore	Scorpio MS
Tommy Lee	Aquarius ES	Pamela Anderson	Scorpio ES
William H. Macy	Aquarius MS	Felicity Huffman	Scorpio MS
Kelly Ripa	Aquarius ES	Mark Consuelos	Scorpio MS
Bernie Taupin	Aquarius MS	Elton John	Scorpio MS
Paulette Washington	Aquarius MS	Denzel Washington	Scorpio MS
Martha Washington	Aquarius MS	George Washington	Scorpio ES
Oprah Winfrey	Aquarius ES	Stedman Graham	Scorpio ES
Oprah Winfrey	Aquarius ES	Gayle King	Scorpio MS

The Aquarius-Scorpio Star mate relationship lasted for a period of 56 years, from 1926 to 1982 and included the most populous baby-boomer group. Judging from the list above, there is a strong dynamic at work between these two VSPs. The attraction in this pair combines the Aquarius VSP who possesses an intensely focused mind bursting with ideas helping, inspiring and creatively feeding the Scorpio VSP, who possesses strong feelings and passions. The Scorpio VSP seeks strong and powerful people in their lives to manifest magical results. In the case of these two fixed signs, the combined increase in fortune can be formidable.

Of interest here is the reigning queen of the airwaves, Aquarius Evening Star Oprah Winfrey, holder of the triple crown of the Venus Star (Sun, Venus and VSP) in one sign. Aquarius pours its information network to the masses in an effortless way, and in the present age of the Gemini VSP where the public is hungry to learn all that they can and consume as much from media as possible, her Star shines brightly. Her two closest personal relationships, Stedman Graham and Gayle King are both Scorpio VSPs, whom she creatively inspires and helps. It is curious, and one might marvel, that the goddess of the air who feeds millions of hungry minds every day still has the capacity to feed (creatively) her two closest personal relationships. Who feeds her? And yet, that is the role of a queen or a goddess – someone whose capacity is so unlimited that she never wearies of her task. Queen Elizabeth and Mother Teresa are also Aquarius VSPs, and similarly made themselves a vessel of pure service to their people.

Tom Cruise, an Aquarius Evening Star, has had two Scorpio Star mates: Katie Holmes, a Morning Star, and Nicole Kidman, an Evening Star. His Neptune in Scorpio squares his own Venus Star, attesting to his huge success in film. That same Neptune conjuncts the Venus Star of his two partners, adding film, drama, idealism, romanticism, and longing to the creative lives they lead. Of course, reality is a different story.

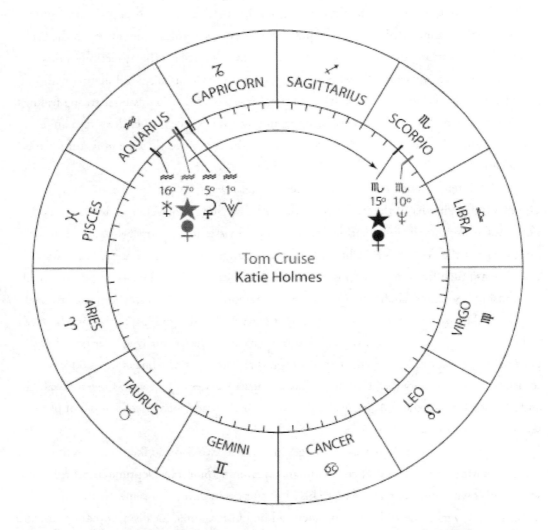

Figure 22.2: THE TOM CRUISE and KATIE HOLMES RELATIONSHIP STAR CHART
CRUISE: 7° AQUARIUS ES (yang/yin)
HOLMES: 10° SCORPIO MS (yin/yang)
CRUISE'S STAR INSPIRES/HELPS HOLMES'S STAR
Holmes's desire (VSP) for: soul & spiritual union, living a dream (Cruise's Neptune)
Cruise's desire (VSP) for: long-term mating (Holmes's Juno)
Cruise's desire (VSP) for home, food, nourishment, children (Holmes's Ceres)
Cruise's desire (VSP) for inner focus, strength, and devotion (Holmes's Vesta)

Aquarius Star/Taurus Star Relationships

See the Taurus Relationship Star, Chapter 18.

Aquarius Star/Aries Star Relationships

See the Aries Relationship Star, Chapter 24.

Aquarius Twin Star Relationships

Research confirmed that Aquarius VSP individuals seem to attract their own kind—their Twin Star. This makes sense on many levels, as Aquarius people desire first to be a friend and then to mate with the person of their dreams. They are social and, as a result, often attract a cult following without even trying. Because they circulate in many ways—from celebrity appearances and community networking to social and political activism—they are served best by partners who keep the home fires burning, not a common attribute of the Aquarius Star. This is not to say that they are incapable of making a nice home together. It's more that they are so busily engaged with careers and outside activities, home and family are the longed-for remedy to an outwardly focused energy that concerns the bigger picture that the Aquarius Star embodies.

Two Aquarius VSP individuals have the best complementary relationship when one partner is a Morning Star and the other is an Evening Star. Aquarius Twin Stars Tim Robbins, a Morning Star, and mate Susan Sarandon, an Evening Star, are twins in more ways than this as they both share the sun sign of Libra. Some celebrity pairs of this type are:

Alec Baldwin	**Aquarius MS**	**Tina Fey**	**Aquarius ES**
Karen Carpenter	**Aquarius MS**	**Richard Carpenter**	**Aquarius ES**
Cindy Crawford	**Aquarius MS**	**Rande Gerber**	**Aquarius ES**
Judy Garland	**Aquarius ES**	**Liza Minelli**	**Aquarius ES**
Ethan Hawke	**Aquarius ES**	**Uma Thurman**	**Aquarius ES**
Marilyn Monroe	**Aquarius MS**	**Joe DiMaggio**	**Aquarius ES**
Jennifer Nettles	**Aquarius MS**	**Kristian Bush**	**Aquarius ES**
Carl Reiner	**Aquarius ES**	**Sid Caesar**	**Aquarius ES**
Tim Robbins	**Aquarius MS**	**Susan Sarandon**	**Aquarius ES**
John Travolta	**Aquarius ES**	**Kelly Preston**	**Aquarius ES**
Donald Trump	**Aquarius ES**	**Melania Trump**	**Aquarius ES**
Natalie Wood	**Aquarius ES**	**Robert Wagner**	**Aquarius ES**

SCORPIO VENUS STAR RELATIONSHIPS

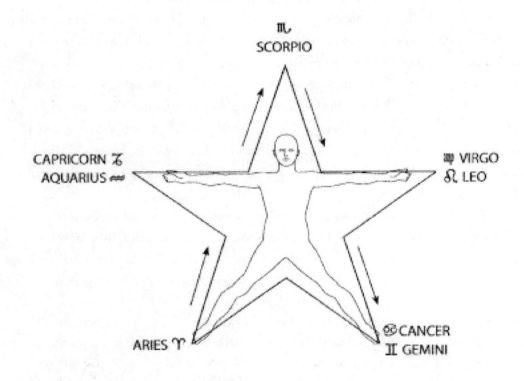

As shown above, the signs that Scorpio interacts with on the star human during the course of the Scorpio Star's lifetime are:

    Feet of Scorpio: Aries; Cancer & Gemini
    Hands of Scorpio: Aquarius & Capricorn; Virgo & Leo

Since only five signs are active on the Venus Star at any given time period, we can break these periods of time for Scorpio's mates into the following:

Figure 23.1: Interactions in the lifetime of the Scorpio Star

FEET OF SCORPIO:

Scorpio-Aries:	1929 to 2027	98 years	LIFE MATES
Scorpio-Cancer:	1926 to 1961	35 years	
Scorpio-Gemini:	1962 to 2027	65 years	

HANDS OF SCORPIO:

Scorpio-Aquarius:	1926 to 1982	56 years
Scorpio-Capricorn:	1986 to 2027	41 years
Scorpio-Virgo:	1926 to 1984	58 years
Scorpio-Leo:	1987 to 2027	40 years

Scorpio Karmic Star Relationships

The star point that Scorpio feeds is shared by two signs: first, Cancer, from 1926 to 1960, and then Gemini, from 1962 to 2027. The Scorpio Star Point is fed by Aries for its lifetime duration, which is reviewed in Chapter 24.

Scorpio Star/Cancer Star Relationships

The first third of the Venus Star's Scorpio transit linked it to the Cancer Star Point, a sign of elemental compatibility (water). In this relationship pairing, there is the promise of both emotional and physical security, desired by both signs. Environments where feelings can be expressed openly, honestly, and deeply are where these two stars shine with one another. Scorpio VSPs are likely to experience painful emotional separations from loved ones during the course of their life. They are also very private about their personal feelings, and can find solace and comfort in the motherly Cancer Star individual who will listen attentively to their confessions. In turn, the Cancer Star, who can usually relate to their own emotionally charged family and/or relationship past, is fed by the Scorpio Star, especially in the area of letting past wounds go and moving on. Though Scorpio feeds Cancer, they both feed each other, joined together on the Venus Star in a 144° biquintile providing a special talent and harmony in living and working together.

An enlightening example of the Cancer VSP-Scorpio VSP pairing is the relationship between Prince Charles and Camilla Parker Bowles. Linked together on the Venus Star in two signs that are elementally compatible and whose signs feed one another, their bond never weakened, enduring through 35 years of separation and marriage to other people. Each of their Venus Stars falls in the other's Sun sign, as can be seen in the following chart.

Scorpio Venus Star Relationships

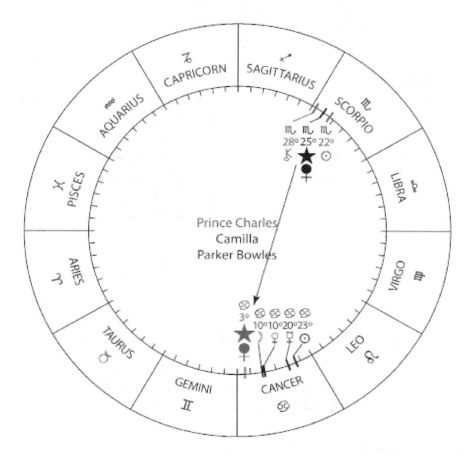

Figure 23.2: THE PRINCE CHARLES and CAMILLA PARKER BOWLES
RELATIONSHIP STAR CHART

PRINCE CHARLES: 3° CANCER MS (YIN/YANG)

PARKER BOWLES: 25° SCORPIO MS (YIN/YANG)

PARKER BOWLES FEEDS PRINCE CHARLES ON THE KARMIC STAR

Prince Charles' desire (VSP) for: nurturing, comfort, food, mothering, children
(Parker Bowles's Moon)

Prince Charles' desire (VSP) for love, romance, to create art and beauty, to live in beautiful
surroundings, for sensual pleasures (Parker Bowles's Venus)

Prince Charles' desire (VSP) for communication, education, travel, playfulness
(Parker Bowles's Mercury)

Charles' desire (VSP) for self-awareness, leadership, light, fame, procreation, self-expression
(Parker Bowles's Sun)

Parker Bowles's desire (VSP) for self-awareness, leadership, light, fame, procreation,
self-expression (Prince Charles' Sun)

Parker Bowles's desire (VSP) for healing, health awareness, caring (Prince Charles' Chiron)

Celebrity examples of this combination include the following:

Tom Arnold	Scorpio ES	Roseanne Barr	Cancer ES
Camilla P Bowles	Scorpio MS	Prince Charles	Cancer MS
Shakira Caine	Scorpio MS	Michael Caine	Cancer MS
Rosalind Carter	Scorpio ES	Jimmy Carter	Cancer MS
George Harrison	Scorpio ES	Eric Clapton	Cancer ES
George Harrison	Scorpio ES	Maharishi Mahesh Yogi	Cancer MS
Coretta Scott King	Scorpio ES	Martin L. King Jr.	Cancer ES
Annie Lennox	Scorpio MS	David A. Stewart	Cancer ES
Ram Das	Scorpio MS	Timothy Leary	Cancer ES

Scorpio Star/Gemini Star Relationships

The second group of Scorpio VSP individuals, born in the era when the Scorpio Star Point feeds the Gemini Star Point (1962 to 2027), comprises a much longer link of sixty-five years. This generation is a different breed than their predecessor Scorpio VSPs, possessing very different motivating principles and objectives than the earlier generation of Scorpio Stars, discussed above. These Scorpio VSPs are neither seeking a mama nor healer to partner with as much as they are concerned with their peer group and siblings. They seek to perfect their ability to express their youthful angst and rebellion. This group is more reluctant to "nest" as in the Scorpio/Cancer connection. They have much more of a wanderlust, moving from place to place, relationship to relationship, or job to job to accumulate as much life experience as possible. Part of this may be due to not wanting to conform to the status quo, telling it like it is, and the desire to remain eternally youthful. It was this period of stars that gave birth to the musical art form known as rap (see Gemini Star, Chapter 11), and these two star mates would love nothing more than to find a mate with whom they can do just that. The Scorpio VSP individuals give depth, focus, strength, and intensity to their Gemini VSP partners, who tend to be involved in numerous projects and activities simultaneously. Moreover, while Scorpio VSP individuals tend to keep things to themselves, their Gemini VSP mates will help them open up and express what's yearning to be free. Celebrity couples belonging to this group include:

Kurt Cobain	Scorpio ES	Courtney Love	Gemini MS
Whitney Houston	Scorpio MS	Bobby Brown	Gemini ES
Heath Ledger	Scorpio MS	Michelle Williams	Gemini MS
Jason Seborn	Scorpio MS	Angie Harmon	Gemini MS

Scorpio Star-Aries Star Relationships

See the Aries Relationship Star, Chapter 24.

Scorpio Creative Star Relationships

Scorpio Star-Virgo Star Relationships

The connection of these two signs on the Venus Star occurred for fifty-eight years, comprising approximately two-thirds of Venus' transit through Scorpio. The Scorpio and Virgo Star Points comprise two-thirds of the baby boomer generation as well. Partners in this type of relationship are generally well suited to one another, as it pairs a water sign with an earth sign. They sit two signs away from each other on the astrological wheel, giving them the opportunities of the sextile (60°) but actually forming an aspect that on average forms the talented quintile (72°) during their long engagement. These two star points can be equally comfortable in a living or a working relationship, and if they are in the same field, all the better for both. From the celebrity groupings below, there is ample evidence of success in creative collaboration on this Creative Star. For instance, Rolling Stones Mick Jagger (Scorpio Star) and Keith Richards (Virgo Star) have been collaborating together for nearly fifty years and their success has surpassed nearly all, if not completely all, of their competition. Each of their Venus Stars conjuncts the other's natal Venus (a match made in heaven). It is worth mentioning that three of the other Rolling Stones, along with Jagger and Richards, comprised all five points of the Venus Star (see Chapter 30). Celebrity relationships of this type include:

Phoebe Cates	Scorpio MS	Kevin Kline	Virgo ES
Jamie Lee Curtis	Scorpio ES	Christopher Guest	Virgo ES
Mikhail Gorbachev	Scorpio MS	Raisa Gorbachev	Virgo ES
Mick Jagger	Scorpio ES	Keith Richards	Virgo MS
Angelina Jolie	Scorpio ES	Brad Pitt	Virgo ES
Nicole Kidman	Scorpio ES	Keith Urban	Virgo MS
Tim McGraw	Scorpio ES	Faith Hill	Virgo MS
Queen Noor	Scorpio ES	King Hussein	Virgo MS
John Phillips	Scorpio ES	Michelle Phillips	Virgo MS
Natasha Richardson	Scorpio MS	Liam Neeson	Virgo MS
Nicolas Sarkozy	Scorpio MS	Carla Bruni	Virgo MS
Arnold Schwarzenegger	Scorpio MS	Maria Shriver	Virgo ES
Jon Stewart	Scorpio MS	Steven Colbert	Virgo ES
Trudie Styler	Scorpio MS	Sting	Virgo MS

Scorpio Star-Leo Star Relationships

This link lasts for forty years comprising the eldest of the Scorpio Stars with the youngest of the Leo Stars. Typically, then, the Scorpio Star will seem older and much more experienced than the youthful Leo Star, no matter what their actual ages. An example of this type of relationship can be shown by the fictional characters portrayed in *Little Miss Sunshine* between grandfather played by Alan Arkin and granddaughter portrayed by Abigail Breslin (herself a Leo Star).

Relationships between individuals of these two fixed signs are often described as magnetic and highly attractive. While this may be true, two fixed signs can also pit people together who are unwilling to make the ongoing compromises that a long-term partnership needs in order to flourish, yet both signs are fixed and motivated to keep a relationship forever. In this particular Venus Star relationship, the insightful Scorpio VSP adds mystery and intrigue and sometimes deep psychological insight to the Leo VSP, a more extroverted, athletic, entertainment-oriented individual. The Scorpio VSP individual can also provide inner strength, honesty, and intensity to the Leo VSP's gleeful and outgoing charm.

Scorpio Star-Aquarius Star Relationships

See the Aquarius Relationship Star, Chapter 22.

Scorpio Star-Capricorn Star Relationships

See the Capricorn Relationship Star, Chapter 26.

Scorpio Twin Star Relationships

Though partners on the Venus Star are usually united by a deep love for one another, the Twin Star relationship of Scorpio also seems to involve two people who enjoy working collaborations, but are not involved in a live-in relationship with each other. Perhaps this is due to the intense privacy needs of the Scorpio VSP, which make collaborative work more comfortable than cohabitation. Twin Stars are sidekicks or doubles, even alter egos of one another, and many of the examples include people whose relationships exemplify that, such as Scorpio VSP entertainers Dana Carvey and Mike Myers of *Saturday Night Live* fame and actors William Shatner and Leonard Nimoy of *Star Trek* fame. One Twin Scorpio Star couple

Scorpio Venus Star Relationships

which stands out is Linda Evans and Yanni, who had a romantic relationship for many years. Their Venus Star Point pattern stands out from the others in that they were both born very close to the inception of the Scorpio VSP and thus project the pure energy of the Venus Star. Yanni, a Morning Star, and Evans, an Evening Star, possess the right combination of yin and yang for balance, but it is the thirteen combined planets and asteroids in Scorpio that may have been just too much to take. Many of their own planets conjunct the other's same planets, including the Venus Star. Their Scorpio energies are as follows:

Linda Evans:
Mars 11° Scorpio
Mercury 18° Scorpio
VSP 23° Scorpio
Sun 25° Scorpio
Venus 26° Scorpio

Yanni:
Mercury 2° Scorpio
Pallas 9° Scorpio
Saturn 13° Scorpio
MH 19° Scorpio
Sun 21° Scorpio
Venus 22° Scorpio
VSP 22° Scorpio
Ceres 27° Scorpio

Some celebrity pairs in the Scorpio Star-Scorpio Star group are:

Joe Biden	Scorpio ES	**Jill Biden**	Scorpio ES
David Bowie	Scorpio MS	**Iman**	Scorpio MS
Dana Carvey	Scorpio MS	**Mike Myers**	Scorpio MS
Francis F. Coppola	Scorpio MS	**Sofia Coppola**	Scorpio MS
Linda Evans	Scorpio MS	**Yanni**	Scorpio ES
Demi Moore	Scorpio MS	**Bruce Willis**	Scorpio MS
William Shatner	Scorpio MS	**Leonard Nimoy**	Scorpio MS
O.J. Simpson	Scorpio MS	**Nicole Brown Simpson**	Scorpio MS
Martin Scorsese	Scorpio ES	**Robert DeNiro**	Scorpio ES
Martin Scorsese	Scorpio ES	**Leonardo diCaprio**	Scorpio MS

24 ARIES VENUS STAR RELATIONSHIPS

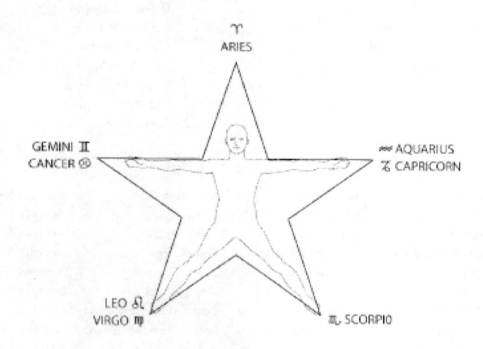

As shown on the star human above, the signs that form a relationship to the Aries Star during the course of its lifetime are:

Feet of Aries: Leo & Virgo; Scorpio
Hands of Aries: Gemini & Cancer; Capricorn & Aquarius

Since only five signs are active on the Venus Star at any one given time period, we can break the different star sign relationships into the following time periods:

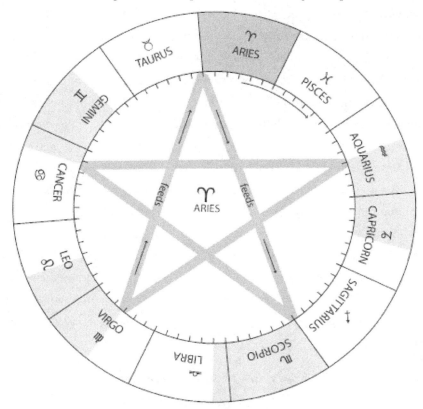

Figure 24.1: Interactions in the lifetime of the Aries Star

FEET on the Karmic Star:
    Aries-Scorpio: 1929 to 2027   98 years   LIFE MATES

    Aries-Virgo: 1927 to 1985   58 years

    Aries-Leo: 1987 to 2037   50 years

HANDS on the Creative Star:
    Aries-Cancer: 1929 to 1961   32 years

    Aries-Gemini: 1964 to 2037   73 years

    Aries-Aquarius: 1929 to 1982   53 years

    Aries-Capricorn: 1985 to 2037   52 years

Here we will consider the signs that are fed or inspired by Aries on its Karmic Star, Scorpio, and on its Creative Stars, Aquarius and Capricorn. The Aries Star, along with its mate the Scorpio Star, is one of the most populous groups of people alive. The Aries Star began in the 1920s and will terminate in the 2030s.

When the Aries VSP began to be activated in 1929, marriage as an institution changed dramatically. This change reflected a shift where the individual's will and desires became more important than the longevity and security of the partnership. Of course, not all Aries VSPs feel this way, but theirs is a star point involved with creating and feeding their own vision, besides feeding the Scorpio point on their life-long quest for self-empowerment and continual transformation. If they are fortunate enough to have a partner that believes in and can support their quest for selfhood, there is a greater prospect of long-term relationship success. In this regard, the Aries VSP desires independence and a career as well as marriage and family. The challenge they undertake to make themselves available for both sometimes costs them one or the other. But they are also gifted with the Venus Star's talent at having an enormous amount of strength and endurance to withstand challenging circumstances. They are not immune to explosive, child-like outbursts if they don't get their way. During the heat of battle, they can be fierce and courageous, never surrendering unless there is no other option. If the fire of relationship engagement gets too heated for too long, they tend to bolt, never looking back. But the Aries VSP is ruled by Mars, who was a lover as well as a fighter, and thus will rarely turn away from the prospects of a promising new day where love and romance prevail.

Aries Karmic Star Relationships

Aries Star-Sagittarius Star Relationships

The Sagittarius Star actually phased out and became the star of Scorpio before the Aries Star began, but there are numerous relationships that paired the elder Sagittarius Star with the younger Aries Star. Some examples are:

Princess Grace	Aries MS	**Prince Rainier**	Sagittarius MS
Joan Plowright	Aries MS	**Sir Laurence Olivier**	Sagittarius MS

Here, the element of fire is represented doubly, creating passion and high-spirited energy. Although Sagittarius is the recipient of the Aries Star energy, it is the Sagittarius Star who is more moderately tempered and the acting elder of this relationship.

Aries Star-Scorpio Star Relationships

The life mates of Scorpio with Aries exist on the Karmic Star for the entire duration of both signs. Individuals of both these signs are survivors, having traveled long and far with considerable personal sacrifice. These two signs are energetically connected by a shared rulership of Mars. The Aries VSP, a fire sign, tends to act on impulse, guided by quick and spontaneous bursts of intuition, while the Scorpio VSP, a water sign, calculates the risk involved with opening one's heart too soon or to the wrong person. Scorpio VSP individuals help Aries people focus on feelings, allowing them to connect with their heart and soul, as well as the deep mysteries of life. The Scorpio VSP can also derive useful instruction from observing their Aries VSP partner go out on a limb and face challenges. Scorpio VSP people feel revitalized in the presence of their eternally youthful and highly charismatic Aries Star Point partner. The Scorpio Star Point can easily facilitate their Aries Star Point partner to have a look inside the deeper feelings that motivate their actions, helping them to examine the reasons behind their need to reach the goal, rather than just focus on the goal.

The defining astrological aspect between the Aries and Scorpio Star Point is the quincunx (150°), an aspect that suggests necessary compromise or separation. In this relationship, the Scorpio VSP is experiencing the need to let go of control and to quell their basic instinct, which is to possess their partner, as an Aries Star Point does not like being possessed and, if acting from their place of power, will not be possessed. The Aries VSP equally needs to make adjustments in their personal behavior, especially concerning being the commander-in-chief in relationships when coupled with the Scorpio VSP.

Some celebrity examples of this pairing are:

Kate Capshaw	Aries MS	**Steven Spielberg**	Scorpio MS
Princess Diana	Aries MS	**Dodi Al-Fayed**	Scorpio MS
Jane Fonda	Aries MS	**Ted Turner**	Scorpio MS
Maggie Gyllenhaal	Aries MS	**Peter Sarsgaard**	Scorpio MS
Goldie Hawn	Aries MS	**Kurt Russell**	Scorpio ES
Nancy Kerrigan	Aries MS	**Tonya Harding**	Scorpio MS
Heidi Klum	Aries ES	**Seal**	Scorpio MS
Anna Kournikova	Aries ES	**Enrique Iglesias**	Scorpio ES
Frida Lingstad	Aries MS	**Benny Andersson**	Scorpio MS
Louis XVI of France	Aries ES	**Marie Antoinette**	Scorpio ES
John McVie	Aries MS	**Christine McVie**	Scorpio ES
Barack Obama	Aries MS	**Joe Biden**	Scorpio ES
Ryan O'Neal	Aries ES	**Farrah Fawcett**	Scorpio MS
Paul Shaffer	Aries ES	**David Letterman**	Scorpio MS
Ben Stiller	Aries ES	**Christine Taylor**	Scorpio MS
Meryl Streep	Aries ES	**Don Gummer**	Scorpio MS

Three notable Aries VSP Morning Star women became members of royal families or family dynasties that catapulted them into the public eye where they remained a public obsession because of their charisma and unique stamp of individuality. They were Grace Kelley, Jacqueline Kennedy Onassis, and Princess Diana. In the case of Princess Diana, the Venus Star offers some interesting inside information. She was first married to Prince Charles, a Cancer Morning Star, in a relationship that indicates the Venus energy dynamic flows from Cancer to Aries. Because there was barely enough, if any, energy emitted from Cancer VSP Charles to Aries VSP Diana, the result was her withering up and potentially dying. But the Aries VSP usually does not die—they fight back or leave—and in Diana's case, she managed to do both. Eventually she was paired with Karmic Star partner Dodi Al-Fayed, a Scorpio Morning Star, in a star pattern that is much more suitable for the Aries Star Point. We will never know how that story would have unfolded, as a tragic accident killed them both in the early days of their love affair.

Another fated and fatal attraction on the Karmic Star cycle between Scorpio and Aries is that of Marie Antoinette (Scorpio Star), who as a child was betrothed to the future Louis XVI of France (Aries Star). She was forced to leave behind her family of origin, her husband, her children, and ultimately to give her own life, a sacrificial victim on the altar of the political times in which she lived. Her star at 4° Scorpio makes a conjunction to her husband's Moon in Scorpio, reflecting her desire for nurturing, comfort, safety, food, mothering, and children.

Aries Star-Virgo Star Relationships

See the Virgo Relationship Star section, Chapter 21.

Aries Star-Leo Star Relationships

See the Leo Relationship Star section, Chapter 27.

Aries Creative Star Relationships

The star point for whom the Aries Star provides creative inspiration and help is shared by two signs: Aquarius (1929 to 1982) and Capricorn (1985 to 2037). Very distinct characteristics apply in terms of how they are motivated and what types of people they desire for friends and mates depending upon which group the Aries Star belongs to.

Aries Star-Aquarius Star Relationships

Aries and Aquarius share the quality of extroversion, as well as a dazzling, self-confident and stylish mannerism, that makes others want to be like them or be with them. As a result, they are likely to attract the attention and following of others. This combination further ignites spontaneous bursts of independence and creativity and a shared passion for invention and experimentation in thought, word, and deed. Creativity and shared interests in a similar cause or profession are the glue that binds them together, and in the case of each of these signs, an independent nature that needs no direction from others can work for or against them. Additionally, these two star signs might be better off as work partners or playmates, steering away from traditional marriage and its requirements.

An example of a pairing that brought new inspiration and help to Aquarius Star Paul McCartney is his post-Beatles marriage to Linda Eastman, whose Aries Star became his helping hand. Previously Paul's star was shown in relationship to John Lennon's star (Beatles co-founder and partner), in which they were linked together on the Karmic Star of Venus. Both relationships helped feed McCartney's own genius and talent and both relationships produced beautiful harmonies for McCartney.

Celebrity examples of the creative Aries/Aquarius pairing include:

Tony Blair	Aries MS	**Cherie Booth**	Aquarius ES
Steffi Graf	Aries MS	**Andre Agassi**	Aquarius ES
Heather Locklear	Aries MS	**Tommy Lee**	Aquarius ES
Linda McCartney	Aries ES	**Paul McCartney**	Aquarius MS
Kate Middleton	Aries ES	**Prince William**	Aquarius MS
Kyra Sedgwick	Aries ES	**Kevin Bacon**	Aquarius MS
Gene Siskel	Aries MS	**Roger Ebert**	Aquarius MS
Britney Spears	Aries ES	**Kevin Federline**	Aquarius ES
Bjorn Ulvaeus	Aries MS	**Agnetha Faltskog**	Aquarius MS

Aries Star-Capricorn Star Relationships

The second generation of the Creative Star that Aries helps and inspires is the Capricorn VSP. This union may promise more stability and long-term security than Aries with the Aquarius star. In this relationship, it is the elder Aries Star that is linked to the younger Capricorn Star. Both signs are still actively being born and many partnerships are arising from this union on the Venus Star. It is the last of the Aries Stars being born in the early twenty-first century, and it is this condition of eldership in the star that imbues them with the characteristic of appointing themselves as the elder, even at a very early age. This works well with a Capricorn VSP, a sign whose nature it is to act older than its years. This is a combination well suited to the creative collaboration of business engagement, especially in fields concerning innovative energy sources, new building models, and architectural models that meet the demands of the new millennium. The Aries VSP can help the Capricorn VSP discover and nurture the inner child. One example of this pairing is writer Stephanie Meyers (Aries ES) with actor Kristen Stewart (Capricorn MS).

Aries Twin Star Relationships

There is no shortage of heat in a relationship containing two Aries Stars. Though greatly magnetized to each other by the passion of the Venus Star Points being located so close together, they are a very different breed, possessing different natures and aspirations. They are just as likely to play vigorously with one another as they are to rage at each other. Because the Twin Star points emanate Venus/Sun energy from the same sign and in such a close proximity to one another, they either look like two stars united in oneness or two stars blocking out the other's light to receive recognition for their own personal achievements and points of view. As indicated by the asterisks below, Twin Venus Stars also occur between Aries and Taurus for the period when the star was changing signs (1920s and 1930s).

Some celebrity pairs in this group are:

Barbara Bush	Aries ES	Jenna Bush	Aries ES
William Clark	Aries ES	Merriwether Lewis	Aries MS
John Edwards	Aries MS	Elizabeth Edwards	Aries ES
Maurice Gibb	Aries ES	Robin Gibb	Aries ES
Caroline Kennedy	Aries ES	Jacqueline Kennedy	Aries MS
Caroline Kennedy	Aries ES	John F. Kennedy	Taurus ES*
Jacqueline Kennedy	Aries MS	John F. Kennedy	Taurus ES*
Robert F. Kennedy Jr	Aries MS	Robert F. Kennedy	Taurus ES*
Beyonce Knowles	Aries ES	Jay-Z	Aries MS
Jacqueline Onassis	Aries ES	Aristotle Onassis	Taurus MS*
J.K. Rowling	Aries ES	Daniel Radcliffe	Aries ES
Paul Simon	Aries ES	Art Garfunkel	Aries ES
Bruce Springsteen	Aries ES	Patti Scialfa	Aries MS

The world of magic and wizardry is a theme of Scorpio, the sign that is fed by the Aries Star. When one star feeds the next, the star receiving the energy becomes the foundational leg. In this case, the brain child is the head (Aries VSP) that finds its support in Scorpio, and it is somewhat fitting that a pair of Aries Stars brought the Harry Potter kingdom to life. Joanne (J.K.) Rowling, the master-mind who penned the wildly successful series was born in July 1965, a Leo Sun and an Aries Evening Star, both fire signs. Rowling's personal story, like many Aries VSPs, is a transformational rags to riches saga that in itself could make for a good read and a similarly enjoyable film.

An example of an Aries Twin Star relationship that reflects great artistic and financial success is that of author J. K. Rowling and actor Daniel Radcliffe. These two Aries Stars pioneered a film dynasty with the Harry Potter series that has greatly influenced an entire generation. It also lends support to how Aries itself feeds Scorpio, in this case the world of mystery and the skillful mastery over magic. If Radcliffe was selected to play Rowling's alter ego, as some film critics have suggested, he was well chosen. But more apparent from the chart connections is a mother-son yearning, as their VSPs intersect with his Moon and Pallas (mother-son) and her Ceres (mother). With an age difference of twenty-four years (three complete Venus Star periods of eight years each), they are well matched twin Aries Evening Stars who also share the same sun sign, Leo.

The other Karmic Star, the one that feeds Aries is Virgo. Rowling's line-up in that sign is formidable, with the personal planets Moon, Mercury and Venus flanking the rare, paradigm shifting Uranus/Pluto conjunction (see accompanying chart, Figure 24.2). Uranus is credited with giving an individual the capacity for extraordinary vision and insight, a Promethean-like cauldron of creative fire. Paired with Rowling's afore-mentioned personal planets in that sign, this creative fire was unleashed to the world in the form of the Harry Potter series and literally spread like a raging bonfire.

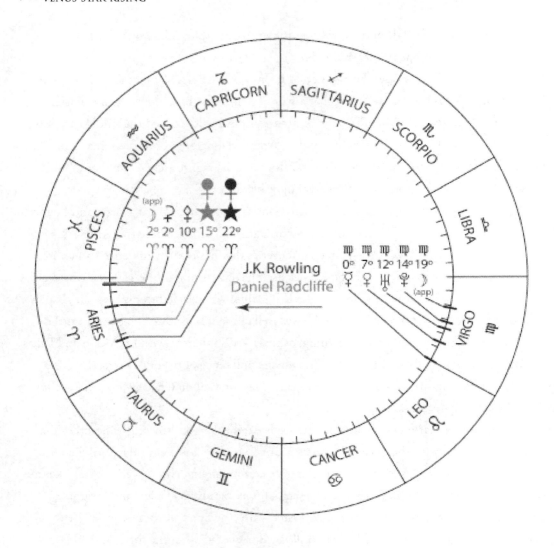

Figure 24.2: THE J. K. ROWLING and DANIEL RADCLIFFE RELATIONSHIP STAR CHART
ROWLING'S VSP: 22° ARIES ES (yang/yin)
RADCLIFFE'S VSP: 15° ARIES ES (yang/yin)
REFLECTING TWINS ON THE ARIES STAR
Rowling's desire for: skills and wisdom (Radcliffe's Pallas)
Rowling's desire for: children, nurturing, comfort, food (Radcliffe's Moon)
Radcliffe's desire (VSP) for: home, food, nurturing, comfort (Rowling's Ceres)

The feeding of one sign to the next extends beyond one person feeding another. An individual is also able to feed oneself. This is aptly demonstrated here, whereby Rowling's abundance of Virgo planets feeds her own Aries Star as well as Radcliffe's Aries Star.

Reaching back to the previous Aries Star period (1678–1786), we encounter two Aries Stars who literally embodied the characteristic of Aries' pioneering spirit and risky, adventurous undertakings in Merriweather Lewis and William Clark of the Lewis & Clark Expedition. Thomas Jefferson had no hesitation in recommending Lewis for the task of exploring the new territories of the Louisiana Purchase that would help map what would ultimately become the expanded boundaries of the United States. Between 1803 and 1805 the journey was undertaken with Lewis at the helm. Jefferson described Lewis as a man of "courage undaunted" and one who possessed firmness, perseverance of purpose, and one who could not easily be diverted from the task he would be undertaking. Double fire, like Rowling cited above, Lewis was a Leo Sun and Aries VSP. His partner and co-leader of the Expedition was Twin Star William Clark, also a Leo Sun and Aries VSP. In this case, their Twin Stars were harmonizing: Lewis was the Morning Star and Clark was the Evening Star.

25 Gemini venus star relationships

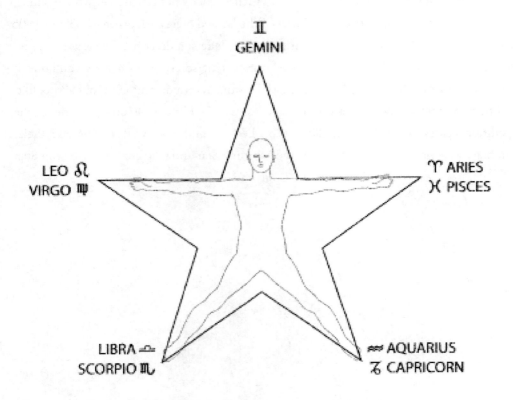

The signs that form a relationship to the Gemini Star during the course of its lifetime, as shown on the star higure above, are:

    Feet of Gemini: Libra & Scorpio; Aquarius & Capricorn
    Hands of Gemini: Leo & Virgo; Aries & Pisces

Since only five signs are active on the Venus Star at any given time period, we can break these relationships into the following increments of time:

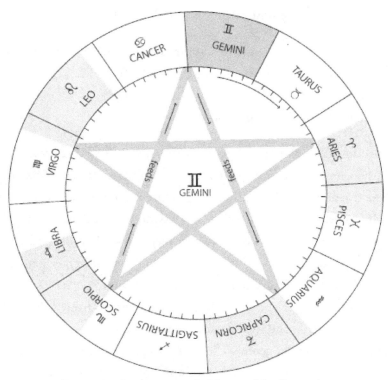

Figure 25.1: Interactions in the lifetime of the Gemini Star

FEET on the Karmic Star:

Gemini-Scorpio:	1962 to 2027	65 years
Gemini-Libra:	2022 to 2073	51 years
Gemini-Aquarius:	1964 to 1982	18 years
Gemini-Capricorn:	1984 to 2073	89 years

HANDS on the Creative Star:

Gemini-Virgo:	1964 to 1984	20 years
Gemini-Leo:	1987 to 2072	85 years
Gemini-Aries:	1964 to 2037	73 years
Gemini-Pisces:	2041 to 2073	32 years

A unique feature of Gemini on the Venus Star is that it partners with more signs than any other star. Like other VSPs that possess a life- mate, Gemini has no one life mate, but eight other star mates during the course of its life. The count increases to nine when one factors in its ability to choose its own sign as a mate. This gives Gemini the ruling status as reaching its arms and legs out to connect with more individuals, or the talents and characteristics represented by the individuals they connect with, on a grand scale.

Gemini Karmic Star Relationships

On the Karmic Star, for a brief period the Gemini VSP feeds Aquarius (1964-1982) and, for the greater part of its cycle, Capricorn (1984-2073).

Gemini Star-Aquarius Star Relationships

The Gemini VSP link to the Aquarius VSP lasted for two decades during what many historians document to be a very unique period of time, 1964 to 1982. This was a time when these two air signs allowed the average citizen, and not just the privileged few, to feel personally empowered to express their views with ease, receiving support from nearly an entire generation of disillusioned youth. Other very powerful astrological influences were operating during that period, but it is worth mentioning that the Venus Star Point activating these two air signs helped to amplify and give meaning to those voices.

A Gemini-Aquarius partnership thrives on the ability to freely voice their concerns, their grievances, their desires, and their dreams to one another without reservation or fear of repercussion. There is creative genius at work in this partnership and the sharing of information is a primary motive in the relationship. People in this pairing are more likely to be friends first, then mates.

Celebrity pairings belonging to this group include:

Ben Affleck	Gemini MS	**Matt Damon**	Aquarius ES
Portia de Rossi	Gemini MS	**Ellen DeGeneres**	Aquarius MS
Prince Harry	Gemini ES	**Prince William**	Aquarius MS
Sarah Jessica Parker	Gemini MS	**Matthew Broderick**	Aquarius ES
Guy Ritchie	Gemini ES	**Madonna**	Aquarius MS

An example of this pair is Gemini VSP Sarah Jessica Parker and her husband Aquarius VSP Matthew Broderick, married since 1997. Not only does her star feed his, their stars are complementary—she a Morning Star and he an Evening Star. These characteristics are seen in the following chart. Even so, long-term success for the marriage is likely to be challenging for these two people-oriented and media-oriented air signs. Broderick's Venus Star in Aquarius is surrounded by two of Parker's female goddesses—Juno, the goddess of marriage and Pallas Athena, the goddess who rejected marriage in favor of autonomy and career. With both urges equally dominant, Ms. Parker must juggle her very busy career with her husband's very busy career and make time for the relationship.

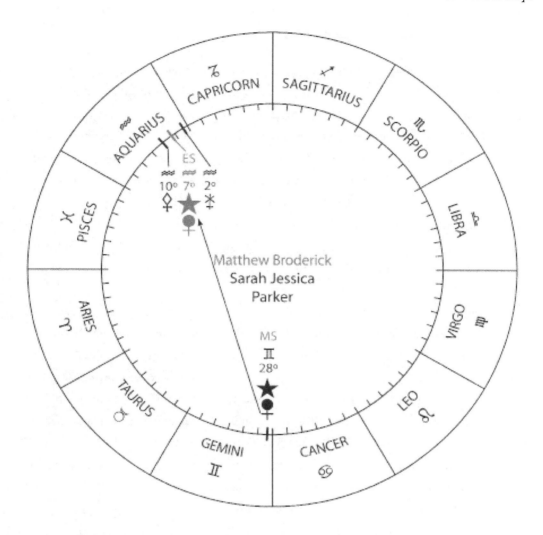

Figure 25.2: THE SARAH JESSICA PARKER and MATTHEW BRODERICK
RELATIONSHIP STAR CHART

Parker: 28° Gemini MS (yang/yang)

Broderick: 7° Aquarius ES (yang/yin)

Broderick's desire (VSP) for: long-term mating (Parker's Juno)

Broderick's desire (VSP) for: wisdom and skills (Parker's Pallas Athena)

Gemini Star-Capricorn Star Relationships

Technically this pair is not defined as life mates, but their link on the Venus Star lasted longer than any other star mate for Gemini (eighty-nine years) and therefore constitutes a firm and enduring exchange of energy.

The Capricorn Star may seem much older than their Gemini Star partner, whether there is an actual age difference or not. This is due, in part, to the grounded, mature, and responsible Capricorn VSP being attracted to and seduced by the more carefree Gemini VSP. The Gemini VSP feeds the Capricorn VSP with a youthful exuberance, encouraging travel and adventure, play and creativity to a more serious and business-oriented Capricorn VSP. The Capricorn VSP adds dignity, maturity, and responsibility to this union and helps to channel all of the Gemini VSP's various interests and ideas into something concrete and tangible.

There is not much data on this pair in the current Venus Star cycle, as these individuals are not yet old enough to have developed a history with each other. The previous Gemini/Capricorn VSP era (eighteenth to nineteenth century) reveals examples of such couples. One example is the seemingly predestined relationship between Empress Josephine and Napoleon Bonaparte. Bonaparte's Venus Star at 13°Gemini forms a biquintile to Josephine's Capricorn Star Point at 21°Capricorn, making theirs a Venus Star soul mate marriage that lasted fourteen years. Their relationship endured long periods of separation and infidelity on the part of both. Still, their connection was powerful for the duration of their lives. Josephine's Capricorn Star provided a foundational rock of security and strength that gave solid grounding to Gemini Star Bonaparte's wandering adventures and conquests in distant lands. Bonaparte's Gemini VSP connects with Josephine's Venus and Jupiter, while her Capricorn Star connects to his Moon and Pluto. Simply put, his amorous desire for her empowered him; she in turn was equally compelled by her Venus Star's desire to connect to power (his Pluto) and nurturing (his Moon) even if she was subjected to his intense outbursts and control. Their connections were:

Gemini	Capricorn
Josephine's Venus 0° Gemini	Bonaparte's Pluto 13° Capricorn
Josephine's Jupiter 2° Gemini	Josephine's Venus Star 21° Capricorn
Bonaparte's Venus Star 13° Gemini	Bonaparte's Moon 29° Capricorn[65]

Gemini Star-Scorpio Star Relationships

See the Scorpio Relationship Star section, Chapter 23.

Gemini Star-Libra Star Relationships

See the Libra Star Relationship section, Chapter 28.

Gemini Creative Star Relationships

Gemini Star-Aries Star Relationships

On the Creative Star cycle, Gemini's point is linked to the Aries point for the better part of its life, from 1964 to 2037, or seventy-three years. This collaboration has stamped its signature on the millennium children and the period itself, adding innovation and youthful exuberance, sport, game, recreation, and giant leaps forward in the communications industry. Thus, for this pair, these breakthrough advances are primary to the success of their relationship. Opportunity for successful collaboration exists between partners of these two star groups, as it forms the 60° relationship, or sextile, on the astrological wheel, but the actual aspect between them on the Venus Star averages 72°, the quintile, an aspect of talent.

The rulership of these two signs are Mercury for Gemini and Mars for Aries, a combination that involves fast thinking, fast talking, and equally fast action, which brings to mind an exciting tennis or ping pong match. In this regard, we note siblings Venus and Serena Williams, a perfect reflection of this Gemini-Aries Venus Star link in which the flow of energy runs from Gemini to Aries. The Aries Star is more likely fast and action oriented while the Gemini Star is very quick at responses and reflexes.

Unless other factors indicate karmic ties, these two star mates come to the relationship as friends, siblings, or creative partners. Disputes or disagreements can occur quickly, but are also resolved just as quickly.

Celebrity pairs of this group include:

Marc Anthony	Gemini ES	Jennifer Lopez	Aries MS
Miley Cyrus	Gemini ES	Billy Ray Cyrus	Aries MS
Jessica Simpson	Gemini MS	Nick Lachey	Aries ES
Venus Williams	Gemini MS	Serena Williams	Aries ES

Gemini Star-Pisces Star Relationships

Once the Aries Star phases out, the Pisces Star takes over in its creative link to Gemini. Both these signs are united on the mutable cross of understanding, modulating back and forth from the realm of air (intellect) to the realm of water (feelings). They are colorful, imaginative spirits who can access the realm of the unconscious. This link lasts for thirty-two years, whereby the "elder" Gemini Stars will be coaching the newly born Pisces Stars. This link is bound to produce imaginative story-telling on a scale heretofore unprecedented, with twenty-first century technology adding spectacular audio/video sequences that might create scenes so virtual as to blur the boundaries between what's imaginary and what's real.

The last link between Gemini and Pisces on the Venus Star was 1789-1822, a time when artist and poet William Blake produced "Songs of Innocence" (1789) and "Songs of Experience" (1794). The next link between Gemini and Pisces will begin in 2041.

Gemini Star-Virgo Star Relationships

See the Virgo Star Relationship, Chapter 21.

Gemini Star-Leo Star Relationships

See the Leo Star Relationship section, Chapter 27.

Gemini's Twin Star Relationships

Gemini itself is known as the "twins" constellation. Therefore, a Twin Star point involving Gemini gives the twin the double they are seeking. There is an ongoing stimulating conversation present in this pair, a virtual idea factory that would excel in the communications field. The following celebrity pairs represent this group:

Amanda Pace	Gemini ES	Rachel Pace	Gemini ES
Gwyneth Paltrow	Gemini MS	Chris Martin	Gemini ES
Cole Sprouse	Gemini ES	Dylan Sprouse	Gemini ES

Two of poet William Blake's (Gemini VSP, Evening Star) most renowned works is called "Songs of Innocence" and "Songs of Experience." Incredibly, this concept describes the Karmic Star feeding from Gemini (innocence) to Capricorn (experience). In these works, Blake addresses the young soul's quest to discover everything one can about life (Gemini) and then counters the work with the dual concept of addressing the impact that life's experience (Capricorn) has had on the soul. The first set appeared in 1789, remarkably when the Gemini Evening Star was in effect and feeding the Capricorn Evening Star of the time. "Innocence" and "Experience" reflect the concept that childhood is a time and a state of protected "innocence". Blake's *Songs of Innocence and of Experience Shewing the Two Contrary States of the Human Soul* were bound and published five years later (1794), adding Experience to Innocence. Blake's works were not celebrated during his lifetime as they then garnered very little attention. But children around the world today are familiar with many of his poems. An excerpt from "The Tyger" follows:

> *Tyger Tyger, burning bright,*
> *In the forests of the night;*
> *What immortal hand or eye,*
> *Could frame thy fearful symmetry?*

26 CAPRICORN VENUS STAR RELATIONSHIPS

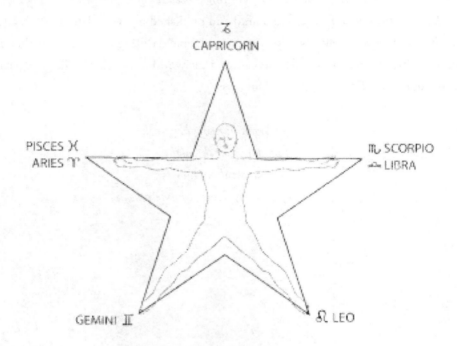

As shown on the star human above, the signs that form a relationship to the Capricorn Star during the course of its lifetime are:

    Feet of Capricorn: Gemini and Leo
    Hands of Capricorn: Pisces & Aries; Libra & Scorpio

Since only five signs are active on the Venus Star at any given period, we can break these relationships into the following increments of time:

Figure 26.1: Interactions in the lifetime of the Capricorn Star

FEET on the Karmic Star:

Capricorn-Gemini:	1984 to 2073	89 years
Capricorn-Leo:	1986 to 2080	94 years LIFE MATES

HANDS on the Creative Star:

Capricorn-Aries:	1985 to 2037	52 years
Capricorn-Pisces:	1790 to 1826	36 years[66]
Capricorn-Scorpio:	1986 to 2027	41 years
Capricorn-Libra:	1771 to 1827	56 years

Capricorn Karmic Star Relationships

The Capricorn VSP-Leo VSP relationship is one of the Venus Star's most stable and enduring, primarily due to the longevity and permanence of its life link on the star.

These two star signs represent two-fifths of the Venus Star, or 40 percent, of the millennium era children. Most of them are too young to have formed any long-term partnerships, but there are numerous examples from the last era of the link between Capricorn and Leo (late eighteenth century and almost all of the nineteenth century). The challenge with reviewing that era is to determine how accurately the birth data has been recorded.

Capricorn is a cardinal yin earth sign that feeds Leo, a fixed yang fire sign: the spindly but sturdy mountain goat feeds the proud and regal lion. Leo is associated with royalty and monarchy while Capricorn is associated with big business and government. Each of these signs commands its own respect for attaining power and authority, and together their power is doubled.

One of the Leo VSP's urges is to produce creative offspring, while the Capricorn VSP is motivated to establish a lineage, ensuring ancestral continuity. The heart-centered lion is fully aware of its passionate nature and loves being surrounded by its cubs or suitors. Thus romance, child bearing, or filling the palace with entertainment and other pleasurable pursuits is always a sure thing for the Leo VSP. The Capricorn Star feeds them practical, sound, earthy wisdom, the appreciation of nature, and the strengthening of age-old traditions through adept means. Some examples from the previous era of Capricorn-Leo include:

John Adams	**Capricorn ES**	**Abigail Adams**	**Leo ES**
Ralph Waldo Emerson	**Capricorn MS**	**Louisa May Alcott**	**Leo ES**
Thomas Jefferson	**Capricorn ES**	**Martha Jefferson**	**Leo MS**

A fine example of these two stars in partnership is the marriage of Capricorn Evening Star John Adams, second president of the U.S., and Leo Evening Star wife Abigail Adams. Abigail's VSP at 27° Leo forms an almost perfect quincunx to John's 29° Capricorn VSP, an aspect that denotes adjustment and separation, which was certainly true of their relationship. John's surrender to the desire to serve his country dutifully required that they experience many years of separation, without undermining their enduring relationship. They fulfilled the archetypal dream of his star by his being intensely involved in the service of his country through political policy-making and leadership (Capricorn). They fulfilled her star motivation by producing numerous offspring (Leo). They had five children, one of whom—John Quincy Adams, a Capricorn Evening Star—followed in his father's footsteps and became the sixth president of the United States. All these aspects can be seen in the following chart.

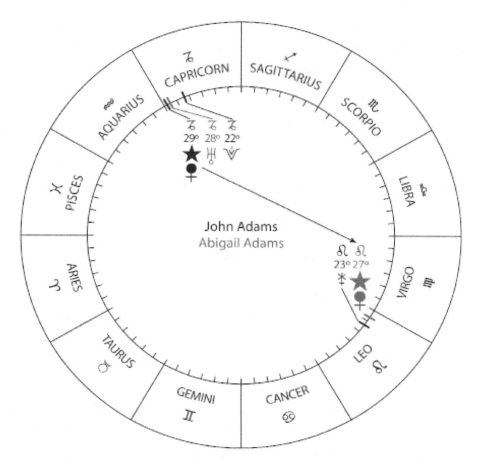

Figure 26.2: THE JOHN and ABIGAIL ADAMS RELATIONSHIP STAR
John feeds Abigail on the Karmic Star
John's Venus Star: 29° Capricorn ES (yin/yin)
Abigail's Venus Star: 27° Leo ES (yang/yin)
Abigail's desire (VSP) for long-term mating, equality in partnership
(John's Juno 23° Leo)
John's desire (VSP) for living outside the boundaries, change, excitement, space
(Abigail's Uranus)

In addition to the Adams marriage cited above, Thomas Jefferson and spouse Martha Wayles Skelton enjoyed the same Venus star relationship. Jefferson's Capricorn Star fed Martha's Leo Star in an almost certain predestined Karmic Star relationship. Adored by one another and married for ten years before her death, he promised he would never remarry. It is reported that Jefferson did not leave his room for three weeks after Martha died.

Jefferson also enjoyed a life-long friendship and collaboration with James Madison, a twin Capricorn Evening Star born one full Venus Star cycle (eight years) after Jefferson. Jefferson referred to Madison as one of his "two great pillars of support." (The other was James Monroe, an Aries Morning Star.)

Capricorn Star-Gemini Star Relationships

See the Gemini Relationship Star section, Chapter 25.

Capricorn Star-Taurus Star Relationships

See the Taurus Relationship Star section, Chapter 18.

Capricorn Creative Star Relationships

On the Creative Star cycle, Capricorn is linked with the star that is shared by two signs: Scorpio in its earlier phase (1986 to 2027) and Libra in its final phase (2022 to 2078).

Capricorn Star-Scorpio Star Relationships

For the first forty-one years of the Capricorn Star, its Creative Star partner and help mate is the Scorpio Star. From an astrological point of view, these are both yin signs that have elemental compatibility (earth and water). In this star connection, partners are attracted to power and see each other as a vehicle for furthering their ambition. Business collaborations would appear to be quite lucrative and long lasting when steered by these two star signs. Additionally, where partners are helping each other out, such as working on a team in a creative or coaching environment or a healing and counseling pair, this can be a very good match.

An example from the previous Capricorn VSP period is First Lady Dolley Madison, a Scorpio Morning Star, who was linked to husband President James Madison, a Capricorn Evening Star. There was an immediate attraction when they met, even though James was seventeen years her senior. They married and, between James' political prowess and Dolley's charm and ingenuity, they became a formidable pair. Dolley showed a discerning political sense and, according to some historians, she is due much of the credit for her husband's election to a second term. For James' part, he allowed Dolley's personality free reign, letting her buck many White House traditions. She established the tradition that the White House would reflect the first lady's tastes and ideas about entertaining. She may have upstaged her husband with her stylish turbans, imported clothes, and enormous popularity, but he was smart enough to use that to his advantage.

Capricorn Star-Libra Star Relationships

When the Scorpio phases out and the Libra Star begins, Capricorn's Creative Star partner will be Libra, which takes effect in 2022. This link of fifty-six years will be what the grandchildren of today's children will experience. Both have a common modality: cardinal, a type of energy that catalyzes a new direction. But gleaning the principles of Capricorn (duty, responsibility) and Libra (fairness and cooperation in partnership), one would surmise that this group will be strongly committed to establishing working partnerships that endure through time.

Capricorn Twin Star Relationships

The Capricorn Twin Star relationship, with its emphasis on duty, government, and adept administration, is exemplified by Queen Victoria and Prince Albert. Here is an example of how two Venus Star Points drew a couple together, for there is very little else in their horoscopes to indicate such bonding, with the exception of Victoria's Juno (desire for long-term mating and equality in partnership) on Albert's Sun (light, fame, leadership). Both were born in 1819 on the same Venus Star (4° Capricorn, a Morning Star).

Further, two Capricorn VSP U.S. presidents were similarly devoted to Capricorn VSP mates: President John Quincy Adams and wife Louisa Adams were Capricorn Evening Stars and Andrew Jackson and wife Rachel were also Capricorn Evening Stars, although her unfortunate death occurred before she became first lady.

Capricorn Twin Stars of the Previous Era

John Quincy Adams	Capricorn ES	Louisa Adams	Capricorn ES
Thomas Jefferson	Capricorn ES	James Madison	Capricorn ES
Andrew Jackson	Capricorn ES	Rachel Jackson	Capricorn ES
Queen Victoria	Capricorn MS	Prince Albert	Capricorn MS

Capricorn Twin Stars of the Current Era

Dakota Fanning	Capricorn ES	Elle Fanning	Capricorn MS
Mary Kate Olsen	Capricorn ES	Ashley Olsen	Capricorn ES
Robert Pattinson	Capricorn ES	Kristen Stewart	Capricorn MS

27 LEO VENUS STAR RELATIONSHIPS

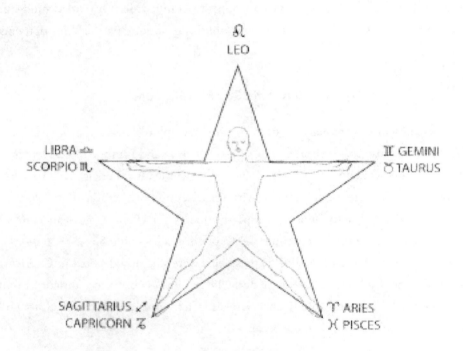

The signs that form a relationship to the Leo Star during the course of its lifetime, as shown on the star human above, are:

Feet of Leo: Sagittarius & Capricorn; Aries & Pisces
Hands of Leo: Libra & Scorpio; Gemini & Taurus

Since only five signs are active on the Venus Star at any given period, we can break these relationships into the following increments of time:

Figure 27.1: Interactions in the lifetime of the Leo Star

FEET on the Karmic Star:

Leo-Capricorn:	1986 to 2080	94 years	LIFE MATES
Leo-Sagittarius:	2081 to 2101	20 years	
Leo-Aries:	1987 to 2037	50 years	
Leo-Pisces:	2039 to 2101	62 years	

HANDS on the Creative Star:

Leo-Scorpio:	1987 to 2027	40 years
Leo-Libra:	2022 to 2100	78 years
Leo-Gemini:	1987 to 2072	85 years
Leo-Taurus:	2076 to 2100	24 years

Noting the time periods above for the links to the Leo Star, the versatile helping hands of the Gemini VSP (85 years) and the sure-footedness of the Capricorn VSP (94 years) provide the longest lasting and strongest relationships for the Leo Star. The Leo-Capricorn-Gemini mix gives individuals born with these Venus Star links in our current era incredible wit, charm, talent, versatility, and success.

Leo Karmic Star Relationships

Leo Star-Aries Star Relationships

The Venus Star link between these two signs exists for fifty years, including the millennium era children, giving the signature of the times and the children born then a double dose of fire. Fire produces warmth, radiance, light, and a desire to express childlike playfulness, recreation, and creativity. A characteristic of this relationship is that both stars can possess blazing hot tempers and become explosive with no warning. The emphasis in this pair is sports, games, play, and creativity as outlets for their energetic and dynamic amounts of self-expression.

Both Leo and Aries can easily become the star of their own life, assigning partners supporting roles. While they both possess the charisma to attract many people to become their supporting players, they may find themselves competing or becoming temperamental when it is their partner, and not themselves, that garners the attention.

The Aries Star has a short fuse, which it lets out in quick, spontaneous outbursts, while the Leo Star, a fixed sign, produces a much slower but deeper burn. Parent/child relationships are particularly vulnerable to this type of fiery, rebellious, and explosive dynamic.

The "elder" Aries Star had been around for five decades before the first of the Leo Stars began to be born. In the Venus Star energy flow, it is the much younger Leo Star who feeds the Aries Star, acting more like the parent or elder of the two. In this case there may be no question that the Leo Star child is the dominant family force and the one who rules.

In previous chapters there has been discussion about how people in the current era can link up with historical figures from previous star eras to tap into one's Venus Star potential. This is the case for President Barack Obama (Aries MS) who was inspired by President Abraham Lincoln (Leo MS) on the Karmic Star. Lincoln's flame was extinguished before he could complete his term of office. Precisely one hundred years after the start of the U.S. Civil War, Barack Obama was born (1961), making history in 2008 when he became the first African-American to be elected president. Consistently throughout his campaign, election, and inauguration, Obama invoked Lincoln's spirit, referring to him as a mentor, role model, and hero, igniting their powerful Leo-Aries Star energy dynamic. Lincoln's Venus Star is 10° Leo and Obama's Sun is 12° Leo, providing vibrancy and strength to their already existing links on the Venus Star.

Leo Star-Pisces Star Relationships

When the Aries Star phases out, Leo links creatively to Pisces. This link lasts for approximately sixty-two years and changes the dynamic in which Leo is motivated. This phase of the Leo Star is the more evolved Leo Star, motivated toward partnering with people who help each other solidify a philosophical or spiritual base that affects the collective consciousness of the planet for creativity and inspiration. The energy flow in this relationship is from bold and dramatic Leo to subtle, sensitive Pisces.

This group has yet to emerge in the current star cycle, as Pisces VSP children will not be born for many years. But history's examples from the last era of the Leo-Pisces link include:

Frederick Engels	Leo MS	**Karl Marx**	Pisces ES
W. S. Gilbert	Leo MS	**Arthur Sullivan**	Pisces ES
Abraham Lincoln	Leo ES	**Mary Todd Lincoln**	Pisces ES
Sarah Bernhardt	Leo MS	**Oscar Wilde**	Pisces MS

The partnership of W.S. Gilbert (Leo MS) and Arthur Sullivan (Pisces ES) provides the perfect example of bold and dramatic Leo to subtle, sensitive Pisces. Gilbert created fantastic stories and characters full of irony and wit. He worked fast, trusted his initial creative instincts (some say to a fault), and turned the surreal into the real. His success before he partnered with Sullivan was spotty at best. Sullivan, too, had some success before his partnership with Gilbert, but not to the point where he could sustain his musical career without having a "day job" as a church organist and composer of hymns, popular songs, and parlor ballads. Gilbert's bold Leo nature was often confrontational, while Sullivan's sensitive Pisces preferred to avoid conflict altogether. Their operas have enjoyed enduring international success and are still performed frequently throughout the world. The two men collaborated on fourteen comic operas between 1871 and 1896 and remain household names today.

Pisces Evening Star VSP Mary Todd Lincoln, married to Leo Evening Star VSP Abraham Lincoln, sixteenth President of the U.S., have Venus Star Point connections as seen in the following chart.

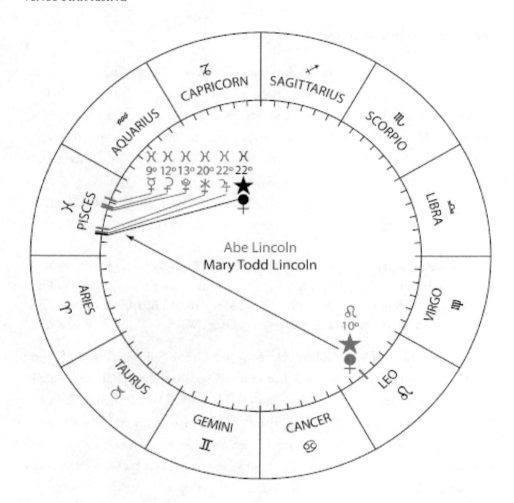

Figure 27.2: THE ABRAHAM LINCOLN and MARY TODD LINCOLN
RELATIONSHIP STAR CHART

Mary Todd Lincoln's VSP 22° Pisces ES (yin/yin)

Abraham Lincoln's VSP 10° Leo ES (yang/yin)

Abraham's star feeds Mary Todd's star on the Karmic Star cycle

Mary Todd's desire for (VSP): long-term mating and partnership (Abraham's Juno)

Mary Todd's desire for (VSP): expansion and hope, gain, and growth (Abraham's Jupiter)

Not only does Abraham's Venus Star feed Mary's Venus Star on the Karmic Star cycle, but her Venus Star in Pisces is a magnet for his stellium of planets in Pisces, including Mercury, Ceres, Pluto, Jupiter, and Juno.

Leo Star-Capricorn Star Relationships

See the Capricorn Relationship Star section, Chapter 26.

Leo Creative Star Relationships

Leo's help mates on the Creative Star are Gemini (1987 to 2072) and Taurus (2076 to 2100).

Leo Star-Gemini Star Relationships

The first of Leo's helping hands on the Creative Star of Venus is the Gemini Star for a period of eighty-five years, which could just qualify them as candidates for life mates. This link creates partnerships between two people that are multi-talented, multi-faceted, enduring, and tend to emphasize creativity. They demonstrate a talent for storytelling, writing, communication, playing music, dancing, and acting.

Within the relationship between these two stars there exists a talent at helping children become free and encouraging them to express their individuality and essence. This also includes working with adults whose childhoods were restricted.

There are too few relationships to examine in the current era, but there are numerous examples from the previous era of Leo and Gemini, some of which include:

Percy Shelley	Leo ES	**Mary Wollstonecraft Shelley**	Gemini ES
Louisa May Alcott	Leo ES	**Henry David Thoreau**	Gemini MS
Sarah Bernhardt	Leo MS	**Victor Hugo**	Gemini MS

In history, an example of such a magnetic and talented pair is poet Percy Bysshe Shelley, a Leo Evening Star and his wife, writer Mary Wollstonecraft Shelley, a Gemini Evening Star, who greatly inspired and helped each other creatively. Another pair who similarly sought inspiration and creative counsel from one another were writers Louisa May Alcott with long-time family friend, Henry David Thoreau.

Leo Star-Taurus Star Relationships

By the fourth quarter phase of the Leo VSP, a phase in which its creative genius proliferates and begins to seed future generations, Taurus becomes the Evening Star and helping hand for Leo. Taurus is an artistic, musically gifted, and sensual sign ruled by Venus, while Leo is a charismatic, creatively endowed, bold, and radiant sign ruled by the Sun. Thus, within these two individuals, there exists a Sun/Venus (the Venus Star) relationship to begin with.

Certainly a by-product of this union would be a joint effort at supplying beauty and elegance, musical genius that possesses a dramatic flair, and equally elegant works of art to future generations. The strong lion and equally strong bull must practice gentleness and tenderness with their partner so they do not completely demolish the other. What they both adore and seek to strengthen in each other is a steady, focused, and productive partnership, which they can invest in for life and rely upon to not crumble in hard times. But such couples can easily get locked into a battle of the wills, because they are fixed in their own ways more strongly than they are able to let go and adapt to someone else's ways.

This link will not occur on the Venus Star until the late twenty-first century (beginning in 2075). A look back to their previous engagement takes us to the period of 1824 to 1849, when the dramatic and bold music of Beethoven's 9th Symphony was first performed for audiences around Europe. Other European composers whose musical genius has endured through the ages and who performed magnificent works of art during this period include: Mendelssohn, Schubert, Rossini, Chopin, Bellini, Donizetti, Berlioz, Wagner, and Verdi, while Jenny Lind captivated audiences with her commanding presence on stage.

Leo Star-Scorpio Star Relationships

See the Scorpio Star Relationship section, Chapter 23.

Leo Star-Libra Star Relationships

See the Libra Star Relationship section, Chapter 28.

Leo Twin Star Relationships

There are few examples of this combination in the 2010 Leo Star era because individuals are young and have not formed any lasting relationships. Leo is identified with the proliferation of offspring, both creative and biological. These relationships work best when the individuals are friends, creative collaborators, or team players rather than life mates, in some part due to the Leo VSP's love of the spotlight, whereby the relationship suffers from competition and envy. Among this group, the best relationship would be between a Leo

Evening Star and a Leo Morning Star, since in such a case there is a harmonizing principle at work.

Two Leo Twin Stars of the previous Leo era produced Russian author Leo Tolstoy and wife Sofia Tolstoy, born sixteen years or two full Venus Star cycles apart. Their Leo Stars' intense creative collaboration produced thirteen children and some of his great works, including *War and Peace*. Sofia helped with the editorial and copy work of this magnum opus, copying it by hand no less than seven times. But their relationship was challenged by Tolstoy's marriage to his people alongside his marriage to Sofia. Sofia did not share his devotion to the people, instead pouring her energy into her children and family, as is fitting for the lioness. Their Leo Twin Venus Stars are located in early Leo alongside his Saturn and natal Venus (withholding of personal love in favor of duty and responsibility), while her natal Venus is close by in Cancer.

28 LIBRA VENUS STAR RELATIONSHIPS

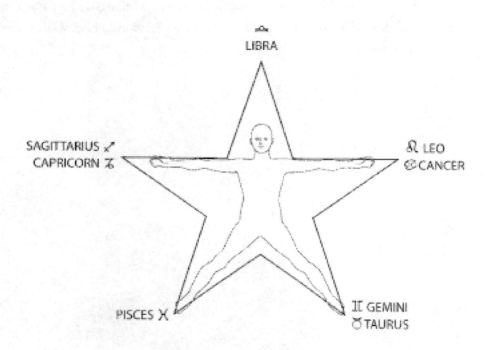

From the star human above, it is easy to observe the Libra Star's interactions with other signs during the course of its life. They are:

    Feet of Libra: **Pisces; Gemini & Taurus**
    Hands of Libra: **Capricorn & Sagittarius; Leo & Cancer**

Libra Venus Star Relationships

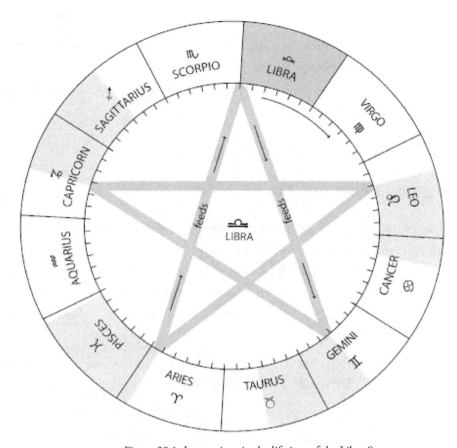

Figure 28.1: Interactions in the lifetime of the Libra Star

The next Libra Star will not begin until 2022. Therefore, we will examine the previous Libra Star era (1771 to 1880). Since only five signs are active on the Venus Star at any given time period, we can break this into the following increments:

FEET of Libra on the Karmic Star:
    Libra-Pisces: 1780 to 1886   106 years   LIFE MATES
    Libra-Gemini: 1771 to 1822   51 years
    Libra-Taurus: 1823 to 1874   51 years

HANDS of Libra on the Creative Star:
    Libra-Capricorn: 1771 to 1827   56 years
    Libra-Sagittarius: 1830 to 1880   50 years
    Libra-Leo: 1771 to 1848   77 years
    Libra-Cancer: 1851 to 1880   29 years

One of Libra's primary dilemmas in life concerns the ability to keep one's equilibrium and focus in a world that constantly challenges Libra's innate sense of fairness and balance. With the Venus Star in Libra, there is a great deal of finesse and talent in achieving this, but Libra's desire to grow and learn through partnership keeps the Libra Star moving through a variety of relationships.

Libra Karmic Star Relationships

Libra Star-Gemini Star Relationships

With true equality, Libra chooses two mates to feed on the Karmic Star cycle of Venus, with precisely the same amount of time devoted to each. Libra's first partner is Gemini, a sign with whom it shares the quality of air. With a double dose of the air element, this partnership is stimulated to support education, communication, and literary and artistic expression. Relationships between people of these two stars would have these principles as their basic values. Examples are:

Lord Byron	Libra ES	**Lady Caroline Lamb**	Gemini MS
George Sand	Libra ES	**Frederic Chopin**	Gemini MS

One Venus Star example from the time when these two signs were previously linked is that of Gemini Morning Star Frederic Chopin and Libra Evening Star George Sand. If anything undermined the longevity of this relationship (it lasted for ten years), it was Libra Star Sand's dilemma of how to keep all the relationships in one's life operating in a harmonious way. Similarly, Lord Byron, a Libra Evening Star, fed Lady Caroline Lamb, a Gemini Star, on the Karmic Star. Byron's pursuit of many simultaneously occurring relationships presented the same challenge.

Libra Star-Taurus Star Relationships

Here are two signs linked together on the Venus Star that both have Venus as their sign's ruling planet. Thus, the crucial elements involved in such a pairing are those represented by Venus herself—a heart-centered approach to each other motivated by shared values of harmony, beauty, peace, sensuality, and equality. With a sure-footed foundation of long-term security provided by Taurus, this is a solid and fulfilling connection. The Libra Star feeds the Taurus Star, so the Libra VSP individual's desire for mating will feed the Taurus VSP's life-long goal of stability. Some examples that turned up with this combination are:

Annie Besant	**Libra MS**	**C. W. Leadbetter**	**Taurus ES**
Mark Twain	**Libra ES**	**Olivia Twain**	**Taurus MS**

Libra Morning Star Annie Besant and Taurus Evening Star C. W. Leadbeater united to form the Theosophical Society. Libra Evening Star Mark Twain and his wife Olivia were devoted to each other and very much in love through their thirty-four-year marriage, which lasted until Olivia's death. Through Olivia, Twain met abolitionists and activists for women's rights and social equality, including writer and utopian socialist William Dean Howells, who became a long-time friend.

Libra Creative Star Relationships

Libra Star-Leo Star Relationships

This relationship on the Creative Star of Venus lasts a very long time (seventy-seven years) and is considered helpful in numerous ways. The energy flows from Libra to Leo on the Venus Star; the two signs form a sextile (opportunity); their elements, air and fire, are compatible and they are linked together for seventy-seven years. Their Venus Star link averages 70°, which brings their relationship into the talented quintile aspect. The result is a relationship in which the mating desires of Libra help the lively, extroverted, and procreative motivations of Leo. This can produce a partnership or creative collaboration that generates many talented offspring or lovely works of art. Libra Evening Star John Keats is paired with good friend and fellow poet Percy Shelley, a Leo Evening Star.

Libra Star-Cancer Star Relationships

This is a much shorter relationship on the Venus Star, lasting a mere twenty-nine years, and forms the more tension-producing aspect (the cardinal square). The cardinal square challenges this partnership to action but the quagmire these two signs can get caught up in is non-action due to the weighing of options by the Libra Star and the emotional responses of the Cancer Star.

Libra helps Cancer by initiating partnerships that are based on ideologies that address social inequities and inhumane conditions of human existence. The Cancer Star provides the emotional content, adding the feeling and nurturing element to any discussion. The Libra VSP is able to keep an objective perspective needed for good decision-making, while the Cancer VSP offers an open channel to emotional richness and depth in a relationship. Examples include:

Annie Besant	**Libra MS**	**Rudolf Steiner**	**Cancer MS**

Libra Twin Star Relationships

Libra Star-Libra Star Relationships

Much of Libra's symbolism has to do with the balanced scales for the simple fact that the Sun enters this sign yearly at the perfect balance of equal day/equal night (the equinox). Thus, much of Libra's temperament and character is focused upon the equality of all things in life. In marriage and relationship, this ingredient is especially needed for long-term success. The relationship between two Libra Stars would greatly amplify this principle. Libra Twin Star relationships, focused on the motivating principles of Libra, are pursuits involving activism, equality, fairness, and balance. The arts and culture, with a dedication to the education and exhibition of arts is another unifying principle in a Libra Twin Star relationship. Examples of this combination are:

Susan B. Anthony	**Libra ES**	**Elizabeth Cady Stanton**	**Libra MS**
Alfred Stieglitz	**Libra MS**	**Georgia O'Keeffe**	**Virgo MS**[67]

The relationship between Georgia O'Keeffe and Alfred Stieglitz garnered a great deal of attention in the early twentieth century when they were involved, but the public's fascination with their unique arrangement has continued to focus on their marriage, one full century later. In a Twin Star relationship, the elder Venus Star feeds the younger, in this case Stieglitz to O'Keeffe. It was immediately apparent that when Stieglitz viewed the artistic genius of O'Keeffe, he proposed a life-long relationship that supported her talent personally and publicly. As a Libra Star, he was committed to supporting many of the artists of the time and, as is the case with other Libra Stars, sought intimate partnerships with them as well. He was also devoted to educating the public about art and photography as an emerging art form.

Another enduring Libra Twin Star relationship existed between Susan B. Anthony and Elizabeth Cady Stanton. Stanton, a Morning Star and Anthony, an Evening Star, were born approximately four years apart—the harmonizing Twin Star relationship. Together they founded the National Women's Suffrage Association and tirelessly campaigned for the equality of women, including women's suffrage, which, although it did not become a reality in their lifetime, benefited future generations.

Libra Venus Star Relationships

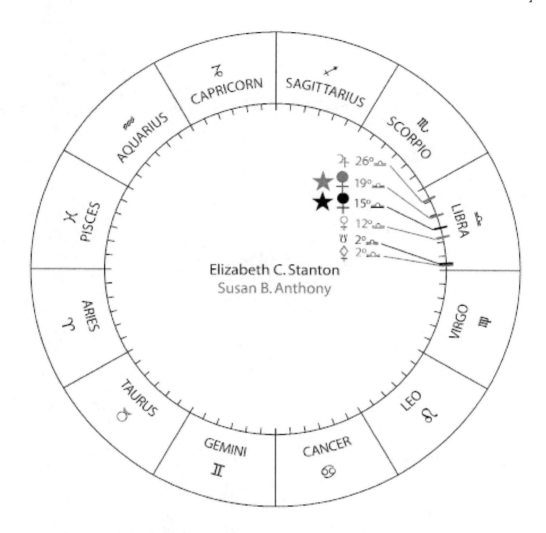

Figure 28.2: THE ELIZABETH CADY STANTON and SUSAN B. ANTHONY RELATIONSHIP STAR CHART

ELIZABETH CADY STANTON: 19° LIBRA MS (yang/yang)

SUSAN B. ANTHONY: 15° LIBRA ES (yang/yin)

Anthony's desire (VSP) for: Stanton's wisdom and skills (Pallas 2° Libra)

Anthony's desire (VSP) to create art, harmony, and peace: Stanton's Venus 12° Libra

Anthony's desire (VSP) for: expansion and hope, gain, and growth (Stanton's Jupiter 26° Libra)

Stanton's desire (VSP) to know again, to replay the past (Anthony's South Node: 2 ° Libra)

29 PISCES VENUS STAR RELATIONSHIPS

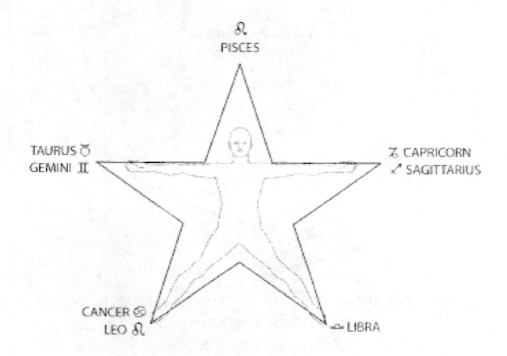

From the star human above, it is easy to observe the Pisces Star's interactions with other signs during the course of its life. They are:

        Feet of Pisces: Leo & Cancer; Libra
        Hands of Pisces: Gemini & Taurus; Capricorn & Sagittarius

Pisces Venus Star Relationships

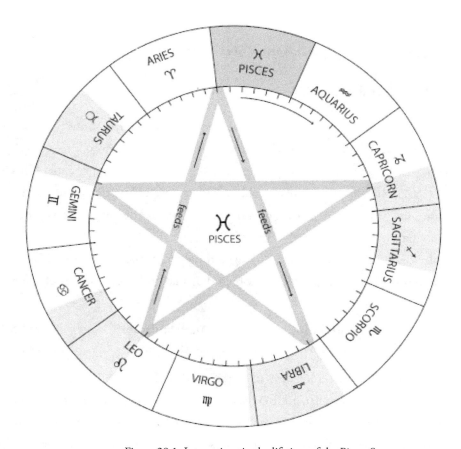

Figure 29.1: Interactions in the lifetime of the Pisces Star

The next Pisces Star will not begin until 2041. Therefore, we will examine the previous Pisces Star era (1790-1886). Since only five signs are active on the Venus Star at any given time, we can break the star partners of Pisces into these time periods:

FEET of Pisces on the Karmic Star:

Pisces-Leo:	1788 to 1850	62 years	
Pisces-Cancer:	1852 to 1886	34 years	
Pisces-Libra:	1790 to 1880	90 years	LIFE MATES

HANDS of Pisces on the Creative Star:

Pisces-Gemini:	1789 to 1822	33 years
Pisces-Taurus:	1825 to 1886	61 years
Pisces-Capricorn:	1790 to 1827	37 years
Pisces-Sagittarius:	1830 to 1887	57 years

335

Pisces Karmic Star Relationships

Pisces Star-Libra Star Relationships

The ninety-year relationship between Pisces and Libra on the Venus Star gives them the status of life mate to one another. The energy flow on the star is from Pisces to Libra, partnering in a caring manner, whereby the watery sign of Pisces feeds airy Libra. This is one of two relationships for Pisces that can be considered exalted on the Venus Star as both signs are associated with Venus. The other is the Pisces-Taurus Creative Star link, which is discussed in Chapter 18.

Both the Pisces VSP and Libra VSP are strongly motivated to compassionate, helping, and healing partnerships, without which they may feel like a fish out of water. Examples of this pair are:

Helen Keller	Libra MS	**Anne Sullivan**	Pisces ES[68]
Charlotte Brontë	Libra MS	**Emily Brontë**	Pisces ES

An example of this combination from the previous Pisces VSP cycle is the relationship between Helen Keller, a Libra Morning Star (double yang) and her teacher and life companion Anne Sullivan, a Pisces Evening Star (double yin). In this relationship the compassion associated with the Pisces VSP was Sullivan's, who had a profound healing influence on Keller, a Libra VSP. Anne Sullivan, visually impaired, was only 20 years old when she became Keller's instructor. It was the beginning of a 49-year-long relationship, evolving into governess and companion. Sullivan taught Keller to communicate by spelling words into her hand and when she realized that the motions her teacher was making on the palm of her hand, while running cool water over her other hand, symbolized the idea of "water." Though challenging at first for both parties, this relationship became nothing short of miraculous, and the term used by Mark Twain to describe Sullivan was "miracle worker". The description was apt, and became the name of a Broadway production (1959) and subsequent film (1962), starring Patty Duke in the role of Helen Keller and Anne Bancroft in the role of Anne Sullivan. Keller, the Libra MS Venus Star Point, devoted her later years to social causes and activism, adopting the same fierce dedication to social issues that we observed in Libra VSPs Susan B. Anthony and Elizabeth Cady Stanton (Chapter 28).

Another example of such a relationship was between sibling writers Charlotte Brontë, a Libra Morning Star, and Emily Brontë, a Pisces Evening Star.

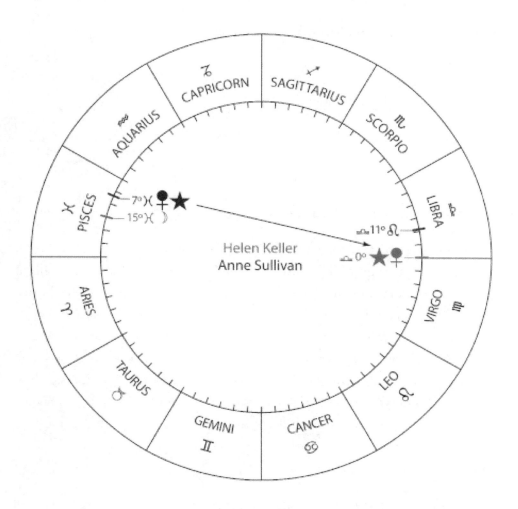

Figure 29.2: THE HELEN KELLER and ANNE SULLIVAN RELATIONSHIP STAR CHART
HELEN KELLER: 0° LIBRA MORNING STAR (yang/yang)
ANNE SULLIVAN: 7° PISCES EVENING STAR (yin/yin)
Sullivan's desire for (VSP) nurturing, comfort, food, feeling, mother/child relationship
(Keller's Moon) at 15° Pisces[1]
Keller's desire (VSP) to know again, to replay the past (Sullivan's Nodes)

Pisces Star-Leo Star Relationships

See the Leo Relationship Star section, Chapter 27.

Pisces Star-Cancer Star Relationships

See the Cancer Relationship Star section, Chapter 20.

Pisces Creative Star Relationships

Pisces Star-Capricorn Star Relationships

The first group on the Creative Star of Venus that Pisces links with is Capricorn. These two signs form a complementary sextile relationship associated with the harmonizing elements of earth and water. In this Venus Star link, imaginative and other-worldly focused Pisces is the inspiration for the practical, dutiful, and responsible Capricorn Star. Although no personal examples were found featuring this pair, the historical period that they were together brought morality into government and legislation. Pisces is the newly born star in this union, pairing with Capricorn in its final third period. These Capricorn VSPs are the elder, blending with the young Pisces VSP. Their relationship requires a blending of both spiritualism and materialism, and their challenge is to reconcile the two.

Pisces Star-Sagittarius Star Relationships

Once Capricorn phased out, the Sagittarius star was born, and it is the second helping hand to Pisces. In this pairing, Pisces has advanced to its final years, while Sagittarius is newly born. In contrast to its Capricorn partner, this union is oriented more toward philosophy and teaching than governing and law-making. It is motivated to bringing forth new ideals and perspectives on man, the divine, and the cosmos. The binding force in this union is the shared interest in philosophical and spiritual ideas and beliefs, creating an overriding cosmic perspective. An example of this type of Venus Star relationship exists between Sagittarius MS Carl Jung and his wife Pisces ES Emma Jung, who spent the better part of their lives involved in mapping the human psyche. Another example is composer Igor Stravinsky (Pisces ES) with designer Coco Chanel (Sagittarius MS).

Pisces Star-Gemini Star Relationships

See the Gemini Star Relationship section, Chapter 25.

Pisces Star-Taurus Star Relationships

See the Taurus Star Relationship section, Chapter 18.

Pisces Twin Star Relationships

The Pisces Star is motivated by spiritual investigation, imagination, romance, mysticism, and the arts, including music. Any two who are paired on the Pisces VSP would hold these qualities as highly valued expressions of life. There is the tendency for the Pisces to lose oneself in others, subsequently blurring the boundary between what parts are their own and what parts are the other.

An example of this type of Pisces Twin Star relationship is the one between Irish poet and playwright Oscar Wilde, a Pisces Morning Star, and companion English poet Lord Alfred Douglas, also a Pisces Morning Star. Born sixteen years apart, or two full Venus Star cycles, they also shared the same Sun sign (Libra), which has a relationship with Pisces on the Karmic Star cycle. The two shared a love of writing, as well as a taste for the dramatic and extravagant. Wilde lavished gifts and attention on Douglas, nursing him like a mother when he was sick. Douglas was spoiled, vengeful, and did not return Wilde's tender care. It's assumed that part of Wilde's attraction was that of a lowly Dubliner for a titled Englishman.

This was certainly no easy relationship for either of them. Douglas first embraced Wilde, then turned against him, and finally condemned their relationship. At the same time, Douglas's father publicly scandalized and legally challenged it. Wilde's Neptune in Pisces connects with both their Venus Stars, leaving him with a milieu of contrasting and confusing feelings as to this romantic, spiritual, and poetic connection that resulted in a scandalous, licentious, and addictive experience.

While this pair reflects the negative star qualities of Pisces, such as addiction, betrayal, and illusion, happily it is not indicative of all Twin Star relationships, nor even of the Pisces Star qualities to which one would aspire.

30
GROUPINGS ON THE VENUS STAR

The ability of the Venus Star to enhance personal relationships is quite extraordinary, as seen from the examples used in this section. If astrology is good at anything, it is good at analyzing and diagnosing relationship indicators from the planetary connections that exist between two people. The Venus Star adds enough extra material to either confirm or deny the longevity or success of any given relationship.

But what has always been puzzling from an astrological point of view is how to effectively work with groups. Groups of families, teams, work partners, creative collaborators such as musical ensembles, and the like have posed challenges for astrology. Working with so many planets, asteroids, and angles per person and so many people in a mix, the outcome can sometimes seem perplexing or overwhelming. The Venus Star changes all of that by detailing how groups of five or more can benefit greatly from positioning themselves on the Venus Star, whereby each member of the group occupies a different point of the star for maximum potency, success, and realization of their goals.

For instance, when researching the Venus Star relationships, I was contacted by a client who owns a small business. There were seven people working in the business at that time. She asked me to look at all their charts to see how the group could be more effective, because at that time they were not producing results for the company, nor were they necessarily working well together. I began looking at the individuals from the point of view of their Venus Stars. What was revealed from this process was extraordinary. Their Star group was as follows:

Owner of Company: Virgo Star
Employee 1: Virgo Star
Employee 2: Aries Star
Employee 3: Aries Star
Employee 4: Cancer Star
Employee 5: Cancer Star
Employee 6: Scorpio Star
Missing Star Point: Aquarius Star

Groupings on the Venus Star

Of the seven people involved, four points of the Venus Star were occupied, leaving one entire Star Point (Aquarius) empty. This was a crucial point to be left empty. Because it was the arm that fed the owner of the company, there was no one feeding her. Additionally, of the four remaining points, two of the seven people occupied the point on the Star that she was feeding (Aries). Most of the time she was frustrated and felt isolated, even though it was her vision and leadership that was necessary to keep the company flourishing.

Additionally, the two people she was feeding were people that she knew she could help personally (as is the want and need of many Virgo Stars), but that soon became her full-time job in the company: feeding and nurturing these two people on a personal and emotional level so that they could fulfill their job duties.

When I revealed the findings of the Venus Star, this made perfect sense to her. In fact, it was such a huge revelation that she sought to relieve the situation immediately. The conclusions we came to were thus: in a simple manner of shuffling, we put the other group member who was also a Virgo Star in the same office as one of the Aries Star people. We selected the other Aries Star and put her into a small grouping that included the Scorpio Star. Thus one Aries Star was being fed by someone, and the other Aries Star was feeding someone else, giving them both a sense of deeper personal connection with their co-workers. I advised the owner of the company to use the Scorpio Star person (in this case, the financial director, as is so fitting for a Scorpio Star) as a group leader who could report to her. In this way, she was benefiting creatively from the help offered by the Scorpio Star to her Virgo Star. Further, even though there were not any Aquarius Stars in the company at the time, there were people who had some strong Aquarius influence, one sun and one moon, who she was able to move to a place of effectiveness for her.

I began studying different groups comprised of five members or more. This technique certainly makes looking at family groupings more insightful as well. For instance, in one family, there are three children and two parents, equaling five people. Again, there was one point of the star that was missing. That missing star was filled in by an aunt and a grandfather, both of whom enjoyed spending time with this family. In another family grouping I analyzed, the two children were feeding the father. The mother was neither feeding, nor being fed by, any of them.

I also looked at political groupings, such as the cabinets in the most recent Bush administration and the Obama administration. Both of these teams consist of members who fill out all five points of the Venus Star. I looked at political families such as the Kennedys, the Windsors, and the Bushes. All of them fared very well and strengthened their abilities to put forth their agendas when all five points of the star were involved in the family.

In the case of the Kennedys and the Windsors, there was a missing star point until Jacqueline married into the Kennedy family and Princess Diana married into the Windsor family. It was only then that the family Venus Star was filled in with all five points. That made sense to me, as both were Aries Star women (the element of fire). These women added luster and sparkle of their own, but also bolstered the family grouping up several notches. Additionally, Jacqueline's Aries Star was the only fire in the family after the death of Joseph Jr., a Sagittarius Star. The Kennedy family was heavily weighted in the earth element, possessing Taurus and Virgo Stars in abundance.

A scan of several five or more member rock bands revealed examples of two groups that are notably present in the workings of the Venus Star. They are the Temptations and the Rolling Stones. It is very interesting that in their first grouping, in both cases, one member was not part of the five-pointed star, but the group created by the replacement of that member yielded the five pointed star.

The Original Temptations:

Eldridge Bryant	Virgo Evening Star
Melvin Franklin	Aquarius Morning Star
Eddie Kendricks	Virgo Evening Star
Otis Williams	Aries Evening Star
Paul Williams	Scorpio Morning Star

The original Temptations included the five members listed above, resulting in two of the members representing the Virgo Star and no member of the Cancer Star. This group released several singles, with the first two being complete flops. The third reached only number 22 on the charts and was followed by four more flops.

In late 1963, Eldridge Bryant was either fired or quit after he attacked fellow band member Paul Williams. Around this time, David Ruffin, a Cancer Morning Star had jumped onstage with the Temptations unannounced one evening and brought the house down. By 1964, they replaced Bryant with Ruffin, the missing point of their five-pointed star. This one personnel change resulted in a change of fortune for the group. Previously they'd been labeled "the hitless Temptations". With Ruffin, they went on to become one of the most successful groups in music history. Their influence on R&B and soul has been compared to the Beatles' influence on pop and rock.

The New Temptations:

Melvin Franklin	Aquarius Morning Star
Eddie Kendricks	Virgo Evening Star
David Ruffin	Cancer Morning Star
Otis Williams	Aries Evening Star
Paul Williams	Scorpio Morning Star

Ruffin was later replaced by Dennis Edwards, a Scorpio ES, but by this time several individuals' misfortunes affected the group as a whole. Also, the replacement of Ruffin by Edwards resulted in the collapse of the Venus Star, so that only four points were represented. Still, admirers of the Temptations will never forget the on-stage chemistry that produced many hits, the most memorable ones including: "The Way You Do The Things You Do", "My Girl", "Papa Was a Rolling Stone" and "Ain't Too Proud to Beg".

The Rolling Stones have an oddly similar story. In its formative years, the band was in flux with several members leaving of their own accord. The most interesting change came when Ian Stewart (an Aquarius ES) was asked to leave. Though Stewart is credited with starting the band with Brian Jones (another Aquarius Star), management ejected him because they didn't think he was cool enough to fit the band's image. Though five other musicians, including Stewart, were in and out of the Stones in the beginning, it was these five points of the Venus Star who remained together and went on to make rock and roll history.

The Rolling Stones:

Mick Jagger	Scorpio Evening Star
Brian Jones	Aquarius Morning Star
Keith Richards	Virgo Morning Star
Charlie Watts	Aries Evening Star
Bill Wyman	Cancer Evening Star

These are the Rolling Stones who created such classics as "I Can't Get No Satisfaction," "Get Off My Cloud," "Paint It Black," "Under My Thumb," "Lady Jane," "19th Nervous Breakdown," "Brown Sugar," "Sympathy for the Devil," and "Honky Tonk Women," among many others. Notice how Jagger and Richards exchange Venus plus the Venus Star Point energies, in Figure 30.1.

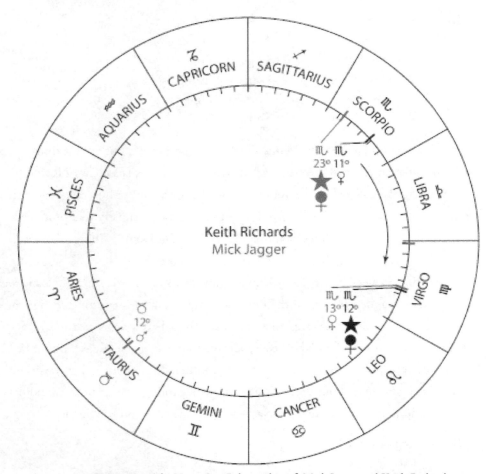

Figure 30.1: The Venus Star Relationship of Mick Jagger and Keith Richards

These two groups—the Temptations and the Rolling Stones—exemplify what is possible when all five points of the Venus Star are present among members who are working together to achieve the same goal. The five points of the Star working together give tremendous help in attaining the kind of commercial success that is possible and furthering the longevity that both groups have enjoyed. This is in spite of both groups having endured members coming and going, as well as certain personality disputes and differences that needed ironing out. It gives the sum of the five points of the star a much greater power than groups of five or more possess when one or more of the points of the star are missing.

It would be negligent here to not mention successful bands or teams that have not had all five points of the star working for them. One example that comes to mind is the Beatles, who, early on, were compared with the Rolling Stones, giving each group some amount of competition. Anyone in the mid 1960s looking at a crystal ball to determine which group would most likely last forever and be performing well into old age would probably have chosen the Beatles over the Stones, but history proves that was not the case. A breakdown of the Venus Star for the Beatles follows:

The Beatles:

George Harrison	Scorpio Evening Star
John Lennon	Cancer Morning Star
Paul McCartney	Aquarius Morning Star
Ringo Starr	Cancer Morning Star

The addition of Brian Epstein's (Aquarius VSP) and George Martin's (Taurus VSP) influence on the group provided one missing point, the Taurus Star. But still there was no Virgo VSP. The pattern that was working in this group was the Karmic Star placement that put both Lennon and Starr in the crucial role of being fed by Harrison and feeding McCartney. After a run of eight years together, the group collapsed and the members went on to form other groups. Nonetheless, the powerful Venus Star exchange between Lennon and McCartney has kept their musical collaboration, some 40 years later, one of the most memorable of the twentieth century. (See Chapter 20, Figure 20.4, for the Lennon-McCartney Venus Star pattern.)

In groups of five or more, making use of the Venus Star is a powerful way to assess the group dynamics. Furthermore, by choosing at least one person to represent each of the five points of the star, it assures that everyone in the group is fairly represented. This gives a much greater chance for group success and longevity because everybody has equal footing, so to speak.

We have seen how the VSP helps us recognize the love principle in our lives and how to use this love principle most effectively by identifying our best talents and enhancing our performance. The VSP helps us to select and develop a romantic relationship; and in assembling groups and teams, the potential for success by utilizing the Venus Star is virtually unlimited.

APPENDIX I

THE VENUS STAR PROGRAM

To develop a personal relationship with your own Venus Star, regardless of whether or not you practice astrology or have consulted an astrologer, follow the suggestions in this section for establishing the Venus Star into your life.

Following are five primary ways to get started.

1. THE VENUS MANTRA

Assuming the position of the Vitruvian Wo(Man), shown below, recite the following:

Oh Venus Star, How Ever Bright You Are
Our Arms Reach To Receive Your Sweet Embrace
Our Feet Are Grounded in Gentle Mother Earth
Our Crown Connects Us to your Lovely Face
Our Hearts Rejoice in Venus' Eternal Grace
© **2005 Arielle Guttman**

2. THE VENUS MUDRA

This is a meditation posture. Stretch your arms out just below the shoulders, and spread your legs as far apart as possible while still comfortable. Ground your feet into Mother Earth. Begin energy flow in the following manner:

1. Feel your right foot anchored to Earth below and send energy up your right leg straight to the top of your head (crown chakra). Breathe.
2. Feel the connection of your crown with the heavens above and send energy down to support the bottom of your left foot. Breathe.
3. Feel your left foot anchored to Earth below and send energy up to your right palm. Breathe.
4. Feel the energy circulating in your right palm and send it across your torso, through your heart center, to your left palm. Breathe.
5. Feel energy circulating in your left palm and send it back down to your right foot to complete the star. Breathe.

This may be accomplished once, or several times in repetition. During the Venus retrograde periods (listed below in Table I) it is highly effective to do this at least once per day during the entire forty day period.

3. THE VENUS PERIOD

Venus turns retrograde for forty days every twenty months, as described in more detail in Chapter 2 "The Mythology and Astrology of Venus." During this retrograde period, Venus and the Sun come into inferior conjunction (closest to Earth), and as they pass through each other as viewed from earth, they create the Star Point that begins the Morning Star cycle. It is especially helpful during such periods to reestablish a vital connection with our core values. The above mantra and mudra should be practiced as often as possible during these forty-day periods.

Further, during the alternating ten-month periods that occur halfway between the twenty-month retrograde periods, Venus and the Sun create another Star Point that begins the Evening Star period while in superior conjunction (farthest from Earth). These dates can be found in Appendix II: "Venus Star Dates and Signs" and are also listed in Table 2. This is another optimum time to focus on Venus practices.

Moreover, Venus rules the signs of Taurus and Libra, which it enters twice a year for nearly one month. When Venus is in those signs (listed in Table 3 below), engaging in Venus practices is also highly recommended.

4. THE VENUS ENVIRONMENT

Using the principles of Venus in your environment can also be beneficial. First, since Venus is the goddess and planet of beauty, grace, and love, if you are surrounded by chaos and cluttered spaces, it is less inviting for Venus energy to enter into the space. For this reason, it is beneficial to practice one of the major principles of *Feng Shui* to have energy flowing productively in your home and workspace, which usually results in increased prosperity, more harmonious relationships, and better health.

Second, you can also use the principles of Venus in your environment by painting, redecorating, or creating an altar to Venus, or by wearing clothes that reflect characteristics of Venus, ones that are flowing and rich in texture and color.

5. A VENUS SONG

Be Who You Really Are

Be who you really are
Play your part so well that you'll truly be a Star
A Star to guide the way for all humanity
A light to free all men from their insanity

Be not afraid, oh children of light
The Stars are all glistening
The Elders are listening
Our dreams can take flight

Be who you really are
Let not the past hold you back
From reaching for the Star
Now is all and all that there will ever be
Open up the eye and you will see

See who we really are
It's not the form in which we're born
That makes us who we are
Seek thyself and search with all our energy
Let our lights burn throughout eternity

Original words and music by Jose Amor © 1976

Appendix I

TABLE 1: VENUS RETROGRADE PERIODS
2000-2025

Venus Retrograde	Begins:	Ends:
Aries Morning Star	March 8, 2001	April 19, 2001
Scorpio Morning Star	October 10, 2002	November 21, 2002
Gemini Morning Star	May 17, 2004	June 29, 2004
Capricorn Morning Star	December 24, 2005	February 3, 2006
Leo Morning Star	July 27, 2007	September 8, 2007
Aries Morning Star	March 6, 2009	April 17, 2009
Scorpio Morning Star	October 8, 2010	November 18, 2010
Gemini Morning Star	May 15, 2012	June 27, 2012
Capricorn Morning Star	December 21, 2013	January 31, 2014
Leo Morning Star	July 25, 2015	September 6, 2015
Aries Morning Star	March 4, 2017	April 15, 2017
Scorpio Morning Star	October 5, 2018	November 16, 2018
Gemini Morning Star	May 12, 2020	June 24, 2020
Capricorn Morning Star	December 19, 2021	January 29, 2022
Leo Morning Star	July 22, 2023	September 3, 2023
Aries Morning Star	March 1, 2025	April 12, 2025

TABLE 2: VENUS EVENING STAR DATES
2000 – 2025

Gemini Evening Star	June 11, 2000
Capricorn Evening Star	January 14, 2002
Leo Evening Star	August 18, 2003
Aries Evening Star	March 30, 2005
Scorpio Evening Star	October 27, 2006
Gemini Evening Star	June 8, 2008
Capricorn Evening Star	January 11, 2010
Leo Evening Star	August 16, 2011
Aries Evening Star	March 28, 2013
Scorpio Evening Star	October 25, 2014
Gemini Evening Star	June 6, 2016
Capricorn Evening Star	January 9, 2018
Leo Evening Star	Aug 13, 2019
Aries Evening Star	March 25, 2021
Libra Evening Star	October 22, 2022
Gemini Evening Star	June 4, 2024

Appendix I

TABLE 3: VENUS TRANSITS TAURUS AND LIBRA
2000 – 2025

Venus Transit	Begins	Ends
Taurus	April 30, 2000	May 25, 2000
Libra	August 30, 2000	September 24, 2000
Taurus	June 6, 2001	July 5, 2001
Libra	October 15, 2001	November 8, 2001
Taurus	March 31, 2002	April 25, 2002
Libra	August 7, 2002	September 7, 2002
Taurus	May 16, 2003	June 9, 2003
Libra	September 15, 2003	October 9, 2003
Taurus	March 5, 2004	April 3, 2004
Libra	October 28, 2004	November 22, 2004
Taurus	April 15, 2005	May 9, 2005
Libra	August 16, 2005	September 11, 2005
Taurus	May 29, 2006	June 23, 2006
Libra	September 30, 2006	October 24, 2006
Taurus	March 17, 2007	April 11, 2007
Libra	November 8, 2007	December 5, 2007
Taurus	April 30, 2008	May 24, 2008
Libra	August 30, 2008	September 23, 2008
Taurus	June 6, 2009	July 5, 2009
Libra	October 14, 2009	November 7, 2009
Taurus	March 31, 2010	April 24, 2010
Libra	August 6, 2010	September 8, 2010
Libra	November 8, 2010	November 29, 2010
Taurus	May 15, 2011	June 9, 2011
Libra	September 14, 2011	October 8, 2011
Taurus	March 5, 2012	April 3, 2012
Libra	October 28, 2012	November 21, 2012
Taurus	April 15, 2013	May 9, 2013
Libra	August 16, 2013	September 10, 2013
Taurus	May 28, 2014	June 23, 2014
Libra	September 29, 2014	October 23, 2014
Taurus	March 17, 2015	April 11, 2015
Libra	November 8, 2015	December 4, 2015

TABLE 3: continued

Venus Transit	Begins	Ends
Taurus	April 29, 2016	May 24, 2016
Libra	August 29, 2016	September 23, 2016
Taurus	June 6, 2017	July 4, 2017
Libra	October 14, 2017	November 7, 2017
Taurus	March 30, 2018	April 24, 2018
Libra	August 6, 2018	September 9, 2018
Libra	October 31, 2018	December 2, 2018
Taurus	May 15, 2019	June 8, 2019
Libra	September 14, 2019	October 8, 2019
Taurus	March 4, 2020	April 3, 2020
Libra	October 27, 2020	November 21, 2020
Taurus	April 14, 2021	May 8, 2021
Libra	August 15, 2021	September 10, 2021
Taurus	May 28, 2022	June 22, 2022
Libra	September 29, 2022	October 23, 2022
Taurus	March 16, 2023	April 10, 2023
Libra	November 8, 2023	December 4, 2023
Taurus	April 29, 2024	May 23, 2024
Libra	August 29, 2024	September 22, 2024

Appendix II

APPENDIX II

VENUS STAR DATES AND SIGNS
1750 to 2050

Sign Abbreviations
A = Aries   Sc = Scorpio   Le = Leo   Ge = Gemini
Cp = Capricorn   Li = Libra   Pi = Pisces   Sg = Sagittarius
Cn = Cancer   Vi = Virgo   Aq = Aquarius   Ta = Taurus
MS = morning star   ES = evening star
Bold = Last Date of Star in that Sign
Bold/Italics = First Date of Star in that Sign

Date	Star	Position		Date	Star	Position
Mar 30 1750 NS	MS	09°A40'		Jan 9 1771 NS	MS	19°Cp13'
Jan 14 1751 NS	ES	24°Cp46'		**Oct 22 1771 NS**	**ES**	**29°Li40'**
Oct 31 1751 NS	MS	08°Sc14'		Aug 12 1772 NS	MS	20°Le23'
Aug 17 1752 NS	ES	25°Le12'		Jun 4 1773 NS	ES	14°Ge19'
Jun 8 1753 NS	MS	17°Ge44'		Mar 23 1774 NS	MS	02°A50'
Mar 31 1754 NS	ES	10°A45'		Jan 7 1775 NS	ES	17°Cp01'
Jan 14 1755 NS	MS	24°Cp09'		**Oct 24 1775 NS**	**MS**	**01°Sc02'**
Oct 27 1755 NS	ES	04°Sc25'		Aug 10 1776 NS	ES	18°Le52'
Aug 17 1756 NS	MS	24°Le46'		Jun 1 1777 NS	MS	11°Ge17'
Jun 9 1757 NS	ES	18°Ge29'		Mar 24 1778 NS	ES	03°A45'
Mar 27 1758 NS	MS	07°A24'		Jan 6 1779 NS	MS	16°Cp44'
Jan 12 1759 NS	ES	22°Cp11'		Oct 20 1779 NS	ES	27°Li18'
Oct 29 1759 NS	MS	05°Sc49'		Aug 10 1780 NS	MS	18°Le11'
Aug 15 1760 NS	ES	23°Le04'		Jun 2 1781 NS	ES	12°Ge12'
Jun 5 1761 NS	MS	15°Ge35'		Mar 20 1782 NS	MS	00°A32'
Mar 28 1762 NS	ES	08°A26'		Jan 4 1783 NS	ES	14°Cp26'
Jan 11 1763 NS	MS	21°Cp41'		Oct 21 1783 NS	MS	28°Li39'
Oct 25 1763 NS	ES	02°Sc02'		Aug 8 1784 NS	ES	16°Le46'
Aug 14 1764 NS	MS	22°Le35'		May 30 1785 NS	MS	09°Ge09'
Jun 6 1765 NS	ES	16°Ge24'		**Mar 21 1786 NS**	**ES**	**01°A24'**
Mar 25 1766 NS	MS	05°A07'		Jan 4 1787 NS	MS	14°Cp16'
Jan 9 1767 NS	ES	19°Cp37'		Oct 18 1787 NS	ES	24°Li58'
Oct 26 1767 NS	MS	03°Sc26'		Aug 7 1788 NS	MS	16°Le01'
Aug 13 1768 NS	ES	20°Le58'		May 30 1789 NS	ES	10°Ge06'
Jun 3 1769 NS	MS	13°Ge27'		**Mar 18 1790 NS**	**MS**	**28°Pi14'**
Mar 26 1770 NS	ES	06°A07'		Jan 1 1791 NS	ES	11°Cp50'

Date	Phase	Position		Date	Phase	Position
Oct 19 1791 NS	MS	26°Li16'		Oct 7 1827 NS	ES	13°Li23'
Aug 6 1792 NS	ES	14°Le40'		Jul 28 1828 NS	MS	05°Le09'
May 27 1793 NS	MS	07°Ge00'		May 20 1829 NS	ES	29°Ta30'
Mar 19 1794 NS	ES	29°Pi02'		Mar 7 1830 NS	MS	16°Pi39'
Jan 1 1795 NS	MS	11°Cp47'		**Dec 20 1830 NS**	**ES**	**28°Sg54'**
Oct 15 1795 NS	ES	22°Li36'		Oct 8 1831 NS	MS	14°Li28'
Aug 5 1796 NS	MS	13°Le49'		Jul 27 1832 NS	ES	04°Le18'
May 28 1797 NS	ES	08°Ge00'		May 17 1833 NS	MS	26°Ta09'
Mar 15 1798 NS	MS	25°Pi55'		Mar 7 1834 NS	ES	17°Pi02'
Dec 30 1798 NS	ES	09°Cp14'		Dec 21 1834 NS	MS	29°Sg23'
Oct 16 1799 NS	MS	23°Li53'		Oct 4 1835 NS	ES	11°Li06'
				Jul 25 1836 NS	MS	03°Le00'
Aug 5 1800 NS	ES	12°Le36'		May 18 1837 NS	ES	27°Ta21'
May 26 1801 NS	MS	04°Ge50'		Mar 5 1838 NS	MS	14°Pi19'
Mar 17 1802 NS	ES	26°Pi39'		Dec 18 1838 NS	ES	26°Sg21'
Dec 31 1802 NS	MS	09°Cp18'		Oct 5 1839 NS	MS	12°Li09'
Oct 14 1803 NS	ES	20°Li18'		Jul 24 1840 NS	ES	02°Le13'
Aug 4 1804 NS	MS	11°Le38'		May 14 1841 NS	MS	23°Ta59'
May 27 1805 NS	ES	05°Ge53'		Mar 5 1842 NS	ES	14°Pi38'
Mar 14 1806 NS	MS	23°Pi37'		Dec 18 1842 NS	MS	26°Sg55'
Dec 28 1806 NS	ES	06°Cp39'		Oct 2 1843 NS	ES	08°Li50'
Oct 15 1807 NS	MS	21°Li31'		Jul 23 1844 NS	MS	00°Le51'
Aug 2 1808 NS	ES	10°Le31'		May 15 1845 NS	ES	25°Ta14'
May 24 1809 NS	MS	02°Ge41'		Mar 2 1846 NS	MS	11°Pi58'
Mar 15 1810 NS	ES	24°Pi16'		Dec 15 1846 NS	ES	23°Sg46'
Dec 28 1810 NS	MS	06°Cp49'		Oct 3 1847 NS	MS	09°Li50'
Oct 11 1811 NS	ES	17°Li58'		**Jul 22 1848 NS**	**ES**	**00°Le09'**
Aug 1 1812 NS	MS	09°Le28'		May 12 1849 NS	MS	21°Ta48'
May 25 1813 NS	ES	03°Ge45'				
Mar 12 1814 NS	MS	21°Pi16'		Mar 2 1850 NS	ES	12°Pi11'
Dec 26 1814 NS	ES	04°Cp04'		Dec 16 1850 NS	MS	24°Sg26'
Oct 13 1815 NS	MS	19°Li10'		Sep 30 1851 NS	ES	06°Li35'
Jul 31 1816 NS	ES	08°Le26'		**Jul 21 1852 NS**	**MS**	**28°Cn41'**
May 21 1817 NS	MS	00°Ge30'		May 13 1853 NS	ES	23°Ta04'
Mar 12 1818 NS	ES	21°Pi53'		Feb 28 1854 NS	MS	09°Pi37'
Dec 26 1818 NS	MS	04°Cp20'		Dec 13 1854 NS	ES	21°Sg11'
Oct 9 1819 NS	ES	15°Li40'		Sep 30 1855 NS	MS	07°Li31'
				Jul 20 1856 NS	ES	28°Cn05'
Jul 30 1820 NS	MS	07°Le19'		May 10 1857 NS	MS	19°Ta38'
May 22 1821 NS	**ES**	**01°Ge38'**		Feb 28 1858 NS	ES	09°Pi44'
Mar 9 1822 NS	MS	18°Pi57'		Dec 13 1858 NS	MS	21°Sg58'
Dec 23 1822 NS	ES	01°Cp30'		Sep 27 1859 NS	ES	04°Li21'
Oct 10 1823 NS	MS	16°Li49'		Jul 18 1860 NS	MS	26°Cn32'
Jul 29 1824 NS	ES	06°Le22'		May 11 1861 NS	ES	20°Ta54'
May 19 1825 NS	**MS**	**28°Ta20'**		Feb 25 1862 NS	MS	07°Pi15'
Mar 10 1826 NS	ES	19°Pi28'		Dec 10 1862 NS	ES	18°Sg39'
Dec 23 1826 NS	**MS**	**01°Cp52'**		Sep 28 1863 NS	MS	05°Li14'

Jul 18 1864 NS	ES	26°Cn01'
May 7 1865 NS	MS	17°Ta28'
Feb 25 1866 NS	ES	07°Pi17'
Dec 11 1866 NS	MS	19°Sg29'
Sep 25 1867 NS	ES	02°Li06'
Jul 16 1868 NS	MS	24°Cn22'
May 9 1869 NS	ES	18°Ta44'
Feb 23 1870 NS	MS	04°Pi52'
Dec 8 1870 NS	ES	16°Sg05'
Sep 26 1871 NS	MS	02°Li55'
Jul 15 1872 NS	ES	23°Cn57'
May 5 1873 NS	MS	15°Ta16'
Feb 23 1874 NS	ES	04°Pi48'
Dec 8 1874 NS	MS	17°Sg00'
Sep 23 1875 NS	**ES**	**29°Vi52'**
Jul 14 1876 NS	MS	22°Cn12'
May 6 1877 NS	ES	16°Ta34'
Feb 20 1878 NS	MS	02°Pi30'
Dec 5 1878 NS	ES	13°Sg33'
Sep 23 1879 NS	**MS**	**00°Li38'**
Jul 13 1880 NS	ES	21°Cn54'
May 3 1881 NS	MS	13°Ta06'
Feb 20 1882 NS	ES	02°Pi19'
Dec 6 1882 NS	MS	14°Sg31'
Sep 20 1883 NS	ES	27°Vi40'
Jul 11 1884 NS	MS	20°Cn03'
May 4 1885 NS	ES	14°Ta22'
Feb 18 1886 NS	**MS**	**00°Pi07'**
Dec 2 1886 NS	ES	11°Sg01'
Sep 21 1887 NS	MS	28°Vi20'
Jul 11 1888 NS	ES	19°Cn49'
Ap 30 1889 NS	MS	10°Ta53'
Feb 18 1890 NS	**ES**	**29°Aq49'**
Dec 3 1890 NS	MS	12°Sg02'
Sep 18 1891 NS	ES	25°Vi27'
Jul 9 1892 NS	MS	17°Cn55'
May 2 1893 NS	ES	12°Ta11'
Feb 16 1894 NS	MS	27°Aq43'
Nov 30 1894 NS	ES	08°Sg29'
Sep 18 1895 NS	MS	26°Vi04'
Jul 9 1896 NS	ES	17°Cn46'
Ap 28 1897 NS	MS	08°Ta41'
Feb 15 1898 NS	ES	27°Aq19'
Dec 1 1898 NS	MS	09°Sg35'
Sep 16 1899 NS	ES	23°Vi16'
Jul 8 1900 NS	MS	15°Cn47'

Ap 30 1901	ES	10°Ta00'
Feb 14 1902	MS	25°Aq20'
Nov 28 1902	ES	05°Sg57'
Sep 17 1903	MS	23°Vi47'
Jul 8 1904	ES	15°Cn42'
Ap 27 1905	MS	06°Ta27'
Feb 14 1906	ES	24°Aq48'
Nov 29 1906	MS	07°Sg06'
Sep 14 1907	ES	21°Vi04'
Jul 5 1908	MS	13°Cn39'
Ap 28 1909	ES	07°Ta46'
Feb 12 1910	MS	22°Aq55'
Nov 26 1910	ES	03°Sg27'
Sep 15 1911	MS	21°Vi30'
Jul 5 1912	ES	13°Cn38'
Ap 24 1913	MS	04°Ta15'
Feb 11 1914	ES	22°Aq18'
Nov 27 1914	MS	04°Sg38'
Sep 12 1915	ES	18°Vi54'
Jul 3 1916	MS	11°Cn31'
Ap 26 1917	ES	05°Ta34'
Feb 9 1918	MS	20°Aq31'
Nov 23 1918	ES	00°Sg57'
Sep 12 1919	MS	19°Vi15'
Jul 3 1920	ES	11°Cn34'
Ap 22 1921	MS	02°Ta01'
Feb 9 1922	ES	19°Aq46'
Nov 24 1922	**MS**	**02°Sg11'**
Sep 10 1923	ES	16°Vi42'
Jul 1 1924	MS	09°Cn22'
Ap 23 1925	ES	03°Ta20'
Feb 7 1926	MS	18°Aq06'
Nov 21 1926	**ES**	**28°Sc27'**
Sep 10 1927	MS	17°Vi00'
Jul 1 1928	ES	09°Cn31'
Ap 20 1929	**MS**	**29°A48'**
Feb 6 1930	ES	17°Aq13'
Nov 22 1930	MS	29°Sc43'
Sep 7 1931	ES	14°Vi33'
Jun 28 1932	MS	07°Cn13'
Ap 21 1933	**ES**	**01°Ta05'**
Feb 4 1934	MS	15°Aq42'
Nov 18 1934	ES	25°Sc59'
Sep 8 1935	MS	14°Vi46'
Jun 29 1936	ES	07°Cn27'
Ap 17 1937	MS	27°A35'
Feb 3 1938	ES	14°Aq41'

Date	Type	Position
Nov 19 1938	MS	27°Sc16'
Sep 5 1939	ES	12°Vi24'
Jun 26 1940	MS	05°Cn04'
Ap 19 1941	ES	28°A51'
Feb 2 1942	MS	13°Aq16'
Nov 16 1942	ES	23°Sc31'
Sep 5 1943	MS	12°Vi33'
Jun 26 1944	ES	05°Cn22'
Ap 15 1945	MS	25°A20'
Feb 1 1946	ES	12°Aq08'
Nov 17 1946	MS	24°Sc50'
Sep 3 1947	ES	10°Vi14'
Jun 24 1948	MS	02°Cn55'
Ap 16 1949	ES	26°A36'
Jan 31 1950	MS	10°Aq51'
Nov 13 1950	ES	21°Sc03'
Sep 3 1951	MS	10°Vi19'
Jun 24 1952	ES	03°Cn18'
Ap 13 1953	MS	23°A07'
Jan 29 1954	ES	09°Aq34'
Nov 15 1954	MS	22°Sc24'
Sep 1 1955	ES	08°Vi07'
Jun 21 1956	MS	00°Cn47'
Ap 14 1957	ES	24°A20'
Jan 28 1958	MS	08°Aq25'
Nov 11 1958	ES	18°Sc37'
Aug 31 1959	MS	08°Vi05'
Jun 22 1960	**ES**	**01°Cn13'**
Ap 10 1961	MS	20°A53'
Jan 27 1962	ES	07°Aq00'
Nov 12 1962	MS	19°Sc59'
Aug 29 1963	ES	05°Vi59'
Jun 19 1964	**MS**	**28°Ge37'**
Ap 11 1965	ES	22°A03'
Jan 26 1966	MS	05°Aq57'
Nov 8 1966	ES	16°Sc10'
Aug 29 1967	MS	05°Vi52'
Jun 20 1968	ES	29°Ge08'
Ap 8 1969	MS	18°A37'
Jan 24 1970	ES	04°Aq27'
Nov 10 1970	MS	17°Sc34'
Aug 27 1971	ES	03°Vi51'
Jun 17 1972	MS	26°Ge29'
Ap 9 1973	ES	19°A47'
Jan 23 1974	MS	03°Aq30'
Nov 6 1974	ES	13°Sc45'
Aug 27 1975	MS	03°Vi39'
Jun 17 1976	ES	27°Ge04'
Ap 5 1977	MS	16°A21'
Jan 21 1978	ES	01°Aq52'
Nov 7 1978	MS	15°Sc08'
Aug 25 1979	ES	01°Vi44'
Jun 15 1980	MS	24°Ge20'
Ap 7 1981	ES	17°A28'
Jan 21 1982	**MS**	**01°Aq03'**
Nov 3 1982	ES	11°Sc20'
Aug 24 1983	**MS**	**01°Vi25'**
Jun 15 1984	ES	24°Ge58'
Ap 3 1985	MS	14°A06'
Jan 19 1986	**ES**	**29°Cp18'**
Nov 5 1986	MS	12°Sc43'
Aug 22 1987	**ES**	**29°Le37'**
Jun 12 1988	MS	22°Ge12'
Ap 4 1989	ES	15°A09'
Jan 18 1990	MS	28°Cp35'
Nov 1 1990	ES	08°Sc57'
Aug 22 1991	MS	29°Le14'
Jun 13 1992	ES	22°Ge53'
Ap 1 1993	MS	11°A49'
Jan 16 1994	ES	26°Cp44'
Nov 2 1994	MS	10°Sc18'
Aug 20 1995	ES	27°Le29'
Jun 10 1996	MS	20°Ge03'
Ap 2 1997	ES	12°A51'
Jan 16 1998	MS	26°Cp07'
Oct 29 1998	ES	06°Sc33'
Aug 20 1999	MS	27°Le01'
Jun 11 2000	ES	20°Ge48'
Mar 29 2001	MS	09°A31'
Jan 14 2002	ES	24°Cp07'
Oct 31 2002	MS	07°Sc53'
Aug 18 2003	ES	25°Le23'
Jun 8 2004	MS	17°Ge54'
Mar 30 2005	ES	10°A31'
Jan 13 2006	MS	23°Cp39'
Oct 27 2006	ES	04°Sc11'
Aug 17 2007	MS	24°Le50'
Jun 8 2008	ES	18°Ge43'
Mar 27 2009	MS	07°A15'
Jan 11 2010	ES	21°Cp32'
Oct 28 2010	MS	05°Sc30'
Aug 16 2011	ES	23°Le18'

Appendix II

Jun 5 2012	MS	15°Ge45'
Mar 28 2013	ES	08°A10'
Jan 11 2014	MS	21°Cp11'
Oct 25 2014	ES	01°Sc49'
Aug 15 2015	MS	22°Le38'
Jun 6 2016	ES	16°Ge36'
Mar 25 2017	MS	04°A56'
Jan 9 2018	ES	18°Cp58'
Oct 26 2018	MS	03°Sc06'
Aug 13 2019	ES	21°Le12'
Jun 3 2020	MS	13°Ge36'
Mar 25 2021	ES	05°A50'
Jan 8 2022	MS	18°Cp42'
Oct 22 2022	**ES**	**29°Li27'**
Aug 13 2023	MS	20°Le28'
Jun 4 2024	ES	14°Ge30'
Mar 22 2025	MS	02°A39'
Jan 6 2026	ES	16°Cp22'
Oct 23 2026	**MS**	**00°Sc44'**
Aug 11 2027	ES	19°Le07'
Jun 1 2028	MS	11°Ge26'
Mar 23 2029	ES	03°A28'
Jan 6 2030	MS	16°Cp16'
Oct 20 2030	ES	27°Li07'
Aug 10 2031	MS	18°Le18'
Jun 2 2032	ES	12°Ge23'
Mar 20 2033	MS	00°A21'
Jan 3 2034	ES	13°Cp46'
Oct 21 2034	MS	28°Li22'
Aug 9 2035	ES	17°Le02'
May 29 2036	MS	09°Ge16'
Mar 21 2037	**ES**	**01°A05'**
Jan 3 2038	MS	13°Cp46'
Oct 17 2038	ES	24°Li47'
Aug 8 2039	MS	16°Le07'
May 30 2040	ES	10°Ge15'
Mar 17 2041	**MS**	**28°Pi03'**
Jan 1 2042	ES	11°Cp13'
Oct 18 2042	MS	26°Li00'
Aug 7 2043	ES	14°Le56'
May 27 2044	MS	07°Ge06'
Mar 18 2045	ES	28°Pi43'
Jan 1 2046	MS	11°Cp18'
Oct 15 2046	ES	22°Li28'
Aug 6 2047	MS	13°Le58'
May 28 2048	ES	08°Ge09'
Mar 15 2049	MS	25°Pi45'
Dec 29 2049	ES	08°Cp37'

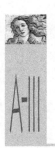

APPENDIX III

VENUS STAR CELEBRITIES, by SIGN

The names in bold type in the lists below
are considered pure Venus Star archetypes,
having been born directly on or very near the star date.

Aquarius Evening Stars

Name	Date
Laurel, Stan	6/16/1890
Kennedy, Rose	7/22/1890
Christie, Agatha	9/15/1890
Marx, Groucho	10/2/1890
Eisenhower, Dwight D.	10/14/1890
Jessel, George	4/3/1898
Luce, Henry	4/3/1898
Meier, Golda	5/3/1898
Lorca, Federico Garcia	6/5/1898
Escher, M.C.	6/17/1898
Gershwin, George	9/26/1898
Lenya, Lotte	10/18/1898
Nelson, Ozzie	3/20/1906
White, T. H.	5/29/1906
Baker, Josephine	6/3/1906
White, Margaret Bourke	6/14/1906
Lindbergh, Anne	6/22/1906
Tenzing, Norgay	5/15/1914
Heyerdahl, Thor	10/6/1914
DiMaggio, Joe	11/25/1914
Meadows, Audrey	**2/8/1922**
Brown, Helen Gurley	**2/18/1922**
Leek, Sybil	2/22/1922
Kerouac, Jack	3/12/1922
Reiner, Carl	3/20/1922
Day, Doris	4/3/1922
Garland, Judy	6/10/1922
Caesar, Sid	9/5/1922

Name	Date
Wagner, Robert	**2/10/1930**
Woodward, Joanne	2/27/1930
Milk, Harvey	5/22/1930
Eastwood, Clint	5/31/1930
Armonstrong, Neil	8/5/1930
Soros, George	8/12/1930
Connery, Sean	8/25/1930
Buffet, Warren	8/30/1930
Charles, Ray	9/23/1930
Annan, Kofi	4/18/1938
Wood, Natalie	7/20/1938
Jennings, Peter	7/29/1938
Rogers, Kenny	8/21/1938
Millman, Dan	2/22/1946
Minelli, Liza	3/12/1946
Cher	5/20/1946
Trump, Donald	6/14/1946
Radner, Gilda	6/28/1946
Bush, George W.	7/6/1946
Stallone, Sylvester	7/6/1946
Clinton, Bill	8/19/1946
Greene, Liz	9/4/1946
Sarandon, Susan	10/4/1946
Kucinich, Dennis	10/8/1946
Carpenter, Richard	10/15/1946
Chopra, Deepak	10/22/1946
Winfrey, Oprah	**1/29/1954**
Groening, Matt	**2/15/1954**
Travolta, John	2/18/1954

Kennedy, Victoria	2/26/1954		Huxley, Aldous	7/26/1894	
Moore, Michael	4/23/1954		Zanuck, Darryl F.	9/5/1902	
Seinfeld, Jerry	4/29/1954		Kroc, Ray	10/5/1902	
McCain, Cindy	5/20/1954		Hubbard, L. Ron	3/13/1910	
Merkel, Angela	7/17/1954		Cousteau, Jacques	6/11/1910	
Cameron, James	8/16/1954		Saarinen, Eero	8/20/1910	
Booth, Cherie	9/23/1954		Mother Theresa	8/26/1910	
Lee, Ang	10/23/1954		Parker, Bonnie	10/1/1910	
Brooks, Garth	**2/7/1962**		**Bishop, Joey**	**2/3/1918**	
Bon Jovi, Jon	3/2/1962		Hatrick, Gloria	3/10/1918	
Broderick, Matthew	3/21/1962		Bailey, Pearl	3/29/1918	
O'Donnell, Rosie	3/21/1962		Ford, Betty	4/8/1918	
Unser, Jr., Al	4/19/1962		Landers, Ann	7/4/1918	
Gerber, Rande	4/27/1962		van Buren, Abigail	7/4/1918	
Ferguson, Craig	5/17/1962		Bergman, Ingmar	7/14/1918	
Sheedy, Ally	6/15/1962		Mandela, Nelson	7/18/1918	
Abdul, Paula	6/19/1962		Bernstein, Leonard	8/25/1918	
Cruise, Tom	7/3/1962		Kennedy, Rose Marie	9/3/1918	
Ford, Tom	8/27/1962		Hayworth, Rita	10/17/1918	
Lee, Tommy	10/3/1962		Agnew, Spiro	11/9/1918	
Preston, Kelly	10/13/1962		Lewis, Jerry	3/16/1926	
Furnish, David	10/25/1962		Hefner, Hugh	4/9/1926	
Bush, Kristian	3/14/1970		Elizabeth II, Queen of England	4/21/1926	
Queen Latifah	3/18/1970		Monroe, Marilyn	6/1/1926	
Carey, Mariah	3/27/1970		Ross, Elizabeth Kubler	7/8/1926	
Consuelos, Mark	3/30/1970		Bennett, Tony	8/3/1926	
Lee, Jason	4/25/1970		Derek, John	8/12/1926	
Trump, Melania	4/26/1970		Hay, Louise	10/8/1926	
Agassi, Andre	4/29/1970		Berry, Chuck	10/18/1926	
Thurman, Uma	4/29/1970		Nader, Ralph	2/27/1934	
Fey, Tina	5/18/1970		Donaldson, Sam	3/11/1934	
Campbell, Naomi	5/22/1970		Steinem, Gloria	3/25/1934	
Beck	7/8/1970		Arkin, Alan	3/26/1934	
Shyamalan, M Night	8/6/1970		Goodall, Jane	4/3/1934	
Phoenix, River	8/23/1970		MacLaine, Shirley	4/24/1934	
Ripa, Kelly	10/2/1970		Moyers, Bill	6/5/1934	
Damon, Matt	10/8/1970		Armani, Georgio	7/11/1934	
Combs, Sean	11/4/1970		Epstein, Brian	9/19/1934	
Hawke, Ethan	11/6/1970		Loren, Sophia	9/20/1934	
Kutcher, Ashton	**2/7/1978**		Cohen, Leonard	9/21/1934	
Federline, Kevin	3/21/1978		**King, Carole**	**2/9/1942**	
Bryant, Kobe	8/23/1978		**Bloomberg, Michael**	**2/14/1942**	
Garcia Bernal, Gael	10/30/1978		Jones, Brian	2/28/1942	
Aquarius Morning Stars			Bakker, Tammy Fae	3/7/1942	
Washington, Martha	6/2/1731	*	Dee, Sandra	4/23/1942	
Graham, Martha	5/11/1894		Streisand, Barbara	4/24/1942	
Hammett, Dashiell	5/27/1894		Weil, Dr. Andrew	6/8/1942	
Edward VIII	6/23/1894		Ebert, Roger	6/18/1942	

McCartney, Paul	6/18/1942		Cruz, Penelope	4/28/1974	
Wilson, Brian	6/20/1942		Jewel	5/23/1974	
Sheldrake, Rupert	6/28/1942		Morissette, Alanis	6/1/1974	
Ford, Harrison	7/13/1942		Jeter, Derek	6/26/1974	
Allende, Isabelle	8/2/1942		Swank, Hilary	7/30/1974	
Keillor, Garrison	8/7/1942		Phillippe, Ryan	9/10/1974	
Jiabao, Wen	9/15/1942		Nettles, Jennifer	9/12/1974	
Franklin, Melvin	10/12/1942		Phoenix, Joaquin	10/28/1974	
Cole, Natalie	**2/6/1950**		Biel, Jessica	3/3/1982	
Tarnas, Richard	2/21/1950		Brown, Kwame	3/10/1982	
Carpenter, Karen	3/2/1950		Clarkson, Kelly	4/24/1982	
Macy, William H.	3/13/1950		Dunst, Kirsten	4/30/1982	
Short, Martin	3/26/1950		Parker, Tony	5/17/1982	
Faltskos, Agnetha	4/5/1950		Lipinsky, Tara	6/10/1982	
Leno, Jay	4/28/1950		Prince William of Wales	6/21/1982	
Gabriel, Peter	5/13/1950		Burton, Hilarie	7/1/1982	
Wonder, Stevie	5/13/1950		Bush, Sophia	7/8/1982	
Taupin, Bernie	5/22/1950		Paquin, Anna	7/24/1982	
Huffington, Arianna	7/15/1950		Roddick, Andy	8/30/1982	
Branson, Richard	7/18/1950		Thorpe, Ian	10/13/1982	
Princess Anne, Princess Royal	8/15/1950		Ne-yo	10/18/1982	
McGraw, Dr. Phil	9/1/1950		**Aries Evening Stars**		
Murray, Bill	9/21/1950		Louix XVI of France	8/23/1754	*
Washington, Paulette Pearson	9/28/1950		Bligh, William	9/9/1754	*
Petty, Tom	10/20/1950		**Wordsworth, William**	**4/7/1770**	*
Hart, Mary	11/8/1950		Clark, William	8/1/1770	*
DeGeneres, Ellen	**1/26/1958**		Beethoven, Ludwig van	12/16/1770	*
Stone, Sharon	3/10/1958		Crockett, David, "Davy"	8/17/1786	*
Hunter, Holly	3/20/1958		**O'Neal, Ryan**	**4/20/1941**	
Baldwin, Alec	4/3/1958		**Ann-Margret**	**4/28/1941**	
Pfeiffer, Michelle	4/29/1958		Dylan, Bob	5/24/1941	
Bening, Annette	5/29/1958		Watts, Charlie	6/2/1941	
Prince	6/7/1958		Lewis, Jim	6/3/1941	
Bacon, Kevin	7/8/1958		Stewart, Martha	8/3/1941	
Bassett, Angela	8/16/1958		McCartney, Linda Eastman	9/24/1941	
Madonna	8/16/1958		Rice, Anne	10/4/1941	
Burton, Tim	8/25/1958		Jackson, Jesse	10/8/1941	
Jackson, Michael	8/29/1958		Simon, Paul	10/13/1941	
Bocelli, Andrea	9/22/1958		Williams, Otis	10/30/1941	
Robbins, Tim	10/16/1958		Garfunkel, Art	11/5/1941	
Mortensen, Viggo	10/20/1958		Rose, Charlie	1/5/1942	
Rock, Chris	**2/7/1966**		Hawking, Stephen	1/8/1942	
Crawford, Cindy	2/20/1966		Angelil, Rene	1/16/1942	
Jackson, Janet	5/16/1966		Ali, Muhammad	1/17/1942	
Hayek, Salma	9/2/1966		**Lange, Jessica**	**4/20/1949**	
Sandler, Adam	9/9/1966		Joel, Billy	5/9/1949	
Mendes, Eva	3/5/1974		Richie, Lionel	6/20/1949	
Beckham, Victoria	4/17/1974		Streep, Meryl	6/22/1949	

Edwards, Elizabeth	7/3/1949	
Knopfler, Mark	8/12/1949	
Gere, Richard	8/31/1949	
O'Reilly, Bill	9/10/1949	
Springsteen, Bruce	9/23/1949	
Liebowitz, Annie	10/2/1949	
Buckingham, Lindsey	10/3/1949	
Weaver, Sigourney	10/8/1949	
Foster, David	11/1/1949	
Raitt, Bonnie	11/8/1949	
Shaffer, Paul	11/28/1949	
Bridges, Jeff	12/4/1949	
Gibb, Maurice and Robin	12/22/1949	
Lewis, Daniel Day	4/29/1957	
Griffith, Melanie	8/8/1957	
Estevan, Gloria	9/1/1957	
Kennedy, Caroline	11/27/1957	
Osmond, Donnie	12/9/1957	
Mahara-Ji: Rawat, Prem	12/10/1957	
Romano, Ray	12/21/1957	
Baker, Anita	1/26/1958	
Rowling, J. K.	7/31/1965	
Sedgwick, Kyra	8/19/1965	
Stiller, Ben	11/30/1965	
Witt, Katarina	12/3/1965	
Bessette, Carolyn	1/7/1966	
Brody, Adrien	**4/14/1973**	
Klum, Heidi	6/1/1973	
Daly, Carson	6/22/1973	
Lewinsky, Monica	7/22/1973	
Beckinsale, Kate	7/26/1973	
Chappelle, David	8/24/1973	
Lachey, Nick	11/9/1973	
Seles, Monica	12/2/1973	
Banks, Tyra	12/4/1973	
Meyers, Stephanie	12/24/1973	
Christiansen, Hayden	**4/19/1981**	
Alba, Jessica	4/28/1981	
Kournikova, Anna	6/7/1981	
Portman, Natalie	6/9/1981	
Angel, Ashley Parker	8/1/1981	
Murray, Chad Michael	8/24/1981	
Bilson, Rachel	8/25/1981	
Knowles, Beyonce	9/4/1981	
Hudson, Jennifer	9/12/1981	
Bledel, Alexis	9/16/1981	
Richie, Nicole	9/21/1981	
Milian, Christina	9/26/1981	

Williams, Serena	9/26/1981	
Akon	10/14/1981	
Cole, Keyshia	10/15/1981	
Bush, Barbara and Jenna	11/25/1981	
Bedingfield, Natasha	11/26/1981	
Spears, Britney	12/2/1981	
Miller, Sienna	12/28/1981	
Brown, Chris	5/5/1989	
Radcliffe, Daniel	7/23/1989	
Panettiere, Hayden	8/21/1989	
Linley, Cody	11/20/1989	
Swift, Taylor	12/13/1989	
Aiken, Liam	1/7/1990	
Aries Morning Stars		
Boone, Daniel	10/22/1734	*
Monroe, James	4/28/1758	*
Lewis, Merriweather	8/18/1774	*
Hepburn, Audrey	5/4/1929	
Roberts, Jane	5/8/1929	
Frank, Anne	6/12/1929	
Cash, June Carter	6/23/1929	
Marcos, Imelda	7/2/1929	
Onassis, Jacqueline Kennedy	7/28/1929	
Arafat, Yasser	8/24/1929	
Palmer, Arnold	9/10/1929	
Plowright, Lady Joan	10/28/1929	
Princess Grace of Monaco	11/12/1929	
Gordy, Jr., Berry	11/28/1929	
Clark, Dick	11/30/1929	
Aldrin, Buzz	1/20/1930	
Hackman, Gene	1/30/1930	
Nicholson, Jack	**4/22/1937**	
Freeman, Morgan	6/1/1937	
Cosby, Bill	7/12/1937	
Thompson, Hunter S	7/18/1937	
Hoffman, Dustin	8/8/1937	
Fonda, Jane	12/21/1937	
Hopkins, Anthony	12/31/1937	
Ulvaeus, Bjorn	4/25/1945	
Dillard, Annie	4/30/1945	
Smith, Michael	4/30/1945	
Presley, Priscilla	5/24/1945	
Simon, Carly	6/25/1945	
Mirren, Helen	7/26/1945	
Martin, Steve	8/14/1945	
Lithgow, John	10/19/1945	
Young, Neil	11/12/1945	
Lyngstad, Frida	11/15/1945	

Hawn, Goldie	11/21/1945	
McVie, John	11/26/1945	
Midler, Bette	12/1/1945	
Keaton, Diane	1/5/1946	
Judd, Naomi	1/11/1946	
Parton, Dolly	1/19/1946	
Siskel, Gene	1/26/1946	
Blair, Tony	5/6/1953	
Brosnan, Pierce	5/16/1953	
Ensler, Eve	5/25/1953	
Edwards, John	6/10/1953	
Allen, Tim	6/13/1953	
Scialfa, Patti	7/29/1953	
Gifford, Kathie Lee	8/16/1953	
Bush, Columba	8/17/1953	
Matalin, Mary	9/19/1953	
Devi, Mātā Amritanandamayī, aka "Ammachi"	9/27/1953	
Jackson, Tito	10/15/1953	
Capshaw, Kate	11/3/1953	
Miller, Dennis	11/3/1953	
Basinger, Kim	12/8/1953	
Bernanke, Ben	12/13/1953	
Kennedy, Jr., Robert F.	1/17/1954	
Boyle, Susan	**4/1/1961**	
Clooney, George	5/6/1961	
Enya	5/17/1961	
Fox, Michael J.	6/9/1961	
Boy George	6/14/1961	
Lewis, Carl	7/1/1961	
Princess Diana	7/1/1961	
Obama, Barack	8/4/1961	
Cyrus, Billy Ray	8/25/1961	
Gandolfini, James	9/18/1961	
Locklear, Heather	9/25/1961	
Jackson, Peter	10/31/1961	
Ryan, Meg	11/19/1961	
Zellweger, Rene	4/25/1969	
Blanchett, Cate	5/14/1969	
Graf, Steffi	6/14/1969	
Lopez, Jennifer	7/24/1969	
Jones, Catherine Zeta	9/25/1969	
Stefani, Gwen	10/3/1969	
Kerrigan, Nancy	10/31/1969	
Jay-Z	12/4/1969	
West, Kanye	6/8/1977	
Tyler, Liv	7/1/1977	
Brady, Tom	8/3/1977	

Ludacris	9/11/1977	
Apple, Fiona	9/13/1977	
Baiul, Oksana	11/16/1977	
Gyllenhaal, Maggie	11/16/1977	
Allen, Lily	5/2/1985	
Tisdale, Ashley	7/2/1985	
Ciara	10/25/1985	
Muniz, Frankie	12/5/1985	
Symone, Raven	12/10/1985	
Marks, Hannah	**4/13/1993**	
Cosgrove, Miranda	5/14/1993	
Gordon, Adam Taylor	6/20/1993	
Norton, Nathan	8/4/1993	
Palmer, Lauren Keyana	8/26/1993	
Gonzalez, Elian	12/6/1993	
Obama, Sasha	6/10/2001	
Cancer Evening Stars		
Pachelbel, Johann	9/1/1653	*
Vivaldi, Antonio	3/4/1678	*
Scarlatti, Guissepe	10/26/1685	*
Shaw, George Bernard	**7/26/1856**	
Wilson, Woodrow	12/28/1856	
van Gogh, Theodore	5/1/1857	
Venizelos, Eleutherios	8/23/1864	
Lautrec, Toulouse	11/24/1864	
Sri Aurobindo	8/15/1872	
Teilhard de Chardin, Fr. Pierre	5/1/1881	
Kennedy, Sr., Joseph Patrick	9/6/1888	
Elliot, T. S.	9/26/1888	
Wolff, Toni	9/18/1888	
Jones, Marc Edmond	10/1/1888	
Carnegie, Dale	11/24/1888	
Chaplin, Charles	4/16/1889	
Piaget, Jean	8/9/1896	
Fitzgerald, F. Scott	9/24/1896	
Gish, Lillian	10/14/1896	
Eisenhower, Mamie	11/14/1896	
Davies, Marion	1/3/1897	
Neruda, Pablo	**7/12/1904**	
Rand, Ayn	2/2/1905	
Prince Andrew	5/13/1905	
Child, Julia	8/15/1912	
Kelly, Gene	8/23/1912	
Johnson, Ladybird	12/22/1912	
Nixon, Richard	1/9/1913	
Bridges, Lloyd	1/15/1913	
Kaye, Danny	1/18/1913	
Parks, Rosa	2/4/1913	

Appendix III

Brynner, Yul	**7/11/1920**	
Bradbury, Ray	8/22/1920	
Rooney, Micky	9/23/1920	
Meadows, Jayne	9/27/1920	
Matthau, Walter	10/1/1920	
Leary, Timothy	10/22/1920	
Friedan, Betty	2/4/1921	
Signoret, Simone	3/25/1921	
Warhol, Andy	8/6/1928	
Fisher, Eddie	8/10/1928	
Kroc, Joan	8/27/1928	
Chomsky, Noam	12/7/1928	
King, Jr., Martin Luther	1/15/1929	
Gehry, Frank	2/28/1929	
Redford, Robert	8/18/1936	
McCain, John	8/29/1936	
Bennett, Joan	9/2/1936	
Kennedy, Joan	9/5/1936	
Holly, Buddy	9/7/1936	
Nelson, David	10/24/1936	
Wyman, Bill	10/24/1936	
Merchant, Ismail	12/25/1936	
Moore, Mary Tyler	12/29/1936	
Tyl, Noel	12/31/1936	
Redgrave, Vanessa	1/30/1937	
Glass, Philip	1/31/1937	
Beatty, Warren	3/30/1937	
Powell, Colin	4/5/1937	
Peltier, Leonard	9/12/1944	
Bissett, Jacqueline	9/13/1944	
Douglas, Michael	9/25/1944	
Carville, James	10/25/1944	
Rice, Tim	11/10/1944	
DeVito, Danny	11/17/1944	
Michaels, Lorne	11/17/1944	
Stewart, Rod	1/10/1945	
Marley, Bob	2/6/1945	
Farrow, Mia	2/9/1945	
Clapton, Eric	3/30/1945	
Akroyd, Dan	**7/1/1952**	
Williamson, Marianne	**7/8/1952**	
van Sant, Gus	7/24/1952	
Swayze, Patrick	8/18/1952	
Stewart, David A.	9/9/1952	
Kennedy, Joseph Patrick III	9/24/1952	
Reeve, Chris	9/25/1952	
Barr, Roseanne	10/3/1952	
Putin, Vladmir	10/7/1952	

Osbourne, Sharon	10/9/1952	
Benigni, Roberto	10/27/1952	
Williams, Lucinda	1/26/1953	
Steenburgen, Mary	2/8/1953	
Bush, Jeb	2/11/1953	
Campion, Nicholas	3/4/1953	
Kidjo, Anjelique	7/14/1960	
Banderas, Antonio	8/10/1960	
Brightman, Sarah	8/14/1960	
Penn, Sean	8/17/1960	
Grant, Hugh	9/9/1960	
Firth, Colin	9/10/1960	
Griffin, Kathy	11/4/1960	
Kennedy, Jr., John F.	11/25/1960	
Moore, Julianne	12/3/1960	
Reeve, Dana	3/17/1961	
Cancer Morning Stars		
Franklin, Benjamin	1/17/1706	*
van Gogh, Vincent	3/30/1853	
Oakley, Annie	8/13/1860	
Guggenheim, Robert Solomon	2/2/1861	
Steiner, Rudolf	2/25/1861	
Tagore, Sir Rabindranath	5/7/1861	
Chamberlain, Neville	3/18/1869	
Mata Hari	8/7/1876	
Casals, Pablo	12/30/1876	
Cayce, Edgar	3/18/1877	
Toklas, Alice B.	4/30/1877	
Roosevelt, Eleanor	10/11/1884	
Truman, Bess	2/13/1885	
Chuchill, Clementine Hozier	4/1/1885	
West, Mae	8/17/1892	
Yogananda, Paramahansa	1/5/1893	
Pickford, Mary	4/8/1893	
Fitzgerald, Zelda	7/24/1900	
Elizabeth, Queen Mother	8/4/1900	
Hayes, Helen	10/10/1900	
Mitchell, Margaret	11/8/1900	
Gable, Clark	2/1/1901	
Hall, Manley P.	3/18/1901	
Berle, Milton	**7/12/1908**	
Johnson, Lyndon B.	8/27/1908	
Coca, Imogene	11/18/1908	
Goldwater, Barry	1/1/1909	
Barrow, Clyde	3/24/1909	
Welty, Eudora	4/13/1909	
Cronkite, Walter	11/4/1916	
Douglas, Kirk	12/9/1916	

Maharishi Mahesh Yogi	1/12/1917		Williams, Montel	7/3/1956	
McCullers, Carson	2/19/1917		**Hanks, Tom**	**7/9/1956**	
Arnaz, Desi	3/2/1917		Hill, Anita	7/31/1956	
Ford, Mary	**7/7/1924**		Cattrall, Kim	8/21/1956	
Marciano, Rocky	9/1/1924		Copperfield, David	9/16/1956	
Bacall, Lauren	9/16/1924		Fisher, Carrie	10/21/1956	
Mastroianni, Marcello	9/28/1924		Bush, Marvin	10/22/1956	
Capote, Truman	9/30/1924		Wilson, Rita	10/26/1956	
Carter, Jimmy	10/1/1924		Derek, Bo	11/20/1956	
Renquist, William	10/1/1924		Ramsey, Patsy	12/29/1956	
Clavell, James	10/10/1924		Couric, Katie	1/7/1957	
Mandelbrot, Benoit	11/20/1924		Princess Caroline of Monaco	1/23/1957	
Newman, Paul	1/26/1925		Van Halen, Eddie	1/26/1957	
Lemmon, Jack	2/8/1925		McKennitt, Loreena	2/17/1957	
O'Connor, Flannery	3/25/1925		Jackson, Marlon	3/12/1957	
Carter, Jenny	12/26/1931		Lee, Spike	3/20/1957	
Chirac, Jacques	11/29/1932		**Capricorn Evening Stars**		
Aquino, Corazon	1/25/1933		Adams, John	10/30/1735	*
Ono, Yoko	2/18/1933		Jefferson, Thomas	4/13/1743	*
Caine, Michael	3/14/1933		Madison, James	3/16/1751	*
Jones, Quincy	3/14/1933		Burns, Robert	1/25/1759	*
Roth, Philip	3/19/1933		Jackson, Andrew	3/15/1767	*
Starr, Ringo	**7/7/1940**		Jackson, Rachel	6/15/1767	*
Stewart, Patrick	7/13/1940		Adams, John Quincy	7/11/1767	*
Brolin, James	7/18/1940		Adams, Louisa	2/12/1775	*
Trebek, Alex	7/22/1940		Balzac, Honore	5/20/1799	*
Lennon, John	10/6/1940		Longfellow, Henry W.	2/27/1807	*
Bush, Laura	11/4/1940		Pasteur, Louis	12/27/1822	*
Boxer, Barbara	11/11/1940		Barton, Mischa	1/24/1986	
Warwick, Dionne	12/12/1940		Conrad, Lauren "L. C."	2/1/1986	
Baez, Joan	1/9/1941		Church, Charlotte	2/21/1986	
Ruffin, David	1/18/1941		Bynes, Amanda	4/3/1986	
Domingo, Placido	1/21/1941		Pattinson, Robert	5/13/1986	
Cheney, Dick	1/30/1941		Olsen, Ashley and Mary Kate	6/15/1986	
Love, Mike	3/15/1941		Lohan, Lindsay	7/2/1986	
Rose, Pete	4/14/1941		Cassie	8/26/1986	
Gore, Tipper	8/19/1948		Stewart, "Boo Boo"	1/21/1994	
McAuliffe, Christa	9/2/1948		Grant, Allie	2/14/1994	
Irons, Jeremy	9/19/1948		Fanning, Dakota	2/23/1994	
Phillips, Mark	9/22/1948		Mikuska, Drew	5/12/1994	
Prince Charles	11/14/1948		Nelson, Hailey Anne	9/14/1994	
Dean, Howard	11/17/1948		**Capricorn Morning Stars**		
Osbourne, Ozzy	12/3/1948		Jones, John Paul	7/9/1747	*
Jackson, Samuel L.	12/21/1948		Empress Josephine	6/24/1763	*
Depardieu, Gérard	12/27/1948		Astor, John Jacob	7/17/1763	*
Belushi, John	1/24/1949		Emerson, Ralph Waldo	5/25/1803	*
Trump, Ivana	2/20/1949		Stowe, Harriet Beecher	6/14/1811	*
Jackson, Randy	**6/23/1956**		Queen Victoria of England	5/24/1819	*

Appendix III

Name	Date	
Howe, Julia Ward	5/27/1819	*
Whitman, Walt	5/31/1819	*
Prince Albert, Prince Consort	8/26/1819	*
Princess Eugenie, Princess of York	3/23/1990	
Castle-Hughes, Keisha	3/24/1990	
Stewart, Kristen	4/9/1990	
Watson, Emma	4/15/1990	
Ramsey, Jon Benet	8/6/1990	
Fanning, Elle	4/9/1998	
Obama, Malia	7/4/1998	
Pettis, Madison	7/22/1998	

Gemini Evening Stars

Name	Date	
von Goethe, Johann	8/28/1749	*
Blake, William	11/28/1757	*
Webster, Daniel	1/18/1782	*
Shelley, Mary Wollstonecraft	8/30/1797	*
Browning, Elizabeth Barrett	3/6/1806	*
Verdi, Giuseppe	10/10/1813	*
Eddy, Mary Baker	7/16/1821	*
Dostoevsky, Fyodor	11/11/1821	*
Barton, Clara	12/25/1821	*
Schliemann, Heinrich	1/6/1822	*
Bana, Eric	8/9/1968	
Berry, Halle	8/14/1968	
Ray, Rachel	8/25/1968	
Ritchie, Guy	9/10/1968	
Anthony, Marc	9/16/1968	
Smith, Will	9/25/1968	
Jackman, Hugh	10/12/1968	
Wilson, Owen	11/18/1968	
Manson, Marilyn	1/5/1969	
Moder, Danny	1/31/1969	
Brown, Bobby	2/5/1969	
Anniston, Jennifer	2/11/1969	
Bardem, Javier	3/1/1969	
Tatou, Audrey	8/9/1976	
Silverstone, Alicia	10/4/1976	
Carter, Vince	1/26/1977	
Shakira	2/2/1977	
Yankee, "Daddy"	2/3/1977	
Martin, Chris	3/2/1977	
Barrino, Fantasia	6/30/1984	
Prince Harry (Henry of Wales)	9/15/1984	
Lavigne, Avril	9/27/1984	
Simpson, Ashlee	10/3/1984	
Cohen, Sasha	10/26/1984	
Omarion	11/12/1984	

Name	Date	
Johannson, Scarlett	11/22/1984	
James, LeBron	12/30/1984	
Duff, Haylie	2/19/1985	
Knightly, Keira	3/26/1985	
Eisenberg, Hallie Kate	8/2/1992	
Sprouse, Cole and Dylan	8/4/1992	
Hutcherson, Josh	10/12/1992	
Cyrus, Miley	11/23/1992	
Bright, Cameron	1/26/1993	
Stone, Jennifer	2/12/1993	
Mavity, Abigail	3/4/1993	
Pace, Amanda and Rachel	10/6/2000	

Gemini Morning Stars

Name	Date	
Mary, Queen of Scots	12/14/1542	*
Bonaparte, Napoleon	8/15/1769	*
Lamb, Lady Caroline	11/13/1785	*
Young, Brigham	6/1/1801	*
Howe, Samuel Gridley	11/10/1801	*
Hugo, Victor	2/26/1802	*
Tennyson, Lord Alfred	8/6/1809	*
Carson, Kit	12/24/1809	*
Gladstone, William	12/29/1809	*
Thoreau, Henry David	7/12/1817	*
Baha-u-llah	11/12/1817	*
Brown, Dan	**6/22/1964**	
Love, Courtney	7/9/1964	
Bonds, Barry	7/24/1964	
Bullock, Sandra	7/26/1964	
Gates, Melinda	8/15/1964	
Reeves, Keanu	9/2/1964	
Flockhart, Callista	11/11/1964	
Countess Sophie of Wessex	1/20/1965	
Lane, Diane	1/22/1965	
Parker, Sarah Jessica	3/25/1965	
Harmon, Angie	8/10/1972	
Affleck, Ben	8/15/1972	
Diaz, Cameron	8/30/1972	
Paltrow, Gwyneth	9/28/1972	
Eminem	10/17/1972	
DeRossi, Portia	1/31/1973	
Kidd, Jason	3/23/1973	
Blaine, David	4/4/1973	
Tatum, Channing	4/26/1980	
Williams, Venus Ebonistar	**6/17/1980**	
Kwan, Michelle	7/7/1980	
Simpson, Jessica	7/10/1980	
Bundchen, Gisele	7/21/1980	

365

Culkin, Macauley	8/26/1980	
Williams, Michelle	9/9/1980	
Ming, Yao	9/12/1980	
Ice T	9/25/1980	
Young Jeezy	9/28/1980	
Cannon, Nick	10/8/1980	
Ashanti	10/13/1980	
Minnillo, Vanessa	11/9/1980	
Aguilera, Christina	12/18/1980	
Gyllenhaal, Jake	12/19/1980	
Pitbull	1/15/1981	
Keyes, Alicia	1/28/1981	
Wood, Elijah	1/28/1981	
Timberlake, Justin	1/31/1981	
Hilton, Paris	2/17/1981	
Groban, Josh	2/27/1981	
MIMS	3/22/1981	
Princess Beatrice of York	8/8/1988	
Hudgens, Vanessa	12/14/1988	
Reivers, Corbin Bleu	2/21/1989	
Lloyd, Jake	3/5/1989	
Moretz, Chloe	2/10/1997	

Leo Evening Stars

Elizabeth I, Queen of England	9/7/1533	*
Paine, Thomas	1/29/1737	*
Adams, Abigail	11/22/1744	*
Audobon, John James	4/26/1785	*
Shelley, Percy Bysshe	**8/4/1792**	*
Braille, Louis	1/4/1809	*
Mendelssohn, Felix	2/3/1809	*
Darwin, Charles	2/12/1809	*
Lincoln, Abraham	2/12/1809	*
Olcott, Col. Henry Steel	**8/2/1832**	*
Alcott, Louisa May	11/29/1832	*
Bandelier, Adolph	**8/6/1840**	*
Rodin, Auguste	11/12/1840	*
Monet, Claude	11/14/1840	*
Renoir, Pierre-Auguste	2/25/1841	*
Wood, Evan Rachel	9/7/1987	
Duff, Hilary	9/28/1987	
Efron, Zac	10/18/1987	
Jonas, Kevin	11/5/1987	
Carter, Aaron	12/7/1987	
Rihanna	2/20/1988	
Osment, Haley Joel	4/10/1988	
Hogan, Brooke	5/5/1988	
Wright, Jordan	10/2/1995	
Breslin, Abigail	4/14/1996	

Leo Morning Stars

Pope Pius VII	**8/14/1740**	*
Tsar Ivan VI, Tsar of Russia	**8/23/1740**	*
Arnold, Benedict	1/14/1741	*
Joseph II, Holy Roman Emperor	3/13/1741	*
Jefferson, Martha	10/30/1748	*
Coleridge, Samuel Taylor	10/21/1772	*
Schubert, Franz Peter	1/31/1797	*
Andersen, Hans Christian	4/2/1805	*
Lind, Jenny	10/6/1820	*
Engels, Friederich	11/28/1820	*
Burton, Sir Richard Francis	3/19/1821	*
Tolstoy, Leo	9/9/1828	*
Gilbert, W.S.	11/18/1836	*
Morgan, John Pierport	4/17/1837	*
Tolstoy, Sofya	8/22/1844	*
Nietzsche, Friedrick	10/15/1844	*
Bernhardt, Sarah	10/22/1844	*
Warren, Karle	2/8/1992	
Lautner, Taylor	2/11/1992	
Osment, Emily	3/10/1992	
Singer, Kelly	3/17/1992	
Kelley, Malcolm David	5/12/1992	
Nero, Haley	3/14/2000	

Libra Evening Stars

Lord Byron	1/22/1788	
Keats, John	10/31/1795	
Hawthorne, Nathaniel	7/4/1804	
Sand, George	7/1/1804	
Liszt, Franz	**10/22/1811**	
Dickens, Charles	2/7/1812	
Eliot, George	11/22/1819	
Anthony, Susan B.	2/15/1820	
Verne, Jules	2/8/1828	
Adams, Evangeline	2/8/1868	
Rossetti, Dante Gabriel	5/12/1828	
Carnegie, Andrew	11/25/1835	
Twain, Mark	11/30/1835	
St. Bernadette of Lourdes	1/7/1844	
Rousseau, Henri	5/21/1844	
Cassatt, Mary Stevenson	5/22/1844	
Abbas-Effendi, Abdu'l-Baha	5/23/1844	
Chekhov, Anton	1/17/1860	
Mahler, Gustave	7/1/1860	
Curie, Marie	11/7/1867	

Libra Morning Stars

Davis, Jefferson	6/3/1808	

Appendix III

Stanton, Elizabeth Cady	11/12/1815	
Bronte, Charlotte	4/21/1816	
Alger, Horatio	1/13/1832	
Carroll, Lewis	1/27/1832	
Zola, Emile	4/2/1840	
Tchaikovsky, Peter	5/7/1840	
Besant, Annie	**10/1/1847**	
Stoker, Bram	11/8/1847	
Gauguin, Paul	6/8/1848	
Freud, Sigmund	5/6/1856	
Tesla, Nikola	7/9/1856	
Munch, Edvard	12/12/1863	
Stieglitz, Alfred	1/1/1864	
Rogers, Will	11/4/1879	
Klee, Paul	12/18/1879	
Mix, Tom	1/8/1880	
Fields, W. C.	1/29/1880	
Woolley, Sir Leonard C.	4/17/1880	
Bailey, Alice	6/16/1880	
Keller, Helen	6/27/1880	

Pisces Evening Stars

Dumas, Alexandre	7/24/1802	
Chopin, Frederic	3/1/1810	
Barnum, P. T.	7/5/1810	
Marx, Karl	5/5/1818	
Bronte, Emily	7/30/1818	
Lincoln, Mary Todd	12/13/1818	
Degas, Edgar	7/19/1834	
Sullivan, Arthur	5/13/1842	
Stevenson, Robert Louis	11/13/1850	
Roosevelt, Theodore	10/29/1858	
Sullivan, Anne	4/14/1866	
Satie, Erik	5/17/1866	
Wells, H. G.	9/21/1866	
Cheiro	11/1/1866	
Houdini, Harry	4/6/1874	
Marconi, G.	4/25/1874	
Hoover, Herbert	8/10/1874	
Holst, Gustav	9/21/1874	
Jung, Emma	3/30/1882	
Stravinsky, Igor	6/17/1882	

Pisces Morning Stars

Lamy, Jean Baptist	10/14/1814	
Grant, Ulysses S.	4/27/1822	
Muir, John	4/21/1838	
Bizet, Georges	10/25/1838	
Eastman, George	7/12/1854	
Wilde, Oscar	10/16/1854	

Henry, O.	9/11/1862	
Lenin, Vladimir	4/22/1870	
Parrish, Maxfield	7/25/1870	
Douglas, Lord Alfred	10/22/1870	
Duncan, Isadora	5/26/1878	
Ben Gurion, David	10/16/1886	

Sagittarius Evening Stars

Dickinson, Emily	**12/10/1830**	**
Blavatsky, Mdm. Helena	8/12/1831	
Cezanne, Paul	1/19/1839	
Bell, Alexander Graham	3/3/1847	
Pulitzer, Joseph	4/10/1847	
Bailey, James Anthony	7/4/1847	
James, Jesse	9/5/1847	
Lowell, Percival	3/13/1855	
Hearst, William Randolph	4/29/1863	
Ford, Henry	7/30/1863	
Proust, Marcel	7/10/1871	
Wright, Orville	8/19/1871	
Einstein, Albert	3/14/1879	
Lawrence, Frieda	8/11/1879	
Sanger, Margaret	9/14/1879	
Rivera, Diego	**12/8/1886**	
Holmes, Ernest	1/21/1887	
Hoover, J. Edgar	1/1/1895	
Ruth, Babe	2/6/1895	
Rudhyar, Dane	3/23/1895	
Valentino, Rudolph	5/6/1895	
Krishnamurti, Jiddu	5/12/1895	
Bush, Prescott	5/15/1895	
Hammerstein II, Oscar	7/12/1895	
Fuller, Buckminster	7/12/1895	
Graves, Robert	7/24/1895	
Richardson, Sir Ralph	**12/19/1902**	
Nin, Anais	2/21/1903	
Crawford, Joan	3/23/1903	
Luce, Claire Booth	4/10/1903	
Spock, Dr. Benjamin	5/2/1903	
Crosby, Bing	5/3/1903	
Hope, Bob	5/29/1903	
Gehrig, Lou	6/19/1903	
Orwell, George	6/25/1903	
Stone, Irving	7/14/1903	
Reagan, Ronald	2/6/1911	
Harlow, Jean	3/3/1911	
Williams, Tennessee	3/26/1911	
Johnson, Robert	5/8/1911	
Rogers, Ginger	7/16/1911	

Name	Date	
Cronyn, Hume	7/18/1911	
McLuhan, Marshal	7/21/1911	
Ball, Lucille	8/6/1911	
Graham, Billy	11/7/1918	
L'Engle, Madeleine	**11/29/1918**	
Rooney, Andy	1/14/1919	
Cole, Nat "King"	3/17/1919	
Seeger, Pete	5/3/1919	
Bowles, Heloise	5/4/1919	
Peron, Eva	5/7/1919	
Liberace	5/16/1919	
Soleri, Paolo	6/21/1919	

Sagittarius Morning Stars

Name	Date	
McKinley, William	1/29/1843	
Evans, Sir Arthur	7/8/1851	
Puccini, Giacomo	**12/22/1858**	
Curie, Pierre	5/15/1859	
Ziegfeld, Florenz	3/21/1867	
Wright, Wilbur	4/16/1867	
Wright, Frank Lloyd	6/8/1867	
Churchill, Winston	**11/30/1874**	**
Schweitzer, Albert	1/14/1875	
Jung, Carl	7/26/1875	
Burroughs, Edgar Rice	9/1/1875	
Gibran, Khalil	1/6/1883	
Kazantzakis, Nikos	2/18/1883	
Fairbanks, Douglas	5/23/1883	
Kafka, Franz	7/3/1883	
Mussolini, Benito	7/29/1883	
Porter, Cole	6/9/1891	
Lewis, C. S.	**11/29/1898**	**
Bogart, Humphrey	1/23/1899	
Astaire, Fred	5/10/1899	
Hemingway, Ernest	7/21/1899	
Hitchcock, Alfred	8/13/1899	
Chanel, Coco	8/19/1883	
Tamayo, Rufino	8/26/1899	
Hepburn, Katharine	5/12/1907	
Olivier, Sir Laurence	5/22/1907	
Wayne, John	5/26/1907	
Carson, Rachel	5/27/1907	
Kahlo, Frida	7/6/1907	
Watts, Alan	1/6/1915	
Holiday, Billie	4/17/1915	
Quinn, Anthony	4/21/1915	
Welles, Orson	5/6/1915	
Paul, Les	6/9/1915	
Warrick, Ruth	6/29/1915	

Name	Date	
Kennedy, Jr., Joseph Patrick	7/25/1915	
Gardner, Ava	12/24/1922	
McMahon, Ed	3/6/1923	
Schirra, Walter	3/12/1923	
Prince Ranier III of Monaco	5/31/1923	
Ergund, Ahmet	7/31/1923	

Scorpio Evening Stars

Name	Date	
Kant, Immanuel	4/22/1724	*
Washington, George	2/22/1732	*
Hayden, F. J.	3/31/1732	*
Antoinette, Marie	**11/2/1755**	*
Mozart, Wolfgang Amadeus	1/27/1756	*
Burr, Aaron	2/6/1756	*
Baba, Sai	**11/23/1926**	
Price, Leontyne	2/10/1927	
Belafonte, Harry	3/1/1927	
Pope Benedict XVI	4/16/1927	
King, Coretta Scott	4/27/1927	
Leigh, Janet	7/6/1927	
Castro, Fidel	8/13/1927	
Carter, Rosalind	8/18/1927	
Chamberlain, Richard	3/31/1934	
Dench, Dame Judith	12/9/1934	
Presley, Elvis	1/5/1935	
Bono, Sonny	2/16/1935	
Lynn, Loretta	4/14/1935	
14th Dalai Lama: Gyatso, Tenzin	7/6/1935	
Sutherland, Donald	7/17/1935	
Phillips, John	8/30/1935	
Erhard, Werner	9/5/1935	
Scorcese, Martin	**11/17/1942**	
Evans, Linda	**11/18/1942**	
Biden, Joe	**11/20/1942**	
Hand, Robert	12/5/1942	
Han, Hak Ja	1/6/1943	
Joplin, Janis	1/19/1943	
Tate, Sharon	1/24/1943	
Harrison, George	2/25/1943	
Fisher, Bobby	3/9/1943	
Major, John	3/29/1943	
Robertson, Robbie	7/5/1943	
McVie, Christine	7/12/1943	
Jagger, Mick	7/26/1943	
DeNiro, Robert	8/17/1943	
Onassis, Christina	12/11/1950	
Rove, Karl	12/25/1950	
Limbaugh, Rush	1/12/1951	

Brown, Gordon	2/20/1951	
Stedman, Graham	3/6/1951	
Russell, Kurt	3/17/1951	
Jackson, Jackie	5/4/1951	
Ride, Sally	5/26/1951	
Biden, Jill	6/5/1951	
Orman, Suze	6/5/1951	
Ventura, Jessie	7/15/1951	
Queen Noor	8/23/1951	
Yanni	11/14/1954	
Curtis, Jamie Lee	11/22/1958	
McGuire, Michael	12/28/1958	
Sade	1/16/1959	
Arnold, Tom	3/6/1959	
Travis, Randy	5/4/1959	
Simpson, Nicole Brown	5/19/1959	
Spacey, Kevin	7/26/1959	
Johnson, Earvin "Magic"	8/14/1959	
Bush, Dorothy	8/18/1959	
Robinson, Chris	12/20/1966	
Sutherland, Kiefer	12/21/1966	
Matthews, Dave	1/9/1967	
Cobain, Kurt	2/20/1967	
McGraw, Tim	5/1/1967	
Giamatti, Paul	6/6/1967	
Kidman, Nicole	6/20/1967	
Anderson, Pamela	7/1/1967	
Ferrell, Will	7/16/1967	
LeBlanc, Matt	7/25/1967	
DiCaprio, Leonardo	11/11/1974	
Seacrest, Ryan	12/24/1974	
Barrymore, Drew	2/22/1975	
Longoria, Eva	3/15/1975	
Fergie	3/27/1975	
Beckham, David	5/2/1975	
Iglesias, Enrique	5/8/1975	
Jolie, Angelina	6/4/1975	
Macguire, Tobey	6/27/1975	
Theron, Charlize	8/7/1975	
Witt, Alicia	8/21/1975	
Hathaway, Anne	11/12/1982	
Kreuk, Kristin	12/30/1982	
Bosworth, Kate	1/2/1983	
Blunt, Emily	2/23/1983	
Underwood, Carrie	3/10/1983	
JoJo	12/20/1990	
Roberts, Emma	2/10/1991	
Spears, Jamie Lynn	4/4/1991	

Scorpio Morning Stars

Cook, Captain James	**11/7/1728**	*
Ross, Betsy	1/1/1752	*
Monroe, Elizabeth	6/30/1768	*
Austen, Jane	12/16/1775	*
Dean, James	2/8/1931	
Morrison, Toni	2/8/1931	
Gorbachev, Mikhail	3/2/1931	
Shatner, William	3/22/1931	
Nimoy, Leonard	3/26/1931	
Das, Ram	4/6/1931	
Mays, Willie	5/6/1931	
Jones, Jim	5/13/1931	
Grof, Stanislav	7/1/1931	
Gorman, R. C.	7/26/1931	
Turner, Ted	**11/19/1938**	
Ullman, Liv	12/16/1938	
Arguelles, Jose	1/24/1939	
Greer, Germaine	1/29/1939	
Capra, Fritzof	2/1/1939	
Coppola, Francis Ford	4/7/1939	
McKellen, Ian	5/25/1939	
Williams, Paul	7/2/1939	
Chicago, Judy	7/20/1939	
McKenna, Terrence	**11/16/1946**	
Versace, Gianni	12/2/1946	
Gummer, Don	12/12/1946	
Andersson, Benny	12/16/1946	
Spielberg, Steven	12/18/1946	
Bowie, David	1/8/1947	
Fawcett, Farrah	2/2/1947	
Caine, Shakira	2/23/1947	
Close, Glenn	3/19/1947	
John, Elton	3/25/1947	
Harris, Emilou	4/2/1947	
Letterman, David	4/12/1947	
Rushdie, Salmon	6/19/1947	
Fleetwood, Mick	6/24/1947	
Barry, Dave	7/3/1947	
Simpson, O. J.	7/9/1947	
Parker-Bowles, Camilla	7/17/1947	
Santana, Carlos	7/20/1947	
Schwartzenegger, Arnold	7/30/1947	
Coelho, Paulo	8/24/1947	
Rice, Condoleezza	**11/14/1954**	
Summers, Lawrence	11/30/1954	
Jackson, Jermaine	12/11/1954	
Lennox, Annie	12/25/1954	

Name	Date	
King, Gayle	12/28/1954	
Washington, Denzel	12/28/1954	
Styler, Trudy	1/6/1955	
Bush, Neil	1/22/1955	
Sarkozy, Nicolas	1/28/1955	
Willis, Bruce	3/19/1955	
Kingsolver, Barbara	4/8/1955	
Al-Fayed, Dodi	4/15/1955	
Carvey, Dana	6/2/1955	
Iman	7/25/1955	
Moore, Demi	**11/11/1962**	
Foster, Jodie	**11/19/1962**	
Stewart, Jon	11/28/1962	
Huffman, Felicity	12/9/1962	
Fiennes, Ralph	12/22/1962	
Jordan, Michael	2/17/1963	
Seal	2/19/1963	
Williams, Vanessa	3/18/1963	
O'Brien, Conan	4/18/1963	
Richardson, Natasha	5/11/1963	
Myers, Mike	5/25/1963	
Depp, Johnny	6/9/1963	
Hunt, Helen	6/15/1963	
Michael, George	6/25/1963	
Falco, Edie	7/5/1963	
Cates, Phoebe	7/16/1963	
Kennedy, Patrick	8/7/1963	
Houston, Whitney	8/9/1963	
Harding, Tonya	**11/12/1970**	
DioGuardi, Kara	12/9/1970	
Blige, Mary J.	1/11/1971	
Sarsgaard, Peter	3/7/1971	
Weisz, Rachel	3/7/1971	
McGregor, Ewan	3/31/1971	
Sehorn, Jason	4/15/1971	
Coppola, Sofia	5/14/1971	
Shakur, Tupac	6/16/1971	
Yamaguchi, Kristi	7/12/1971	
Taylor, Christine	7/30/1971	
Holmes, Katie	12/18/1978	
Brandy	2/11/1979	
Hewitt, Jennifer Love	2/21/1979	
Jones, Norah	3/30/1979	
Ledger, Heath	4/4/1979	
Hudson, Kate	4/19/1979	
Cavallari, Kristin	1/14/1987	
Lil Bow Wow	3/9/1987	
McCartney, Jesse	4/9/1987	

Name	Date	
Stone, Joss	4/11/1987	
Sharapova, Maria	4/19/1987	
Castro, Raquel	**11/17/1994**	
Greenfield, Chloe	7/7/1995	
Taurus Evening Stars		
Geronimo (Goyathlay)	**5/29/1829**	
Hickok, Wild Bill	5/27/1837	
Cody, Buffalo Bill	2/26/1846	
Leadbetter, C. W.	2/16/1854	
Roosevelt, Edith	8/6/1861	
Goldman, Emma	6/27/1869	
Gandhi, Mahatma	10/2/1869	
Matisse, Henri	12/31/1869	
Hesse, Herman	7/2/1877	
Sandburg, Carl	1/6/1878	
Buber, Martin	2/8/1878	
Lawrence, D. H.	9/11/1885	
Patton, George S.	11/11/1885	
Perls, Fritz	7/8/1893	
Tung, Mao Tse	12/26/1893	
Rockwell, Norman	2/3/1894	
Benny, Jack	2/14/1894	
Cooper, Gary	**5/7/1901**	
Bush, Dorothy Walker	7/1/1901	
Armstrong, Louis	8/4/1901	
Sullivan, Ed	9/28/1901	
Disney, Walt	12/5/1901	
Mead, Margaret	12/16/1901	
Dietrich, Marlene	12/27/1901	
Bing, Sir Rudolph	1/9/1902	
Lindbergh, Charles	2/4/1902	
Flynn, Errol	6/20/1909	
Tandy, Jessica	7/7/1909	
Nelson, Harriette	7/18/1909	
Fitzgerald, Ella	**4/25/1917**	
Pei, I. M.	**4/26/1917**	
Kennedy, John F.	5/29/1917	
Martin, Dean	6/7/1917	
Marcos, Ferdinand	9/11/1917	
Hillerman, Tony	5/27/1925	
Curtis, Tony	6/3/1925	
Bush, Barbara	6/8/1925	
Griffin, Merv	7/6/1925	
Sellers, Peter	9/8/1925	
King, B. B.	9/16/1925	
Thatcher, Margaret	10/13/1925	
Carson, Johnny	10/23/1925	
Burton, Richard	11/10/1925	

Appendix III

Winters, Jonathan	11/11/1925	
Hudson, Rock	11/17/1925	
Kennedy, Robert F.	11/20/1925	
Davis, Sammy Jr.	12/8/1925	
Van Dyke, Dick	12/13/1925	
Martin, Sir George	1/3/1926	
Burnett, Carol	**4/26/1933**	
Nelson, Willie	**4/30/1933**	
Brown, James	**5/3/1933**	
Feinstein, Dianne	6/22/1933	
Polanski, Roman	8/18/1933	
King, Larry	11/19/1933	
Taurus Morning Stars		
Brahms, Johannes	**5/7/1833**	
Haeckel, Ernst	2/16/1834	
Conrad, Joseph	12/3/1857	
Yeats, William Butler	6/13/1865	
Cavell, Edith	12/4/1865	
Kipling, Rudyard	12/30/1865	
Carter, Howard	**5/9/1873**	
Stein, Gertrude	2/3/1874	
DeMille, Cecil B.	8/12/1881	
Picasso, Pablo	10/25/1881	
Woolfe, Virginia	1/25/1882	
Johndro, Lord Edward	1/30/1882	
Roosevelt, Franklin Delano	1/30/1882	
Joyce, James	2/2/1882	
Barrymore, John	2/15/1882	
Cocteau, Jean	7/5/1889	
Earhart, Amelia	7/24/1897	
Day, Dorothy	11/8/1897	
Fonda, Henry	**5/16/1905**	
Sartre, Jean Paul	6/21/1905	
Garbo, Greta	9/8/1905	
Hughes, Howard	12/24/1905	
Onassis, Aristotle	1/20/1906	
Ford, Gerald	7/14/1913	
Leigh, Vivian	11/5/1913	
Ponti, Carlo	12/11/1913	
Berrigan, Daniel	**5/9/1921**	
David, Hal	5/25/1921	
Prince Philip, Duke of Edinburgh	6/10/1921	
Reagan, Nancy	7/6/1921	
Kennedy, Eunice	7/10/1921	
Glenn, John	7/18/1921	
Haley, Alex	8/11/1921	
Roddenberry, Gene	8/19/1921	
Allen, Steve	12/26/1921	

Meadows, Audrey	2/8/1922	
Virgo Evening Stars		
Catherine the Great	5/2/1729	*
Crowley, Aleister	10/12/1875	
Rilke, Ramer Maria	12/4/1875	
Truman, Harry	5/8/1884	
Brice, Fanny	10/29/1891	
Miller, Henry	12/26/1891	
Tolkein, J. R. R.	1/3/1892	
Hardy, Oliver	1/18/1892	
Buck, Pearl	6/26/1892	
Coward, Noel	12/16/1899	
Bunuel, Luis	2/22/1900	
Weill, Kurt	3/2/1900	
Tracy, Spencer	4/5/1900	
Wray, Fay	**9/15/1907**	
Autry, Gene	9/29/1907	
de Beauvoir, Simone	1/9/1908	
Davis, Bette	4/5/1908	
Seymour, Frances Ford	4/14/1908	
Stewart, James	5/20/1908	
Fleming, Ian	5/28/1908	
Bridges, Dorothy	**9/19/1915**	
Miller, Arthur	10/17/1915	
Shriver, Robert	11/9/1915	
Sinatra, Frank	12/12/1915	
Piaf, Edith	12/19/1915	
Gleason, Jackie	2/26/1916	
Shore, Dinah	2/29/1916	
Peck, Gregory	4/15/1916	
Crick, Francis	6/8/1916	
Khan, Pir Vilayat Inayat	6/19/1916	
Lawford, Peter	**9/7/1923**	
Berrigan, Philip	10/5/1923	
Heston, Charlton	10/24/1923	
Shephard, Alan	11/18/1923	
Callas, Maria	12/2/1923	
Brando, Marlon	4/3/1924	
Kennedy, Patricia	5/6/1924	
Bush, George H. W.	6/12/1924	
Philbin, Regis	**8/25/1931**	**
Walters, Barbara	9/25/1931	
Turner, Ike	11/5/1931	
Rajneesh, Bagwan Shree	12/11/1931	
Gorbachev, Raisa	1/5/1932	
Kennedy, Edward	2/22/1932	
Cash, Johnny	2/26/1932	
Taylor, Elizabeth	2/27/1932	

371

Reynolds, Debbie	4/1/1932		Obama, Michelle	1/17/1964	
Sharif, Omar	4/10/1932		Linney, Laura	2/5/1964	
Cuomo, Mario	6/15/1932		Palin, Sarah	2/11/1964	
Oswald, Lee Harvey	10/18/1939		Binoche, Juliette	3/9/1964	
Cleese, John	10/27/1939		Prince Edward	3/10/1964	
Slick, Grace	10/30/1939		Crowe, Russell	4/7/1964	
Turner, Tina	11/26/1939		Colbert, Stephen	5/13/1964	
Kendricks, Eddie	12/17/1939		Judd, Wynonna	5/30/1964	
Bakker, Jim	1/2/1940		Cox, Courteney	6/15/1964	
Brokaw, Tom	2/6/1940		**Arquette, David**	**9/8/1971**	
Koppel, Ted	2/8/1940		**McCartney, Stella**	**9/13/1971**	
Pelosi, Nancy	3/26/1940		**Armstrong, Lance**	**9/18/1971**	
Pacino, Al	4/25/1940		**Pinkett-Smith, Jada**	**9/18/1971**	
Nelson, Rickie	5/8/1940		Ryder, Winona	10/29/1971	
King, Stephen	**9/21/1947**		Martin, Ricky	12/24/1971	
Kline, Kevin	10/24/1947		O'Neal, Shaquille	3/6/1972	
Clinton, Hillary Rodham	10/26/1947		Garner, Jennifer	4/17/1972	
Dreyfuss, Richard	10/29/1947		Langdon, Royston	5/1/1972	
Richardson, Bill	11/15/1947		Mya	10/10/1979	
Danson, Ted	12/29/1947		Blake, James	12/28/1979	
Goldberg, Natalie	1/4/1948		Nordegren, Elin	1/1/1980	
Baryshnikov, Mikhail	1/27/1948		Rogers, Amerie	1/12/1980	
Guest, Christopher	2/5/1948		Carter, Nick	1/28/1980	
Crystal, Billy	3/14/1948		Valderrama, Wilmer	1/30/1980	
Webber, Andrew Lloyd	3/22/1948		Ricci, Christina	2/12/1980	
Tyler, Steven	3/26/1948		Clinton, Chelsea	2/27/1980	
Gore, Al	3/31/1948		Chingy	3/9/1980	
Perlman, Rhea	3/31/1948		Wall, Paul	3/30/1980	
Cliff, Jimmy	4/1/1948		**Virgo Morning Stars**		
Nicks, Stevie	5/26/1948		Handel, George Friedrich	2/23/1685	*
Ma, Yo Yo	10/7/1955		Bach, Johann Sebastian	3/21/1685	*
Gates, Bill	10/28/1955		O'Keefe, Georgia	11/15/1887	
Shriver, Maria	11/6/1955		Assagioli, Roberto	2/27/1888	
Goldberg, Whoopie	11/13/1955		Rockne, Knute	3/4/1888	
Wilson, Cassandra	12/4/1955		Simpson, Wallis	6/19/1895	
Wright, Steven	12/6/1955		**Muni, Paul**	**9/22/1895**	
Gibson, Mel	1/3/1956		Peron, Juan	10/8/1895	
Maher, Bill	1/20/1956		Freud, Anna	12/3/1895	
Rogers, Mimi	1/27/1956		Burns, George	1/20/1896	
Zahn, Paula	2/24/1956		**Colbert, Claudette**	**9/13/1903**	**
Kelley, David E.	4/4/1956		Dixon, Jean	1/5/1904	
Garcia, Andy	4/12/1956		Grant, Cary	1/18/1904	
Borg, Bjorn	6/6/1956		Davis, Adelle	2/25/1904	
McGuire, Mark	10/1/1963		Campbell, Joseph	3/26/1904	
Maples, Marla	10/27/1963		Gielgud, John	4/14/1904	
Schiavo, Terri	12/3/1963		Oppenheimer, Robert	4/22/1904	
Pitt, Brad	12/18/1963		Dali, Salvador	5/11/1904	
Cage, Nicholas	1/7/1964		Cosby, Camille	4/27/1905	

Appendix III

Name	Date
Pollock, Jackson	1/28/1912
Nixon, Pat	3/16/1912
Trudeau, Pierre	10/18/1919
Pahlavi, Mohammad Reza	10/26/1919
Asminov, Isaac	1/2/1920
Fellini, Federico	1/20/1920
Kennedy, Kathleen	2/20/1920
Moon, Sun Myung	2/25/1920
Pope John Paul II	5/18/1920
Kennedy, Jean Ann	2/20/1928
Garcia-Marquez, Gabriel	3/6/1928
Albee, Edward	3/13/1928
Angelou, Maya	4/4/1928
Watson, James D	4/6/1928
Kennedy, Ethel	4/11/1928
Bacharach, Burt	5/12/1928
Westheimer, Dr. Ruth	6/4/1928
Ivory, James	6/7/1928
Guevara, Che	5/14/1928
Andrews, Julie	10/1/1935
Hussein, King of Jordan	11/14/1935
Allen, Woody	12/1/1935
Reynolds, Burt	2/11/1936
Darin, Bobby	5/14/1936
Gossett, Jr., Lou	5/27/1936
Walesa, Lech	9/29/1943
Chase, Chevy	10/8/1943
Deneuve, Catherine	10/22/1943
Shepard, Sam	11/5/1943
Ramsey, John	12/7/1943
Kerry, John	12/11/1943
Richards, Keith	12/18/1943
Davis, Angela	1/26/1944
Walker, Alice	2/9/1944
Demme, Jonathan	2/22/1944
Ross, Diana	3/26/1944
Waters, Alice	4/28/1944
Lucas, George	5/14/1944
Giuliani, Rudy	5/28/1944
Phillips, Michelle	6/4/1944
Hynde, Chyrissie	**9/7/1951**
Almodovar, Pedro	9/24/1951
Sting	10/2/1951
Mellencamp, John	10/7/1951
Zemeckis, Robert	5/14/1952
Neeson, Liam	6/7/1952
Cowell, Simon	10/7/1959
Osmond, Marie	10/13/1959
Ferguson, Sarah	10/15/1959
Roper, Richard	10/17/1959
Ullman, Tracey	12/30/1959
Prince Andrew	2/19/1960
Bono	5/10/1960
Scott Thomas, Kristin	5/24/1960
Valenzuela, Fernando	11/1/1960
Hill, Faith	9/21/1967
Urban, Keith	10/26/1967
Roberts, Julia	10/28/1967
Rossdale, Gavin	10/30/1967
Smith, Anna Nicole	11/28/1967
Fox, Jamie	12/13/1967
Bruni, Carla	12/23/1967
Mills, Heather	1/12/1968
LL Cool J	1/14/1968
MacLachlan, Sarah	1/28/1968
Presley, Lisa Marie	2/1/1968
Brolin, Josh	2/12/1968
Dion, Celine	3/30/1968
Judd, Ashley	4/19/1968
Buble, Michael	**9/9/1975**
Woods, Tiger	12/30/1975
Witherspoon, Reese	3/22/1976
Capriati, Jennifer	3/29/1976
Hilton, Nicky	10/5/1983
Santana, Juelz	2/18/1984
McPhee, Katherine	3/25/1984
Moore, Mandy	4/10/1984
Ferrera, America	4/18/1984
Sigler, Jamie-Lynn	5/15/1984

* denotes people born in previous Venus Star cycle
** denotes people born just prior to star date, but very close to it

APPENDIX IV

HOUSES OF THE VENUS STAR POINT

Chapters 4-15 delved deeply into the nature, character and motivating life principles of the Venus Star Point's placement through the zodiac. Another dimension to explore is which House the Venus Star Point occupies in a chart. Figure 3.1 shows Sign/House associations, and the list below expands the association by providing further detail into the House position. The Venus Star Point by House gives a person a life-long passion and driving ambition towards expressing their genuine talent in the ways described below.

First House (read also Aries Star Point, Chapter 10)
Standing out and being noticed; initiating or launching new enterprises; putting ideas into instant action; travelling down roads where few have gone before; taking courageous and fearless risks to achieve personal goals. Shadow: blindness to everything else but one's own agenda.

Second House (read also Taurus Star Point, Chapter 4)
Building something magnificent and solid from the ground up; a persistent and tenacious development to achieve personal security and financial independence; developing and maintaining relationships and structures that endure through time; an avid interest in beauty and art. Shadow: grasping too tightly to people or things.

Third House (read also Gemini Star Point, Chapter 11)
Developing educational opportunities for self and others; enhancing learning skills through speech, writing and dissemination of information; a passion to enhance communication skills as a means of peace-making among family members and team members; a close sibling relationship. Shadow: sibling rivalry and competition might spark rumors, lies and negative press.

Fourth House (read also Cancer Star Point, Chapter 6)
Developing roots, security and a strong family core; securing your dream home and property and nurturing its growth; a passionate relationship with food as an avocation or vocation; deep relationship with mother. Shadow: childhood wounds that suppress real feelings, even into adulthood.

Fifth House (read also Leo Star Point, Chapter 13)
Marking your place in life through exhibiting your personal stamp of creativity and talent on a very public stage; entertaining others endlessly; a playful and affectionate connection with people, children and animals all of whom are irresistible to your charms. Shadow: Becoming the self-appointed Queen or King who subjects one's rule to the people in your life as devoted worshippers.

Sixth House (read also Virgo Star Point, Chapter 7)
Becoming indispensible to those around you through the many skills you possess; a unique ability to work with a variety of healing techniques and provide service to others; Earth's bountiful harvest is yours for the taking and is dispensed carefully and lovingly to those whom you care for. Shadow: when path of service is not aligned to heart, one can become quite frustrated, anxiety-ridden and subsequently ill.

Seventh House (read also Libra Star Point, Chapter 14)
Building, developing and sustaining life-long partnership is your goal; peaceful co-existence and equality in relationship is your gift; creating artistic and pleasing environments and resolving conflict disputes are your specialty. Shadow: idealizing partnership at any price; peace for the sake of peace; inability to confront the opposition head-on when needed.

Eighth House (read also Scorpio Star Point, Chapter 9)
Securing personal power through one's intimate relationships; possessing an uncanny ability to penetrate the veil between states of material and non-material reality; a shaman's way of viewing the world; a knack for deep research, uncovering long buried mysteries and secret motives. Shadow: an unconscious ability to manipulate others for personal gain.

Ninth House (read also Sagittarius Star Point, Chapter 5)
Developing and promoting an expanded world view that allows many different belief systems to flourish; travel and cohabitation with people of different cultural or spiritual viewpoints.

You are a philosopher and freedom-loving adventurer, at heart, and are not afraid to engage in dangerous and risky undertakings. Shadow: engaging in a dogmatic set of beliefs that preach doctrine rather than demonstrate tolerance.

Tenth House (read also Capricorn Star Point, Chapter 12)
A talent for expressing yourself through career success and notoriety; the ability to manage and organize groups and work teams, large or small. You have developed a creative style of mentoring, parenting and teaching skills as powerful resources. Shadow: With lack of authority and recognition, you wither, fearful that people can't love you for yourself rather than the power you possess.

Eleventh House (read also Aquarius Star Point, Chapter 8)
You possess a passion and talent for social responsibility; your intellect and voice inspire others to engage in local, national or global issues of concern; you strongly resist being one of the sheep, taking intentional steps toward being unique and living outside of the box. Shadow: A stubborn resistance to alternative views can blind you to facts and ideas that might have merit.

Twelfth House (read also Pisces Star Point, Chapter 15)
You are committed to a life of spiritual processes and disciplines that bring peace and tranquility. Involved in overcoming addictions, resolving past-life issues and healing emotional wounds for the purpose of liberating the Soul. A gifted healer and spiritual advisor for others by overcoming fears and anxieties. Shadow: desire for easy escape mechanisms, such as addiction can become a life-long crutch of dependency to serve as protection from facing real, true feelings.

ENDNOTES

1 These terms, "dominator model" and "partnership model," coined eloquently in Riane Eisler's seminal work *The Chalice and the Blade* (San Francisco, Harper & Row, 1987), describe the changes referred to here.

2 Mario Livio, *The Golden Ratio: The Story of Phi, the World's Most Astonishing Number,* quoting British physicist Sir James Jeans (New York, Random House, 2002), 10

3 Christopher Knight and Robert Lomas, *The Book of Hiram: Freemasonry, Venus and the Secret Key to the Life of Jesus* (Sterling Publishing, New York, 2003), 41-42

4 To learn more about labyrinths, see Dr. Lauren Artress, *Walking A Sacred Path: Rediscovering the Labyrinth as a Spiritual Tool* (New York, Riverhead Books, 1995)

5 Graham Hancock and Santha Faiia, *Heaven's Mirror* (New York, Three Rivers Press, 1998)

6 Susan Milbrath, *The Star Gods of the Maya: Astronomy in Art, Folklore and Calendars* (Austin, TX, University of Texas Press, 1999), 52

7 This mathematical sequence has been applied in countless ways in the modern world.

8 Marcus Vitruvius Pollio was the first century BCE architect who originally drew this analogy, which has been extensively copied, most notably by Leonardo da Vinci, whose drawing resides in Venice's Galleria dell' Accademia.

9 Michael S. Schneider, *A Beginner's Guide to Constructing the Universe: The Mathematical Archetypes of Nature, Art, and Science* (New York: Harper Perennial, 1994), 96

10 Ibid., 98-99

11 Ean Begg, *Cult of the Black Virgin,* rev. ed. (London, Arkana Penguin, 1996), 142

12 Michael Baigent, *From The Omens of Babylon: Astrology and Ancient Mesopotamia* (London, Arkana Penguin Books, 1994)

13 Ibid.

14 To determine if your Venus is a Morning Star or Evening Star, simply note the relationship in your horoscope to your Sun. If Venus is zodiacally ahead of the Sun, she is an Evening Star. If Venus is placed zodiacally behind the Sun, she is a Morning Star.

15 Robert Hand, "Planetary Periods" (lecture, Australis 1997 Congress, Adelaide, Australia, 1997)

16 Deborah Houlding, "The Beauty of the Venus Cycle," *The Mountain Astrologer* Feb/Mar 2010, 77, quoting Abraham Ibn Ezra's 12th century *The Book of Reasons* (Leiden, The Netherlands, Brill, 2007)

17 Susan Milbrath, *The Star Gods of the Maya,* 52

18 Barbara G. Walker, *The Woman's Encyclopedia of Myths and Secrets* (San Francisco, Harper & Row, 1983) 866–67

19   Lynn Picknett and Clive Prince, *The Templar Revelation: Secret Guardians of the True Identity of Christ* (New York: Touchstone, 1998), 157

20   Alan Butler, *The Goddess, the Grail, and the Lodge: The Real DaVinci Code and the Origins of Religion* (Winchester, UK, 0 Books, 2004), 140

21   Ibid., 140

22   Ibid., 144-146

23   Wikimedia Commons under Creative Commons Attribution-Share Alike 2.5 generic

24   Graham Hancock, *Fingerprints of the Gods* (New York, New York, USA, Three Rivers Press, 1995), 158-159. citing J. Eric Thompson, *The Rise and Fall of Maya Civilization* (Pimlico, London, 1993). Thompson is credited with being one of the foremost scholars of the Mayan calendar, deciphering its start date and end date.

25   Adrian G. Gilbert and Maurice M. Cotterell, *The Mayan Prophecies* (Rockport, Massachusetts, USA, Element Books, 1995), 33. There are other references to the "first rising of or birth of Venus as a planet," most notably the controversial work by Dr. Immanuel Velikovsky, *Worlds in Collision* (New York, Dell Publishing Co., 1973).

26   John Major Jenkins, *Galactic Alignment* (Rochester, Vermont, USA, Bear & Company, 2002). This is Jenkins' second work dedicated to the rare astronomical alignment of 2012. The first work, *Maya Cosmogenesis 2012* (Rochester, Vermont, USA, Bear & Company, 2002) details what clues the Maya meticulously recorded and left for future generations to unravel.

27   Kenneth Johnson comment in a conversation with the author after visiting the Mayan elders of today in the Guatemalan highlands. Johnson is the author of *Jaguar Wisdom*, which links astrology and Mayan mythology with the Mayan calendar.

28   *The Dresden Codex* is a book of Mayan astronomy from the eleventh or twelfth century. It reveals the precision with which the Maya recorded celestial cycles, particularly of the planet Venus. *The Dresden Codex* describes extremely accurate calculations of the location of Venus.

29   Gilbert & Cotterell, *The Mayan Prophecies*, 38

30   The importance of such outer planet alignments correlating to historical changes cannot be overstated. For an excellent treatise on the impact of outer planet occurrences on Earth, refer to Richard Tarnas's *Psyche and Cosmos: Intimations of a New World View* (New York: Viking Press, 2006).

31   Dennis Tedlock, *Popul Vuh: The Mayan Book of the Dawn of Life* (New York, Simon & Schuster, 1985)

32   Susan Milbrath, *The Star Gods of the Maya*, 52

33   Daniel Giamario, "A Shamanic Investigation of Venus and Mars, Part Two," *The Mountain Astrologer*, Feb/March 1997, 51-60

34   Knight and Lomas, *The Book of Hiram*, 238-240

35   *Phaedrus*, Plato, 360 BCE, translated by Benjamin Jowett (http://www.e-text.org/text/Plato%20-%20PHAEDRUS.pdf)

36   Bob Dylan, "The Times They Are A-Changin,'" *The Times They Are A-Changin'*, (Sony Records, 1964)

37   John Lennon, "Mother," *Imagine* (Capitol Records, 1988)

Endnotes

38   John Lennon, "Woman," *Imagine* (Capitol Records, 1988)

39   *Forrest Gump*, directed by Robert Zemeckis (Paramount Pictures, 1994)

40   *Philadelphia*, directed by Jonathan Demme (TriStar Pictures, 1993)

41   *I Am Sam*, directed by Jessie Nelson (New Line Cinema, 2001)

42   *Milk*, directed by Gus Van Sant (Focus Features, 2008)

43   Bob Dylan, "Gotta Serve Somebody," *Slow Train Coming* (Columbia Records, 1979)

44   *Scoop,* written and directed by Woody Allen (Focus Features, 2006)

45   *Broadcast News,* written and directed by James L. Brooks (20th Century Fox, 1987)

46   encarta.msn.com/encyclopedia.../age_of_enlightenment.html I

47   *The Dark Knight*, directed by Christopher Nolan (Warner Brothers, 2008)

48   The Sabian symbols are a channeled series of images that appeared around the inception of the Aries Star and are applied to each degree of the 360 degree zodiac wheel. *The Sabian Symbols in Astrology: A Symbol Explained for Each Degree of the Zodiac* was the first work published in 1953 by Marc Edmond Jones (republished in 1978 by Shambhala Publications, Boulder, CO and London). Since then, at least four other works have been published illuminating these symbols, some of which are listed in the bibliography.

49   Dan Brown, *The Da Vinci Code* (New York, Doubleday Group, 2003)

50   Bob Dylan, "The Times They Are A-Changin'"

51   The Harmonic Convergence was an astronomical alignment that occurred on August 17, 1987, ostensibly linked to an ancient prophecy concerning the Mayan calendar and the significance of the calendar's frequent reference to the year 2012.

52   James Redfield, *The Celestine Prophecy* (New York, Warner Books Inc., 1993)

53   Many books of the early twenty-first century have speculated that the founding fathers of America were part of the brotherhood of Freemasonry and were aware, if even superficially, that Venus traced a pentagram in her orbit every eight years. See bibliography for sources.

54   *Queen Elizabeth*, directed by Henri Desfontaines and Louis Mercanton (Paramount Studios, 1912)

55   *The Wizard of Oz*, directed by Victor Fleming (MGM Studios, 1939)

56   *The Lion King*, directed by Roger Allers and Rob Minkoff (Walt Disney Pictures, 1994)

57   *Little Miss Sunshine*, directed by Jonathan Dayton and Valerie Faris (Fox Searchlight Pictures, 2006)

58   Charles Dickens, *A Tale of Two Cities* (London, Chapman & Hall, 1859)

59   Carnegie Corporation of New York, "Our Founder," (http://www.carnegie.org/sub/about/biography.html)

60   Ignatius Donnelly, *Atlantis: The Antediluvian World* (New York, Harper & Brothers, 1882)

61   Elson M. Haas, MD, *Staying Healthy with the Seasons* (Berkeley, CA: Celestial Arts, 1981), 166

62   Ibid.

63   Ibid., 26

64   Scorpio was fed on the Karmic Star by Taurus only briefly. The Taurus Star's much longer life-link feeds Sagittarius.

65   Bonaparte's Moon at 29° Capricorn is an estimate, based on a noon birth time. His actual Moon will be within 5 to 6 degrees of this point.

66   Since there will not be a link on the Venus Star from Capricorn to Pisces until 2041 and from Capricorn to Libra until 2022, we will observe their previous Venus Star relationships.

67   Although different signs are indicated, this pair falls under the same VSP, Libra/Virgo, born three full Venus Star cycles apart. Their VSPs are: 5° Libra (Stieglitz) and 28° Virgo (O'Keeffe).

68   The exact times of birth for Sullivan and Keller are not available. The Moon for Keller using an average time of noon occurs at 15 degrees Pisces.

Glossary of Terms

Aspect: derived from Latin signifying "to look at" or "to gaze upon," an aspect is the angular relationship between one orbiting body and another, measured in degrees of the circle, such as conjunction (0°), trine (120°), quintile (72°), etc.

Biquintile: an aspect of 144° denoting talent, and a regularly occurring aspect in the creation of the Venus Star

Cazimi: an Arabic term meaning "in the heart of the Sun," when a planet is within 0.5° of the Sun and said to be greatly strengthened. In this volume the Venus Star Points referred to are actually cazimi (0°00'), whereby Venus has penetrated the heart of the solar disk.

Conjunction: an aspect or position occupied by two planets that are located within a very close range of one another (usually 0° to 10°) in celestial longitude, indicating a blending or merging of the energies of each of the two bodies involved

Contra-parallel: see declination

Declination: distance in degrees and minutes that a planet is located from the celestial equator; when two planets are located within one degree of each other relative to the celestial equator they are said to be parallel (both bodies north or both bodies south) or contra-parallel (one body north and one body south). Parallels and contra-parallels greatly increase the potency of the two planets in relationship.

Degree: separations of the circle (360° in all) denoting the location of a planet or Venus Star Point at a particular time

Direct: when a planet appears to be moving forward, or counter-clockwise, around the wheel through the natural order of the zodiac

Eclipse: the passage of the Moon across the Sun (solar eclipse) or the Earth across the Moon (lunar eclipse), thus obscuring all or part of either of these bodies from Earth's view

Evening Star: a term applied to the appearance of Venus in the evening sky, visible after sunset

Feeding: The Venus Star Point progresses from one sign to the next in its creation of its Star, thus "feeding" its energy from one point to the next

Harmonic: the circle of the zodiac of 360° divided by whole numbers. The Venus Star Points referred to in this book are typically related to the fifth harmonic.

Heliacal rising: a Greek term (from "helios") meaning a planet that rises before the Sun, and newly visible from its separation from the Sun

Inferior conjunction: the coming together of a planet such as Venus with the Sun, occurring between Sun & Earth at perigee (closest to Earth)

Morning Star: Venus in the morning sky, visible before sunrise and occurring after the inferior conjunction of Venus with the Sun

Opposition: an aspect of 180° denoting two bodies that are directly across from one another creating a polarity

Parallel: see declination

Ptolemaic: aspects used in astrology that derive from dividing the circle by 1 (conjunction); 2 (opposition); 3 (trine); 4 (square) and 6 (sextile)

Quincunx (also called inconjunct): an aspect of 150° denoting adjustment, separation or restructuring, and a regularly occurring aspect in the creation of the Venus Star

Quintile: an aspect of 72°, or the circle divided by 5 (the fifth harmonic) denoting special talent and creativity, and a regularly occurring aspect from one Venus Star Point to another, in sequential order

Retrograde: when a planet appears to be moving backwards, or clockwise, around the wheel, against the natural order of the zodiac

Sesqui-square: an aspect of 135°, also called a tri-octile, denoting a conflicting set of circumstances resulting in stress and over-reaction, and a regularly occurring aspect in the creation of the Venus Star

Square: an aspect of 90°, denoting a stressful relationship between two orbiting bodies, which requires action and attention to reduce the tension implied by this condition

Star Point: see Venus Star Point

Stationary: when a planet appears to stand in one spot without moving, just prior to it turning retrograde or direct

Superior conjunction: the coming together of a planet such as Venus with the Sun occurring on the far side of the Sun, at apogee (farthest from Earth)

Transit: the term derives from the Latin "to go over" or "to cross over," it is the passage of a planet through a certain area of the zodiac

Trine: an aspect of 120°, denoting harmony and flow

Tri-octile: see sesqui-square

Venus Star: the five points of the Star that Venus traces in the sky during the course of an eight-year period

Venus Star Point (VSP) or Star Point: one point of the five-pointed star that Venus transits, such as a sign or degree of a sign

Venus Transit: these rare transits occur in pairs in an 8 year separation, approximately 120 years apart, when Venus passes its shadow across the face of the Sun.. There are two of these occurrences in the twenty-first century: June 2004 and June 2012

Yod: a geometric pattern involving planets at three angles: two 150° quincunxes and one 60° sextile. This pattern has also been referred to as a Finger of God. Figure 2.22 illustrates this pattern and calls attention to the three Venus-related signs that make up this pattern at certain intervals of the Venus Star cycle, thus giving this pattern a distinctive Venusian flavor.

SELECTED BIBLIOGRAPHY

Artress, Lauren. *Walking a Sacred Path: Rediscovering the Labyrinth As a Spiritual Tool.* New York: Riverhead Books, 1995.

Aveni, Anthony. *Conversing with the Planets: How Science and Myth Invented the Cosmos.* New York: Times Books, 1992.

Baigent, Michael. *From the Omens of Babylon: Astrology and Ancient Mesopotamia.* London, England: Arkana Penguin Books, 1994.

Baring, Anne, and Jules Cashford. *The Myth of the Goddess: Evolution of an Image.* London, England: New York: Arkana Penguin Books, 1993.

Begg, Ean. *The Cult of the Black Virgin*, rev. ed. London, England; New York: Arkana Penguin Books, 1996.

Brown, Dan. *The Da Vinci Code.* New York: Doubleday, 2003.

Butler, Alan. *The Goddess, the Grail and the Lodge: The Real Da Vinci Code and the Origins of Religion.* Winchester, UK, New York: O Books, 2004.

Calleman, Carl Johan. *The Mystery of 2012: Predictions, Prophecies, and Possibilities.* Boulder, CO: Sounds True, 2007.

Campbell, Joseph. *The Mythic Image.* Princeton, NJ: Princeton University Press, 1975.

Cross, Matthew, and Robert Friedman, M.D. *The Golden Matrix.* Stanford, CT: Golden Matrix Publishing, 2003.

Donnelly, Ignatius J. *The Antediluvian World.* New York: Harper & Brothers, 1882.

Eisler, Riane. *The Chalice and the Blade.* San Francisco: Harper & Row, 1987.

Falvey, Tom. "Venus," *The Mountain Astrologer* (June/July 1997): 84–86.

Fuller, R. Buckminster in collaboration with Applewhite, E. J. *Explorations in the Geometry of Thinking: Synergetics.* New York: Macmillan Publishing Company, 1982.

Gadon, Elinor W. *The Once and Future Goddess: A Sweeping Visual Chronicle of the Sacred Female and Her Reemergence in the Cultural Mythology of Our Time.* San Francisco, CA: Harper and Row Publishers, 1989.

Giamario, Daniel. "A Shamanic Investigation of Venus and Mars, Part One." *The Mountain Astrologer* (Feb/Mar 1997): 13–23.

———. "A Shamanic Investigation of Venus and Mars, Part Two." *The Mountain Astrologer* (Feb/Mar 1997): 51–60.

Gilbert, Adrian G. and Maurice M. Cotterell. *The Mayan Prophecies.* Rockport, MA: Element Books, 1995.

Grossinger, Richard. *The Night Sky: The Science and Anthropology of the Stars and Planets.* Los Angeles, CA: Jeremy P. Tarcher, 1981.

Guttman, Ariel and Kenneth Johnson. *Mythic Astrology Applied: Personal Healing Through the Planets.* St. Paul, MN: Llewellyn Publications, 2004.

———. *Mythic Astrology: Archetypal Powers in the Horoscope.* St. Paul, MN: Llewellyn Publications, 1993.

Hancock, Graham. *Fingerprints of the Gods.* New York: Three Rivers Press, 1995.

Hancock, Graham and Santha Faiia. *Heaven's Mirror: Quest for the Lost Civilization.* New York: Three Rivers Press, 1998.

Huntley, H. E. *The Divine Proportion: A Study in Mathematical Beauty.* New York, NY: Dover Publications, 1970.

Houlding, Deborah. "The Beauty of the Venus Cycle" *The Mountain Astrologer* (Feb/Mar 2010).

Jenkins, John Major. *Maya Cosmogenesis 2012.* Rochester, VT: Bear & Company, 1998.

———. *Galactic Alignment.* Rochester, VT: Bear & Company, 2002.

Karouzou, Semni. *National Museum: Illustrated Guide to the Museum*, trans. David Hardy. Athens, Greece: Ekdotike Athenon S.A., 1977.

Knight, Christopher, and Robert Lomas. *The Book of Hiram: Freemasonry, Venus, and the Secret Key to the Life of Jesus.* New York: Sterling Publishing, 2003.

———. *Uriel's Machine: Uncovering the Secrets of Stonehenge, Noah's Flood, and the Dawn of Civilization.* Gloucester, MA: Fair Winds Press, 1999.

Lawlor, Robert. *Sacred Geometry: Philosophy and Practice.* New York: Thames and Hudson, 1982.

Livio, Mario. *The Golden Ratio: The Story of Phi, The World's Most Astonishing Number.* New York: Broadway Books, 2003.

Lundy, Miranda. *Sacred Geometry.* New York, NY: Walker and Company, 2001.

Mann, A. T. *The Round Art: The Astrology of Time and Space.* New York: Galley Press, 1979.

Martineau, John. *A Little Book of Coincidence.* New York: Walker & Company, 2001.

McNutt, Mark S. "Venus Lucifer and Venus Hesperus." *The Mountain Astrologer* (March 1993): 49–50.

Melchizedek, Drunvalo. *The Ancient Secret of the Flower of Life*. AZ: Light Technology Publishing, 2000.

———. *The Ancient Secret of the Flower of Life*. Flagstaff, AZ: Light Technology Publishing, 1998.

Michell, John. *The Dimensions of Paradise: The Proportions and Symbolic Numbers of Ancient Cosmology*. Kempton, IL: Adventures Unlimited Press, 2001.

Michelson, Neil F. *The American Ephemeris for the 21st Century*. San Diego: ACS Publications, 1997.

———. *The American Ephemeris for the 20th Century*. San Diego: ACS Publications, 1991.

Milbrath, Susan. *Star Gods of the Maya: Astronomy in Art, Folklore and Calendars*. Austin, TX: University of Texas Press, 1999.

Ovason, David. *The Secret Architecture of Our Nation's Capital: The Masons and the Building of Washington, D.C.* New York: Perennial/Harper Collins, 2002.

Picknett, Lynn, and Clive Prince. *The Templar Revelation: Secret Guardians of the True Identity of Christ*. New York: Touchstone, 1998.

Purce, Jill. *The Mystic Spiral: Journey of the Soul*. New York: Thames and Hudson, 1974.

Quoniam, Pierre. *The Louvre*, trans. Barbara Shuey. Paris, France: Editions de la Réunion des musées nationaux, 1983.

Reid, Robert. "The Generic Sun-Venus Cycle: Developing the Expression of Love and Beauty." *The Mountain Astrologer* (April/May 2000): 93–101.

Rudhyar, Dane. *An Astrological Mandala: The Cycle of Transformation and Its 360 Symbolic Phases*. New York: Vintage Books, 1974.

Safra, Jacob E., chairman of the Board, and Jorge Aguilar-Cauz, President. *Encyclopaedia Brittanica Almanac 2006*. Chicago, IL: Encyclopedia Brittanica, 2005.

Schneider, Michael S. *A Beginner's Guide to Constructing the Universe: The Mathematical Archetypes of Nature, Art, and Science*. New York: Harper Perennial, 1995.

Schuchhardt, Walter-Herwig. *The Universe History of Art and Architecture: Greek Art*, transl. George Weidenfeld & Nicolson Ltd, London. New York: Universe Books, 1972.

Seltman, Charles. *The Twelve Olympians*. New York: Apollo Editions, 1962.

Sullivan, Erin. *Retrograde Planets: Traversing the Inner Landscape*. London, England: Arkana Penguin Books, 1992.

Tarnas, Richard. *Cosmos and Psyche: Intimations of a New World View*. New York: Viking Press, 2006.

Thompson, J. Eric S. *The Rise and Fall of Maya Civilization.* London, Pimlico, 1993.

Velikovsky, Immanuel. *Worlds in Collision.* New York: Dell Publishing Co., 1973.

Walker, Barbara G. *The Women's Encyclopedia of Myths and Secrets.* San Francisco: Harper & Row, 1983.

Whitney, David C. *The American Presidents.* Garden City, NY: Doubleday and Company, 1985.

Wolkstein, Diane, and Samuel Noah Kramer. *Inanna, Queen of Heaven and Earth: Her Stories and Hymns from Sumer.* New York: Harper and Row Publishers, 1983.

LIST OF REFERENCES FOR CELEBRITY BIRTH DATA

INTERNET SOURCES	BOOK SOURCES
astrodatabank.com	ACG Book of Maps (Llewellyn Worldwide) 1989
famousbirthdays.com	Almanac of Famous People, 5th ed., Baer and Walker, Gale Research Inc., Detroit, MI c. 1994.
wikipedia.com	Almanac of Famous People, 7th ed. Jennifer Massman, ed. C. 2001, Gale Group Farmington Hills, MI.
womenshistoryabout.com	Chambers Biographical Dictionary ed. Magnus Magnussen, 5th ed. 1990, W & R Chambers, Ltd., Edinburgh
	Clifford Chart Data: Solar Fire V Astrological Software
	Encyclopedia Britannica
	Encyclopedia Britannica Almanac, 2006
	Gale Group/Almanac of Famous People
	Jim Maynard's Celestial Guides: 2000, 2003, 2004, 2005, 2006, 2007
	Penfield, 2001. Data Collection
	The American Presidents, David C. Whitney
	Time (Leaders issue) 4/13/1998
	Treas. Soc. 1875, NYC.
	Data for charts & Venus Star Point dates: Solar Fire Software, a product of Esoteric Technologies (esotech.com)

ACKNOWLEDGEMENTS

Figures 1.0 and 1.1: Pattern of the Venus/Earth Orbit is from A Little Book of Coincidence by John Martineau. New York: Walker & Company, 2001. It is published with the permission of Bloomsbury USA.

Figures 1.2 and 1.6: The Venus-Earth Mandala (calculated for October 7, 1981 to September 17, 1983), as programmed by Neil F. Michelsen for his book Tables of Planetary Phenomena, now in Third Edition, Starcrafts Publishing, © 2007 The Michelsen-Simms Family Trust. Used by permission of the publisher.

Figure 1.3: The Heart and Star of the Venus Orbit, and Figure 3.4: The Orbital Pattern of Venus as Viewed From Earth were created by Deborah Houlding for her upcoming book (to be released in 2011) portions of which have been published in the Mountain Astrologer. The image is used with the permission of Deborah Houlding.

Geometric drawings in figures 1.15, 1.18, 1.19, and 1.23 were created by Joseph Amormino and are used with his permission.

Photographs in figures 1.17, 1.24, and 2.9 are used with permission of the photographer Arielle Guttman.

Images in figures 1.8, 2.2, 2.3, 2.5, 2.6, and 2.9 from Wikimedia Commons under GNU Free Documentation License.

Figures 2.12 and 2.13 were created by Jaye Oliver and are used with her permission.

Image of the rosary in figure 2.14a from Wikimedia Commons under Creative Commons Attribution-Share Alike 2.5 generic.

All other images are in the public domain

All horoscope charts were produced using Solar Fire Software, a product of Esoteric Technologies (www.esotech.com.au). All other charts and Star Man images were conceived by Arielle Guttman and created by Jaye Oliver.

INDEX

Numerals

1.6 ratio 26–30
See also divine proportion; Fibonacci; golden mean; golden section; phi ratio
1960s 50, 74, 109, 113, 125, 137, 138, 151, 170, 172, 173, 265, 345
2012 xi, 48–52, 70, 71, 81, 167, 193, 198, 349, 351, 357, 378, 379

A

Abel 170
Achilles 157
    Achilles' heel 157
Adams, Abigail 75, 197, 316, 317
Adams, John 75, 188, 189, 316, 317
Adams, John Quincy 188, 316, 319
Adams, Louisa 319
Adonis 42
Africa 33, 87, 185, 200
African American 87, 156, 322
Age of Aquarius 137, 212
Age of Enlightenment 138
Age of Pisces 212
Age of Reason 138
Age of Taurus 91
air
    element of 90, 111, 130, 166, 204, 206, 221, 252, 259, 278, 284, 330, 331
    in mythology 97
    sign 128, 135–139, 168, 173, 174, 181, 230, 308, 312
    travel 100, 137, 174

Alahi salaam, Musa 57
Albert, Prince (husband of Queen Victoria) 180, 319
Albert Edward, Prince of Wales 195
alchemy 142, 146
Alcott, Louisa May 325
Aldebaran 87
Al-Fayed, Dodi 300
Algol 87
Allen, Tim 159
Allen, Woody 120, 121
America
    astrological sign of 112
    history 91, 111, 112, 123, 133, 161, 173, 181, 188
See also Americas; North America; United States
American Gallery 279
American Idol 200
American Revolution 73, 138, 188, 199, 210
Americas 33, 222
    history 99
See also America; North America; United States
Amor, Jose 348
Andersen, Hans Christian 195
Angelil, Rene 224, 274, 275
Angel Island 112
Anthony, Susan B. 208, 210, 224, 332, 333, 336
anti-Galactic Center 49
Apache 88
Aphrodite 36–42, 37–39, 41, 42, 206
    "celestial goddess" 40

"common goddess" 40
Pandemos 40, 44
Urania 40, 44
See also Venus
Apollo 206
Aquino, Corazon 109
archetype 15, 66
    Aquarius 134
    Aquarius Star 128, 133
    Aries 154, 156, 157, 162
    Cancer 104
    Capricorn 178
    Gemini 166, 168
    Leo 192
    Libra 204, 206
    pure 78
    Sagittarius 94, 97
    Scorpio 142
    Taurus 84, 87, 88
    Venus 15, 38, 39, 86
    Virgo 116
Ares 40
See also Mars
Aries
    star period 72
    Venus Star Point 153–164
    Venus Star relationships 296–305
Arkin, Alan 294
Armstrong, Louis 253
Arnaz, Desi 109, 258
Art Nouveau 195
Ascendant
    and Venus Star 242
    astrological factor 247
Ashtaroth 37
See also Sumeria
Asklepius 150
Astarte 37–39
See also Sumeria
astrology 340
    and mythology 15, 37, 42
    and Venus 14, 54–57
    contemporary 130, 144, 178
    Greek 43
    Mayan calendar 48–52
    practice of 65
    traditional 130
    Vedic 144, See also dashas
See also astronomy; geometry; quantum physics; Rudhyar, Dane
astronomy
    and geometry 25
    and Venus xii, 14
    and Venus Star Point theory 15
See also astrology; geometry; quantum physics
Athena 43, 158, 162, 308, 309
Atlantis 223, 379
axis 25, 30, 172, 173

B

baby boomer 71, 159, 282, 284, 293
Babylon 33, 37, 39, 377, 383
bagua 231
Baigent, Michael 42
Ball, Lucille 109, 120, 258
Bancroft, Anne 336
Batman 150, 157
Beatles 107, 265, 301, 342, 344, 345
See also Harrison, George; Lennon, John; McCartney, Paul; Starr, Ringo
Beatrice, Princess of York 170
Beethoven, Ludwig van 75, 210, 326
Begg, Ean 42
Beginner's Guide to Constructing the Universe, A 32
See also Schneider, Michael
Bell, Alexander Graham 136
Bellini 326
Berlioz 326
Bernhardt, Sarah 190, 195, 323, 325
Besant, Annie 331
biquintile 54, 56, 290, 310
birth dates, table
See Table of Birth Dates
Black Madonna
See Black Virgin
Black Virgin 150, 377, 383
See also religion

Index

Blake, William 171, 312, 313
Blanchett, Cate 159
Blavatsky, Helena 101, 223
Boleyn, Ann 196
Bolivar, Simon 222
Bonaparte, Napoleon
See Napoleon Bonaparte
Book of Hiram, The 24, 57, 377, 378, 384
Botticelli 36, 39–41
Bowie, David 148, 151
Bowles, Camilla Parker 268, 290–292
Breslin, Abigail 201, 294
Broderick, Matthew 308, 309
Bronte, Charlotte 336
Bronte, Emily 336
Brown, Dan 78, 171, 379
Browning, Elizabeth Barrett 171
Bryant, Eldridge 342
Buddhism
See religion
Burns, George 120
Bush administration 341
Bush, Barbara 250
Bush family 341
Bush, George W. 132
Butler, Alan 48, 378
Byron, Lord 330

C

caduceus 142
See also serpent
Cain 170
calendar
    Mayan 48–52
    numerical values of Venus 30–36
California 91, 100, 199
See also Gold Rush
Campbell, Joseph 122
Cancer
    Venus Star Point 103–114
    Venus Star relationships 262–270
Capricorn
    Venus Star Point 98–99, 177–190
    Venus Star relationships 98–103, 314–319
cardinal 50, 156, 158, 268, 316, 319, 331
    axis 172, 173
Carnegie, Andrew 207, 208
Carter, Howard 91
Carter, Jimmy 109
Carvey, Dana 294
Cash, Johnny 151
Cassatt, Mary 210
Castor 166, 168, 170
Catholic Church, Roman
See religion
Cazimi 381
Ceausescu, Nicolae 186
celestial heartbeat x
Celestine Prophecy, The 187, 379
centaur 94, 97, 100
Ceres
    and Aries VSP 303, 304
    and Virgo VSP 118, 120
    and VSP relationships 242
    in Aquarius 222, 286
    in Leo 111
    in Pisces 324
    in Scorpio 295
Chanel, Coco 338
Charles, Prince of Wales 107, 109, 113, 200, 268, 290–292, 300
Chavez, Cesar 133
China 33, 136, 185, 186
Chinese
    five-pointed star theory 236
    medicine 231, 232
    model 230, 232
    people 43
See also medicine
Chirac, Jacques 109
Chiron
    and Aquarius VSP 134
    and Venus Star relationships 242
    in Sagittarius 97, 111
    in Scorpio 291
    in Taurus 254, 255
Chopin, Frederic 195, 326, 330

Christianity
See religion
See also Black Virgin; church, Medieval
Christ (Jesus) 150, 378, 385
church 132, 138
    authority of 221
    law 222
    Medieval 47
See also religion
Church, Charlotte 183
Churchill, Winston 79, 161
Ciccone, Madonna 131, 134
civil rights movement 162
Civil War, American 88, 210, 322
Clark, William 305
classical era 38, 157
Clinton, Bill 132, 186, 199, 283
Clinton, Hillary Rodham 282, 283
Cobain, Kurt 148
Colbert, Stephen 120
Cold War 186
conjunction
    inferior 44
    superior 44
See also individual planets; quincunx
Cooper, Gary 88
Coppola, Francis Ford 148
Corinth 39
Cosby, Bill 159
cosmic order 77, 94
Costello, Elvis 195
Cousteau, Jacques 133
creation 22, 32, 56, 231, 236, 381, 382
    artistic 26, 201
    cosmic 61, 69, 104, 381
    sheng 231, 232
    stories 53
See also mandorla; vesica piscis; womb of creation
Creative Star 233, 235, 239, 240
See also relationship chapters for Creative Star and individual signs
Crete 91
Cronus 181, 232

Cruise, Tom 285, 286
Crystal, Billy 120
Curie, Marie 259
Curie, Pierre 259
Curtis, Jamie Lee 148
cycle 146, 196, 212
    creation 236
    creative star 311, 318
    evolutionary 108, 170, 212
    of life 146, 158, 216
    of Venus 24, 48, 100, 137, 147, 187, 188, 207, 210, 211, 217, 222, 231, 232, 250, 269, 272, 310, 318, 323, 336, 347
See also retrograde
Cyprus 39
Cytheria 39
Czechoslovakia 186

D

Dalai Lama 186
Dali, Salvador 118
Darth Vader 150
Darwin, Charles 222, 223
dashas xii
See also astrology, Vedic
Da Vinci Code, The
See Brown, Dan
da Vinci, Leonardo 30
Davis, Adelle 118
Dean, James 148, 151
declination 53, 381, 382
Delphi 42, 206
De Niro, Robert 148
Depp, Johnny 148, 151
depth psychology 150
destruction 161, 231, 232
See also ko
Diana, Princess of Wales 159, 200, 268, 300, 342
DiCaprio, Leonardo 78, 148
Dickens, Charles 207, 211, 213, 379
Dion, Celine 274, 275
Dione 40, 44

direct 25, 56, 58, 71, 382
direct (motion) 381
Divine Mother 104
divine proportion 26, 29
See also 1.6 ratio; Fibonacci; golden mean; golden section; phi ratio
dodecahedron 32, 33
dominator model 377
Donizetti 326
Donnelly, Ignatius 223
Dostoevsky, Fyodor 171, 173
Douglas, Lord Alfred 339
Dresden Codex, The 49, 378
Dr. Ruth 121
Duff, Haylie 170
Duff, Hilary 170
Duke, Patty 336
Dylan, Bob 74, 158, 159, 173

E

Earhart, Amelia 88
earth
    element of 70, 86, 90, 111, 118, 169, 180, 210, 221, 251, 252, 254, 267, 318, 338, 342
    mother 87, 116, 118
    periods x, 50, 225
    sign 70, 87, 90, 98, 107, 180, 182, 210, 230, 250, 251, 272, 273, 276, 293
Earth
    and Aquarius VSP 128
    and Aries VSP 156
    and Capricorn VSP 178
    and Gemini VSP 168
    and Leo VSP 194
    and Pisces VSP 216
    and Sagittarius VSP 96
    and Scorpio VSP 148
    and Taurus VSP 86
    and VSP relationships xi, xii, 14–16, 21–23, 25, 27, 30, 40, 43, 45, 46, 56–58, 65, 78, 106, 118, 125, 347
    evolution x
    harmony xi
    historical events 50, 74, 75, 91
    in mythology 40–46
    orbit 24, 53
See also Gaia
Earth/Venus 34
    mandala 23
eclipse 50, 381
    cycle 49
    lunar 49
    point 50
    solar 53
Edison, Thomas 136
Edward, Duke of Windsor 200
Edwards, Dennis 343
Egypt 26, 33, 91
Eighth House 79, 222, 375
Einstein, Albert 29, 136, 223
Eleventh House 376
Elizabeth I, Queen 201
Elizabeth II, Queen 134, 285, 379
Elizabeth, the Queen Mother 109
Ellis Island 112
energy 347
    and Venus x–14, 48, 57, 58, 61, 65, 72, 78, 83, 86, 93, 103, 113, 115, 127, 141, 153, 165, 177, 191, 203, 215, 230–232, 236, 244, 245, 247, 295, 300, 302, 322
    cosmic 15, 56, 65, 113, 128, 130, 142, 144, 147, 156, 225, 231
    in relationships 70, 158, 159, 183, 192, 196, 197, 219, 241, 242, 254, 277, 278, 284, 287, 298, 303, 310, 311, 319, 322, 323, 327, 331, 336
See also feminine, energy
England, Elizabethan 196, 200
Enki 170
Enlil 170
Epstein, Brian 345
equiangular spiral 29
equinoctial gate 120
Eros 48, 61, 62
Euclid 29

Eugenie, Princess 170
Europe 136, 185, 199, 208, 210, 233, 279
    history 99–112, 138, 200, 222, 326
Evans, Linda 295
Evans, Sir Arthur 91

F

Facebook 201
Fanning, Dakota 183
Fanning, Elle 183
Fates, the 15
feminine
    causes 149, 158, 210
    energy 49, 142
    sacred 150, 171
    sign 87, 147
    type 44, 192, 224
    Venus 40
feminine, the 48, 52, 74, 104, 110
Feng Shui 230, 231, 348
Fibonacci, Leonardo 29
See also 1.6 ratio; divine proportion; golden mean; golden section; phi ratio
Fields, W. C. 207
Fifth House 375
finger of god 60, 382
See also yod
Finger of the Goddess 56, 60, 61
fire
    cosmic 98
    element of 70, 94, 96, 111, 154, 156, 192, 194, 199, 210, 221, 254, 258, 259, 298, 322, 331, 342
    era of 199
    sign 156, 196, 199, 230, 250, 299, 303, 316
First House 99, 157, 374
fixed sign 250, 322
Fonda, Jane 159
Ford, Gerald 88
Fourth House 98, 375
Fox, Michael J. 159
Foxx, Jamie 120
France 26, 39, 40, 47, 222, 299, 300, 385

Freemasonry 186, 377, 379, 384
French Revolution 73, 138, 199, 222
Freud, Sigmund 150, 208, 223, 259
Furies, The 39

G

Gaia 44, 84
See also Earth
Galactic Alignment
See Jenkins, John Major
Galactic Center 49
See also Milky Way
Gandhi 82, 87, 88, 370
Gates, Bill 277
Gates, Melinda 277
Gauguin, Paul 210
Gemini
    twins archetype 170
    Venus Star Point 165–176
    Venus Star relationships 306–313
geometry xii, 14
    and Venus 14, 25, 32, 70
    sacred xii, 30
See also astrology; astronomy; quantum physics
George, King of England 181
Germany
    Berlin Wall 136, 185
    Nazi 161
Giamario, Daniel 56
Gilbert, W. S. 323
Glenn, John 88
God 22, 46, 57, 97, 98, 124, 138, 171
goddess 14, 30, 38–45, 47, 48, 50, 60, 78, 107, 116, 145, 147, 162, 218, 249, 285, 308, 348
See also Aphrodite; Venus

Goethe, Johann von 171, 175
Goldberg, Whoopi 120
golden mean 29, 30
See also 1.6 ratio; divine proportion; Fibonacci; golden section; phi ratio
golden section 29

See also 1.6 ratio; divine proportion; Fibonacci; golden mean; phi ratio
Gold Rush 91, 100, 199
See also California
Gone with the Wind 87
Goodall, Jane 133
Gore, Al 125
Gothic cathedrals 26, 47
Grace, Princess of Monaco 159, 298, 300
Graham, Stedman 284, 285
Great Depression 100, 124, 148, 161
Great Goddess 37, 46, 149, 150
Great Pyramid 26
Greece 33
    classical era 38
    mythology 15, 37, 38–42
    Olympic games 42
Guggenheim Museum 26

H

Habitat for Humanity 109
Hades 138
See also Pluto
Haiti 222
Haley, Alex 87
hand of the goddess
See Finger of the Goddess
Hand, Robert 43, 44
Hanks, Tom 78, 109
Harmonia 40
Harmonic Convergence 187, 198, 379
harmonics 54, 55
Harrison, George 345
Harry, Prince 134, 170
Hawking, Stephen 29, 163
Hawn, Goldie 159
heart center x, 17, 84, 94, 154, 279, 347
Heaven 138
heaven(s) x, 28, 61, 347
heliacal rising 56
Hemingway, Ernest 98
Henry VIII, King 196
Hephaestus 40, 41
See also Vulcan

Hera 149
See also Great Goddess; Juno
Hercules 157
Hero Twins 53
Hesiod 39
Hidalgo, Padre Miguel 222
hieros gamos 41
Hilton, Nicky 170
Hilton, Paris 170
Hitler, Adolf 161
Hoffman, Dustin 159
Hollywood 109, 200
Holmes, Katie 285, 286
Holocaust (European) 160
Holy Grail 47
Holy Spirit 46
Howells, William Dean 331
Hughes, Howard 87
Hugo, Victor 171, 174, 195, 325
Hyades 87

I

Ibn Ezra, Avraham 45
Ilyas, Prophet 57
Inanna 37–39, 147, 386
inconjunct 55, 382
India 33, 87
Indian (American) 100
    lands 201
industrial age 74, 136
Industrial Revolution 14, 138
Iron Curtain 136
Ishtar 37–39, 42, 43
Isis 38
Islam
See religion

J

Jackson, Andrew 188, 319
Jackson, Michael 131, 134
Jackson, Rachel 319
Jagger, Mick 293, 343, 344
Jason 157
Jedi 150

395

Jefferson, Thomas 188, 305, 317, 318
Jenkins, John Major 49
Joel, Billy 158
Jolie, Angelina 148
Jones, Brian 343
Josephine, Empress 310
Jove 96
See also Jupiter; Zeus
Judaism
See religion
Jung, Carl 98, 150, 223, 338
Jung, Emma 338
Jungian concept 41
Juno
    and Chiron 254, 255
    and Pisces VSP 222, 324
    and Saturn 185
    and Scorpio VSP 149
    and Sun 319
    and Venus Star relationships 234, 242
    in Aquarius 286, 308, 309
    in Aries 111
    in Leo 317
    square 113
See also Great Goddess; Hera
Juno/Chiron conjunction 254
Jupiter 199
    and Juno 162
    and Maya 53
    and VSP relationships 241
    in Gemini 310
    in Leo 90, 222
    in Libra 333
    in Pisces 224, 225, 324
    in Sagittarius 96
    in Scorpio 111
    in Taurus 253
See also Jove; Zeus

K

Kahlo, Frida 260, 261
Karmic Star 233–237
See also relationship chapters for Karmic Star and individual signs

Keaton, Diane 159
Keats, John 331
Keillor, Garrison 133
Keller, Helen 202, 336, 337
Kennedy, Edward 108, 121
Kennedy, Ethel 122, 373
Kennedy, Jacqueline (Onassis) 159, 253–255, 300, 302, 342, 363
Kennedy, Jean Ann 121
Kennedy, John F. 88, 108, 122, 173, 253
Kennedy, John F. Jr. 108
Kennedy, Joseph Jr. 122, 342
Kennedy, Joseph Sr. 108, 121
Kennedy, Kathleen 121
Kennedy, Patricia 121
Kennedy, Robert Sr. 88, 108
Kennedy family 341, 342
Kidman, Nicole 148, 284, 285
King, B.B. 250
King, Gayle 284, 285
King, Larry 250
King, Martin Luther Jr. 109
King, Stephen 121, 124
Kinsey, Alfred 151
Klee, Paul 210
Knight, Christopher 24, 377, 384
Knowles, Beyonce 159
ko 231, 232
See also destruction

L

labyrinth 26, 27
Lamb, Lady Caroline 330
Latin America 185, 200, 222
Leadbetter, C. W. 331
Ledger, Heath 148, 150
Leigh, Janet 148
Leigh, Vivien 87
Lennon, John 106, 265, 266, 269, 301, 345
Leno, Jay 133
Lent 57
Lewis, C. S. 42, 98
Lewis, Merriwether 305
life mate 130, 146, 198, 209, 307, 336

Limbaugh, Rush 133
Lincoln, Abraham 322–324
Lincoln, Mary Todd 323, 324
Lind, Jenny 195, 326
Lindbergh, Charles 88, 137
Lion King, The 200
Liszt, Franz 210
Livio, Mario 22
Lomas, Robert 24, 377, 384
Long Count 49
Lopez, Jennifer 159
Louisiana Purchase 305
Louis XVI, King of France 300
Louvre Museum 40
Lucas, George 122, 150
lunar
    calendar 30
    eclipse 49
    landing 137
    nodes 30, 162, 181

M

MacLaine, Shirley 133
Madison, Dolly 318
Madison, James 318, 319
Madonna
See Black Virgin
See Ciccone, Madonna
Maher, Bill 120
Mahler, Gustav 210
Mandela, Nelson 133, 186, 199
mandorla 32
See also creation; sheng; vesica piscis; womb of creation
manifest destiny 99
mantras 17
Marie Antoinette 75, 300
Mars
    and Leo VSP 199
    and Libra VSP 207
    and Maya 53
    and Pluto 146, 207
    and Venus 42, 52, 74
    and Virgo VSP 275

    and VSP relationships 241
    in Aries 98, 156, 298, 311
    in Gemini 173
    in Leo 222
    in mythology 40
    in Scorpio 144, 146, 181, 295
    in Taurus 90, 207, 254
    in Vedic astrology 144
See also Ares
Mars/Pluto 145, 207
Mars/Saturn/Uranus/Pluto T-sqaure 173
Mars/Uranus/Jupiter 222
Martin, Ricky 151
Martin, Steve 159
Mary Magdalene 150
Mary (mother of Jesus) 47, 116
masculine, the 52
Maya 30, 39, 45, 48–54, 198
McCartney, Linda Eastman 301
McCartney, Paul 131, 133, 265, 266, 269, 301, 345
McGregor, Ewan 148
medicine 109, 116, 124, 282
    Chinese 230–233
See also Chinese medical model
Mediterranean 39
Mendelssohn, Felix 195, 326
Mercury
    and Maya 53
    and Virgo VSP 118
    and VSP relationships 241
    in Capricorn 185
    in Gemini 168, 277, 311
    in Leo 198, 199, 324
    in mythology 118, 168
    in Sagittarius 98, 111, 260, 261
    in Scorpio 295
    in Taurus 91, 253, 291
    in Virgo 303, 304
Mercury/Mars 224
MesoAmericans 43
Mesopotamia 39
Mexican War of Independence 222

Middle East 185
Midheaven 162, 242
Milky Way, Center of 49
See also Galactic Center
Monet, Claude 194
Monroe, James 188, 318
Monroe, Marilyn 131
Moon 14, 21, 26, 30, 48, 52, 380, 381
    and Cancer VSP 106
    and Leo VSP 198, 199
    and Libra VSP 209
    and Maya 53
    and Neptune opposition 212
    and Pisces VSP 337
    and Sagittarius VSP 99
    and Scorpio VSP 291
    and Virgo VSP 275
    and VSP relationships 234, 241
    in Aquarius 265, 266
    in Capricorn 310
    in Libra 224
    in Scorpio 300
    in Taurus 185
    in Virgo 162, 303, 304
Mother Earth 84, 118, 346, 347
Mother Goddess 46
Mother Teresa 133, 285
Mozart, Wolfgang Amadeus 75
Mucha, Alphonse 195
mudras 17
Muhammad 57
Mussolini, Benito 161
mutable sign 250
Myers, Mike 294
Myspace 201
mythology
    of Venus xi, xii, 14, 15, 37–63
See also Maya; individual gods

N

Napoleon Bonaparte 310
Napoleonic era 199
natal chart 54, 57, 59
National Women's Suffrage Association 332

nautilus shell 24
Near East 37
Nelson, Willie 250
Neptune
    and Aquarius VSP 286
    and VSP relationships 241
    conjunction 98
    discovery of 218
    in Capricorn 185, 186
    in Libra 162
    in mythology 206
    in Pisces 111
    in Virgo 124, 275
See also Poseidon
Neptune/Pluto conjunction 136, 137
Neptune/Saturn (square) 148, 149
Neptune/Uranus (square) 225
Neptune/VSP 285
    120, 148, 162
New Age 187, 198, 212
Newman, Paul 109
New Mexico 279
New Testament 57
New World 99, 100, 112, 222, 378, 386
New York 279
New York Stock Exchange 91
See also stock market
Nicholson, Jack 78, 157, 159
Nimoy, Leonard 294
Ninth House 98, 99, 375
node 90, 181
    and VSP relationships 242
North America 201, 233
See also America; Americas; United States
Nostradamus 74
Novus Ordo Seclorum 188

O

Obama administration 341
Obama, Barack 156, 158, 322
occult 100, 148, 150
See also spiritualism
O'Hara, Scarlett 87
O'Keeffe, Georgia 121, 279, 332

Old Testament 57
Olsen, Ashley 183
Olsen, Mary Kate 183
Olympus 40, 41, 97
Onassis, Aristotle 87, 254, 255
Onassis, Jacqueline
See Kennedy, Jacqueline
Ono, Yoko 107, 269
opposition 54, 99, 162, 174, 212, 222, 224, 251, 254, 267, 375, 382
orbit
See individual planets; Moon; Sun
O'Reilly, Bill 158
Orwell, George 223
Osbourne, Ozzie 109, 269
Osbourne, Sharon 109, 269
Osiris 170
Ouranos 44
See also Uranus

P

Pace, Amanda 170
Pace, Rachel 170
Pallas
    and Aries VSP 303, 304
    and Libra VSP 333
    and VSP relationships 242
    in Aquarius 222, 308, 309
    in Leo 111
    in Scorpio 295
See also Athena; Venus
Pan-Hellenic Games 42
Parker, Sarah Jessica 308, 309
Parthenon 26
partnership model x, 186, 377
Pattinson, Robert 183
Pei, I. M. 87
Peloponnese 39
Penn, Sean 110
pentagon 32, 34
pentagonal pattern x
pentagonal star 29
Pentagon, the 34
pentagram xii, 21, 33, 34, 44, 56, 188, 379

Perelandra
See Lewis, C. S.
Peron, Evita 133
Perseus 157
Philip, Prince 250
phi ratio xii, 30
See also 1.6 ratio; divine proportion; Fibonacci; golden mean; golden section
planetary period
    Vedic system xi
    Western system xii
See also dashas
Plato 29, 61, 223, 378
platonic solids 32
Pleiades 87
Pluto
    and Aquarius VSP 138
    and Cancer VSP 111, 112
    and Gemini VSP 173, 310
    and Leo VSP 137, 199
    and Libra VSP 207
    and Pisces VSP 222
    and Sagittarius VSP 98
    and Scorpio VSP 144–146, 151
    and Taurus VSP 91
    and VSP relationships 242
    discovery of 50, 148
    in mythology 75, 160
    in Pisces 324
    in Sagittarius 175
    in Scorpio 144–146, 151, 181
    in Virgo 125
    square VSP 211
    T-square 173
See also Hades
Pollux 166, 168, 170
Pope John Paul II 186
Popol Vuh 53
See also Maya
Poseidon 218
See also Neptune
Potter, Harry 147, 161, 303
power
    and astrological influence 16, 21, 25,

33, 34, 65, 185, 194, 210, 316, 344
  cognitive 120
  feminine 48, 74, 147, 162
  higher 94, 216
  in history 112, 136, 137, 148, 161
  places of 26
  transformational 112, 142, 146, 187
Precessional Age 23
Presley, Elvis 131, 133
Prince (musician and actor) 131, 134
principle 47, 57, 147, 149, 150
  feminine 14, 43, 147, 149, 150, 224
  Feng Shui 348
  harmonizing 327
  life 17, 65, 77, 79
  male 52
  motivating 97, 98, 107, 132
  of attraction 229, 247
  of Venus Star relationship 348
  Venus Star relationship x, 43, 57, 72, 233, 236, 244
progression
  and the Aquarius Star 139
  definition of 57, 139, 232
  of the seasons 232
Prohibition 100, 125
Prometheus 98
Puccini 195
Pygmalion 42
Pythagoras 29
Pythia Games 42

Q

quantum physics 15, 125
See also astrology; astronomy; geometry
quincunx 54–56, 60, 61, 274, 299, 316
See also conjunction
quintile 54–56, 277, 293, 311, 331, 381

R

Radcliffe, Daniel 161, 302–304
Ramsey, Jon Benet 183
Reagan, Nancy 250
Reagan, Ronald 100

Reconstruction 123
Redfield, James 187, 379
religion
  and astrological influences 174, 175
  and the sacred feminine 150, 224
  Buddhism 57
  Catholic Church, Roman 124, 138, 186
  Christianity 38, 47, 57, 150
  goddess 44
  Greek Orthodox Church 57
  influence of 59, 97, 124, 139, 225
  in history 222
  Islam 38, 57
  Judaism 38, 39, 57
See also Black Virgin; church, Medieval; mythology
Remus 170
Renaissance 30, 38, 39, 98
Renoir, Pierre 194
retrograde
  and Maya 53–56
  and the cycle of Venus xi, 15, 23–27, 24, 25, 26, 27, 49, 53, 54–59, 56, 57, 58, 59, 69, 71, 85, 95, 105, 117, 129, 143, 155, 167, 179, 193, 205, 217, 347, 349, 382
Richards, Keith 293, 343, 344
Rivera, Diego 260, 261
Roaring Twenties 91, 100
Robbins, Tim 287
Roberts, Julia 122
Rodin, Auguste 194
Rolling Stones, The 293, 342–344
Romania 186
Romano, Ray 159
Rome 37, 38, 40, 47
Romulus 170
Roosevelt, Eleanor 109
Roosevelt, Franklin 88, 89, 161
Roots
See Alex Haley
rosary 48, 388
rose

anagram 48
shape of 21
symbol of 47, 48
Rossetti, Dante Gabriel 210
Rossini 326
Rousseau, Henri 210
Rowling, J. K. 158, 159, 161, 302, 303, 304
Royal Swedish Opera 195
Royal Theatre School 195
Rudhyar, Dane 98
Ruffin, David 342, 343
Russian Revolution 136, 200

S

Sabian symbol 159, 161, 187
sacral centers x
Sagittarius
    Venus Star Point 93–102
    Venus Star relationships 256–262
Sand, George 330
Santana, Carlos 151
Sarandon, Susan 287
Sartre, Jean Paul 89
Saturday Night Live 294
Saturn
    and Aquarius VSP 130, 131, 133
    and Aries VSP 161, 162
    and Capricorn VSP 180, 185, 186
    and Gemini VSP 173
    and Leo VSP 199, 327
    and Maya 53
    and mythology 181, 232
    and Pisces VSP 224
    and Sagittarius VSP 98
    and Scorpio VSP 148, 295
    and Virgo VSP 275
    and VSP 234
    and VSP relationships 241
    in Pisces 50, 221–222
    in Taurus 111
Schwarzenegger, Arnold 200
Schliemann, Heinrich 91
Schneider, Michael 32
Schubert 326
Scorpio
    Venus Star Point 141–152
    Venus Star relationships 288–296
Scorsese, Martin 148
Scotland 208
Second House 374
serpent 142, 150
sesqui-square 54, 55, 382
See also tri-octile
Seth 170
Seventh House 88, 90, 161, 185, 254, 375
sextile 54, 60, 283, 293, 311, 331, 338, 382
sexual revolution 151
Shakespeare 5, 42, 200
Shatner, William 294
Shelley, Mary 171, 325
Shelley, Percy 194, 196, 325, 331
sheng 231, 232
See also creation; mandorla; vesica piscis; womb of creation
Sixth House 185, 375
Skelton, Martha Wayles 317
slavery 90, 100, 222
Smothers, brothers 277
Social Security 88, 89
solar system 97, 118
See also Sun
Solomon's Temple 26
solstice
    summer 120, 172
    winter 49, 178
South Africa 186
Soviet empire 186
Spears, Britney 157
Spider Man 157
Spielberg, Steven 148
spiral 24, 25, 29, 30
spiritualism 100, 338
See also occult
Springsteen, Bruce 158, 159
Sprouse, Cole 170
Sprouse, Dylan 170
square 54

See also individual planets and signs
Stallone, Sylvester 200
Stanton, Elizabeth Cady 210, 332, 333, 336
Starr, Ringo 345
Star Trek 294
Stefani, Gwen 159
Steinem, Gloria 133
Stewart, Ian 343
Stewart, Kristin 183, 302
Stewart, Martha 158
Stieglitz, Alfred 279, 332
Stiller, Ben 159
Stockholm 195
stock market 91, 148
    crash 148
See also New York Stock Exchange
Stravinsky, Igor 338
Streep, Meryl 158
Streisand, Barbra 131, 284
Sullivan, Annie 336, 337
Sullivan, Arthur 323
Sumeria 37, 39, 147
Inanna
See also Ashtaroth; Astarte
Sun
    and Cancer VSP 111
    and Leo 326
    and Libra VSP 209
    and the transit of Venus 52–53
    and Virgo VSP 275
    and VSP relationships 241
    heliacal rising 56
    in Capricorn 185
    in mythology 53
    in Sagittarius 261
    in Scorpio 291, 295
See also Apollo; individual signs; solar system
Sun/Venus 52
Superman 157

T

Table of Birth Dates 77
Tarot 187, 196
Taurus

Venus Star Point 83–92
    Venus Star relationships 248–256
Tchaikovsky, Pyotr Ilich 207, 210
Tedlock, Dennis 53, 378
Temptations, The 342–344
Tennyson, Lord Alfred 171
Tenth House 162, 376
Tesla, Nikola 136
Thatcher, Margaret 88
Theosophical Society 331
Theseus 157
Third House 99, 121, 374
Thoreau, Henry David 171, 325
Tiananmen Square 185
Tibet 186
Tolstoy, Leo 327
Tolstoy, Sofia 327
Torah 60
Trebek, Alex 109
trine 54, 210, 274, 381, 382
tri-octile 54–56, 382
See also sesqui-square
triple crown 78, 79, 121, 285
Troy 91
T-square 173, 212
Turner, Ike 278
Turner, Tina 278
Twain, Mark 210, 331, 336
Twain, Olivia 331
Twelfth House 199, 376
Twin Star 233, 235, 238, 239
See also relationship chapters for Twin Star and individual signs

U

United States
    flag 33
    history 17, 34, 99, 112, 137, 174, 188, 208, 210, 305, 322,
    presidents 108, 174, 188, 254, 316, 319, 323
See also America; Americas; individual presidents; North America
Uranus

and Aquarius 130–134
and Aries VSP 161, 162
and Cancer VSP 112, 113
and Capricorn VSP 185, 186, 317
and Leo VSP 199
and Libra VSP 206
and Venus Star 134
and Virgo VSP 277
and VSP relationships 241
discovery of 50
in Leo 134, 222, 224
in mythology 39
in Taurus 111
in Virgo 125
T-square 173, 225

See also Ouranos
Uranus/Neptune conjunction 187
Uranus/Neptune/Pluto
  alignment 50
  trine 210
Uranus/Pluto
  conjunction 303
  square 50, 52
Uranus/Pluto/Venus Star conjunction 50
U.S.
See United States
U.S. Constitution 188
U.S. Department of Defense 34
U.S. government 34
USSR 136
See also Soviet empire

V

Van Damme, Jean-Claude 200
Velvet Revolution 186
Venus
  and VSP relationships 241
  as planet 14
  as star 14
  celestial 39
  in Cancer 291
  in Capricorn 185
  in Libra 333
  in Sagittarius 261
  in Scorpio 295
Venus de Milo 4, 39, 40
Venus/Earth
  orbit 21, 22, 24, 25
Venus Hesperus 44
Venus Pandemos 45, 206
Venus Phosphorus Lucifer 44
Venus Star
  square 50
Venus Star Point
  definition of 15
Venus Star/Saturn
  square 149
Venus Star/Uranus
  conjunction 113, 134
Venus/Sun 302
  conjuction xi
Venus Urania 39, 45
Verdi 326
Verne, Jules 211
vesica piscis 32
See also creation; mandorla; sheng; womb of creation
Vesta
  and VSP relationships 242
  in Aquarius 222, 286
  in Aries 98
  in Capricorn 185
  in Taurus 111
Victoria, Queen 180, 319
Victorian age 136
Victorian era 91, 180
Virgo
  Venus Star Point 115–126
  Venus Star relationships 270–280
Vitruvian Man 30, 31
volcanism 41
Vulcan 40, 41
See also Hephaestus

W

Wagner, Wilhelm Richard 326
Walters, Barbara 159
water

element of 111, 142, 216, 218, 219, 221, 264, 267, 284, 338
sign 104, 107, 128, 230, 269, 276, 290, 293, 299, 312
symbol of 106
Wayne, John 100
Weber, Andrew Lloyd 148, 277
Webster, Daniel 171
White House 318
Wilde, Oscar 195, 214, 339
William, Prince 134, 170
Williams, Paul 342
Williams, Serena 170, 311
Williams, Venus 78, 170, 171, 311
Willis, Bruce 148
Wilson, Brian 131
Windsor family 341, 342
Winfrey, Oprah 78, 133, 284, 285
Wizard of Oz, The 379
womb of creation 32, 104
See also creation; mandorla; sheng; vesica piscis
women's suffrage 90, 224, 332
Woods, Tiger 121, 125
Woodstock Generation 138
World War II 112
wounded healer 97, 134, 254
Wright, Orville 100
Wright, Steven 120
Wright, Wilbur 100, 137
Wright brothers 260

Y

yang 78, 192, 204, 229, 230, 232, 241, 255, 261, 264, 266, 275, 286, 295, 304, 309, 316, 317, 324, 333, 336, 337
Yanni 295
yin 78, 87, 204, 229, 230, 232, 241, 255, 261, 264, 266, 273, 275, 276, 286, 295, 304, 309, 316–318, 324, 333, 336, 337
yod 60, 61
See also finger of god
YouTube 195, 201

Z

Zeus 40, 44
See also Jove; Jupiter

Photo: Elsie Maio

ARIELLE GUTTMAN began her research into astrology in 1974 and continues her practice today with a global clientele. She is a consultant, teacher, and tour leader, conducting workshops globally and leading tours to sacred sites in Greece and France. She has presented seminars in North America, Europe, Australia, New Zealand and Dubai UAE. She is the founder and past president of the Astrology Forum of Santa Fe and also founded the Sophia Center in Santa Fe, a school devoted to wisdom teachings. Venus Star Rising is her fifth book on astrology.

Her previous books are:
Astro-Compatibility (1986)
The Astro*Carto*Graphy Book of Maps (with Jim Lewis, 1989)
Mythic Astrology (with Kenneth Johnson, 1993, 2004)
Mythic Astrology Applied with Kenneth Johnson (2004)

To find out more about Arielle's programs and tours to Greece, visit her website:

www.sophiavenus.com

For current updates on Venus Star Rising special programs, book updates and seminars, visit the website:

www.VenusStarRising.com

CPSIA information can be obtained
at www.ICGtesting.com
Printed in the USA
LVHW060253290622
722372LV00011B/439

9 780983 059851